Frontiers in Economic History

Economic historians have contributed to the development of economics in a variety of ways, combining theory with quantitative methods, constructing new databases, promoting interdisciplinary approaches to historical topics, and using history as a lens to examine the long-term development of the economy. Frontiers in Economic History publishes manuscripts that push the frontiers of research in economic history in order to better explain past economic experiences and to understand how, why and when economic change occurs. Books in this series will highlight the value of economic history in shedding light on the ways in which economic factors influence growth as well as social and political developments. This series aims to establish a new standard of quality in the field while offering a global discussion forum toward a unified approach in the social sciences.

More information about this series at http://www.springer.com/series/16567

Giovanni Battista Pittaluga • Elena Seghezza

Building Trust in the International Monetary System

The Different Cases of Commodity Money and Fiat Money

Springer

Giovanni Battista Pittaluga
Department of Political Science
University of Genoa
Genoa, Italy

Elena Seghezza
Department of Political Science
University of Genoa
Genoa, Italy

ISSN 2662-9771 ISSN 2662-978X (electronic)
Frontiers in Economic History
ISBN 978-3-030-78490-4 ISBN 978-3-030-78491-1 (eBook)
https://doi.org/10.1007/978-3-030-78491-1

This Springer imprint is published by the registered company Springer Nature Switzerland AG.
The registered company address is: Gewerbestrasse 11, 6330 Cham, Switzerland

The function of a coin is originally bound to its material in what is almost a personal union; but when a public authority guarantees its value, it acquires independence and exchange, and trade in the material from which it is made becomes open to everybody, precisely to the extent that its function as money is assured by the collectivity. . . . The value of money is based on a guarantee represented by the central political power, which eventually replaces the significance of the metal.

Simmel G., The Philosophy of Money. Routledge, 1978, third ed., p. 184

To Enrica and Stefano

Preface

A few years ago, when writing a paper on the prospects of the euro and the likelihood of its rivalling the dollar, we realized that an answer to this question was not possible without first considering the theory of the origin and evolution of international money.

These two aspects of currency development are profoundly interconnected, since rather than a single type of international money, various types can be distinguished. At one end of the spectrum, we can place commodity money, that is, money whose face value corresponds to its intrinsic value, while at the other extreme we have fiat money, that is, money with no intrinsic value but nonetheless accepted as having value and purchasing power.

It seemed to us that the transition from one type of money to another could be explained in the light of the neo-institutionalist theory. The development of trade, the formation of states with fiscal capacity, changes in their internal socio-political balance, technological development, and other factors lead to a demand for monetary innovation. The nature of this demand, internationally as well as nationally, has been for forms of money with ever greater degrees of flexibility of supply. Such a demand could only be satisfied by ever more "abstract" forms of money, i.e. those with a face value higher than their intrinsic value.

However, for these forms of money to be accepted as a medium of exchange, there has to be confidence in the stability of their value over time. The question therefore arises of who and how this confidence can produce.

At a national level, the solution to this question lies in the existence of a state that accepts fiat money as payment for the obligations of its citizens towards it and therefore has an interest in establishing and maintaining its value. At the international level, the problem of generating confidence in fiat money is more complex, both because there is no supranational authority to do it and because issuing fiat money offers the issuer the possibility of earning revenue from seigniorage, thus strengthening its power.

For these reasons, to explain the origin and evolution of international money, we are driven to look to the underlying assumptions of international relations theory. Only taking these into account, it does become clear when the balance of power in the international arena permits the creation of an institutional framework able to meet the demand for certain kinds of monetary innovations and produce trust in them, thereby allowing them to be accepted as a medium of exchange.

This implies that the analysis of the prospect of a currency, the possibility of its becoming or remaining an international money, first requires us to consider the different types of money involved and, ultimately, the different ways of producing trust in it, which makes it possible to accept it as a medium of exchange in international transactions.

Genoa, Italy
April 2021

Giovanni Battista Pittaluga
Elena Seghezza

Contents

Chapter 1
Introduction: The Main Features of the International Money's Evolution

In recent years, especially after the global financial crisis (GFC) of 2008, the debate on reforms to the international monetary system and the prospects for the dollar, which is now the key currency, has gained momentum.

Any contribution to this debate must include basic theoretical assumptions about the origins of international money, the stability of its value and the monetary system based on it.

The prevailing theories on these aspects can be traced to two main strands of thought. The first strand is based on Menger's theory that a good becomes money when it is widely accepted as a medium of exchange. Its acceptance depending on the probability of encountering another individual who uses it. In an international context, therefore, the greater the economic size of a country, the more likely it is that its currency will be accepted as a medium of exchange. In the second half of the nineteenth century, sterling became an international currency because of England's prominent share in foreign trade. For a similar reason, the dollar became an international currency after the Second World War.

A second strand of thought for the origins of international money can be traced back to the so-called theory of hegemonic stability. According to one version of this theory, the hegemonic country, i.e. the country with dominant economic and political power, imposes its currency as the international money on follower countries, pursuing only its own interest. In another variant of the hegemonic theory, the hegemonic country solves the collective action problem that the smaller follower countries are unable to solve. In fact, it induces the other countries to cooperate in order to achieve higher levels of welfare for all. In the theory of hegemonic stability, the dominance of the pound in the nineteenth century and that of the dollar after the Second World War is considered to be equivalent and traced back to the hegemonic role of England and the USA, respectively.

Both the Mengerian theory and the theory of hegemonic stability in their explanations of the origin of international money ignore the type of money used. In fact, at the international level, as at the national level, the evolution of money has been marked by a persistent trade-off between what Jevons called the "recognizability" of

G. B. Pittaluga, E. Seghezza, *Building Trust in the International Monetary System*, Frontiers in Economic History, https://doi.org/10.1007/978-3-030-78491-1_1

its value and the elasticity of its supply with respect to trends in productive activity. The continuous growth of trade and demand for money by the private and public sectors has favoured the introduction of monetary innovations whose supply is increasingly flexible, i.e. types of money that are less and less tied to commodity money.

The value of such types of money, however, can be distorted by fraudulent behaviour on the part of the producer. Hence the problem of how to ensure confidence in types of money whose face value is higher than their intrinsic value. In the case of such a money without a commodity anchor, i.e. a fiat money, or with an uncertain commodity anchor (which we will call quasi-fiat money), the problem arises of producing trust in the stability of its value and of the monetary system based on it. The production of trust involves costs which, at the national level, are borne by the state. At the international level, however, there is no supranational authority to bear these costs and a state will only perform this role if it is profitable for it to do so. The latter derives from its ability to exploit the right of seigniorage, what Giscard d'Estaing in the early 1960s called, with reference to the US dollar, an "exorbitant privilege". The exploitation of international seigniorage poses the issue of asymmetrical relative gains. The acceptance of this asymmetry, which can lead to alterations in the existing geopolitical balance, is difficult when there is a multipolar balance in the international arena. In this case, the countries attribute great weight to relative gains. It is, on the other hand, relatively easy to accept if there is a large difference in power between one country, the hegemon, and the other states, the "followers", which have an incentive to accept the currency of the hegemon country as international currency because this favours trade and their economic growth without significantly altering the balance of power.

The transition in international trade from commodity money to fiat money has, therefore, entailed a profound change in the mechanisms of trust production. Over time, the problem has been solved by institutional mechanisms.

In the gold standard of the nineteenth century, the problem of creating confidence in money was solved by providing for its convertibility into gold. Banknotes, at that time, gave the right to obtain from the issuing bank a predetermined quantity of this precious metal. This guaranteed the stability of their value over time. The adoption of the gold standard therefore emerged spontaneously by all advanced countries during the 1870s. In it, sterling, being both a perfect substitute for gold and the most frequently used currency in trade, became the international currency. Hence this process can be explained on the basis of Mengerian theory. It remains, however, to be explained why the advanced countries adhered to the gold standard and abandoned the bi-metallic system.

Attempts to explain this transition have focused mainly on the efficiency of the two systems in ensuring price stability. In this context, the most widely accepted explanation today is that adherence to the gold standard stemmed from a desire to solve the problem of time inconsistency, i.e. the propensity of governments to resort to inflationary surprises and to exploit seigniorage. From this perspective, currency convertibility was a credible commitment mechanism.

Knafo (2013) appropriately objects that this explanation is flawed by its tending to use hindsight, that is looking at the past from the point of view of the present. Indeed, in the last decades of the nineteenth century, advanced states had an adequate fiscal capacity and financed their extraordinary expenditures, mainly war expenses, not with currency debasement, but with debt. The higher the fiscal capacity of the state, the greater its debt capacity. From this perspective, government's aim was to encourage the development of the domestic banking and financial system. This would help to strengthen the nation economically and politically. Price stability was a function of this goal. By adhering to the gold standard, governments gained control over the amount of domestic money and could thus encourage the development of the banking system, following the example of England after the Bank Charter Act of 1844.

Cooperation between states during the gold standard was limited, taking place only at specific moments and on a bilateral basis, dictated by the desire to avoid crisis spillover effects.

The gold standard ended with the First World War. After the war there was a need for a new international monetary order. England, and in particular the governor of the British central bank, Montagu Norman, insisted on a return to the gold standard. The return to a pre-war system was defined at the Genoa Conference in 1922.

The new international monetary system, the so-called gold-exchange standard, was, like the gold standard, a system of fixed exchange rates and convertible currencies, but it differed from the earlier system in several respects. The main one being that the new system was based on a two-tier system: the key currencies, sterling and dollars, were exclusively convertible into gold, while other currencies were convertible into both gold and the key currencies. This solution was due to the fact that after the First World War gold reserves were mainly concentrated in the USA, the other advanced countries having spent their gold reserves to cover their war expenses.

The gold-exchange standard was short-lived, lasting only from 1925 to 1931. The commonly accepted explanation for its collapse is that the emergence of strong trade unions and mass parties was incompatible with a monetary system whose operation required a high degree of price and wage flexibility. Added to this factor were the complications in inter-state relations that emerged after the Treaty of Versailles. The substantial isolation in which France found itself in the years following the signing of the Treaty of Versailles, its fears about the re-emergence of the German threat, led it to sterilize capital inflows, accumulate large gold reserves and to use these reserves as an instrument of financial "statecraft" against England to counter its openings to Germany in foreign policy.

The USA, for different reasons from France, also defended its gold reserves vigorously.

Declining confidence in the stability of the gold-exchange standard convinced other countries to replace their foreign exchange reserves with gold. This led to a significant decrease in the international monetary multiplier. The resulting decline in world money supply deepened the recession in the advanced countries of the early 1930s and helped turn it into the Great Depression.

The period between the two World Wars was without an international money. On the one hand, the new socio-political balance prevailing within advanced countries brought with it the demand for monetary innovations, i.e. for an international money with a higher supply elasticity than commodity money; on the other hand, the transition to a more flexible international money was problematic because of a multipolar balance in the international arena. In this context, there was no country in a position to generate trust in a quasi-fiat money and no agreement among them that a country could act as a hegemon and exploit international seigniorage. In the absence of an international money, currency blocs formed within which a country exercised leadership functions.

The conditions for the existence of a quasi-flat international money arose after the Second World War. The Bretton Woods Agreement of 1944 was the first instance of the "legalization" of international monetary affairs. They created a monetary system based on a quasi-flat currency, trust in the stability of which was ensured by institutional mechanisms defined in a treaty between a group of countries.

The Bretton Woods Agreements were more precisely a political exchange in which the hegemonic country assumed responsibility for guaranteeing the value of the currency it issued and at the same time acquired the privilege of international seigniorage, and the follower countries accepting the fact that the hegemonic country would enjoy this privilege, benefited from the economic advantages entailed in the existence of an international money.

Over time, the Bretton Woods system frayed. Different explanations have been given for the collapse of the Bretton Woods system. On the basis of the so-called Triffin dilemma, many scholars have traced it to the loss of confidence in the convertibility of the dollar into gold.

In 1971 President Nixon suspended the convertibility of the dollar. Adherents of the theory of hegemonic stability attribute the declining stability of the system to the decline of US military-political power and thus to the decline of its coercive or coordinating capacity. In reality, it is more reasonable to argue that over time, the economic and political costs to the USA of producing confidence in the system had become excessive.

In the years after the suspension of dollar convertibility the attempts to return to a system of fixed exchange rates proved futile. The emergence of a floating exchange rates regime based on fiat currencies meant a significant widening of governments' margins of freedom in managing monetary policy, margins which were subsequently abused resulting in the Great Inflation of the 1970s. This period was characterized by a high degree of international monetary disorder. Confidence in the stability of the value of the dollar and the monetary system based on it weakened. Out of this disorder emerged a strong demand for institutional changes to ensure domestic price stability. This demand was met by reforms of central banks aimed at increasing their independence and the introduction of rules for the conduct of monetary policy.

These reforms fostered a period of price and output stability with low exchange rate volatility between mid-1980s and 2007, known as the Great Moderation. In the same period, as a result of political choices, technological innovations and the liberalization of capital movements, the financial interdependence of advanced and emerging countries increased very markedly.

This gave rise to two types of potential imbalances. The first occurred in emerging countries, which were, more often than in the past, subject to sudden stops and hence currency and financial crises. The second type of imbalance mainly affected advanced countries. In these countries, the increase in gross capital flows led to credit booms and financial bubbles. The most striking outcome of these processes was the global financial crisis of 2008 and the euro area sovereign debt crisis of 2010–2011.

Despite these crisis factors, the dominance of the dollar in the international monetary system has not been undermined. In fact, in some respects it has been re-enforced. The growing financial interdependence of the advanced countries has favoured the emergence of a hierarchical structure in the monetary system, with the US currency at the top, the other reserve currencies (euro, yen, pound sterling, Swiss franc, etc.) at a lower level and, finally, the remaining currencies.

Reference

Knafo, S. (2013). *The making of modern finance*. Routledge.

Chapter 2
Money and the International Monetary System: Origins and Evolution

2.1 Introduction

An international money is a public good that allows both private and public entities coming from different countries to interact in the economic and financial sphere using it as a means of exchange, i.e. the ultimate means of payment,[1] a unit of account or a store of value.[2] The existence of an international money therefore is the *sine qua non* of the existence of an international monetary system, or to cite the description given by Eichengreen (1996, p. 3), "the glue that binds national economies together".

To understand the nature and evolution of the international monetary system it is first necessary to explain how an international money emerges. The theories in this regard can be divided into two strands of thought. The first strand traces the origin of international money to an act of coercion by which a hegemonic power either imposes it directly on follower states, or in another view, allows them to overcome the collective action problem and adopt a cooperative behaviour regarding it. This hypothesis, supported by the scholars of the Hegemonic Stability Theory[3] and those of International Political Economy,[4] insists on the role of the power that the hegemonic country has at its disposal. In this hypothesis, therefore, the hegemon has both the ability and the willingness to exercise its power to promote the use of its national currency as an international money by the follower countries, taking advantage from this.

The second strand of thought can be traced back to the view of Menger (1892). The Menger theory, analytically developed in recent times by the search-theoretic models, holds that international money is a good that is adopted as a means of

[1] See Shiller (2003).

[2] See Dorucci and McKay (2011).

[3] See, among others, Kindleberger (1973) and Gilpin (1981).

[4] See Strange (1971a, 1971b) and Cohen (1971).

G. B. Pittaluga, E. Seghezza, *Building Trust in the International Monetary System*, Frontiers in Economic History, https://doi.org/10.1007/978-3-030-78491-1_2

payment in an impersonal way through the interaction of individuals. Acceptance of a commodity as money becomes more likely the greater the likelihood of encountering a counterpart who will accept it. In the international market, therefore, the currency that tends to emerge as the international currency is the one most frequently used in trade, i.e. typically that of the largest country.

In the two approaches mentioned,[5] there is a tendency to ignore the specific type of money underlying a monetary system. In fact, both nationally and internationally, there has been a gradual transition from forms of money with a low elasticity of supply (with respect to the trend of productive activity) to those with a higher elasticity of supply, such as fiat money.

In this transition, however, the problem arises of how to ensure the stability of the value of forms of money that have little or no intrinsic value compared to their face value. Considering what has just been said, it seems that when we talk about money, and therefore also about international money, a distinction must be made between the different types of money. In fact, the conditions in which a commodity money is used are different to those in which a fiat money is adopted. In the first case, since the face value corresponds to its intrinsic value, there is no problem in guaranteeing the confidence in the stability of the value of the asset used as a means of payment. On the other hand, in the case of fiat money, or a money for which the intrinsic value and face value differ (possibly significantly), the problem of the stability of its value is of crucial importance.

While the search-theoretic models explain the use of a commodity money in international exchanges, since they do not consider the problem of how trust is maintained in a currency with an intrinsic value lower than its face value, they have difficulty in explaining the origin of forms of money with no (or limited) intrinsic value (such as the dollar today).

In the few studies of search-theoretic models in which it is asserted that a good can be accepted as money only if there is confidence in the stability of its value, it is assumed that the costs of ascertaining the "recognizability" of this asset, that is its quality, fall on private individuals. In this context, therefore, the state has no role.[6]

Two drawbacks arise from this. On the one hand, it is not possible not to take into account the fact that the type of international money cannot be incompatible with the socio-political balance prevailing within the states. Emblematic is the case of the interwar period, when, as evidenced by Eichengreen (1992), the emergence of strong trade unions and mass parties made the fluctuations in prices and wages necessary for the functioning of a monetary system anchored to gold politically unacceptable.

On the other hand, given that they give no role to the state in the emergence of an international money they neglect the importance that relations between states play in

[5]The distinction between these two theories of the origin of international money mirrors the distinction between metallist and chartalist theories with regard to the origin of domestic money. See Goodhart (1998).

[6]See Lester et al. (2011, 2012) and Zhang (2014).

the acceptance of a fiat[7] or quasi-fiat[8] international money and in preparing the institutional architecture and adopting policies necessary to allow the functioning of the international monetary system.

The distinction between different types of money is also absent in the case of hegemonic stability theory, in both the neo-liberal and neo-realist versions reference is made to the power of the hegemonic country as a determining factor for the existence of an international money.

The international political economy literature focuses on what is meant by power.[9] However, in this literature, as in that based on the hegemonic stability hypothesis, the focus is primarily on the supply side of an international public good that can be used as money. From this perspective, it becomes problematic to explain the evolution of the international money.

However, this evolution can be explained by taking into account, in addition to supply, the demand for monetary innovation. When this latter aspect is considered, it is easier to explain how different is the types of power that favours the emergence of one type of money rather than another.

The joint consideration of the demand for monetary innovation and the supply of institutions and policies aimed at guaranteeing trust in the stability of their value helps to explain how, at the international level, we have gradually passed from the use of commodity money to ever more "abstract" forms of money, that is to a currency with an intrinsic value that is ever lower when compared to its face value. If, on the one hand, this process has made it possible to have types of money with an increasing flexibility of supply, on the other hand, it has posed the problem of how to maintain confidence in the stability of their value over time.[10]

When, faced with a demand for monetary innovations, there is no means to create the rules and institutions necessary to guarantee stability of value, a situation arises in which these innovations go unsatisfied. In some cases leading to a situation where no international money exists.

2.2 The Functions of the International Money

The international money, as has been said, is a public good that can be used outside its country of origin as a medium of exchange, unit of account and store of value.[11] These functions, although similar to those typical of the national currency, are, however, exercised by the international currency in a different way. This is evidenced in Table 2.1.

[7]That is a money with no intrinsic value.

[8]That is a currency that is pegged to a commodity money, but whose cover ratio is discretionary.

[9]For an illustration of this point see Cohen (2015).

[10]See Knafo (2006).

[11]See Dorucci and McKay (2011).

Table 2.1 The roles of international money functions

Level of analysis	Medium of exchange	Unit of account	Store of value
Private	Foreign exchange trading, trade settlement	Trade invoicing	Investment
Official	Foreign exchange interventions	Exchange rate anchor	Reserve

Source: Cohen (2015)

In its capacity as a medium of exchange, international money can be used as a vehicle in exchanges between individuals and as a means of intervention in the interbank market and in the exchange rate market by central banks.

International commercial contracts are invoiced in the international currency, which thus acts as the invoicing currency. As such it performs the function of a unit of account. An analogous function is performed by the international currency when it serves as a peg in exchange rate policies.[12]

Finally, the international currency can be used by both individuals and states as a store of value. In particular, individuals and states tend to hold financial assets denominated in the international currency given its high liquidity and the stability of its value.

The key currency of an international monetary system normally performs all six of the aforementioned roles. Other currencies can only exercise some of these roles internationally. This is the case, for example, of reserve currencies, or currencies which, due to the stability of their value, are present in the official reserves of central banks. In the current system, the currencies that are mostly used as a means of exchange in international transactions are the US dollar, the euro and the yen. Among these currencies, however, only the dollar exercises all the roles typical of a key currency.[13] Therefore, unlike national currencies, an international money is not used exclusively. However, it nevertheless plays a predominant role.

Apart from the difference just referred to, the main difference between national currencies and the international money is that the use of the former is imposed by a state which guarantees its value, while the value of the latter is neither imposed nor guaranteed by any supranational authority. This difference is particularly relevant in the case of money whose intrinsic value is lower than its face value, as in the case of fiat or quasi-fiat money. In fact, confidence in these types of money requires that the issuing country protects the property rights of holders of this type of money through rule of law and policies that ensure confidence in the stability of its value. The absence of a supranational authority acting like a state helps to explain why monetary innovations involving the use of abstract moneys were first introduced and accepted at the national level and then, with certain conditions prevailing, internationally.

[12]That is to say when you anchor the exchange rate of your own currency to the currency of a foreign country.

[13]See Goldberg (2010).

2.3 The Main Theories of the Origin of International Money

As in the case of money at the national level, also in the case of international money the theories of its origin can be traced to two main streams of thought.[14] In a first we find the theories that emphasize the importance of the existence of a hegemonic country, whose currency is imposed or accepted by other countries as the international money. This view is principally found in the various versions of the hegemonic stability theory. A second group of theories considers international money to be the outcome of market forces. The search-theoretic models can be traced to this view, which derives from Menger's theory of money.

2.3.1 The International Money in the Hegemonic Stability Hypothesis

According to the hegemonic stability theory, an international money can exist only if there is a hegemonic country. This, according to Eichengreen (1987), is comparable to a dominant company: it is a country whose size is sufficient to influence the prices and quantities of world markets and whose market power significantly exceeds that of individuals.[15] The basic hypothesis of this theory is that the distribution of power between states is the primary determinant of whether or not an international money exists.[16]

There are three distinct traditions of thought in this theory which, despite their differences, share the common idea that without a hegemon there is no international monetary order.[17] The first of these traditions belongs to Kindleberger (1973), according to whom the production of a public good such as money is subject to a problem of collective action. In fact, a small country is unlikely to produce it, since its currency is unlikely to be accepted as an international money. In this context, small countries will tend to behave like "free riders", hoping that others will produce the international money. In a world where there are only small or medium-small states, all countries adopt this behaviour and hence it is unlikely that an international money emerges. Only a hegemonic country has the power and motivation to provide

[14]See Goodhart (1998).

[15]See Eichengreen (1987).

[16]This theory has many points in common with the Chartalist theory illustrated by Knapp (1924) in *The State Theory of Money*. This theory rejects the hypothesis that money emerges spontaneously through an impersonal market mechanism. For chartalists, money is introduced with an act of empire by the state. In imposing taxes, the latter establishes the unit of account in which the tax obligation can be paid by citizens. This unit of account gives rise to money. See Goodhart (1998).

[17]For a critical analysis of hegemonic monetary stability theories see Eichengreen (1987).

an international money and ensure a world monetary order. This is the collective goods version of the hegemonic stability theory.

Based on these assumptions, Kindleberger, in his volume *The World in Depression, 1829–1939*, traces the ultimate cause of the Great Depression to the refusal of the USA to play the role of hegemon in the gold-exchange standard which Britain had previously exercised in the gold standard: " ... [T]he 1929 depression was so wide, so deep, and so long because the international economic system was rendered unstable by British inability and US unwillingness to assume responsibility for stabilizing it ...".[18] According to Kindleberger, the monetary stability of the world economy occurs when the hegemon exercises certain functions,[19] including, most importantly, that of lender of last resort, as a "benevolent planner". In this context, however, it is not clear why the hegemon should bear the costs involved in producing an international money. However, another version of the hegemonic stability theory, the so-called neo-realist version of this theory, takes this into account. In this theory, states are not assumed to have a common and shared interest in monetary stability. In fact, if the existence of an international money helped raise the welfare of all countries, some states would nonetheless gain more relative to others, which would favour an alteration of the balance of power. It follows that the introduction of an international money can only take place with an act of imposition by the hegemon which pursues, exclusively, its own interests.[20] The leading country[21] uses its power to force other countries to abide by the rules that allow the system to function and its currency to be widely accepted (Table 2.2).

The collective goods version of the hegemonic stability theory, initially proposed by Kindleberger (1973), was revived and developed by Keohane, who, in his influential book *After Hegemony*[22] gave a version defined as neo-liberal. In this version of hegemonic stability theory the hegemon induces other countries to adopt cooperative behaviour from which flows a general increase of well-being. The hegemon has an incentive to produce an international money and an international monetary system as, for it, the costs of producing the international public good are lower than the benefits it derives from it.

The neo-liberal version of the hegemonic stability theory differs from Kindleberger's position in two ways. First, unlike in Kindleberger, the hegemon produces the international public good not out of altruism, but because it has a net gain from it. Second, neo-liberals identify the international public good not in the ability to manage financial crises, as in Kindleberger, but rather in the creation of

[18]See Kindleberger (1973, p. 289).

[19]That is of: "(1) maintaining a relatively open market for distress goods; (2) providing countercyclical, or at least stable, long- term lending; (3) policing a relatively stable system of exchange rates; (4) ensuring the coordination of macroeconomic policies; (5) acting as a lender of last resort by discounting or otherwise providing liquidity in financial crisis". See Kindleberger (1973, p. 289).

[20]See Gilpin (1987).

[21]Lake (1993) specifies that the leader country differs from the hegemon because it produces the infrastructures that ensure international stability, that is, it produces a public good.

[22]See Keohane (1984).

Table 2.2 Versions of the hegemonic stability theory

Phases	Neo-realist security version	Neo-liberal collective goods version
Crisis phase of the international monetary system	Competition between powers and the absence of a system	Collapse of the previous monetary system
Creation of the international monetary system	The hegemon imposes a monetary order based on its currency	The existence of the hegemon makes it possible to overcome the problems of collective action
Operation of the international monetary system	The hegemon guarantees the functioning of the system based on its currency	The costs of cooperation are reduced
Decline of the hegemon	The system based on the currency issued by the hegemon declines, albeit with inertial delays	The system and the underlying institutions survive as there is an interest in cooperating anyway
Multipolar equilibrium	Competition between powers and the absence of a monetary system	As above the system survives as there is an interest in cooperating anyway

international rules and institutions. Such rules and institutions can survive the decline of hegemon as states recognize the benefits of cooperation.

Beyond the limits of the hegemonic stability theory which have been highlighted by various scholars,[23] it is important to underline that this theory focuses mainly on the origin of international money. In this context, the evolutionary process of money into increasingly abstract forms remains obscure. It is therefore unsurprising that some followers of hegemonic stability theory make no distinction between the hegemony exercised by Britain in the gold standard with that of the USA in the Bretton Woods system,[24] this despite the profound differences between the two systems, the gold standard being based on the convertibility of the pound into a commodity money, while the Bretton Woods system was based on a quasi-fiat money, the dollar.

It is again the scarce importance attributed to the different forms of money that led the exponents of the neo-realist version of the hegemonic stability theory to trace the collapse of Bretton Woods to the political decline of the USA.[25]

This view has sparked a wide ranging debate on the concept of power.[26] As part of this debate, Strange highlighted the necessity to distinguish between "relational power" and "structural power".[27] While the first type of power refers to the ability of a state to influence the behaviour of other states within a given regime, structural power is "... the power to choose and to shape the structures of the global political

[23]See, in particular, Snidal (1985).

[24]See Gilpin (1975, 1981). On this aspect see also Ikenberry (2006).

[25]See Gilpin (1975), Keohane (1984) and Krasner (1976, 1983).

[26]See Calleo (1982) and Strange (1987).

[27]For an analysis of these different forms of power see Guzzini (1983).

economy within which other states, their political institutions, their economic enterprises, and (not least) their professional people have to operate".[28]

2.3.2 International Money and Search-Theoretic Models

As mentioned in the introduction, in Mengerian theory, and thus in search-theoretic models the use of a particular good as money depends on the probability that the other party accepts the same good in subsequent exchanges.[29] The more numerous are the individuals who accept the good as payment instrument, the higher is the probability of meeting a partner who wants to exchange goods by accepting this good as ultimate payment. This results in a decrease in the transactions' costs of exchanges.

In this context, therefore, money, like all other institutions, emerges from the market, through the repeated and random interaction of individuals. The acceptability of money is independent of its objective characteristics: it is a social institution.[30] Most search-theoretic models explain the origin of money within a state. This basic scheme was first extended to international money by Matsuyama et al. (1993). In their model they consider two countries, each with its own money.

The population of the two countries is growing and each of the two governments issues money by buying goods from individuals, that is, it exploits the right of seigniorage. Individuals meet randomly with the intent to trade. In exchanges one individual (the seller) sells a good by receiving money from another individual (the buyer). This money can be national or foreign. The probability that two individuals from the same country will meet is higher than that of two individuals from different countries.

Taking these premises into account, Matsuyama et al. (1993) analyse under what conditions foreign money is accepted and thus becomes an international money. They show that the possibility of using a foreign currency in equilibrium is higher the more integrated the two economies are and the larger one economy is compared to the other.

---

[28]See Strange (1987, p. 565). According to her, structural power lies in four different forms: 1. "... with the person or group able to exercise control over ... other people's security from violence"; 2. with those able to control the system of production of goods and services; 3. with those able to determine the structure of finance and credit through which ... it is possible to acquire purchasing power without having either to work or to trade it; 4. with those who have most influence over knowledge ...". In the international arena the state that is dominant in most of these aspects is the most powerful one.

[29]See, in particular, Kiyotaki and Wright (1989, 1991, 1993), Trejos and Wright (1993), Shi (1995, 1997) and Iwai (1996).

[30]In Menger's approach, therefore, the state plays no role in the emergence of money. Similar conclusions come from the search-theoretic models.

Thus, if we consider two commercially integrated countries such as the USA and Mexico, since it is easy for a Mexican seller to meet a Mexican buyer, while it is difficult for an American buyer to meet a Mexican seller, pesos do not circulate in the USA. At the same time, if the frequency with which Mexican buyers meet American sellers is sufficiently high, the dollar circulates as an international currency in the two countries.

In the scheme of Matsuyama et al. (1993), and also in some of its developments,[31] the origin of international money depends exclusively on demand and, therefore, on market mechanisms. International money emerges when there is a high integration between countries and the economic size of one country is significantly greater than that of the other.

Matsuyama et al. (1993) can be taken as reference to explain the use of commodity money as international money. The acceptance of the pound sterling as an international currency in the gold standard can be explained by its high degree of substitutability with gold, and with the significant weight of the British economy in world trade. However, their theory is less effective when used to explain the use of fiat or quasi-fiat type international money, since it does not take into account the problem of trust in a payment instrument without intrinsic value. However, this problem is taken into account in some recent contributions by search-theoretic models.[32] In these contributions the problem of the quality of money, or its "cognizability", is posed, The latter is defined as follows by Jevons (1875/1876): "By this name we may denote the capability of a substance for being easily recognized and distinguished from all other substances. As a medium of exchange, money has to be continually handed about, and it will occasion great trouble if every person receiving currency has to scrutinise, weigh it and test it. If it requires any skill to discriminate good money from bad, poor ignorant people are sure to be imposed upon ...".

Taking this issue into account, Lester et al. (2011, 2012), developing the Lagos and Wright (2005) scheme,[33] hypothesize the existence of two forms of payment with different degrees of acceptability: fiat money and a real asset. The latter can be counterfeited if the buyer realizes that the seller is unable to confirm its quality. Aware of this, the seller does not accept the real asset as payment. Unless private individuals find it convenient to bear the costs of obtaining reliable information on the quality of real assets, then fiat money remains the only means of payment available. Based on these assumptions, with reference to both national and

[31]See, for example, Li and Matsui (2009).

[32]See, in particular, Lester et al. (2011, 2012).

[33]In this scheme, as in that of Rocheteau and Wright (2005), the hypothesis of indivisibility of money is removed and it is assumed that agents can operate exchanges in decentralized markets bargaining and in centralized markets *à la* Walras in which prices are competitive. The consideration of decentralized markets makes it possible to explain the role of financial assets in facilitating exchanges, while that of centralized markets make it possible to establish the price of financial assets. See also Nosal and Rocheteau (2011).

international markets, Zhang (2014), like Lester et al. (2011, 2012), shows that the good whose quality is cognizable at lower costs becomes money.

The contributions of Lester et al. (2012) and Zhang (2014), taking into account the problem of the quality of a means of exchange, represents an important step forward in the explanation through search-theoretic models of the conditions in which a good can be accepted as money and providing among these conditions its "cognizability", according to Jevons' expression. However, acquiring the latter carries a cost. In this context, it is inevitable to raise the question of who bears this cost. Zhang (2014) assumes that it is borne by individuals. It is relatively low in the case of a commodity money. In the case of quasi-fiat or fiat money, this cost inevitably increases, as the producer could behave fraudulently by issuing a quantity of money that compromises the stability of its value. In a context of this type, high production costs of "cognizability" of the money will tend to make it unacceptable.

The reduction of these costs can only be obtained by exploiting economies of scale in the production of "cognizability", that is of trust in the stable value of money. This can be achieved by concentrating in the state the responsibility for the production of trust in a currency which has an intrinsic value lower than its face value. This is what actually happened for national currencies. However, in the international arena, given the absence of a supranational authority, the production of cognizability for a fiat or quasi-fiat money is subject to various conditions, which are illustrated in the next section.

2.3.3 *Building Trust in a Fiat Money in the International Context*

In the previous section we saw how the use of a commodity money at the international level can be explained by extensions of the search-theoretic models, such as those found in the contributions of Matsuyama et al. (1993) and Li and Matsui (2009). On the other hand, the acceptance as an international money of a national currency of the fiat or quasi-fiat type requires a series of conditions which are illustrated analytically in the model shown in the Appendix.

These conditions first of all imply the creation of an institutional architecture aimed at guaranteeing trust in fiat money. The costs of making a fiat currency internationally recognizable fall on the issuing country. These costs essentially consist in defining institutions and policies that protect the property rights of the holders of the currency and of the assets denominated in it.

Internally, this protection comes from the existence of a high level of respect for the rule of law and from a relatively conservative monetary policy.[34] The latter implies the intention of keeping the inflation rate low, i.e. avoiding the inflationary erosion of the real value of the issued currency.

[34]See Walter (2006).

In addition to the constraints on the conduct of monetary policy, there are added costs for the issuing country to render its currency internationally recognizable. These costs are attributable, first of all, to the creation of an adequate internal and international institutional architecture. Among the domestic institutions to ensure confidence in a fiat money a crucial role is played by the rule of law. It is a fact that, if the country does not have a high level of "rule of law" internally, it is unlikely that a large and active financial market can develop in it, which is an essential prerequisite of the liquidity of financial assets denominated in a specific currency.[35]

However, the creation of an adequate internal rule of law may conflict with the policymakers' need to exercise control over the allocation of resources and the economic development model they pursue. Finally, in order for a currency to become an international money, the issuing country must bear the costs of creating an adequate internal rule of law as well as those necessary to ensure compliance with rules and institutions by the member countries of an international monetary system based on fiat money.

The production of trust through the creation of an adequate domestic institutional framework and virtuous policy choices inevitably entails costs. Clearly a country has an incentive to bear these costs only if the benefits it derives from the issuance of the international currency are greater than the costs. These benefits in the case of the issuance of a fiat currency consist mainly in the enjoyment of the privilege of international seigniorage.

Since a country's privilege of international seigniorage can affect the balance of power in its favour, it is necessary that other countries attribute little importance to this fact, focusing instead on the benefits that derive to them from the existence of an international money. This situation occurs when there is a significant initial power imbalance between the issuing country of the international currency and the other adhering countries. Indeed, asymmetric relative gains can alter the balance of power between the country issuing the international currency and the others. Unlike what happens in the presence of a multipolar equilibrium, when in the relations between states there is a country that enjoys a significantly higher "state capability" than the others, it is easier for an international money of a fiat or quasi-fiat type to emerge.[36] An international money of this type, therefore, emerges for the interest of the two parties, i.e. the leader country and the follower countries, to initiate a political exchange from which both parties benefit.

The hypothesis just illustrated also allows us to explain the historical evolution of the international money. In the presence of a commodity money, such as gold, the problem of "cognizability" of money does not arise. In this case, as evidenced in the search-theoretic models, it is almost exclusively the economic dimensions of

[35]It is certainly no coincidence that, as shown by Gourinchas and Rey (2007) in this post-war period, the return on foreign assets held by the USA is persistently higher than the return on that country's liabilities held abroad. Therefore, the accumulation by other countries of dollar-denominated assets represents a form of interest subsidy. See Kaminska and Zinna (2014).

[36]That is a currency whose face value is partially hedged and at the discretion of the issuing country.

the states that matter. In this context, the commodity money adopted by the largest country prevails. This is the case in England and the gold standard.

After the First World War, however, changes in internal political and social conditions and in international relations gradually made it impossible to return to the gold standard. Therefore, the demand for more flexible forms of money emerged at the national level, which would involve lower adjustment costs in the event of macroeconomic imbalances and, more generally, in relation to the trend of the economic cycle.

In a context of this type, an incompatibility emerged between the type of money used inside countries and the international money, anchored to a commodity money and, therefore, not very flexible. The interwar years were characterized by the absence of an international money and the establishment of some monetary blocs. After the Second World War, with the emergence of American leadership, it was possible with the Bretton Woods Agreements to "legalize" monetary relations between countries. These Agreements not only satisfied the US objective of creating an international money and more generally of creating the conditions for a significant development of international trade,[37] but also those of follower countries to pursue relatively autonomous national economic policies, aimed principally at achieving full employment, and enjoying protection for their national security.[38] The result was a political-economic exchange that was advantageous for all parties.[39]

In this exchange the leader country took on the costs of producing trust in the international money it issued and was able to take advantage of international seigniorage, while the follower countries accepted the relative gains obtained by the leader country from the privilege of international seigniorage, since they benefited from a public good, the international money, and could thus increase their foreign trade, income and domestic well-being.

In light of the interpretation proposed here, the introduction into the Bretton Woods system of a quasi-fiat money depended not, therefore, on the imposition of a hegemonic country, as neo-realist version of hegemonic stability theory would suggest, since follower countries obtained to safeguard large margins of monetary autonomy. However, the acceptance of the dollar as the key currency of the Bretton Woods system did not even stem from a cooperative agreement between states aimed at ensuring a higher level of economic well-being for their citizens, as the neo-liberal version of the hegemonic stability theory argues. Rather, in the political exchange underlying the Bretton Woods Agreements and then in the actual implementation of those Agreements, an important role was played by the aspect of international security and the balance of power between states. It is a fact that states, in addition to maximizing the economic well-being of their citizens, pursue the goal of maximizing their security. "In a self-help system each of the units spends a portion

---

[37]As argued by such scholars as Gilpin (1981) and Block (1977).

[38]See Ikenberry (1993).

[39]See Mastanduno (2009).

of its effort, not in forwarding its own good, but in providing the means of protecting itself against others. . . . When faced with the possibility of cooperating for mutual gain, states that feel insecure must ask how the gain will be divided. They are compelled to ask not 'will both of us gain?' but 'who will gain more?'".[40]

In the international arena, the country that today is a friend may tomorrow be an enemy. In this context, the question of relative gains becomes important. The follower countries accepted that the USA had the privilege of seigniorage in the Bretton Woods system because they attached little weight to the fact that that country would be able to exploit this privilege to increase its political and military power in the international arena: this was because on the one hand, the power disparity between the leader and follower countries was already vast, and, on the other hand, the leader country was largely responsible for addressing their international security needs.

The political agreement at the heart of the Bretton Woods system continued in the years following the suspension of the dollar in 1971, i.e. in the phase of the dollar standard still in place. The focus on the problem of relative gains makes it possible to explain not only the prerequisites for the existence of an international money, but also those of its absence. Where there is a multipolar equilibrium, that is several countries with similar levels of power, the weight they attach to relative gains is high. The ability of a country to enjoy the privilege of seigniorage could alter the existing balance of power. In this context, it is difficult to see how an international currency of the fiat or quasi-fiat type could exist. Emblematic in this sense is the situation that arose in the period between the two Wars. In this period, in the absence of an international currency, monetary blocs emerged. Within these blocks a mechanism similar to that previously outlined at the global level occurs: there was, in fact, a leading country whose fiat currency tended to play the key currency role in the area.

2.4 The Evolution of International Money

Different types of money underlie different international monetary systems. In the previous section the origin of international money under a static approach was discussed, we have not analysed the reasons for the evolution of money, especially its transition from commodity money to increasingly abstract forms of money that is money with an intrinsic value which may be significantly lower than its face value.

There is a tendency among some scholars to compare money to language, arguing that just as the language most widely used in the world is the result of a convention, so too is international money. Kindleberger (1967, p. 10) writes: "The selection of the dollar as the lingua franca of international monetary arrangements, then, is not

[40]See Waltz (1979, p. 105).

the work of men but of circumstances".[41] As Giannini (2011, p. 8) writes: "The analogy is misleading. Once a social convention has developed, it is self-supporting because it is in the interest of all the members in the society to observe it. This is not true of money. The stock of money can be likened to a durable good that produces a flow of services for the person holding it …". A sudden increase in the money supply, for example, significantly reduces the flow of services it offers.

Since money is an institution and not a convention, the evolution of money both nationally and internationally can be explained within a theoretical framework that explains the reasons for institutional changes. North (1992, p. 10) writes: "The sources of change [of institutions] are the opportunities perceived by entrepreneurs. They stem from either external changes in the environment or the acquisition of learning and skills and their incorporation in the mental constructs of the actors. Changes in relative prices have been the most commonly observed external sources of institutional change in history, but changes in taste have also been important".[42]

In the context just outlined, the evolution of international money is the result of a process of adaptive efficiency in which two principal moments can be identified. The first moment is characterized by pressures for the introduction of a monetary innovation that would favour a decrease in the transaction costs of exchanges. The strength of these pressures depends on the bargaining power of the interest groups that favour it. Crises increase the effectiveness of these pressures and, therefore, favour the adoption of monetary reforms. The second moment is represented by the supply of the monetary innovations and the institutions that allow the existence of these innovations. In fact, "a demand for reform is not necessarily matched by a supply of reform. This is because the concept of supply of reform involves the political sphere".[43] At the national level, a decisive role in the adoption of reforms is played by the states. At the international level, the way in which a political environment favouring the introduction of monetary reforms is formed is more complex. Its complexity varies according to the type of money involved.

Under certain circumstances, the origin of an international money may depend on a third moment, beyond those just mentioned. This moment is when the imitative process of the states towards monetary reforms implemented at the national level in other states allows an international money to emerge almost spontaneously. This occurs when a monetary reform within a country is effective in reducing the transaction costs of exchanges and other countries consider it convenient for them to adopt it internally.

In the past centuries, the form of money traditionally used in international trade was a commodity money, silver or gold. While, on the one hand, this type of money is exempt from the problem of producing trust in it, on the other hand, it has two drawbacks. The first of these is related to the costs of producing it and to the fact that

---

[41] A similar statement is found in Rey (2019, p. 15): "… the dollar is to currencies what English is to languages".

[42] See also North (1971, 1990).

[43] See Giannini (2011, p. xxviii).

the commodity used as money is no longer available for alternative uses. The second disadvantage of commodity money is due to its low supply elasticity with respect to output. This aspect is well highlighted by Friedman (1951, p. 206) when he writes: "The vices of strict commodity standards are the other side of their virtues. Being automatic, they may not provide sufficient flexibility or adaptability to prevent substantial swings in prices or in income".

The low supply elasticity of commodity money with respect to output tends to slow down the growth of trade and, therefore, the economic growth of countries due to the downward rigidity of prices and wages. The downward rigidity of these variables has increased over time with the emergence of unions, mass political parties who are traditionally opposed to a downward flexibility of wages, and, at the industrial level, with the emergence of monopolies with a high market power. The increasing use of multi-period contracts has also contributed to the rigidity of the prices of many goods and services.

A given quantity of commodity money could make an increasing number of exchanges possible only if prices and wages were flexible. Such flexibility would only be possible if contracts were continuously renegotiated. However, renegotiation would result in very high transaction costs in exchanges. Economic growth would be significantly affected. In the context just outlined, the pressures to introduce innovations that would make it possible to increase the elasticity of the money supply have been persistent over time.[44]

These pressures became particularly intense with the development of internal and international trade during the nineteenth century. The widespread use of banknotes, perhaps the most important monetary innovation ever, is to be seen in this context. The acceptance of this medium of exchange was, however, conditioned by the existence of an institutional architecture that guaranteed the stability of its value.

This architecture could be created as part of the state building process of nation states. The adoption by England of the Bank Charter Act in 1844, on the one hand, allowed the political class of that country to centralize money supply and stabilize its amount by anchoring it to gold, and on the other hand, favoured the spread of bank cheques. The monetary reforms adopted by England were subsequently imitated by other countries in the context of the process of state capacity building which was associated with the formation of nation states. The spread of the gold standard allowed the political class to promote the development of the internal monetary and financial market and, therefore, to pursue high economic growth and, with it, a higher level of international economic and political influence. The gold standard emerged largely automatically from the adoption of internal monetary and institutional reforms.

[44]See Giannini (2011). In historical periods in which the use of commodity money was prevalent, in order to increase the elasticity of the money supply, governments resorted to different means such as the debasement of the minting alloy, the use of different types of money for internal and international use, the establishment of a unit of account alongside the physical currencies used as a means of payment. See Cipolla (1957), Giannini (2011) and Goodhart (1989).

The demand for monetary innovation, in addition to an increase in the transaction costs of economic exchanges, can come from an increase in the transaction costs of a political nature, induced by changes in the internal socio-political balance. As will be seen, the social and political changes that took place after the First World War were not compatible with the rigidity of the gold standard rules and there was a demand for monetary innovation that would allow greater flexibility in economic policy. In the 1930s, however, attempts to create an institutional framework that could guarantee confidence in a quasi-fiat or fiat international money failed due to the, then prevalent, multipolar equilibrium in the international arena. Similar attempts, however, were successful after World War II when the USA had become the dominant power.

The example just given shows how the transition to increasingly abstract forms of money has been more problematic at the international level than at the national one. This problem arises from the fact that the acceptance of an abstract money at the international level, and the creation of an institutional architecture that produces trust in it, depends on the relations between states and on the balance of power that characterizes them. This explains the delay with which, starting from the period following the First World War, the international monetary system took to adapt to the monetary innovations introduced within the states. This situation contrasts with what happened previously when the introduction of monetary innovations was prompted by the development of international trade. At that stage it was the structure of the monetary systems within the states that changed following changes in the international payment system.[45] The inversion of the causal link just illustrated must obviously be traced back to the formation of national states.

The process of state building capacity related to the formation of states not only allowed policymakers to acquire the control of money as well as create rules and institutions that would ensure the stability of its value, but also influenced the forms that money would take. In the first place, with the formation of nation states, a situation arose in which the international money had to be compatible with the internal one. In this new context, the existence of an international money and its typology came to depend on the objectives of the nation states and the political class that guided them. Such goals could be economic growth and expansion of the country's power or, more simply, the survival of the ruling elite.

Second, in the definition of an institutional architecture that assures confidence in a quasi-fiat or fiat money, the role of the relationships between states is crucial. Indeed, the existence of an international fiat or quasi-fiat money depends on the existence of a certain balance of power between the leader and the follower countries, in particular on the existence of a leader country. In the neo-liberal perspective of hegemonic stability theory, the existence of a leader makes it possible to overcome the problems of free-riding. From this perspective, it can be considered that

[45]See North and Thomas (1973).

this function of coordination can be exercised, instead of by a single country alone, by a few large countries.

The theoretical scheme proposed in Sect. 2.3.3 assumes, according to the prevailing international relations literature,[46] that cooperation between states, particularly between great powers, is problematic because of the problem of relative gains. This problem becomes crucial in the case of fiat or quasi-fiat currencies, since the issuing country enjoys the privilege of seigniorage. In this context, the initial power discrepancy between the leading and the follower countries implies that the latter attribute little weight to the higher relative gains that the issuing country enjoys. This aspect leads us to believe that the simultaneous existence of a plurality of international currencies, predicted by some scholars, is unlikely to occur.[47]

2.5 From an International Money to an International Monetary System

The existence of an international money, or key currency, is the prerequisite for the existence of an international monetary system. Like international money also the international monetary system is a public good.[48] It is therefore important to clarify the conditions under which such a public good can be produced. The role of an international monetary system "is to lend order and stability to foreign exchange markets, to encourage the elimination of balance of payments problems, and to provide access to international credits in the event of disruptive shocks".[49]

This definition identifies well which are the functions performed by an international monetary system. Its structure depends on four fundamental characteristics, namely:

i. the type of international money;
ii. the exchange rate regime;
iii. the degree of international mobility of capital;
iv. the rules, institutions and conventions that ensure its functioning and stability.

Reference to features *ii.* and *iii.* makes it possible to clarify how an international monetary system works. As is known, according to the macroeconomic trilemma of Mundell (1963) and Fleming (1962)[50] in the conduct of monetary policy one cannot simultaneously have monetary autonomy, fixed exchange rates and perfect capital mobility. It is therefore necessary to give up at least one of the conditions mentioned. For example, when the target was to respect a fix exchange rate (as was the case

[46] See Waltz (1979).
[47] See Bergsten (2011), Eichengreen (2011b), World Bank (2011) and Chitu et al. (2014).
[48] See Dorucci and McKay (2011).
[49] See Eichengreen (1996, p. 3).
[50] See Giannini (2011) and Schenk (2014).

Table 2.3 Solutions to the trilemma in recent international monetary systems

	Fixed exchange rates	International capital mobility	Autonomy of monetary policy
1870–1914	x	x	
1919–1931	x	x	
1931–1939			x
1945–1971	x		x
After 1971		x	x

before the Second World War), constraints must be placed on capital movements or monetary autonomy must be renounced. Conversely, the adoption of flexible exchange rates is compatible with the international mobility of capital and the preservation of monetary discretion. Table 2.3 shows the solutions given to the macroeconomic trilemma in the monetary systems that emerged from 1870 to today.

The choice of which of the conditions of the trilemma to abandon depend, above all, on the relative importance attributed to the enjoyment of monetary autonomy or to the stable exchange rate. Between 1870 and 1914, when the classical gold standard was in effect, governments attached paramount importance to exchange rate stability. Minimizing exchange rate risk favoured, in fact, the growth of commercial exchanges and international capital flows.

Conversely, after the First World War, governments attached increasing importance to domestic economic conditions, in particular the unemployment rate and the stability of citizens' income. In this context, a regime of fixed exchange rates and high international capital mobility proved incompatible with the maintenance of high monetary sovereignty. Monetary disorder and frequent recourse to competitive devaluations in the interwar period led policymakers to return to a fixed exchange rate system with the Bretton Woods Agreements. In that monetary system, the monetary sovereignty of the states was safeguarded by the possibility of resorting to restrictions on capital movements. In the dollar standard, the monetary system currently in force, the monetary autonomy of states derives from the adoption of flexible exchange rates, while the constraints on capital movements, in advanced countries at least, were removed in the 1980s.

Point *iv.* concerns the set of conventions, rules and institutions that ensure, in addition to the functioning, the stability of the international monetary system. This set changes in relation to point *i.*, the type of international money used. Therefore, the evolution of the latter is inevitably reflected in point *iv.* As pointed out in Sect. 2.4, the international money, which initially consisted of a commodity money, has taken on ever more abstract forms over time. This process was accompanied by a growing articulation and complexity of the rules and the institutional structure aimed at guaranteeing the functioning and stability of the international monetary system. It initially reflected the state capacity building process of nation states. Subsequently, post-WWII, a balance of power emerged which made it possible to define rules and create an institutional architecture which, partially substituting the absence of a supranational monetary authority, guaranteed the stability of a monetary system based on fiat money.

In the Middle Ages and up to the sixteenth century, the gold coins of the states had a limited circulation, which corresponded to the limited state capacity of the issuing states. The low state capacity implied both a territorial limitation over which the state exercised its authority and a modest fiscal capacity. The first of these aspects helps to explain why in the Middle Ages and the Renaissance the extent of seigniorage available to kings and princes was limited.[51] The second aspect, namely the modest fiscal capacity of states in the modern age, often induced sovereigns to finance themselves by debasing the intrinsic value of money and, therefore, by the inflationary tax.

The states, given the limited power which they possessed, suffered the monetary innovations that were induced by the development of international trade. In this context, the weight of the markets prevailed over that of the states. The latter exercised their power only internally both in order to keep their competitiveness high and to affect the distribution of income. In this regard, Cipolla (2013) showed how, in fourteenth century Florence, two different types of coin were used: gold for trade with foreign countries and silver for internal trade, particularly the payment of wages. Changes in the exchange rate between these two types of money allowed the elite to intervene in the distribution of income.

The states acquired the ability to influence the international monetary order when, in the nineteenth century, they became nation states, unifying the domestic monetary system and taking control on money supply. The prerequisite for the choice of advanced countries to adopt the gold standard in the 1870s was the availability of a high degree of fiscal capacity. Together with the possession of an adequate level of gold reserves, this made it possible to defend the convertibility of national currencies and to preserve the stability of their value. The latter, combined with the higher flexibility of the money supply allowed by the gold standard compared to bimetallism, allowed the nation states to develop domestic monetary and financial systems, thus satisfying the demand for financing from the private and public sectors, supporting the country's economic growth and its power in the international arena. With the gold standard the causal relationship between state and market in defining the international monetary system was reversed; henceforth, it will be states who define the internal and external institutional framework that is at the basis of an international monetary system.

In the context that has arisen, the choices of states in monetary matters are mainly determined by the internal and international objectives pursued by the political elite. These objectives are conditioned, on the one hand, by the prevailing socio-political balance inside and, on the other hand, by the balance of power in the international arena.

After the First World War, under pressure from England, the Allies reconstituted an international money order which, from many points of view, was similar to the

[51]See Goodhart (1989).

pre-war system. However, this system turned out to be incompatible with the new socio-political reality prevailing in advanced countries. The advent of strong trade unions, the extension of electoral suffrage, the formation of mass parties made the economic and social costs of the adjustment mechanisms provided by a monetary system such as the gold-exchange standard based on a commodity money, unacceptably high.

In this context, there was a growing demand for an international money with greater supply flexibility than that provided by the gold-exchange standard. It would have made easier to smooth out the costs of the adjustment measures of any imbalances. The collapse of the gold-exchange standard was not due, as Kindleberger (1973) suggests, to the refusal of the USA to exercise a leadership similar to that exercised by England in the gold standard, but rather to the fact that it was not compatible with the new internal socio-political reality of the advanced countries. This reality required the abandonment of the past system, to which a part of the elite of the time, in particular the British, was stubbornly linked. As Keynes writes: "A preference for a tangible gold currency is no longer more than a relic of a time when governments were less trustworthy in these matters than they are now, and when it was the fashion to imitate uncritically the system which had been established in England and had seemed to work so well during the second quarter of the nineteenth century".[52]

The demand for a more flexible money, and an international monetary system based on it, remained unsatisfied not only because part of the elite could not conceive of an international monetary system other than the gold standard, but also because there was a lack of balance of power between states that would have made it advantageous for a country to bear the costs of building trust in such a system.

After the Second World War, due to the new balance of power between states, the conditions emerged for the adoption of an international fiat money and to guarantee the functioning of the monetary system based on it. In particular, American leadership made it possible with the Bretton Woods Agreements to create rules and institutions capable of guaranteeing trust in an international monetary system based on currencies anchored only indirectly to a commodity.

The Bretton Woods Agreements constituted the first form of "legalization" of international monetary affairs.[53] This implies the commitment of the adhering countries to adopt behaviour consistent with maintaining the stability of the monetary system. It therefore provides for a transfer of sovereignty by the adhering countries. In exchange for which, however, the member countries would enjoy two public goods: the use of an international money and a stable international monetary system.

As noted by Abbot and Snidal (1998), the legalization of international monetary relations is a tool to enhance the credibility of a system of this type, since it increases the cost of the violation of the commitments made by the participating countries.

---

[52]See Keynes (1913, p. 51).

[53]See Simmons (2000).

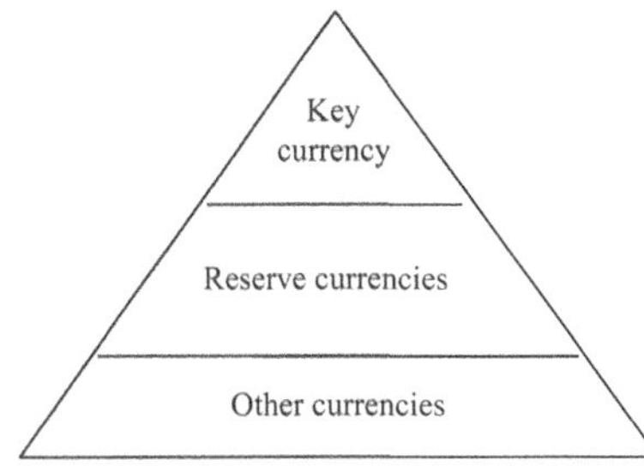

Fig. 2.1 The hierarchical structure of currencies in an international monetary system based on fiat or quasi-fiat money

Under the Bretton Woods system this task was assigned to the International Monetary Fund (IMF). In fact, this institution was assigned the function of supervising the management of exchange rates and changes in parities. Subsequently, the IMF mainly took on tasks of surveillance and management of the financial and currency crises of emerging countries and, in recent times, also of advanced countries. The authority of the IMF was, and is, assured by the political support of the USA.[54]

Recourse to international treaties and agreements is seen today as the standard method in the construction not only of the international monetary system, but also of regional monetary systems. Emblematic in this sense are the Maastricht Treaty and the creation of the European Monetary Union.

The method of legalization of international monetary affairs has proved particularly effective due to the possibility it gives to modify rules and institutions in response to destabilizing shocks and to carry out reforms that improve the stability of the existing monetary system.[55]

Whatever the origin of an international monetary system, in general, alongside the key currency, other high quality currencies are used in international trade. Even in the classic gold standard, despite the dominant role of the pound and Britain, France and Germany also contributed to the stability of the system as a whole and, in particular, to the areas over which they had political influence.

It follows that often in an international monetary system there is a tendency to consolidate a hierarchy among the currencies used in international exchanges. This hierarchy takes the form of a pyramid based on the different roles that various currencies have in the international monetary system. At the top of the pyramid (Fig. 2.1) is the currency of the leading state, which acts as the key currency of the system that is the international money. At a lower level are the currencies of the countries that better protect the property rights of their holders. Assets denominated in these currencies are therefore held in the official reserves of many countries. Furthermore, these same currencies, in many cases, circulate as a means of payment

---

[54]See Henning (2009) and Woods (2006).

[55]It has been appropriately observed that: "... the legalization of international monetary relations helps governments make credible policy commitments to market actors ... the central mechanism encouraging compliance is the desire to avoid reputational costs associated with reneging on a legal obligation". See Simmons (2000, p. 574).

and unit of account in certain limited geographical areas. Finally, at the base of the pyramid are the currencies of the other countries that are part of the system.

Various international political economy scholars tend to explain the hierarchical structure of the international monetary system based on the classification made by Strange (1971a, 1971b). On the basis of this classification, there are four categories of currencies at the international level: master currencies, or currencies issued by hegemonic countries, which impose them on the rest of the world; the top currencies, widely used in international trade for the dominant economic role of the issuing country; the negotiated currencies, the use of which results from a negotiation between the issuer country and other countries, in which the issuer offers forms of support in exchange for the use of its currency; the neutral currencies, issued by economically strong countries, although not predominant. Strange's classification, subsequently taken up and expanded by Cohen (1998), is essentially based on the degree of international power enjoyed by the issuing country.

The hierarchical structure of the currencies used in international trade can be explained differently depending on the existing monetary system and the type of money on which it is based. Thus, it can be assumed that in the gold standard, since all the currencies of the acceding countries are convertible into gold, the lower rank of the franc and mark with respect to the pound depends on the lower degree of substitutability with gold of these currencies than the English currency. On the other hand, in the current monetary system, based on a fiat money, the hierarchical superiority of the dollar against other reserve currencies, such as the euro and the yen, derives from the fact that the countries issuing these currencies, on the one hand, preside over the stability of their areas of influence, thus contributing to the stability of the dollar-based monetary system, but on the other hand, they have financial systems that are highly interdependent with the American one and, as such, are exposed to the financial cycle of the American currency and therefore have an incentive to maintain the stability of the global financial system.

2.6 Benefits and Costs of the Country that Issues the International Money

In the past, various economists and politicians have foreseen the possibility that there is only one international currency, whether it be of the fiat or quasi-fiat type. Post-WWII President Roosvelt instructed the Secretary of the Treasury, Henry Morgenthau Jr., to prepare a plan for the creation of an international currency. The White Plan gave the currency the name "unitas"; the Keynes Plan called it "bancor". More recently Mundell (2012) took up this idea calling the new money "intor".

The issue of a world currency, however, is somewhat problematic. The main problem that hinders the existence of a currency of this type is the distribution, among the different countries, of the benefits and costs deriving from issuing it. The problem of relative gains re-emerges as do difficulties of cooperation between states in the monetary sphere.

In fact, the country that issues a fiat or quasi-fiat type international currency enjoys benefits that far outweigh the costs it bears. It was referring to them that Giscard d'Estaing, speaking of the role of the dollar in the Bretton Woods system, said that the USA enjoyed an "exorbitant privilege".[56]

The role of leader of an international monetary system has undoubted benefits for the country that issues the key currency, however, this country also bears costs. These costs are mainly related to the production of trust both in the currency it issues and in the monetary system based on it. The main benefits and costs that the leading country incurs are reported below.[57]

2.6.1 *The Benefits*

The main benefits of issuing an international currency are as follows:

2.6.1.1 Seigniorage

This is defined as the excess of the nominal value of a currency over the cost of producing it. Seigniorage is generated when foreign subjects accept a currency, or an asset denominated in it, in exchange for goods and services.[58] For example, at present, in the case of the USA, it is estimated that about 60% of the notes issued by the Federal Reserve are held by non-residents.

A second form of seigniorage comes from the differential between the interest rate on foreign assets and that on assets denominated in the international currency.[59] This differential depends on the different liquidity premium on the various currencies. In some empirical studies it has been estimated at 300 or more basis points per year.[60]

[56] Eichengreen (2011a).

[57] See Cohen (2012).

[58] See Cohen (2009, p. 10).

[59] See Aliber (1964) and Chinn and Frankel (2007).

[60] See Gourinchas and Rey (2007) and ECB (2010). In other empirical studies, however, it is argued that the gains from interest rate differentials are modest in magnitude, see Dobbs et al. (2009) and Cooper (2009).

2.6.1.2 High Macroeconomic Flexibility

The use of a currency as an international money allows the issuing country to finance current account imbalances simply by issuing additional currency.[61] This possibility makes foreign constraints on the conduct of the monetary and fiscal policy of the country issuing the international currency less stringent and hence this country is less exposed than other countries to the discipline factor represented by the foreign market.

2.6.1.3 International Monetary Power

The possession, on the part of the issuing country, of the privilege of seigniorage and high macroeconomic flexibility has led many scholars of International Political Economy (IPE) to conclude that this country enjoys a high degree of international monetary power.[62] What this power consists in, however, is not simple. As Zimmermann (2013, p. 149) writes: "It is simply assumed that a national currency that takes on an international role enhances the power of the issuing country .... However, substantiating in what sense the possession of a global currency actually bestow power on the issuing country is not so easy". A debate on the definition of monetary power is found mostly in the IPE literature.[63] On the basis of this literature, monetary power takes on two different connotations.[64] In a first, international monetary power means the ability of a state not to be conditioned by other states in its policy choices.[65] This implies being able to proceed to adjustment policies later and smoothly.

In the second connotation, having international monetary power means being able to influence the decisions of other states, inducing them to do what they would otherwise not do.[66] Such influence may take the hard form of relational power or that of soft structural power. Some scholars, such as Kirshner (1995), focus on the first type of power and the deliberate use of certain monetary instruments to achieve state objectives. An example of the exercise of relational monetary power is the behaviour of the USA during the Suez Canal crisis of 1956. As is known, in October of that year Israel, France and England militarily occupied the canal. In addition to Egypt

[61]See Cohen (2012) and Chey (2012).

[62]See Kirshner (1995) and Andrews (2006).

[63]See, in particular, Strange (1971b), Cohen (2013), Helleiner (2008), Kirshner (2008), and Norrlof (2014).

[64]See Cohen (2015).

[65]See Cohen (2006) and Helleiner and Kirshner (2009).

[66]Obviously, having autonomy in domestic economic policy choices is an indispensable prerequisite for exercising influence over other states. As Cohen (2012, p. 18) writes: "First and foremost, policymakers must be free (or at least relatively free) to pursue national objectives in the specific issue area or relationship without outside constraint, to avoid compromises or sacrifices to accommodate the interests of others".

and the Soviet Union, the USA opposed the occupation fearing a widening of the conflict. Without intervening militarily, through their central bank, the USA exerted downward pressure on the pound. Another more recent exercise of hard monetary power is the possibility of granting or denying dollar loans to countries affected by financial crises. Typical is the behaviour of the Fed in response to the financial crisis of 2008–2009 when it granted swap lines in dollars to emerging countries in order to avoid a serious banking crisis in them, but chose not to do so towards others, such as India, which had also asked for similar support measures.[67]

The country issuing an international currency can exercise its soft structural power defining the structure of the international monetary system and directing changes in order to maintain the primacy of its currency.[68] Simmons (2001) gives an example of this form of power in his analysis of international capital market regulations. In this analysis she shows that the definition of these regulations was strongly influenced by the financial power of the USA: "[America] has the potential to change significantly the context for financial markets and hence it affects regulators in the rest of the world".[69]

2.6.1.4 The Microeconomic Benefits

Consumers, businesses and financial institutions in the country that issues the international currency enjoy a competitive advantage. Banks enjoy the benefit that they can issue liabilities at interest rates lower than those on the liabilities of banks of foreign countries. Businesses can benefit from the fact that most foreign transactions are conducted in their national currency and they are therefore not exposed to foreign exchange risk. Consumers benefit from the fact that when their national currency becomes the international money, its value increases and consequently their purchasing power increases.[70]

---

[67]See Allen and Moessner (2010) and Allen (2013).

[68]Another form of monetary power enjoyed by the country issuing the international currency is represented by the prestige it enjoys from the widespread use of its currency. This prestige translates into the transmission of its values and culture to other countries. As Mundell (1993, p. 10) wrote: "Great powers have great currencies". Taking this form of soft power into account, Hirschman (1945) traces the structural power of the country that issues the international currency to its ability to influence the perception of its own interests by the states that use this currency in trade with other countries.

[69]See Simmons (2001, p. 596).

[70]See Trejos and Wright (2001) and Kannan (2009).

2.6.2 *Costs*

The country that issues an international money, in addition to enjoying significant benefits, also bears costs. Among these the main ones are the following.

2.6.2.1 Conditions in the Conduct of Monetary Policy

The fact that non-residents hold the currency used as an international currency makes the demand for it unstable. This can affect the effectiveness of the monetary policy of the country issuing the international currency whether its central bank target is a monetary aggregate or an interest rate. This type of conditioning, however, becomes less significant the larger the money market of the country issuing the international currency is.[71]

2.6.2.2 Political Responsibility

The country that issues the international money also implicitly assumes responsibility for the stability of the international monetary system. By assuming this responsibility, the leading country ensures the smooth functioning of the international payments system and, therefore, promotes trade and economic growth. This responsibility is particularly important in a monetary system based on an abstract money. In this case, in fact, the leader country must guarantee compliance with the rules and institutions that ensure the stability of the monetary system. In the production of this public good, it inevitably incurs costs.

Another type of cost arising from the responsibility to ensure the stability of the international monetary system is the impact on its monetary policy. In the conduct of its monetary policy, the leading country cannot ignore the repercussions that its stance has on international monetary and financial stability. Similarly, in the presence of crises in part of the international monetary system or of a global nature, an accommodative monetary policy may be required on the part of the country issuing the international money, but such a policy could conflict with the internal needs of that country.

2.6.2.3 The Trade-Off Between Issuing the International Money and Building Trust in It

If the country that issues the fiat or quasi-fiat international money wants its currency to retain a prominent role in exchanges, it must guarantee an increase in its supply

[71]In the case of the USA, given the size of its money market, this conditioning is considered modest. See Genberg (2010).

corresponding to that of foreign exchanges. However, such growth can be detrimental to confidence in the stability of its future value.

With reference to the Bretton Woods system, Triffin (1947) showed that the American authorities were faced with a dilemma in the management of the dollar. As will be seen in Chap. 5, in this system the American currency was expected to be convertible into gold at a fixed exchange rate. In this context, the USA should therefore have held an amount of gold reserves sufficient to satisfy this requirement. Since in the decades immediately following the Second World War the rate of growth of foreign trade was significantly higher than that of their gold reserves, according to Triffin (1960), the USA was faced with a dilemma. If they had not met the increase dollar demand to support the growth of world trade, they would have penalized this growth and, therefore, the growth of world output. Conversely, if they allowed the growth of the supply of dollars to match the growth of world trade, they would have gradually reduced the share of dollars in circulation covered by gold reserves. In this way they would undermine confidence in the convertibility of dollars into gold and induced non-residents to get rid of their stocks of US currency, thus causing a pronounced depreciation.

With reference to the post-Bretton Woods monetary system, the dollar standard, confidence in the stability of the value of the US currency can be threatened by the large and persistent U.S. current account deficit. Hence, on the one hand, the need for this country to reduce these deficits, but, on the other hand, the concern that by doing so it will lead to a shortage of international liquidity.

2.7 Conclusions

The prevailing theories of international money, namely the search-theoretic models and the various versions of the hypothesis of hegemonic stability, while they explain the origins, do not offer an explanation of its evolution over time and the reasons for it.

Since money is an institution, its evolution is the result of a process of adaptive efficiency in which different moments can be recognized. The first moment is represented by the demand for monetary innovations with respect to the current regime. This demand emerges when the current monetary system gives rise to high economic or political transaction costs. In some cases, the pressure for the introduction of monetary innovations is made evident by monetary and financial crises, even dramatic ones.

Whatever its origin, the demand for monetary innovation can only be satisfied by a political supply of rules and institutions that produce confidence in the new form of money and the monetary system based on it. This is the second moment. When the political supply of an institutional framework that produces confidence in the required reforms is lacking, the demand remains unsatisfied. In a situation of this type, a situation of monetary disorder prevails; the system of international payments can deteriorate and a situation emerges in which an international money is lacking.

At the international level, as at the national level, money has become more and more abstract, passing from commodity money, to quasi-fiat money, to fiat money. This process has made it possible to significantly increase the elasticity of the money supply, but at the same time it has posed the problem of how to build trust in it. Under the gold standard, the elasticity of the international money supply was low and equally, the problem of trust was irrelevant since the currency was convertible into gold. This type of money was recognizable, that is, its quality was publicly known. In the Bretton Woods system, the international money became a quasi-fiat money anchored to a commodity but without establishing a predefined cover ratio. This constraint has gradually become looser over time.

The supply elasticity of a currency of this type is high, but the problem of preserving confidence in the stability of its value is also significant, as is the preservation of confidence in the functioning and stability of the monetary system which is based on it.

The Bretton Woods Agreements represent the "legalization" of monetary affairs that is an agreement between states in which rules and institutions are defined to ensure confidence in the stability of the value of a quasi-fiat international money and its associated monetary system.

In the international context, in the absence of a supranational authority, similar agreements aimed at producing trust in an abstract money, rather than to forms of cooperation (difficult due to the problem of relative gains), are comparable to a political exchange between states. The Bretton Woods system was based on precisely such a political exchange, as is the current international monetary system, the dollar standard. The political exchange which underpins a monetary system based on a quasi-flat or fiat money, however, can only take place if at least two conditions are met. The first of these is that the leading country can benefit from supporting an international monetary system in which participating countries use fiat currencies. This happens if the return that the leading country has by exploiting seigniorage exceeds the costs incurred by it to enforce compliance with rules and institutions.

The second condition for an international monetary system based on fiat money to exist is that the follower countries accept the relative gain that the leading country acquires from the exploitation of international seigniorage. This condition is met when the political-military power imbalance between the leading country and the follower countries is very high.

The two conditions just illustrated explain not only the origin and nature of the Bretton Woods system and the dollar standard, but also why an international money was missing in the interwar period. After the First World War, in fact, changes in internal political and social conditions and in relations between states gradually made the return to the gold standard impractical. The demand for more flexible forms of money, which entailed lower adjustment costs in the event of macroeconomic imbalances, asserted itself at the national level. The demand for monetary reform—despite the numerous monetary conferences held in the 1920s, the role attributed to the League of Nations in the stabilization of some countries and the establishment of the Bank for International Settlements[72]—did not emerge explicitly, also because Britain and its central bank stubbornly insisted on a return to the gold standard. However, the emergence of an international monetary system based on money of this type required rules and institutions that would guarantee confidence in its operation and stability. Given the multipolar equilibrium prevailing in that period, the weight attributed to relative gains was significant. It was therefore problematic for any country to bear the costs of producing confidence in an international money with a degree of flexibility compatible with that of domestic money. In the absence of pressure for the introduction of monetary innovations and an adequate political response, a situation arose in which an international money was lacking. The absence of an international leader and the tensions between states favoured the emergence of several monetary blocs in which leadership was exercised by a great power that guaranteed the stability of each bloc.

References

Abbot, K., & Snidal, D. (1998). Why states act through formal international organizations? *Journal of Conflict Resolution, 42*, 3–32.

Aliber, R. Z. (1964). The costs and benefits of the US role as a reserve currency country. *Quarterly Journal of Economics, 78*, 442–456.

Allen, W. A. (2013). *International liquidity and the financial crisis*. Cambridge University Press.

Allen, W. A., & Moessner, R. (2010). *Central bank cooperation and international liquidity in the financial crisis of 2008-09*. BIS working paper n. 310.

Andrews, D. M. (2006). *International monetary power*. Cornell University Press.

Bergsten, C. F. (2011, February 15). Why the world needs three global currencies. *Financial Times*.

Block, F. (1977). *The origins of international economic disorder. A study of United States international monetary policy from World War II to present*. University of California Press.

Calleo, D. P. (1982). *The imperious economy*. Harvard University Press.

Chey, H. (2012). Theories of international currencies and the future of the world monetary order. *International Studies Review, 14*, 51–77.

Chinn, M., & Frankel, J. A. (2007). Will the euro eventually surpass the dollar as leading international reserve currency? In R. H. Clarida (Ed.), *G7 current account imbalances: Sustainability and adjustment*. University of Chicago Press.

Chitu, L., Eichengreen, B., & Mehl, A. (2014). When did the US dollar overtake sterling as the leading international currency? *Journal of Development Economics, 111*, 225–245.

Cipolla, C. M. (1957). *Moneta e civiltà mediterranea*. Neri Pozza.

Cipolla, C. M. (2013). *Il fiorino e il quattrino. La politica monetaria a Firenze nel Trecento*. Il Mulino.

Cohen, B. (1971). *The future of sterling as an international currency*. Macmillan.

Cohen, B. (1998). *The geography of money*. Cornell University Press.

Cohen, B. (2006). The macrofoundations of monetary power. In D. M. Andrews (Ed.), *International monetary power*. Cornell University Press.

Cohen, B. (2009). *Currency and state power*. Paper presented at the conference in honor of Krasner SD. Stanford University, December 4–5.

[72]See Einzig (1932).

Cohen, B. (2012). The benefits and costs of an international currency: Getting the calculus right. *Open Economies Review, 23*, 13–31.

Cohen, B. (2013). The coming global monetary (dis)order. In D. Held & C. Roger (Eds.), *Global governance at risk*. Polity Press.

Cohen, B. (2015). *Currency power: Understanding monetary rivalry*. Princeton University Press.

Cooper, R. (2009). *The future of the dollar*. Peterson Institute for International Economics, Policy Brief n. PB09–21.

Dobbs, R., Skilling, D., Hu, W., Lund, S., Manyika, J., & Roxburgh, C. (2009). *An exorbitant privilege? Implications of reserve currencies for competitiveness*. McKinsey Global Institute Report.

Dorucci, E., & McKay, G. (2011). *The international monetary system after the financial crisis*. ECB Occasional Paper Series n. 123.

ECB. (2010, May). The great inflation: Lessons for monetary policy. *Monthly Bulletin*, 99–110.

Eichengreen, B. (1987). *Hegemonic stability theory of the international monetary system*. NBER working paper n. 2193.

Eichengreen, B. (1992). *Golden fetters: The gold standard and the great depression, 1919–1939*. Oxford University Press.

Eichengreen, B. (1996). *Globalizing capital: A history of the international monetary system*. Princeton University Press.

Eichengreen, B. (2011a). *Exorbitant privilege: The rise and fall of the dollar and the future of the international monetary system*. Oxford University Press.

Eichengreen, B. (2011b). The renminbi as an international currency. *Journal of Policy Modeling, 33*, 723–730.

Einzig, P. (1932). *The Bank for International Settlements*. Macmillan.

Fleming, J. M. (1962). Domestic financial policies under fixed and under flexible exchange rates. *IMF Staff Papers, 9*, 369–380.

Friedman, M. (1951). Commodity reserve currency. *Journal of Political Economy, 59*, 203–232.

Genberg, H. (2010). The calculus of international currency use. *Central Banking, 20*, 63–68.

Giannini, C. (2011). *The age of central banks*. Edward Elgar.

Gilpin, R. (1975). *US power and the multinational corporation: The political economy of foreign direct investment*. Basic Books.

Gilpin, R. (1981). *War and change in world politics*. Cambridge University Press.

Gilpin, R. (1987). *The political economy of international relations*. Princeton University Press.

Goldberg, L. S. (2010). Is the international role of the dollar changing? *Federal Reserve Bank of New York Current Issues in Economics and Finance, 16*, 1–7.

Goodhart, C. A. E. (1989). *Money, information and uncertainty*. Macmillan.

Goodhart, C. A. E. (1998). The two concepts of money: Implications for the analysis of optimal currency areas. *European Journal of Political Economy, 14*, 407–432.

Gourinchas, P. O., & Rey, H. (2007). From world banker to world venture capitalist: US external adjustment and the exorbitant privilege. In R. Clarida (Ed.), *Current account imbalances sustainability and adjustment*. University of Chicago Press.

Guzzini, S. (1983). Structural power: The limits of neo-realist power analysis. *International Organization, 47*, 443–478.

Helleiner, E. (2008). Political determinants of international currencies: What future for the US dollar? *Review of International Political Economy, 15*, 354–378.

Helleiner, E., & Kirshner, J. (2009). The future of the dollar: Whither the key currency? In E. Helleiner & J. Kirshner (Eds.), *The future of the dollar*. Cornell University Press.

Henning, C. R. (2009). *US interests and the International Monetary Fund*. Peterson Institute for International Economics Policy Brief n. PB 09-12.

Hirschman, A. O. (1945). *National power and the structure of foreign trade*. University of California Press.

Ikenberry, G. J. (1993). The political origins of Bretton Woods. In M. Bordo & B. Eichengreen (Eds.), *A retrospective on the Bretton Woods system: Lessons for international monetary reform*. University of Chicago Press.

Ikenberry, G. J. (2006). *Liberal order and Imperial ambitions. Essays on American power and world politics*. Polity Press.

Iwai, K. (1996). The bootstrap theory of money: A search theoretic foundation of monetary economics. *Structural Change and Economic Dynamics, 7*, 451–477.

Jevons, W. (1875/1876). *Money and the mechanism of exchange*. Appleton.

Kaminska, I., & Zinna, G. (2014). *Official demand for US debt. Implications for US real interest rates*. IMF working paper n. 14/66.

Kannan, P. (2009). On the welfare benefits of an international currency. *European Economic Review, 53*, 588–606.

Keohane, R. O. (1984). *After hegemony: Cooperation and discord in the world political economy*. Princeton University Press.

Keynes, J. M. (1913). *Indian currency and finance*. Frankfurt am Main: Verlag (Ed. 2020).

Kindleberger, C. (1967). *The politics of international money and world language*. Princeton University, Dept. of Economics, Essays in International Finance n. 61.

Kindleberger, C. (1973). *The world in depression, 1929–1939*. University of California Press.

Kirshner, J. (1995). *Currency and coercion: The political economy of international monetary power*. Princeton University Press.

Kirshner, J. (2008). Dollar primacy and American power: what's at stake? *Review of International Political Economy, 15*, 418–438.

Kiyotaki, N., & Wright, R. (1989). On money as a medium of exchange. *Journal of Political Economy, 97*, 927–954.

Kiyotaki, N., & Wright, R. (1991). A contribution to the pure theory of money. *Journal of Economic Theory, 53*, 215–235.

Kiyotaki, N., & Wright, R. (1993). A search-theoretic approach to monetary economics. *American Economic Review, 83*, 63–77.

Knafo, S. (2006). The gold standard and the origins of the modern international monetary system. *Review of International Political Economy, 13*, 78–102.

Knapp, G. (1924). *The state theory of money*. Macmillan.

Krasner, S. (1976). State power and the structure of international trade. *World Politics, 28*, 317–347.

Krasner, S. (1983). *International regimes*. Cornell University Press.

Lagos, R., & Wright, B. (2005). A unified framework for monetary theory and policy analysis. *Journal of Political Economy, 113*, 463–484.

Lake, D. (1993). Leadership, hegemony, and the international economy: Naked emperor or tattered monarch with potential? *International Studies Quarterly, 37*, 459–489.

Lester, B., Postlewaite, A., & Wright, R. (2011). Information and liquidity. *Journal of Money, Credit, and Banking, 43*, 355–377.

Lester, B., Postlewaite, A., & Wright, R. (2012). Information, liquidity, asset prices and monetary policy. *Review of Economic Studies, 79*, 1209–1238.

Li, Y., & Matsui, A. (2009). A theory of international currency: Competition and discipline. *Journal of Japanese and International Economics, 23*, 407–426.

Mastanduno, M. (2009). System maker and privilege taker: US power and the international political economy. *World Politics, 61*, 121–154.

Matsuyama, K., Kiyotaki, N., & Matsui, A. (1993). Toward a theory of international currency. *Review of Economic Studies, 60*, 283–307.

Menger, K. (1892). On the origin of money. *Economic Journal, 2*, 239–255.

Mundell, R. (1963). Capital mobility and stabilization policy under fixed and flexible exchange rates. *Canadian Journal of Economics and Political Science, 29*, 475–485.

Mundell, R. (1993). *EMU and the international monetary system: A transatlantic perspective*. Austrian National Bank working paper n. 13.

Mundell, R. (2012). The case for a world currency. *Journal of Policy Modelling, 34*, 568–578.
Norrlof, C. (2014). Dollar hegemony: A power analysis. *Review of International Political Economy, 21*, 1042–1070.
North, D. (1971). Institutional change and economic growth. *Journal of Economic History, 31*, 118–125.
North, D. (1990). *Institutions, institutional change and economic performance*. Cambridge University Press.
North, D. (1992). *Transaction costs, institutions, and economic performance*. International Center for Economic Growth Publication.
North, D., & Thomas, R. (1973). *The rise of the Western world: A new economic history*. Cambridge University Press.
Nosal, E., & Rocheteau, G. (2011). *Money, payments and liquidity*. MIT.
Rey, H. (2019). *International monetary system and global financial cycles*. Banca d'Italia, Lezioni Paolo Baffi di Moneta e Finanza. Rome, November 22.
Rocheteau, G., & Wright, R. (2005). Money in search equilibrium, in competitive equilibrium, and in competitive search equilibrium. *Econometrica, 73*, 175–202.
Schenk, C. (2014). Sterling and monetary policy 1870-2010. In R. Floud, J. Humphries, & P. Johnson (Eds.), *The Cambridge economic history of modern Britain* (Vol. 2). Cambridge University Press.
Shi, S. (1995). Money and prices: A model of search and bargaining. *Journal of Economic Theory, 67*, 467–496.
Shi, S. (1997). A divisible search model of fiat money. *Econometrica, 65*, 75–102.
Shiller, R. (2003). *The new financial order*. Princeton University Press.
Simmons, B. A. (2000). The legalization of international monetary affairs. *International Organization, 54*, 573–602.
Simmons, B. A. (2001). The international politics of harmonization: The case of capital market regulation. *International Organization, 55*, 588–620.
Snidal, D (1985). The limits of hegemonic stability theory. *International Organization 39*, 579–614.
Strange, S. (1971a). *Sterling and British policy: A political study of an international currency in decline*. Oxford University Press.
Strange, S. (1971b). The politics of international currencies. *World Politics, 23*, 215–231.
Strange, S. (1987). The persistent myth of lost hegemony. *International Organization, 41*, 551–574.
Trejos, A., & Wright, R. (1993). Search, bargaining, money and price: recent results and policy implications. *Journal of Money, Credit and Banking 25*, 558–576.
Trejos, A., & Wright, R. (2001). International currency. *The B.E. Journal of Macroeconomics, 1*, 1–17.
Triffin, R. (1947). National central banking and the international economy. *Postwar Economic Studies, 7*, 46–81.
Triffin, R. (1960). *Gold and the dollar crisis: The future of convertibility*. Yale University Press.
Walter, A. (2006). Domestic sources of international monetary leadership. In D. Andrews (Ed.), *International monetary power*. Cornell University Press.
Waltz, K. N. (1979). *Theory of international politics*. Addison-Wesley.
Woods. (2006). *The globalizers: The IMF, the World Bank and their borrowers*. Cornell University Press.
World Bank. (2011). *Multipolarity: The new global economy*. The International Bank for Reconstruction and Development/The World Bank.
Zhang, C. (2014). An information-based theory of international currency. *Journal of International Economics, 93*, 286–301.
Zimmermann, H. (2013). Can the euro rival the dollar? In A. W. Cafruny & H. M. Schwartz (Eds.), *Exploring the global financial crisis*. Lynne Rienner.

Chapter 3
The Classical Gold Standard

3.1 Introduction

The classic gold standard lasted from 1871 to 1914. This system was based on a commodity money, gold, to which the adhering countries undertook to keep their currency convertible. This commitment corresponded to an unwritten law according to which if a state, for some reason, suspended convertibility, it should re-establish it as soon as possible. This implied that in the long run, governments would have to expand the quantity of money according to the growth of gold reserves. In fact, between 1870 and 1914, worldwide, the total quantity of money increased in line with these.

Prior to 1870, only four countries had adopted the gold standard: England, Australia, Canada and Portugal. Most other countries based their monetary systems on a bi-metallic system, which provided for a fixed parity between gold and silver.

In the 1870s, a significant number of countries switched from the bi-metallic system to the gold standard. The process started with Germany's accession to the gold standard in 1871, this was made possible thanks to the indemnity which it obtained from its victory over France, whereby it was able to set aside huge gold reserves.

In order to hinder Germany's redeployment of foreign exchange reserves in favour of gold and inflict capital losses on it, France decided to limit the minting of silver coins.[1] As a result, the price of silver began to decline. Fearing a progressive loss of value of their silver reserves, the Scandinavian countries adopted the gold standard shortly after Germany in 1873. A few years later, in 1878, together with Belgium and Switzerland, France itself abandoned the bi-metallic system to join the gold standard. By around 1880 most of the advanced countries were part of the system.[2]

---

[1] See Flandreau (1996).

[2] See Eichengreen and Flandreau (1998), Gallarotti (1995), Meissner (2005), and Reti (1998).

G. B. Pittaluga, E. Seghezza, *Building Trust in the International Monetary System*, Frontiers in Economic History, https://doi.org/10.1007/978-3-030-78491-1_3

The process of accession to the gold standard of the peripheral countries was slower and more troubled. Some of them, like Japan and Russia, only adopted the gold standard at the end of the nineteenth century while others, such as Argentina and Brazil, adhered to the gold standard intermittently. Some, like Spain, never adopted the gold standard.

The nature of the classic gold standard is that there was no international agreement that committed the member states to respect its rules.[3] Countries joined the system unilaterally, without agreeing with other countries either their membership or the parity of their currency.

Various assumptions have been made about the transition from bi-metallism to gold mono-metallism with the debate on this issue focused mainly on an assessment of the efficiency of these two monetary systems in ensuring price stability. According to some scholars, since bi-metallism ensured price stability more efficiently than the gold standard, the transition from one system to the other was an "accident" provoked by the political rivalry between France and Germany. Other scholars, relying on the theory of time inconsistency, have argued that the gold standard was a credible commitment mechanism to prevent inflationary surprises by the government.

Any explanation of the reasons for the adoption of the gold standard must take into account that it took place at a time of nation state formation and consolidation. The adoption of the gold standard can be seen as part of the process of state capacity building of that period, in particular "... as a political response to the problems resulting from the development and expansion of modern banking".[4] In short, by adopting the gold standard, governments were able to take control of money supply, at a time when the use of bank money was becoming widespread, as a means to direct it to meet, not only their own financial needs but also those of the private sector.

The orderly growth of the banking and financial system presupposed the stability of prices and the value of money, including bank money. This stability had therefore become an objective of governments which, thanks to their fiscal capacity, increasingly obtained resources, rather than through currency debasement, by borrowing. In the advanced countries, therefore, the state assumed the role of guarantor of the stability of the new form of money in order to promote the financial and economic growth of the country and, through that, its power in the international arena.

Rather than explaining the adoption of the gold standard in advanced countries, the commitment mechanism hypothesis seems particularly useful in explaining its diffusion in peripheral countries. Some of whom, in fact, adopted the gold standard to attract foreign capital and reduce the cost of their borrowing on international markets. Many peripheral countries, however, did not have adequate fiscal capacity to maintain the convertibility of their currencies. As a result, they were subject to

---

[3]See Simmons (2000, p. 575).

[4]See Knafo (2006, p. 89).

frequent currency and financial crises. The comparatively low state capacity of some peripheral countries, which had close trade and financial relations with advanced countries, meant that they bore a large part of the adjustment costs of macroeconomic imbalances, acting as a form of "shock absorbers".

3.2 Bi-metallism

Historically, monetary systems have almost always been based on commodity money, generally metals, primarily gold and silver. The latter represented for centuries the most widespread form of money in Europe, while gold was used only in international transactions involving very large sums.

The bi-metallic system was prevalent worldwide for centuries before it was supplanted by the gold standard.[5] There is, still, only a sparse literature on the characteristics and operating modes of this system. Friedman (1990a, p. 87) aptly notes that few textbooks mention bi-metallism: "... typically taking it for granted that a gold standard is the only kind of commodity standard that needs to be mentioned".

Bi-metallism was based on the coexistence of gold and silver in the payment system. From the 1820s until the early 1870s the legal gold/silver exchange rate fluctuated around 15.5 to 1.[6] As Figure 3.1 shows, it was only after 1873 that silver depreciated significantly relative to gold.

In the bi-metallic system both gold and silver could be traded by private individuals on bullion markets. The gold-silver exchange rate in these markets could diverge from the legal exchange rate and, in this case, arbitrage opportunities emerged. In line with Gresham's law, the money that was legally overvalued tended to replace the undervalued one. This process can be illustrated with an example.[7] Suppose that gold had a relatively high price on the bullion market compared to that in the form of coins. In this case it was profitable to sell gold coins on the bullion market, receive silver bullion in return and take the silver bullion to be minted into currency. In this way the arbitrageur obtained a quantity of silver coins with a face value higher than the gold coins he had had at the beginning.

The arbitrage just described encouraged the convergence of gold-silver exchange rates in the bullion market to the legal exchange rate. In fact, thanks to this type of operation, on the one hand, the supply of gold increased and, on the other hand, correspondingly, the demand for silver increased. Simply put, the bi-metallic arbitrage stabilizes the gold-silver exchange rate in the bullion market at the mint level.[8]

---

[5]On the characteristics of this system there was a considerable debate already in the nineteenth century. See, among others, Laughlin (1896), Darwin (1898), and Fisher (1911).

[6]For an illustration of the trend over time of the gold-silver exchange rate see Flandreau (1996).

[7]See Flandreau (2003).

[8]How arbitrage worked is described in detail by Oppers (1993).

Fig. 3.1 Gold-Silver price. Source: Measuring worth dataset

Obviously, arbitrage operations had costs, in particular costs of transporting precious metals, fees to the mint for minting coins, and so on. These costs resulted in upper and lower gold-silver exchange rate points.[9] Within this range this exchange rate could fluctuate without the absolute dominance of one precious metal over the other.

Taking this into account, Oppers (2000) compares the functioning of the bi-metallic system to a target zone. As in a system of this type, in fact, "... the mere existence of a bi-metallic mint tended to stabilize the market ratio of gold and silver; the anticipation of arbitrage stabilized market ratio even when it was away from the mint ratio".[10]

In the stabilization of the gold-silver exchange rate and, therefore, of the bi-metallic system, France played a crucial role. As Fisher (1911, pp. 133–134) writes referring to the discovery of gold mines in California in the mid-nineteenth century: "By 1850 ... bimetallism would have broken and resulted in silver mono-metallism ... except the fact that ... gold had just been discovered in California. The consequence of the new and increased gold production was a reverse movement, an

[9]The gold points represented the fluctuating limits of a currency. They were determined by the transport and insurance costs to be incurred to transfer the gold between the place where the bill was drawn to that where it was payable. Attempts to measure gold-silver points have yielded controversial results. See Friedman (1990b), Redish (1992), Flandreau (2003), and Oppers (1993).

[10]See Oppers (2000, p. 531). According to Oppers, exchange rate stability was even more credible in the bi-metallic system than in a target-zone system since not only central banks but also private individuals could take advantage of arbitrage opportunities. On the stability of the bi-metallic system, in addition to Oppers (1995, 2000) see Velde and Weber (2000). For a review of the different positions on bi-metallism as a self-equilibrating system see Diebolt and Parent (2008).

inflow of gold into the French currency and an outflow of silver... It seemed probable that France would be entirely drained of her silver currency and came to a gold basis ... But the new gold mines were gradually exhausted ...".

France and the bi-metallic block, in which it played a dominant role and the epitome of which was the Latin Monetary Union,[11] acted as a sort of arbitrageur of last resort with respect to the world monetary system and, as such, absorbed the imbalances that were created in the bullion market. This gave credibility to the system and encouraged private individuals to engage in stabilizing forms of speculation.[12]

France's prominent role in stabilizing the gold-silver exchange rate can be traced to three factors.[13] First, France at that time was of significant economic importance. Secondly, after the disappointing experience of the "assignats", it had developed a strong preference for commodity money. Third, France had high monetary credibility. Not even during the Napoleonic wars against a large part of Europe did it suspend the convertibility of its currency.[14] While conversely, at the time of those wars, Britain had suspended the convertibility of the pound sterling only re-establishing it in 1821.

Throughout history, the theoretical debate on the advantages and disadvantages of bi-metallism and mono-metallism has focused mainly on the effects of the two systems on the transaction costs of exchanges and on price trends. The first of these two aspects will be dealt with in the next section, since the hypothesis that the gold standard allowed to reduce transaction costs is one of the explanations of the transition from bi-metallism to gold standard.

As regards the effects of bi-metallism on price trends, a discrete number of scholars share Fisher's view (1911, pp. 126–127): "... in a series of years, the bi-metallic level [of the real value of the monetary unit] remains intermediate between the changing levels which the two metals would separately follow. Bi-metallism spreads the effect of any single fluctuation over the combined gold and silver markets ...".

On several occasions the bi-metallic system proved itself capable of absorbing shocks in the production of gold and silver without any repercussions on the general level of prices.

In 1848, following the discovery of gold mines in California, the production of this precious metal increased significantly. There was widespread concern that the world economy would be hit by gold inflation. Britain, by adopting the gold standard, was particularly exposed to this increased supply of money. However, what was feared did not occur. In fact, in France, under the free coinage of silver and gold, people adopted arbitrage operations, importing gold and exporting silver. In this way the gold- silver exchange was stabilized. The effect of the higher supply of

---

[11]See Einaudi (2000, 2001).

[12]See Flandreau (1997a).

[13]See Friedman (1990a, 1990b).

[14]See Walker (1896).

Table 3.1 Wholesale price indices for main industrial countries

Year and period	USA	United Kingdom	Germany	France
Indexes (1913 = 100)				
1849	82	86	67	94
1873	137	130	114	122
1896	64	72	69	69
1913	100	100	100	100
Changes (in percent)				
1849–1873	67	51	70	30
1873–1896	−53	−45	−40	−45
1896–1913	36	39	45	45

Source: Cooper (1982)

gold due to the discovery of Californian mines was simply a change in the composition of the currency in circulation in that country: an increase in the share of gold coins corresponded to a decrease in the share of silver coins.[15]

Some scholars trace the world deflation that occurred between 1873 and 1894 (Table 3.1) to the "demonization" of silver and a shortage of gold compared to demand.[16]

This phase of deflation led to an intense conflict between creditors and debtors and revitalized the debate on the preferred monetary system. The controversy reached its climax in the USA with the presidential election of 1896, in which the populist Democratic candidate William Jennings Bryan, whose famous phrase "you shall not crucify mankind upon a cross of gold", was defeated by the Republican candidate William McKinley, who proposed US adoption of the gold standard.[17] With reference to these troubled years[18] Friedman (1990b, p. 1175), based on the results of a counterfactual estimate, argues: "If my estimates are anywhere near correct, a bi-metallic standard . . . would have produced a steadier price level than did the gold standard that was adopted".

Friedman's thesis, according to which bi-metallism would have guaranteed greater stability than the gold standard, has been supported in recent times by other scholars.[19] From this perspective, therefore, as will be seen in the next section, the replacement of bi-metallism with the gold standard, by some economists[20] can be considered an "accident" caused by political circumstances.

[15]See Meissner (2015).

[16]See Oppers (1996) and Flandreau (2003).

[17]In Britain the debate was less heated, but led to the establishment of the "Gold and Silver Commission" that reported in 1889.

[18]On the crisis phases of those years see Friedman and Schwartz (1963).

[19]See, in particular, Flandreau (1996) and Wiegand (2019).

[20]See Flandreau (1996).

Table 3.2 Year in which main European Countries adopted the gold standard

Country	Year	Country	Year
Portugal	1854	Finland	1877
Germany	1872	Belgium	1878
Sweden	1873	France	1878
Denmark	1873	Switzerland	1878
Norway	1873	Italy	1884
Netherlands	1875		

3.3 The End of Bi-metallism and the Emergence of the Gold Standard in Advanced Countries

In the 1870s, in the space of only a few years, all the advanced countries of the time joined the gold standard, the transition from bi-metallism to the new international monetary system therefore took place in an extremely short period of time. In fact, almost within a decade, the international monetary system passed from a regime in which both gold and silver were used as base for metallic currencies to a regime where the largest European industrial countries—Britain, France and Germany—used only a single metallic currency, gold (Table 3.2).

Various explanations have been given of the transition from bi-metallism to the gold standard in advanced countries. These explanations are often associated with differing assessments of whether this represented an improvement in the efficiency of the international monetary system. The main ones are outlined here.[21]

3.3.1 *The Fundamental Theory*

In this hypothesis it is argued that due to the discoveries of silver mines in Nevada and Mexico in the mid-nineteenth century and the innovations in production technologies, the supply of silver had increased significantly, consequently the market price of silver fell.

Kindleberger (1984) argues that this led to distrust in the possibility of maintaining the gold-silver exchange stable. Michel Chevalier himself, one of the leading and most influential French monetary experts of the time and a great supporter of bi-metallism,[22] in the mid-1870s changed his opinion in favour of the gold standard after the mining discoveries just mentioned.

Appropriately Flandreau (1996) notes that France had such liquidity of gold that it could stabilize the relative price of silver, as it had done at the time of the increased supply of gold in the 1850s after the discovery of gold mines in California.

[21]For a detailed survey of these explanations see Flandreau (1996).

[22]See Chevalier (1859).

3.3.2 The Flight to a Safe Haven

After the victory of the battle of Sedan in 1870, Germany imposed on France the payment of a war indemnity of 5 billion francs and, in 1871, adopted a monetary reform with which it adhered to the gold standard. Germany's decision resulted in a massive influx of gold (into Germany) and at the same time a massive outflow of silver from it. The decrease in the price of silver on the market after 1871 led to arbitrage transactions in France and in the countries of the Latin Monetary Union in which silver was sold in exchange for gold at the official rate of 15.5. In this context, the French government and those of the Latin Monetary Union countries began to worry that bi-metallic arbitrage operations could lead to a shift to effective silver mono-metallism in the countries they governed. This process would have meant a worsening of their terms of trade.[23]

Given these concerns, in 1873 France and Belgium suspended the free coinage of silver.[24] That decision triggered a sort of run on silver. Several advanced countries, in fact, fearing a strong depreciation of this precious metal and therefore huge capital losses on their foreign exchange reserves, decided to adopt the gold standard.[25] That is a "scramble for gold"[26] occurred as a result of which in 1875 most advanced countries adopted the gold standard.

Oppers (1996) and Flandreau (1996) criticized the explanation just given arguing that France had sufficient gold reserves to allow it to buy the total sale of Germany's silver reserves, thus stabilizing the gold-silver exchange rate at around 15.5. As a result of these interventions, France would have found itself with a lower gold share of its foreign exchange reserves,[27] but bi-metallism would have survived.

3.3.3 The Hypothesis of Transaction Costs

This hypothesis starts from the assumption that the gold standard represented a more efficient tool than the silver standard in international trade since this was the system used by the country which had the largest share of foreign trade. This assumption is consistent with the Mengerian theory of the origin of money illustrated in Chap. 2. Within this hypothesis, therefore, the basic question is not why countries moved

[23]See Gallarotti (1995).

[24]In this way they adopted a "limping gold standard", in which existing former standard silver coin retained full legal tender. Central banks, in this way, could redeem their notes in silver as well as gold.

[25]See Gallarotti (1995).

[26]See White (1893).

[27]Flandreau (1996) estimates that this share would have dropped from 85 percent in 1870 to 80% in 1880. Oppers (1996) draws similar conclusions.

Table 3.3 Import share of the main European countries in 1867 (percent of total imports)

	France	Belgium	Zollverein	Austro-Hungary	Netherlands
UK	10.0	10.4	12.5	26.3	43.6
France	–	29.6	7.0	15.6	7.8
Italy	11.1	0.2	0.1	9.3	0.1
Zollverein	8.6	13.9	–	28.7	23.1
Austria- Hungary	1.2	0.3	29.9	–	0.3
Belgium	2.7	–	4.2	1.5	6.2
Netherlands	3.2	2.2	6.0	0.5	–
Russia	9.4	6.3	17.4	2.6	8.6

Source: Morys (2012)

from the silver standard to the gold standard, but rather why this transition occurred in the 1870s.

An answer to this question was given by Redish (1990, 2000). According to this scholar, the adoption of the gold standard by Britain stemmed from the desire to overcome the instability of bi-metallism, largely due to changes in the market price of gold and silver. This problem could be overcome when it became possible to use silver exclusively for small transactions and gold for other transactions. This possibility emerged when, thanks to an invention of the engineer Matthew Boulton, a way was found to use steam to mint small denomination coins in a standardized way. These coins were no longer made from precious metals. Their value was fixed relative to high-value gold coins into which they were convertible. However, the technological problem referred to by Redish had been solved some 40 years earlier. If this explanation were true France and the German states should have abandoned the silver standard long before they did.

Nonetheless, network externalities based on trade do not seem to offer adequate confirmation of the transaction cost hypothesis. As Table 3.3 shows, in fact, the share of imports from Britain to France and the Zollverein (the German customs union) in 1867 was relatively small. By contrast, the close commercial ties between France and Belgium, as well as those between the Zollverein and Austria-Hungary and Russia emerge clearly from this data. Curiously, the Netherlands, which had intense trade ties with Britain, was the only country to vote against gold monometallism at the 1867 International Monetary Conference.[28]

3.3.4 *The Political Economy Hypothesis*

According to some scholars, the industrialization process that took place in many European countries in the nineteenth century was accompanied by a change in the political influence of the social classes that formed part of the elite. As noted by Clough and Cole (1946), the gold standard was particularly favourable to the

[28]See Morys (2012).

interests of the industrial and financial class, while bi-metallism was better suited to the interests of farmers, particularly landowners. The latter, given the time interval between sowing and harvesting, were structurally in debt. Industrialists and financiers, on the other hand, were net creditors.

It was widely believed that the bi-metallic system was beneficial for debtors for two main reasons. First, there was a widespread belief that a multi-metal standard would favour a wider money supply. Second, in the bi-metallic system, debtors could take loans in the metal that was valued (gold) and repay them in the metal that was depreciating (silver). Given this belief, it is not surprising that creditors were in favour of gold mono-metallism.

De Cecco (1974) reached similar conclusions, considering the trend in the period after 1873 of the exchange rates of countries with the gold standard and those with the silver standard, he came to the conclusion that while landowners/farmers preferred this second standard, industrialists were in favour of the first. Indeed, in the years following 1873, silver depreciated steadily and significantly relative to gold.

Therefore, countries that had adopted the silver standard would have enjoyed an increasing degree of export competitiveness. This was, according to De Cecco, of particular interest to European farmers who found themselves opposing the invasion of American wheat. The industrial bourgeoisie, on the contrary, tended to favour the gold standard for two main reasons, the first, that the industrialization process required large imports, primarily of raw materials. An exchange rate that was appreciated in real terms, because it was based on the gold standard, would have reduced the cost of these imports. On the other hand, the industrial bourgeoisie also held its wealth in financial assets, the value of which was exposed to inflationary erosion. This risk, given the tendency of silver to depreciate, would be reduced if the gold standard was adopted.

Even Gallarotti (1995) insists on changes to internal economic and political balance induced by industrialization. "... The spectrum of domestic politics changed significantly in the developed world in the 19th century. The rise of political liberalism was a manifestation of the political rise of the urban industrial class .... With the shift in the political balance of power came a concomitant shift in monetary preferences from a standard oriented around a bulky and inflationary metal (i.e. silver) to one oriented around a light and non- inflationary metal (i.e. gold)".[29]

This hypothesis, although tempting, does not explain some aspects of the transition from bi-metallism to gold mono-metallism. First, several studies have shown that before 1873, that is, before the transition to gold mono-metallism began, the dynamics of silver production and its price did not tend to favour inflationary processes.[30] Second, in light of this it remains unexplained why in the 1850s, when gold became particularly abundant, and potentially inflationary, following the California mining discoveries, there was no transition from bi-metallism to silver. Finally, this hypothesis does not explain why the turning point between the two systems occurred precisely in 1873.

[29]See Gallarotti (1995, p. 10). See also Frieden (1991, 2015).

[30]See Flandreau (1996) and Morys (2006).

3.3.5 The Hypothesis of the Status Symbol

This explanation insists that the adherence of advanced countries to the gold standard stemmed from cultural rather than economic reasons.[31] As Gallarotti (1995, p. 9) writes: "... nations come to see monetary standards as economic and political status symbol. Gold mono-metallism came to confer higher status, while silver and bi-metallism came to confer low status. ... The example of Britain was especially compelling because ... elites were drawing associations between Britain's monetary practices and its industrial success".[32] Schumpeter (1954), in the *History of Economic Analysis*, wondered why countries, such as Austria-Hungary, Italy and Russia, characterized by high inflation rates and paper currencies, were willing to make such profound sacrifices and delay their development in order to adopt the gold standard. In his opinion this question becomes even more difficult to answer if one considers that there was no pressure for such a choice, since all interest groups that had political influence (landowners, industrialists, workers) would be harmed.

The only answer to this question, according to Schumpeter, may be of an extra-economic nature. Compared to the past, characterized by recurring inflation and devalued currencies, the gold standard had become "a symbol of sound practice and a badge of honour and decorum".[33] At the time of the international monetary conference of 1867, gold was regarded as "the natural standard of the stronger and richer nations, and silver of the weaker and poorer nations".[34]

The status acquired by gold surely stemmed from the example of England. It was believed that one of the factors that had contributed to the pronounced economic growth of that country was its adoption of mono-metallism.[35] This was certainly the conviction of the German elite who, after the victory over France in 1870, decided to adopt the gold standard.[36] The elevation of Britain to a model country was a manifestation of its soft power. As Gallarotti (2010, p. 168) writes: "The 'scramble for gold' was a classic manifestation of Britain's soft power. Monetary elites generally shared the belief that Britain's lead in industrialization was principally driven by adopting a gold standard".

3.3.6 The Strategic Hypothesis

This explanation rejects the premise of the transaction costs hypothesis according to which the gold standard was a more efficient monetary system than bi-metallism.

[31]See, among others, Mertens (1944) and Milward (1996).

[32]See also Milward (1996).

[33]See Schumpeter (1954).

[34]See Russell (1898, p. 148).

[35]See Chevalier (1859).

[36]See Milward (1996).

Indeed, according to several scholars,[37] while the vagaries of gold supply determined wide fluctuations in the price level, the imperfect correlation between gold and silver supply shocks, allowing a diversification of the risk, would have guaranteed a higher stability of prices and, therefore, of the economic cycle. In addition to this, in the opinion of these scholars, the transition from bi-metallism to the gold standard, in determining a significant increase in the demand for this precious metal, contributed to a deflationary slump from 1873 to the mid-1890s within the gold block. During this period there were severe distribution conflicts between creditors and debtors and global sub-par growth.[38]

The transition from bi-metallism to the gold standard was driven, rather than by economic factors, by political events in the international arena. In the years preceding the adoption of the gold standard, with the development of world trade, a need was felt to have a common monetary standard. This obviously involved transition costs from one regime to another. However, the transition from the gold standard to the bi-metallic standard entailed costs similar to those of the transition from the bi-metallic to the gold standard.

If France had joined the gold standard, it would have had to sell at least 1 billion francs in silver,[39] meaning large capital losses. On a strictly political level, France would also have had to give up the role of arbitrageur for the gold-silver exchange rate thanks to which, being able to exercise forms of financial statecraft vis-à-vis other countries, it enjoyed greater international monetary power.

Germany, in turn, had large amounts of trade with gold nations, primarily Britain. However, as part of the bi-metallic system, the stability of the exchange rate of the mark against the pound was under the control of France. To switch to the gold standard, Germany would have had to sell about 2 billion of silver on the market which would have exposed it to significant losses if France had not been accommodating. Given the scarcity of gold reserves held by Germany, such losses would have been unsustainable. As Bamberger (one of Bismarck's most listened to economic advisers) wrote in 1871: "... the difficulty was never to ask: 'where to find the gold' but 'where to put the silver?' Where is the hole in which we can throw 300 or 400 million of silver that we need to get rid off, without throwing them into the water outright?".[40]

The victory at Sedan put Germany in a position to ask France for an indemnity of 5 billion French francs for which payments could be made in silver coin. If France had demonetized silver, it would have defaulted and become liable to occupation.[41]

The accommodating behaviour of France was guaranteed until such time as the indemnity had been paid in full. This took place on September 5, 1873. The next day France placed a strict limit on the issuing of silver francs and consequently, the price

[37]See Drake (1985), Friedman (1990a), Flandreau (1996), and Oppers (1996).

[38]See Wiegand (2019).

[39]See Flandreau (1996, 2003).

[40]See Bamberger (1871, p. 250).

[41]See Helfferich (1898).

of silver began to decline. The aim of the French authorities was to make Germany's transition to the gold standard costly, since at that time they held 2 billion French francs in silver.

It is probable, as Flandreau (1996) argues that the French government had not adequately considered the consequences of limiting the minting of silver coinage, in particular its repercussions on the survival of bi-metallism.

Germany, predicting the unaccommodating behaviour of France after it had completed the payment of the indemnity, accelerated the adoption of the gold standard as far as possible by completing the monetary reform in July 1873.

The monetary choices of France and Germany can be interpreted as an uncooperative game, in which the two players try to derive the maximum relative advantage from their choices. From this perspective, Germany's decision to join the gold standard seems entirely rational. Its permanence in the bi-metallic system would, in fact, have presupposed long-term cooperation with France, which seems unlikely given the war the two countries had just fought. Less rational appears to be France's choice to limit the minting of silver coins. In this way it undermined confidence in the stability of the gold-silver exchange rate and favoured a "scramble to gold" by those countries that had previously adopted the bi-metallic system. In this way it lost the role of arbitrageur of the international monetary system, a role which passed to England.

If the efficiency of a system is measured by the degree of elasticity of the money supply, then the transition from bi-metallism to gold mono-metallism was probably not from a less efficient system to a more efficient one. In this sense, Flandreau rightly defined this transition as an "accident of history".[42] The transition in question highlights the importance of international relations with respect to the prevalence of one monetary system or another.

3.3.7 The Commitment Mechanism Hypothesis

Some scholars have explained the origin of the gold standard in terms of the theory of time inconsistency.[43] According to this theory, if a monetary authority announces money growth at the beginning of the year consistent with zero inflation, and then fails to respect this announcement, resulting in a monetary surprise which captures seigniorage revenue, individuals gradually lose faith in the announcements as being no longer credible and, as a result, they incorporate a higher-than-zero inflation rate in their expectations. Monetary authorities, at this point, if they want to prevent an increase in the unemployment rate, must practise a loose monetary policy and accept that the inflation rate is above zero. They are no longer able to "surprise" individuals and the economy is plagued by an inflationary bias. Both Bordo and Kydland (1995)

[42]On this aspect see also Flandreau and Oosterlinck (2012).

[43]See Bordo and Kydland (1977) and Bordo and Rockoff (1996).

and Bordo and Rockoff (1996) tend to see the gold standard as a rule, or rather a commitment mechanism "... to prevent governments from following the otherwise time-inconsistent policies of creating surprise fiduciary money issues ...".[44]

From this perspective, the gold standard is seen as a contingent rule. A country could suspend the convertibility of its currency into gold in emergency situations, such as war. The public, however, understood the exceptional nature of the situation and expected that, once the emergency was over, convertibility would be restored.

3.3.8 The Neo-Institutionalist Hypothesis

In a recent contribution Meissner (2015) tries to explain the transition from bi-metallism to the gold standard as being based on the path dependence concept of North's neo-institutionalist theory. "The path of institutional change, which determines the long-run evolution of societies, is based by the constraints derived from the past and the unanticipated consequences of the innumerable incremental choices of entrepreneurs ...". Through an impersonal process of interaction between individuals, institutions that reduce transaction costs tend to replace less efficient institutions. Since, as shown by Velde and Weber (2000), bi-metallism, since it biased the relative price between non-species gold and silver, was inferior from a welfare perspective, and it was supplanted by the gold standard.

The advocates of the strategic hypothesis tend to compare bi-metallism and the gold standard using, as a measure of efficiency, their influence on inflation or on prices of other precious metals. The commitment mechanism hypothesis argues that the gold standard made it possible to eliminate the inflationary bias resulting from the time inconsistency problem. However, the efficiency of monetary systems can also be assessed from a dynamic, rather than a static, perspective by referring to their ability to support economic growth.

"... [T]he prime mover of monetary change has been the needs of trade. All the major monetary innovations have taken place during a sharp growth of trade ... particularly international trade ... A rapid expansion of trade, particularly where there is a predominance of deferred transactions and long- term relations between the parties, raises the appreciation of the mal-adaption costs of existing payment technologies, thereby creating the right incentives for the development of new, more adaptable technologies".[45]

In an economic system where part of the contracts are long term, part of the prices are rigid, and, where the quantity of money is given (as happens in monetary systems based on commodity money) then economic growth is penalized. As Friedman (1951, p. 19) writes: "The vices of strict commodity standards are the other side of

[44]See Bordo and Rockoff (1996, p. 391).

[45]See Giannini (2011, pp. 19–20).

their virtues. Being automatic, they may not provide sufficient flexibility or adaptability to prevent substantial swings in prices or in income".

The lack of flexibility in the money supply gives rise not only to instability in the price level but also to high transaction costs. As Clower (1969) observes, given that the price of money is given by the inverse of the average of the price level of goods, an imbalance between supply and demand of money can only be eliminated through a renegotiation of the contracts stipulated in the different markets.[46]

The convertible banknote, given the flexibility its supply, made it possible to reduce the transaction costs of exchanges. However, for this payment instrument to be accepted, the convertibility clause needed to be credible. This could only happen if there was an institutional framework that would prevent the issuer from behaving fraudulently, not respecting convertibility (microeconomic risk) or issuing an excessive amount of notes (macroeconomic risk).[47]

This framework was created by the state that took control of money supply, making use of innovative institutions such as central banks to guarantee the convertibility of banknotes to gold at a predetermined price.

Bi-metallism was a less favourable system for the diffusion of the banknote since, as Kindleberger (1984) notes, the central bank reserved the right to convert the banknotes into gold or silver according to the exchange rate that it considered most favourable. The holder of the banknotes was therefore uncertain about its value. This uncertainty was increased by the fact that on a global level the stability of the gold-silver exchange ratio was guaranteed by France, the only country that had adequate reserves for this purpose. The conversion value of the banknotes therefore depended on its interests and behaviour.

From the perspective just outlined, the transition from bi-metallism to the gold standard is seen as part of a process aimed at increasing the elasticity of the supply of money and, therefore, better supporting economic growth. This process was made possible, in the second half of the nineteenth century, by the formation of nation states and by the state building capacity that characterized it.[48]

3.4 The Consolidation of the Gold Standard in England

Before becoming the basis of the international monetary system, the gold standard emerged as a national monetary system, establishing itself in England earlier than elsewhere. In fact, after the Napoleonic wars in 1821 Britain decided to return to the convertibility of the pound sterling into gold, as originally established by Newton's monetary reform of 1717.

---

[46]See Giannini (2011, p. 12).

[47]See Giannini (2011, p. 56).

[48]See Helleiner (2003).

Various interpretations have been given of the definitive adoption of the gold standard by Britain.

The purely technical explanation of the adoption of gold mono-metallism given by Redish is unsatisfactory in two respects. First, it emphasizes the problem of the shortage of small denomination coins,[49] a problem not considered crucial by the British elite.[50] Secondly, England's adoption of the gold standard cannot be reduced to a technical fact, since the adoption of bi-metallism was the subject of lively discussion in this country at the time. Even in the late thirties and early forties of the nineteenth century there were sectors of the elite that supported the opportunity of a return to bi-metallism.[51] Thirdly, the technical hypothesis of the adoption of the gold standard clashes with the fact that it does not explain why the gold standard, given its convenience, was adopted in most European countries long after Boulton's invention. Finally, it does not explain why the adoption of the gold standard in England was accompanied by a series of reforms of the banking system and of the mechanisms for issuing money.

The explanation of England's adoption of the gold standard given by Cain and Hopkins (2001) is different. According to these scholars, it was an aspect of the policy pursued by "gentlemanly capitalism", based on the alliance of aristocrats and workers, in order to favour the free movement of capital and financial interests at the expense of industrial ones. The explanation of Cain and Hopkins recalls in some way the hypothesis of political economy, illustrated in Sect. 3.3.4 and intended to explain the adoption of the gold standard in core countries. However, it tends to see the English aristocracy as a compact bloc, neglecting the clash between finance and landowners over the adoption of the gold standard.[52] Furthermore, the interpretation of Cain and Hopkins clashes with the fact that in the first half of the nineteenth century several English leaders, also expressing of gentlemanly capitalism, railed against the policy of the Bank of England which they accused of over-issuing money.[53]

In reality, the adoption of the gold standard in England was the result of a long process marked by a crucial innovation in the payment system: the convertible banknote. The latter was a negotiable promissory note payable to the bearer, the value of which depended on the respect of the convertibility clause. Since its issue was managed with some discretion, convertible banknotes made it possible to significantly increase the flexibility of the money supply.

---

[49]See Sargent and Velde (2001).

[50]The British mint was often reluctant to mint small denomination coins given the low profits derived from their production. See Selgin (2008).

[51]See Fetter (1965, p. 181).

[52]On this aspect, see Knafo (2013, p. 35).

[53]See Knafo (2013).

The process that led to the establishment of an institutional framework that generated confidence in the convertible banknote was relatively long and was punctuated by crises and reforms by the British Parliament. In fact, shortly after its return to the gold standard in 1825, England was hit by a severe banking crisis that jeopardized the convertibility of the pound.

Some years after this crisis, in 1833, when the concession to issue money to the Bank of England was due for renewal, Parliament redefined the powers of the central bank, granting the status of legal tender to the currency it issued, entrusting it with the role of custodian of the country's gold reserves, and dis-applying the usury limits on interest rates applied in its discount transactions. These provisions set the conditions for the Bank of England to perform the functions of lender of last resort.[54] Given the new powers granted to the central bank, Parliament reserved the right to revoke the concession and the privileges associated with it at any time, this provision was intended to incentivize the central bank to put public interests before private ones.

Despite the provisions of the 1833 law, two other serious banking crises occurred in 1837 and 1839. In the case of 1839, the convertibility of the English currency was only preserved thanks to a loan of 2 million pounds worth of gold from the Bank of France. Public opinion saw this as a humiliation, the fact that the integrity of the Bank of England and the country's permanence in the gold standard depended on the support of a country which, less than 60 years earlier, had been in the throes of monetary disorder for the issuance of *assignats.*

The serious banking crises just mentioned provoked a major debate between the followers of the currency school[55] and those of the banking school.[56] Among the former, a prominent role was played by Loyd who, in 1850, became Lord Overstone. In his writing he pointed out that in 1825, 1837 and 1839, the country's gold reserves were depleted because when reserves began to decline the Bank of England, rather than reduce its issuance (as prescribed from the price-species mechanism) had expanded it.[57] This behaviour was in large measure due to the so-called Palmer rule, according to which "variations in the amount of the circulation shall correspond to variations in the amount of bullion. By this means, and by this means only, can we obtain a paper currency varying in amount exactly as it would have varied had been wholly metallic".[58] This new rule had proved itself ineffective because it failed to distinguish between the deposits and notes liabilities of the Bank of England.

[54]See Calomiris et al. (2016).

[55]The main exponents of which were Loyd, Ramsey, McCullock and Torrens.

[56]Leading exponents were Tooke, Wilson (editor of the Economist) and John Stuart Mill.

[57]See Overstone (1837a, 1837b, 1840).

[58]See Morgan (1943).

This aspect was strongly expressed by the exponents of the currency school, in particular Torrens and Overstone, according to whom "when the Bank found that its gold reserves were being drawn out through its deposits, it should have reduced its note circulation ... by deliberate contraction of its discounts or by sale of government securities in the open market".[59]

This principle was included when the government renewed the Bank of England's concession through the Bank Charter Act of 1844 which placed a limit on the cash that the central bank could issue. Above this limit, emissions had to be covered with 100% metal reserves.[60] In order to guarantee the link between issued currency and gold reserves, the central bank was divided into two departments: the issue department (monetary department) and the discount department (banking department).

With the Bank Charter Act of 1844 and its application, politics assumed full control of money with:[61]

i. the attribution of the monopoly to issue money to the central bank and, therefore, the centralization of money supply;
ii. the establishment of a quantitative constraint (based on metal reserves) on the amount of money that the central bank could issue.

These two principles were followed as a model in the successive monetary reforms of several other European countries. First, in France in 1848, then in Germany in 1875, in Sweden in 1897 and so on.[62]

The Bank Charter Act put predefined limits on the amount of money in notes which the Bank of England could issue. However, it did not set rules on the management of deposits, in this way it encouraged the use of bank money as a means of payment. Around the middle of the nineteenth century, cheques began to spread in Europe and the USA as a means of payment.[63] The use of bank money allowed a significant increase in the elasticity of money supply. However, to be accepted this type of money required a higher level of confidence than that based on the banknote. On the one hand, in fact, the assets of banks are opaque: the value of a bank, therefore, is not known to depositors. On the other, the fact that the deposit has a certain nominal value and that it can be repaid at any time can expose the bank to situations of illiquidity or insolvency.

---

[59] See Viner (1960, p. 228).

[60] At the same time, the opening of new issuing institutions was prohibited and the prohibition of provincial banks from establishing themselves in the London area was reaffirmed.

[61] See Knafo (2013, p. 147).

[62] See De Kock (1974).

[63] See Kindleberger (1984) and Cameron (1967).

Only 3 years after the Bank Charter Act was passed in 1847, the Bank of England was faced with such a situation. Given the limits set by the Bank Charter Act, it was unable to meet the banks' demand for liquidity. The impasse was overcome thanks to a letter from the Treasury that allowed the central bank to discount liberally even if this involved violating the 1844 law,[64] the liquidity shortage quickly disappeared and the stability of the British banking system was preserved.[65]

In the views expressed in the literature[66] there is a consensus that the Bank of England consolidated its role as lender of last resort in the early 1870s. However, already in the Overend-Gurney crisis it lent freely. The intervention of the Bank of England was justified by its governor, Lancelot Holland, speaking before the Board with these words: "We could not flinch from the duty, which we conceived was imposed upon us of supporting the banking community, and I am not aware that any legitimate application for assistance which was made to this house was refused".[67]

The ways in which the Bank of England was to operate as lender of last resort were codified by Bagehot in *Lombard Street* in 1873. The process by which the institutional architecture underlying the domestic gold standard took shape in England is part of the state building process that characterized that country.

If, on the one hand, the attribution to the Bank of England of the monopoly to mint money meant centralizing the money supply, on the other, the exercise by the same institution of the function of lender of last resort favoured the acceptance and diffusion of bank money. In this way, England was able to develop an articulated monetary and financial system.

The accession to the gold standard of Germany in 1873 and then of the Scandinavian countries in 1875 and of France in 1878 implied a recognition that the monetary institutions which had been established in England in this long process (characterized by various experiments) were more efficient than those based on bi-metallism because, on the one hand, they allowed the state to acquire control over the quantity of money and, on the other, they made the supply of means of payment more reactive with respect to the evolution of demand.

The acquisition of control of money supply by the state implied both the centralization of its supply and autonomy regarding changes in the price of silver with respect to gold whether this was determined by the market or manipulated by France. From this perspective, it would seem reasonable to agree with those who link adhesion to the gold standard of advanced countries to the state building process underway, especially in Europe, in the second half of the nineteenth century.[68] The government's control of the quantity of money also implied a certain subordination of the central bank to the government. As Kisch and Elkin (1928, p. 27) write, before

[64]See Giannini (1995).

[65]See Morgan (1943).

[66]See Fetter (1965), Clapham (1954), and Sayers (1957).

[67]See Bagehot (1873).

[68]See Helleiner (1999).

the First World War there was a tendency in Europe "... to stress the control of the state over the central bank ... to regard a state or semi-state bank as analogous to a state railway system or a state tobacco monopoly".

There were several reasons for this subordination of central bank to the state. On the one hand, the governments of many advanced countries set out to promote an accelerated process of industrialization and to provide it with adequate financial support. In certain cases, primarily in the case of Germany, there was the objective of closing the gap with England: the Reichsbank was also intended to contribute to the achievement of this objective.

On the other hand, in all the advanced countries, central banks were called upon to support governments in their policy of consolidating nation states and, in some cases, of imperial expansion. The prerequisite for this policy was that these countries, in particular the core countries, enjoyed a high level of monetary and financial capacity. Hence the need, on the part of the governments of the time, to gurantee prices and exchange rate stability. Thus, a country's monetary power in terms of gold reserves and borrowing capacity in the event of war were to be preserved and, if possible, increased.

As stated above, and as noted by Knafo (2006, 2013), in the case of core countries, to believe that adopting the gold standard constituted a commitment aimed at restraining the propensity of policymakers to resort to inflationary surprises,[69] and emphasising the fact that in this system central banks were independent,[70] is to project the future into the past, and into a past in which suffrage was limited and the political costs of deflationary policies were contained.

3.5 The Rules of the Game

The essence of the gold standard was that each country defined the price of its currency in terms of gold and committed itself to keeping that price fixed over time. Thus, the value of the pound corresponded to 113 g of gold, that of the French franc to 0.290 g of gold, that of the Reichsmark to 0.358 g of gold and so on.

By adhering to the gold standard, a country undertook to respect the so-called *rules of the game*[71] shown in Box 3.1.

---

[69]See Bordo and Kydland (1995) and Bordo and Rockoff (1996).

[70]See, for example, Schenk and Straumann (2016).

[71]This expression was first used in the more extended version of "rules of the gold standard game" by Keynes (1930, vol. II, p. 306).

Box 3.1 The Rules of the Pre-war International Gold Standard

Rule	Description
1	Fix an official gold price, or mint parity, and convert freely between domestic money and gold at that price
2	Do not restrict the export or import of gold by private citizens, nor impose any other exchange restrictions on current or capital account transactions
3	Back national banknotes and coinage with earmarked gold reserves, and condition long-run growth in deposit money on availability of general gold reserves
4	In short-run liquidity crisis from an international gold drain, have the central bank lend freely to domestic banks at higher interest rates (Bagehot's rule) [See Bagehot (1873)]
5	If rule 1 is temporarily suspended, restore convertibility at traditional mint parity as soon as practicable, if necessary by deflating the domestic economy
6	Allow the common price level (nominal anchor) to be endogenously determined by the worldwide demand for and supply of gold

Source: McKinnon (1993)

With the adherence of a number of countries to the first three rules, the gold standard took on the status of an international monetary system. In fact, if each of them undertook to convert their national currency into a predetermined amount of gold (Rule 1), if the price of gold in that currency was determined by the market, subject only to the "gold points"[72] (Rule 2) and if the internal currency of the country corresponded to its gold reserves (Rule 3), there was an international monetary system based on fixed exchange rates between national currencies.[73] Rules 4–6 had a predominantly internal value: they, in fact, indicated how central banks and treasuries should behave within the gold standard. Rules 4 and 5 foresaw, respectively, that in given circumstances central banks would have to act as lender of last resort and that a country, if for some reason it suspended the convertibility of its currency, should re-establish it as soon as possible. Rule 6 ruled out the possibility for governments to manipulate the price of gold. The latter would be determined by the market and, therefore, given the fixed exchange rate regime, the domestic price level of the individual countries was endogenous.

The fundamental pillar of the gold standard was the commitment of the acceding countries to respect rules 1–5. These rules ensured the stability of the exchange rate in the long run. Britain suspended the convertibility of the pound sterling three times between 1871 and 1914: in 1847, 1857 and 1866. In all three cases, convertibility was restored within a short time.[74]

[72]The gold points represented the limits of fluctuation of a convertible currency. They were determined by the transport and insurance costs to be incurred to transfer the gold between the place where the bill was drawn to that where it was payable.

[73]See Eichengreen (1985).

[74]See Bordo (1981).

The widespread confidence in rule 5 meant that when a government found it necessary to raise the domestic interest rate to attract gold, investors considered investing in that country's securities as low risk. Therefore, small increases in the interest rate were sufficient to attract capital from abroad in order to cover payment deficits. In this context, given the high credibility of rule 5 compliance, current account imbalances were mainly adjusted by short-term capital flows, rather than transferring gold. Simply put, speculation was a stabilizing force in the pre-war gold standard.

It must be asked what encouraged governments to maintain the credibility of compliance with rules 1–5.[75] A first form of commitment mechanism was to include the principle of gold convertibility into the country's constitution, the case of Sweden being a prime example.[76] A second form of commitment was reputational. The maintenance of fixed exchange rates and stable prices, when not actually decreasing, corresponded to wealth distribution goals and to the influence of the rentier class in internal politics.[77] However, in the case of the core countries, the concern to maintain a high reputation on the international financial markets responded to the need to maintain and consolidate their power in the international arena. Grossman (1988, p. 7) writes with reference to Britain: "Without denying the importance of distributional considerations, given Britain's long history of recurring war of attrition against continental foes, it is easy to argue that a central consideration influencing British postwar [after the Napoleonic Wars] was the desire to maintain a trustworthy reputation for honouring war debts, without which efficient financing of the next war would not have been possible".

3.6 The Gold Standard as a System of International Balance of Payments Adjustment

With the accession of the main European countries to gold mono-metallism, an international monetary system was defined which, for the first time, even if not based on international treaties and agreements, implied appropriate institutions and policies for the adhering countries to guarantee the convertibility of their national currencies.

This system to which, as will be seen later in this chapter, many peripheral countries also adhered, lasted from 1873 to 1914. With the beginning of the First World War, in order to meet the costs of the war, most countries suspended the convertibility of their currencies.

Traditionally, the balance of payments adjustment mechanism is identified with Hume's *price-species-flow model*.[78] In this model it is assumed that the movement of goods in international trade depends on relative price levels, as explained by the

[75]See Bordo and Kydland (1995).

[76]See Jonung (1984).

[77]See, with reference to Britain, Alesina (1988).

[78]See Hume (1752).

Ricardian theory of comparative advantage. In this context, an imbalance in external accounts can only be corrected by a change in relative prices. The domestic price level of each country is assumed to be determined by the quantity of money in circulation, as predicted by the quantity theory of money. On the other hand, in the price-species-flow model, referring to a monetary system based on commodity money, the quantity of money in circulation in a country that adhered to the gold standard corresponded to its gold reserves.

From this perspective, therefore, if a country was affected by a current account deficit, it would sell gold abroad to cover this imbalance. In this way, its gold reserves and the currency in circulation within it would decrease. This would be followed by a decrease in the level of domestic prices as suggested by the quantity theory. The change of relative prices of goods on the international market would lead to corresponding changes in demand for imports and exports which would bring the foreign accounts of the country into equilibrium.

The mechanism just illustrated had three important features.[79] First, the mechanism through which the imbalances were adjusted was entirely automatic. Markets were assumed to be perfectly competitive: perfectly flexible prices and wages guaranteed full employment. Second, the adjustments to trade imbalances were fully symmetrical. In the country experiencing current account deficits, prices fell due to the loss of reserves and a decrease in money, while in the country in surplus prices rose for the opposite effect. Third, it assumed a world in which only goods could be traded internationally. Factors of production were mobile within countries, but not internationally. This implied that any trade imbalances needed to be eliminated immediately. They could not, in fact, be covered by foreign debt.

Even if in the hypothesis of the *price-specie-flow* mechanism capital flows were not taken into account, during the nineteenth century, particularly in the last decades of the century, the amount of financial investment abroad gradually increased. This process was described by John Stuart Mill in 1848: "... it is a fact now beginning to be recognized, that the passage of the precious metals from country to country is determined much more than was formerly supposed, by the state of the loan market in different countries, and much less by the state of prices".[80]

Only after the First World War did the Cunliffe Committee present a version of the model in which capital flows were also taken into account and, in which, central banks could influence their direction by varying the policy interest rate.[81] Thus, if a country had a current account deficit, its central bank, through an increase in the discount rate, could attract short-term funds and replenish its gold reserves and thereby maintain the high confidence in the convertibility of its currency.

The balance of payments adjustment model just described presupposed automatisms that excluded a countercyclical behaviour on the part of central banks. The empirical evidence does not support this hypothesis. In particular, Bloomfield

[79]See Panic (1992).

[80]See Mill (1848 [ed. 1965, p. 515]).

[81]See Committee on Currency and Foreign Exchange after War (1919).

(1959), focusing on the correlation between the discount rate and the level of reserves, showed that there was no significant correlation between these variables. Indeed, this analysis revealed asymmetrical behaviour by central banks. These institutions were active in periods of capital outflows, while in periods of inflows they did not vary the discount rate that is they undertook forms of sterilization of capital inflows. The behaviour just described suggests that the main objective of central banks was, in fact, the protection of their gold reserves.[82]

The above considerations invalidate the traditional view that the gold standard was the period in which markets determined policy, particularly monetary policy. Indeed, as shown in Table 3.4, England and Germany consistently reported current account surpluses in the period 1880–1913. Nevertheless, the number of years in which the central banks of these countries raised the discount rate are far greater than that in which they lowered it.

By contrast, Scandinavian countries very often recorded current account deficits during the same period but despite this, the number of years in which the discount rate was adjusted upwards is far lower. In these countries, it also appears that between 1880 and 1913 the average annual growth of money supply was higher than that of England (Table 3.5).

From the data reported in Tables 3.4 and 3.5 it would seem that it was often central banks with their interest rate policy and other instruments that influenced market performance and not vice versa.

Bloomfield's conclusions were confirmed in the empirical analysis by Goodhart (1972) and Dutton (1984) relating to England, which seem to indicate the presence of anti-cyclical measures by that central bank and, therefore, a violation by it of the "rules of the game".[83] More recent contributions highlight the fact that on several occasions central banks resorted to forms of sterilization, thus pursuing objectives that are, in part, different from that of the convertibility of their own currencies.[84] However, in the long run, the central banks of the core countries (i.e. Britain, France and Germany) considered preserving the convertibility of their currencies as their primary goal.[85]

3.7 Cooperation Between States and Central Banks

Various scholars trace the credibility and stability of the gold standard to cooperation between states and central banks. Scammel writes: "... [T]he nineteenth century saw the steady growth of an international financial fraternity, which expressed itself

[82]See Eichengreen (1985) and Ford (1989).

[83]Pippenger (1984) argues that this policy of the Bank of England was aimed at maintaining high profits for its shareholders.

[84]See Giovannini (1986), Jeanne (1995), and Davatyan and Parke (1995).

[85]See Eichengreen (2004).

Table 3.4 Some inconsistencies of the Classical Gold Standard (number of years)

	Current account balance		Money supply		Central bank discount rate		Consumer prices	
	Surplus	Deficit	Increase	Reduction	Increase	Reduction	Increase	Reduction
UK	34	0	28	6	29	14	15	12
Germany	34	0	28	6	21	12	20	13
Italy	24	10	27	7	n.a		18	14
USA	18	16	30	4	n.a		7	5
Norway	10	24	29	4	14	13	19	12
Sweden	7	27	34	0	13	14	19	15
Denmark	2	32	26	4	15	14	15	19

Source: Panic (1992)

Table 3.5 Trend of some macroeconomic variables (1880–1913)

	Current account (% GDP)	Discount rate (%)	Money supply growth (%)	Inflation (%)
UK	4.5	3.5	2.0	0.1
Germany	1.8	4.1	6.5	0.7
USA	0.7	n.a	5.6	0.2
Italy	0.6	n.a	3.3	0.6
Sweden	−2.5	4.7	5.4	0.5
Norway	−2.5	4.7	5.9	0.5
Denmark	−2.6	4.3	2.6	−0.1

Source: Panic (1992)

through international banking and the cooperation of the great central banks of the leading countries".[86]

Similar considerations are found in Eichengreen, according to whom: "The credibility of the pre-war gold standard rested on international cooperation ... Major crises [were] contained through overt, conscious cooperation among central banks and governments".[87]

As we saw in Chap. 2, the emergence of cooperation in the international arena in a multipolar context (which was the prevailing situation during the gold standard period) is infrequent, since countries in this context place great weight on relative gains. This theoretical assumption is confirmed by the pre-war gold standard period: in this monetary system the cooperation between governments and central banks was episodic and motivated, when it happened, by the sole objective of defending national interests.[88]

3.7.1 Cooperation Between States

Monetary cooperation between governments prior to the twentieth century was modest. In the period of the pre-war gold standard it was limited to some regional agreements and to the organization of a series of international conferences with inconclusive results.

In the context of international monetary agreements, the Latin Monetary Union was of pre-eminent importance, established in 1865 between France, Belgium, Switzerland and Italy, with the Papal States, Greece and Romania joining later.[89]

[86]See Scammell (1965 [ed. 1985, p. 105]).

[87]See Eichengreen (1992, pp. 7–8).

[88]See Flandreau (1997b).

[89]The other important monetary agreement in the period considered was the Scandinavian Monetary Union, established in 1873 to stabilize the exchange rate between Sweden, Denmark and Norway, i.e. between countries with high commercial interdependence.

With this Union it was decided to standardize the coinage among users of the franc.[90] The absence of standardized coinage, in fact, led to arbitrage opportunities and unwanted movements of silver from one country to another.[91]

The intent of Napoleon III, promoter of this monetary union, was not only of a technical nature, but was also aimed at strengthening the international prestige of France, envisioning a dominant role in a union extended to a large number of countries.[92] It was in pursuit of this goal that he promoted the Paris Monetary Conference of 1867, coinciding with the Universal Exhibition of that year.

In carrying out the work of the conference, differing positions emerged among the participants. The British delegation stated simply that it had listened to the proposals and would then report to the government. The French insisted that the franc-gold should be the international numeraire, the USA was in favour of the coexistence of francs and dollars. In essence, the work ended without conclusion apart from a generic declaration in favour of the adoption of gold as international money.

With the rush to the gold standard occurring in the first half of the 1870s, silver began to be marginalized as a means of payment. Consequently, its price dropped markedly. At the same time and for the same reason, the global demand for gold increased significantly. The shortage of gold encouraged a phase of deflation.

These two processes created economic and social tensions within the advanced countries and, in order to alleviate these tensions, pressure emerged for the adoption of measures to support the price of silver and even for a return to the bi-metallic system. In the wake of this pressure, and above all on the initiative of France and the USA, three international conferences were organized in 1878, 1881 and 1896. However, conflicting views emerged in the negotiations conducted by the major powers, and the prevalence of non-cooperative positions of the participating states resulted in the substantial failure of these conferences.[93]

3.7.2 Cooperation Between Central Banks

In Sect. 3.3.8 of this chapter the hypothesis was put forward that adherence to the gold standard in most advanced countries was an indication of strengthening of state capacity. With the concentration in the central banks of the monopoly for issuing banknotes, the government and parliament acquired control over money supply. This allowed them to preserve the convertibility of the national currency, protecting the country from the automatic adjustment mechanism of the gold standard[94] and maintaining a degree of autonomy in the conduct of economic policy.

---

[90]See Einaudi (2001).

[91]See Kindleberger (1984) and Gallarotti (1995).

[92]See Einaudi (2001).

[93]For an illustration of the different positions of the states see Gallarotti (1995).

[94]See Helleiner (2003).

It is not surprising, therefore, that a number of scholars,[95] carrying out in-depth analysis of the relationships between central banks in pre-war gold standard, came to the conclusion that the cooperation between these institutions was episodic and never assumed an institutional value.[96] As Bloomfield (1968, p. 27) observes: "Monetary authorities showed little or no overt awareness of a mutual response for the smooth functioning of the international gold standard". Attempts to coordinate monetary policies, as we shall see, were made in the gold-exchange standard, but no such efforts took place in the case of the classic gold standard. Cooperation between central banks was purely episodic limited to some cases of crisis and always took the form of bilateral arrangements which ended as soon as the critical moment had passed.

Central banks, as they also carried out ordinary banking activities, in many cases obtained liquidity, rather than from other central banks, from commercial banks, if possible in their own country.[97] In managing liquidity, central banks followed a kind of "pecking order", first, they sought to obtain liquidity from their own resources. Then, they had recourse to the internal market and ultimately, if it was not possible to obtain the liquidity they needed, they turned to their governments or the international market.

Since this hierarchical order of preference was known, the request for help from another central bank was considered a sign of weakness, and a serious loss of prestige. No wonder, therefore, that in 1873, when Germany offered to support the Bank of England in case of need, Britain flatly refused this offer. On the occasion of the 1907 crisis, the Bank of France provided loans to the Bank of England, which was intent on dealing with that crisis.[98] In the face of this intervention, the English press was keen to clarify that this support had not been requested and that it was exclusively an initiative by France which was worried that the tensions on the London market would extend to the Paris market.[99]

The above leads to the conclusion that in the pre-war gold standard central banks tended to focus mainly on interests of their own country rather than on the world monetary system.

This means that when a crisis occurred, the support given by a foreign central bank was dictated by "narrow self-interest", in particular by the fear of the spillover effects of the crisis on its financial market.[100] On the other hand, in the case of generalized financial crises, the objective of protecting their gold reserves prevailed among central bankers. In these cases, as Viner writes (1937, pp. 274–275): "[They]

[95]See, in particular, the recent contributions on this issue of Flandreau (1997b) and Gallarotti (1995).

[96]On this aspect see Viner (1937), King (1936) and Bloomfield (1963).

[97]See Gallarotti (1995).

[98]On the behaviour of the Bank of France in the classical gold standard see Gallarotti (2005).

[99]See Kindleberger (1984, p. 188).

[100]See Bloomfield (1963).

Table 3.6 Growth and composition of foreign exchange assets, 1900–1913 (in millions of dollars)

All institutions	End of 1900	End of 1913	Change
Sterling	121.0	441.4	320.4
Francs	27.2	275.1	247.9
Marks	24.2	136.9	112.7
Other currencies	71.4	212.0	140.6
Unallocated	160.4	557.1	396.7
Total	404.2	1622.5	1218.3

Source: Lindert (1969)

engaged in competitive increases on their discount rates and in raids on each other's reserves".

Towards the end of the nineteenth century "nation entered into geopolitical competition, gold stocks came to be seen as a 'national war treasure' which were to be kept up in case of conflict".[101] It follows that the high correlation between the discount rates set by the central banks of the gold standard core countries can be considered the result, rather than of cooperation, of a fierce competition aimed at protecting their own gold reserves. It was precisely from this competitive behaviour, rather than from a "conscious" cooperation, that the stability of the gold standard was derived.[102] Within the latter, the dominance of sterling was by no means absolute. This is demonstrated by the composition of foreign exchange assets held by both state and private institutions between 1900 and 1913 (Table 3.6).[103]

Therefore, "[w]hile greater balances were held in London than in any other international financial center, a larger share was held in France and Germany than has been generally realized. The frequent portrayal of London as the only major reserve center before World War I exaggerates somewhat".[104]

The composition of the official reserves confirms the fact that although sterling was the most important reserve currency, its primacy was not unrivalled. As can be seen the currency composition of the official reserves of different countries reflected, to a large extent, the political influence of the major powers. In Europe, as a reserve currency, sterling had less weight than the franc and the mark. By contrast, its primacy was undisputed in the other continents (Table 3.7).

[101] See Gallarotti (1995, p. 84).

[102] See Brown (1940).

[103] See Lindert (1969).

[104] See Lindert (1969, p. 76). Similar conclusions are found in Bloomfield (1963).

Table 3.7 Reported foreign official holdings of major currencies, end of 1913 (in millions of 1913 dollars)

	England	France	Germany	Other countries	Countries not specified	Total
Europe	76.4	262.1	115.5	44.9	164.5	663.4
Rest of the world	355.2	13.0	36.8	17.4	46.3	468.7
Total	431.6	275.1	152.3	62.3	210.8	1132.1

Source: Lindert (1969)

3.8 Did Britain or Its Central Bank Play a Hegemonic Role in the Gold Standard?

In the previous section we saw that in the gold standard the cooperation between states and central banks was modest. It is inevitable, therefore, to ask whether a country, specifically Britain, and its central bank exercised a hegemonic role in this monetary system.

In the neo-realist view and for many international political economy scholars, the gold standard was established and managed hegemonically by Britain. According to Gilpin (1981, p. 138), in fact, in the second half of the nineteenth century "[a] primary objective of British foreign policy became the creation of a world market economy based on free trade, freedom of capital movements, and a unified monetary system", specifically the gold standard. A substantially similar opinion is found in Cohen (1977, p. 81), according to whom in the gold standard "... Britain not only dominated the international monetary order, establishing and maintaining the prevailing rules of the game, but also gave monetary relations whatever degree of inherent stability they possessed".[105]

Extensive literature has shown that it was not among the aims of the British government to exercise political, or even monetary, hegemony over the rest of the world. Between 1820 and 1913, Britain's military expenditure as a proportion of national income was the lowest of the great powers.[106] In the "concert of Europe" Britain did not play a prominent role.[107] For much of the second half of the nineteenth century the most feared states were Russia and France, whose ability to intervene in the political affairs of the continent was high. In this context, it is not surprising that, as Gallarotti (1995, pp. 88–89) observes, the English Parliament was not very interested in international monetary affairs. It also paid little attention to the international monetary conferences held between 1867 and 1892.[108]

---

[105] A similar opinion is found in Krasner (1976).

[106] See Hobson (2002, p. 309).

[107] See Holsti (1992).

[108] See Hansard's Parliamentary Debates from 1860 to 1914.

International monetary affairs were not even of interest to the Foreign Office whose main objective was to maintain peace and the balance of power in continental geo-strategic relations. Appropriately O'Brien (2002) argues that Britain never assumed political responsibility for creating and maintaining the classical gold standard.

Several scholars have shown that Britain's hegemonic role in the gold standard was exercised not so much by the country's government and parliament as by its central bank. Two different views can be found on this aspect, according to some, the Bank of England influenced foreign financial markets indirectly due to the strategic role of the London stock market (indirect hegemony) while, according to others, it consciously and deliberately exercised an influence on the functioning of the international monetary system (direct hegemony).

An expression of this second point of view is found in Keynes in *The Treatise on Money*, where he writes: "During the latter half of the nineteenth century, the influence of London on credit conditions throughout the world was so predominant that the Bank of England could almost have claimed to be the conductor of the international orchestra".[109] This view was then developed by Kindleberger (1973, 1984), according to whom the British central bank in the period of the classic gold standard acted as a "benevolent" hegemon, providing public goods, discounting its paper in crises and maintaining a flow of investment capital. Kindleberger's view that the Bank of England in the case of monetary disturbances protected the weaker powers by exporting capital to them is shared by various other scholars.[110]

In a 1976 contribution, Skidelsky wrote: "... not only Britain 'managed' the pre-war economic system, but it is unimaginable that such a system could have developed in the nineteenth century without such management".[111] More recently Eichengreen (1987) has shown how the Bank of England played the role of leader through its smooth operations.

This hypothesis, however, clashes with the fact that the Bank of England, as a private commercial bank, pursued profit objectives, having to pay dividends to its shareholders. The pursuit of this objective was often emphasized by the Bank's top management.[112] As Sayers observes, the British central bank did not have "... any special regard for what the gold standard... required".[113]

The same tendency of the British central bank to hold a modest amount of reserves, or of low-yielding assets, can be explained in the light of its dual nature that is combining the privilege of issuing legal tender with its original nature as a commercial bank like any other. Given the modest amount of reserves held, it happened more often that the Bank of England, rather than providing liquidity to

109 See Hobson (2002, p. 309).

110 See Beyen (1949) and Ford (1962).

111 See Skidelsky (1976, p. 162). See also Bergsten (1975).

112 See Clapham (1944) and Fetter (1965).

113 See Sayers (1976, vol. I, p. 45)

Table 3.8 The composition of reported official reserves, end of 1913 (converted into millions of 1913 dollars)

	Gold	Silver	Foreign exchange	Total reserves
United Kingdom	164.9	n.a	n.a	164.9
France	678.9	123.5	3.2	805.6
Germany	278.7	65.9	49.6	394.2
Three main creditors	1122.5	189.4	52.8	1364.7
Other Europe	1757.0	309.4	610.6	2677.0
Western Hemisphere	1764.9	525.2	64.8	2354.9
Africa, Asia, Australia	201.8	108.5	403.9	714.2
All considered countries[a]	4846.2	1132.5	1132.1	7110.8

Source: Lindert (1969)
[a]35 countries

Table 3.9 Share of the world trade for the main countries, 1860–1913

	United Kingdom	France	Germany	USA
1860–1880	25.1	10.7	9.2	8.3
1881–1885	19.1	10.7	10.4	10.0
1891–1895	18.0	9.2	11.0	10.5
1901–1905	16.4	7.6	11.6	10.5
1911–1913	14.1	7.5	12.2	10.1

Source: Kuznets (1966)

the system, received it from other central banks, such as the Bank of France, with much higher reserves (Table 3.8).

While the hypothesis that the Bank of England exercised direct hegemony in the gold standard seems questionable, the hypothesis that it exercised indirect hegemony in that monetary system seems plausible. There is no doubt that in the classic gold standard the pound played a leading role as a means of payment. The widespread use of the pound worldwide was caused by various factors. First, Britain had the largest share of world trade (Table 3.9).

Second, Britain funded a large part of foreign trade. According to calculations by Keynes (1914), in 1914 the international trade bills financed by London banks amounted to 350 million pounds.[114] The use of the pound sterling in a large part of foreign trade was favoured, in addition to the prevailing role of Britain in international trade, by the high degree of development of the British money market compared to that of other advanced countries, due to the widespread use of cheques and bank money in Britain. The low value shown for the cover ratio, i.e. the gold-money ratio, is evidence of this (Table 3.10).

The fact is that Britain was the largest lender country in the world (Table 3.11) mainly because a large formal and informal empire contributed to the breadth of the sterling-based international money market. India and Japan, in particular, held their reserves in sterling, effectively adopting a gold-exchange rate.

[114]See also Aliber (2000).

Table 3.10 Gold-money ratio

	France	United Kingdom	USA
1889	0.256	0.026	0.117
1899	0.267	0.032	0.112
1910	0.304	0.029	0.105

Source: De Cecco (1974)

Table 3.11 Foreign investment of major lending countries, 1870–1913 (in millions of dollars)

	1870	1885	1900	1913
Great Britain	4900	7800	12,100	19,500
France	2500	3300	5200	8600
Germany	na	1900	4800	6700
Netherlands	500	1000	1100	1250
USA	na	na	500	2500

Source: Kindleberger (1984)

The combination of the above factors explains the development of the sterling-based international money market. This development, however, could not have occurred without confidence in the stability of the pound's value. This trust was based on the reputation acquired over time by the British currency whose exchange rate against gold had remained unchanged since the Newton reform of 1717. This credibility of the pound meant that it was considered risk-free and perfectly replaceable with the commodity money/gold.

On the basis of the above, it can be concluded that the international money prevailing in the gold standard, i.e. the pound sterling, can be traced to the Mengerian theory or the first generation search-theoretic models, illustrated in Chap. 2.

The large domestic and international money market for sterling enabled Britain to defend its reserves and the convertibility of sterling with changes in the bank rate. When current account imbalances occurred, the Bank of England raised the bank rate. Following this, a net capital inflow into Britain occurred and the exchange rate of the pound was pushed up and its convertibility into gold preserved. Given the credibility of the pound, frequent and modest changes in the bank rate were enough to cause significant capital movements. This helps explain why Britain could hold significantly less reserves than other core countries.[115]

Given its prominent role in the international money market, foreigners, both individuals and central banks, held large amount of sterling reserves, part of which were deposited with British banks. As Lindert (1969, p. 28) writes: "The increasingly keen competition for gold reserves made it more difficult to acquire gold than to give it up. Consequently, most European countries . . . found it in their interests to supplement 'gold devices' with foreign exchange sales to keep temporarily adverse

[115]As Lewis (1978, pp. 47–48) writes: "The Bank of England kept very little gold (in relation to money supply) — some say gold yielded no interest while others are more charitable, whatever the reason, the consequence was that the Bank was forced to react to slight losses of gold, changing the bank rate an incredible number of times per year". See also De Cecco (1974).

payments balances from causing gold losses". Therefore, foreign exchange reserves constituted a sort of shock absorber.

In order to preserve their reserves, the core countries would, as a first solution, make use of changes in the discount rate. It is certainly no coincidence that Bloomfield (1959) found a high correlation between the levels of policy interest rates of Britain, France and Germany. To further protect their gold reserves many advanced countries used other instruments in addition to changes in the discount rate. In some countries, in fact, disincentives were used to discourage the conversion by private individuals of banknotes into gold.[116] France, having a large amount of reserves in both gold and silver, discouraged the conversion of banknotes into precious metal, reserving the right to redeem these claims in the less valued metal.

Foreign exchange reserves were held in sterlings, French francs and marks. As Lindert (1969) observes, the use of the sterling in the composition of foreign exchange assets, while prominent, was not exclusive. In fact, the use of the French franc and the German Reichsmark was not negligible (Table 3.7).

In the classic gold standard, therefore, there was a hierarchy of currencies used in the international payments system. At the top of the system was the pound. Immediately below the English currency were the French and German ones. While it is true that the pound had the rank of international money, it is equally true that both the French franc and the German Reichsmark enjoyed their own areas of influence. This hierarchy between currencies ensured the stability of the gold standard,[117] as Lindert writes (1969, p. 78): "This hierarchy of short-run financial influence, through which funds moved from lesser to greater financial centers as interest rates rose everywhere, helped to minimize monetary friction among major centers by passing the short run financial adjustment burden along to the peripheral countries", these latter countries bore a large part of the burden of adjustments. Nonetheless, they held their reserves almost exclusively in foreign exchange reserves and since they did not have central banks, they were unable to influence capital flows with changes in policy interest rates and to oppose the policy choices of advanced countries, in particular of core countries.

3.9 Macroeconomic Outcomes of the Gold Standard in Advanced Countries

The gold standard, in particular between 1881 and 1913, saw a period of price and output stability, the inflation rate was extremely low in the advanced countries. Consequently, inflation differentials between countries were limited. This indicates that, at least in the medium to long term, the price-species-flow mechanism had worked. As the standard deviation of price growth in these countries shows, the

[116]See McGouldrick (1984) and Jonung (1984).

[117]See Cleveland (1976).

Table 3.12 Main macroeconomic indicators during the gold standard

Country	Inflation		Real GDP per capita growth		Money growth		Long-term interest rates	
	Mean	Std. dev.	Mean	Std. dev.	Mean	Std. dev.	Mean	Std. dev.
USA	0.3	3.1	1.8	5.1	6.1	4.1	3.8	0.3
United Kingdom	0.3	3.1	1.1	2.4	2.1	1.7	2.9	0.2
Germany	0.6	2.6	1.7	2.9	5.7	4.7	3.7	0.2
France	0.0	4.9	1.5	4.6	2.1	4.7	3.2	0.3
Japan	4.6	5.5	1.4	3.8	7.2	14.5	n.a	n.a
Canada	0.4	1.4	2.3	2.8	7.4	5.3	3.5	0.4
Italy	0.6	3.2	1.0	4.0	3.2	3.1	4.2	0.5

Source: Bordo (1993)

volatility of inflation rates had also been contained. Low price growth in the advanced countries was matched by high stability in long-term inflation rates. In a context where uncertainty about the evolution of exchange rates and inflation rates was low, real GDP growth was high in advanced countries (Table 3.12).

3.10 The Gold Standard and the Peripheral Countries

In addition to the core countries and those with high per capita income many "peripheral" countries adhered to the gold standard (Table 3.13).

It is inevitable to ask why these countries made this choice. As will be seen below, the reasons varied, as did the outcomes. The peripheral countries that had a low state capacity were exposed to currency and financial crises that forced them to abandon the convertibility of their currency only to then re-establish it, sometimes after considerable delay. The institutional weakness of most of the peripheral countries also forced them to act as shock absorbers for the crises that from time to time affected the core countries. The ways in which this function was exercised are illustrated below.

3.10.1 The Reasons for Peripheral Countries Joining the Gold Standard

As seen in Sect. 3.3.7, according to some economists the decision to make a currency convertible into gold was to provide a credible pre-commitment mechanism to discourage the government from resorting to monetary surprises aimed at capturing seigniorage revenue.

Bordo and Rockoff (1996) refer to the hypothesis just mentioned to explain the reasons for various peripheral countries adhering to the gold standard. Participation,

Table 3.13 Peripheral countries on classical gold standard

Country	Period	Standard	Reason for change	Change in parity?
Canada	1853–1914	Gold	War	No
Australia	1852–1915	Gold	War	No
USA	1792–1861	Bi-metallic (de facto gold after 1834)		No
	1862–1878	Paper (greenbacks)	War	
	1879–1917[a]	Gold	War	No
Italy	1862–1866	Bi-metallic	Lax fiscal policy, war	No
	1866–1884	Paper		
	1884–1894	Gold	Lax fiscal policy	Yes
	1894–1914	Paper		
Spain	1868–1883	Silver	Crisis	Yes
	1883–1914	Paper		
Portugal	1854–1891	Gold	Crisis	Yes
	1891–1914	Paper		
Argentina	1867–1876	Gold		No
	1876–1883[b]	Paper	Lax fiscal policy	
	1883–1885	Gold		Yes
	1885–1899	Paper	Lax fiscal policy	
	1899–1914	Gold	War	Yes
Brazil	1857–1888	Paper		
	1888–1889	Gold		Yes
	1889–1906	Paper	Revolution	
	1906–1914	Gold	War	Yes
Chile	1870–1878	Bi-metallic	Crisis	Yes
	1878–1895	Paper		
	1895–1898	Gold	War threat	Yes
	1898–1925	Paper		

Source: Bordo and Schwartz (1996)
[a]Gold Embargo 1917–1919, standard not suppressed
[b]Failed attempt to restore convertibility in 1881

for these countries, was equivalent to a "good housekeeping seal of approval". This would have allowed them to finance themselves on international markets at lower interest rates than would otherwise have been possible.[118]

Bordo and Rockoff (1996), and other scholars,[119] gave empirical confirmation of this hypothesis. Other authors, however, have contested the hypothesis of "good housekeeping seal of approval". Some other scholars, instead, have taken up the

[118]On the importance of this aspect see Maxfield (1997).

[119]See Obstfeld and Taylor (2004) and Meissner (2005).

hypothesis of Hobson (1914) according to which the reduction of the debt burden enjoyed by many peripheral countries in the period of the classical gold standard was due to the improvement of the "fundamentals" recorded in that period by these countries.[120] Ferguson and Schularik (2006), on the other side, showed that, if British colonies such as Canada and Australia were excluded from the estimation sample, there was no evidence that, by adhering to the gold standard, peripheral countries could benefit from lower interest rates on foreign loans.[121]

What could be the cause of such radically different empirical evidence? Ferguson and Schularik (2012) trace the principal reasons for these differences to the sample taken as a reference in the estimates, the different control variables used, or simply to the gold "coding" issue.

Here it is believed, however, that the differing empirical results mentioned depend on the fact that peripheral countries joined the gold standard for different reasons. Certainly, some countries joined the system in order to have better access to the international financial markets and to obtain financing at lower interest rates. In other cases, however, adherence to the gold standard mainly responded to internal redistributive logic. This is the case with countries that exported food and mineral products, particularly those from Latin America. In these countries adhesion to, and permanence in, the gold standard was strongly conditioned by the trend of the balance of payments. Phases of the price commodity boom were favourable to the permanence of these countries in the gold standard. This is not only because these phases allowed them to accumulate adequate reserves of precious metal, but also was a means to hinder redistributive processes unfavourable to the dominant interest groups.

The different reasons that led many countries to join the gold standard on a lasting basis and others to join it intermittently are exemplified by two ideal-type countries: Argentina and Japan.[122]

Argentina joined the gold standard in 1867 without, however, having developed a state capacity adequate to comply with the rules of the system.[123] In particular, at the time of joining it had only a modest amount of gold reserves and its fiscal capacity was strongly dependent on customs revenue, which constituted over 60% of the total government revenue.

In the following years the country was characterized by persistent public and current account deficits. Consequently, in 1876, it was forced to abandon the convertibility of its currency. This was re-established in 1883 only to be suspended again 2 years later due to the country's fiscal indiscipline. The Barings crisis of 1890

---

[120]See Flandreau and Zumer (2004).

[121]With other reasons, the hypothesis of 'good housekeeping seal of approval' is also contested by Mitchener and Widenmeyer (2015), Sussman and Yafeh (2001), and Mauro et al. (2006).

[122]For a comparison of the different reasons that led these countries to join the gold standard see Bryan (2010).

[123]See Marichal (1989) and Della Paolera and Taylor (2001).

and the default on foreign debt prompted the elite to take a series of measures aimed at increasing Argentina's state capacity.

Among these measures was the approval, in November 1891, of the law establishing the *Caj de Conversión,* an institution which can be compared to a currency board, this was given the exclusive right to issue money. This right was, at the same time, taken away from the banks which had benefited from it by over-issuing money. The monetary reform allowed Argentina to centralize the supply of money. Other reforms, also in 1891, concerned public finance. In particular, it was established that duties had to be paid in gold and for the first time, taxes on consumption were introduced.

The set of fiscal measures made it possible to increase tax revenues and make them less conditioned by the volatility of customs revenue.[124] At the same time, a rigorous monetary policy made it possible to reduce inflation and stabilize the exchange rate. The consolidation process was aided by the positive cycle of food prices and in 1899 Argentina returned to the convertibility of the peso.

Despite the reforms, the share of taxes on total government revenues remained small compared to that resulting from tariffs. At the same time, the supply of money was not controlled by any authority, but depended mainly on the balance of foreign trade. The state building process in Argentina remained, therefore, very limited.

The above leads one to ask why Argentina adhered to the gold standard repeatedly during the nineteenth century without being able to respect its rules.

The most plausible answer to this question is that this decision was prompted by domestic political reasons. In particular, as Ford (1962, p. 169) writes: "... in Argentina before 1914, the landed and export-producing oligarchy, aided by the particular economic and political structure, willingly abandoned or adopted the gold standard whenever it was to their benefit and profit".[125]

In the phases when the prices of raw materials and foodstuffs on international markets were rising, the peso tended to appreciate considerably. An appreciation of the peso, if not opposed, would have involved a redistribution of income in favour of the workers and to the detriment of the landowners. The latter, therefore, at these stages of the cycle exerted pressure to calm the appreciation of the exchange rate. The adoption of the gold standard and the accumulation of reserves were the preferred way to achieve this goal.

Unlike Argentina, Japan preceded its accession to the gold standard by a process of state capacity building that began with the Meiji revolution of 1868 and lasted about 30 years. Japan joined the gold standard only in 1897. As is well known, in the second half of the nineteenth century, the Far East became an area of great interest to the Western powers and the international scenario in which Japan had been operating for a long time changed significantly.

The growing external threat contributed, in no small measure, to the profound changes in the internal political balance. In 1868 a coup, known as *Meiji restoration*,

[124]At the same time, cuts in public spending were introduced.

[125]See also Ford (1960).

brought a new political class to power, whose goal was the modernization and industrialization of Japan to preserve its independence from external threats.

The sense of the project of the Meiji regime, established with the revolution of 1868, can be summarized in the expression: *Fukoku Kyōhei* (enrich the country, strengthen the military). This expression indicates that Japan's economic growth was a means of achieving its military buildup[126] and, therefore, at least in an initial phase, to safeguarding the independence of the country from the potential threat of conquest by Western powers which had manifested itself in the second half of the nineteenth century.

The strengthening of the country was pursued through a process of building state capacity. In fact, extensive institutional reforms were initiated by the Meiji regime, often in imitation of the successful experiences of Western countries.[127]

Most of these institutional reforms were carried out under the pressure of Matsukata Masayoshi.[128] The tax administration and the tax structure were the first point of attack. In this context Matsukata, as Japanese Minister of Finance, on the one hand, strengthened the bureaucratic apparatus, centralizing the collection of indirect taxes,[129] and on the other, healed state finances by approving huge cuts in public spending and substantial increases in the tax levy. The introduction of new taxes, especially indirect ones, allowed a significant increase in the central state's tax revenues. The process of state capacity building continued in 1882 with the establishment of the Bank of Japan, on the model of the central bank of Belgium.[130] In addition to the issuing monopoly, the new central bank was assigned the primary task of making the national currency convertible into gold, by eliminating the plurality of domestic currencies in circulation and proceeding with the gradual re-absorption of the paper money in circulation.

By having a central bank, the Japanese government was able to control the quantity of money and the level of prices. The centralization of the supply of money and the achievement of a high fiscal capacity were determining factors in the process of modernization and industrialization of Japan. However, it was only after the victorious war with China and receiving an indemnity from China of 30 million pounds (equivalent to 364 million yen) that the Meiji leadership decided in 1897 to join the gold standard. The availability of substantial gold reserves and an adequate state capacity made, in fact, the probability of the country's default very low.

---

[126]As Vishwanathan (1975, p. 41) writes: "The Western challenge had to be met not by retreating into a shell but by arming Japan .... The slogan *Fukoku Kyokei* was the expression of the need for deliberate efforts at modernization".

[127]See Hunter (2003).

[128]At the time of his appointment as Minister of Finance, he publicly expressed his conviction that the most urgent financial measure to be adopted was to free the country from the evil of the inconvertibility of money. See Matsukata (1899, pp. iv–v).

[129]See He (2013, p. 106).

[130]That is to say a central bank that enjoyed much less independence that the Bank of England. See Tamaki (1995) and Schiltz (2012).

Table 3.14 Adoption of the gold standard and state capacity in some peripheral countries

Country	Year of adoption	Revenue from customs duties[a]	Central bank reserves[b]	Exchange rate volatility[c]
Argentina	1883	64	3.8	na
Argentina	1899	54	0.2	0.57
Brazil	1888	59	1.4	0.37
Brazil	1906	57	0.8	0.69
Japan	1897	8	6.1	na
Russia	1897	12	12.6	0.04

Source: Flandreau and Zumer (2004)
[a]Percentage of total public revenue
[b]Percentage of GDP
[c]Average of volatility in the 5 years preceding the accession to the gold standard

In the years following 1897, the issuance of Japanese government bonds on the international financial markets followed one another with considerable frequency. In 1913, the amount of long-term government securities was 1530 million yen—over 30% of that year's GDP and about 57% of total government debt.[131]

The ability to access substantial foreign funding had two beneficial effects for Japan. On the one hand, this form of debt allowed the country to buy goods abroad, especially military equipment, and thereby acquire the ability not only to protect its independence, but also to acquire greater influence in Southeast Asia. On the other hand, the proceeds from foreign loans favoured an increase in consumption and imports, encouraging the growth and industrialization of the country.

The two ideal-type cases just illustrated allow a distinction to be made in the peripheral countries between those, such as Japan and Russia, which, by adhering to the gold standard, aimed at easier access to international financial markets and those, such as Argentina, Brazil and Chile, which adhered to this system without adequate fiscal capacity and an adequate amount of gold reserves, mainly for distribution reasons and who often, when it suited the ruling classes, suspended convertibility (Table 3.14).

3.10.2 The Interdependence Between Core and Peripheral Countries in the Gold Standard

The peripheral countries contributed to the stability of the gold standard, bearing a large part of the adjustment costs. This cost transfer could take place thanks to the high financial interdependence between core and peripheral countries. Indeed, as

[131]Pittaluga and Seghezza (2016) show that Japan was able to borrow abroad even when its debt became unsustainable thanks to the alliance with England which, in the face of its financial support, delegated to this country the military protection of its interests in the Far East.

Fishlow writes (1985, p. 383): "From 1870 to 1914 ... a truly global economy was forged for the first time, extending from the core of Western European industrializers to late-comers in Eastern Europe to raw material suppliers on the periphery". Between 1870 and 1913 over $30 billion were invested abroad by the core countries. The motivations for these investments were partly economic and partly political. The economic ones consisted of the significant gains that could derive from investments in countries rich in natural resources, such as Latin America. The political motivations lay in using the financial tools to build friendship or alliance. Feis (1930) underlines the difference in behaviour between England, whose financial investments abroad were mainly aimed at economic profit, and those of France and Germany, whose loans to foreign countries in many cases had political purposes. Think of the financial support offered by France to Russia after Bismarck's ban on the Reichsbank's accepting Russian bonds as covenants or that of Germany to the countries of Eastern and central Europe. In this context, in correspondence with an unfavourable balance of payments and tensions on the amount of its gold reserves, the Bank of England raised the bank rate thus discouraging capital exports and encouraging the repatriation of British foreign loans. This helps explain the year on year fluctuations in the country's foreign loans, which went from $480 million in 1872 to $60 million in 1877, back to $480 million in 1890 and down to $110 million in 1898, only to increase continuously in the following period up to $250 million in 1904 and booming in the following years up to $1100 million in 1913.[132]

The use of increases in the bank rate by the Bank of England in determining a decrease in capital flows to peripheral countries inevitably had repercussions on the balance of payments of the debtor countries. As a result, these countries were affected by a decrease in incomes and imports. Furthermore, the decrease in gold and foreign exchange, leading to a reduction in the reserves of local banks, favoured a decline in money and credit, or triggered a phase of deflation. These trend processes were aggravated by the fact that most peripheral countries lacked an institutional framework, in particular a central bank, which could mitigate their intensity and impact.

Another mechanism by which the peripheral countries contributed to the stability of the core countries is that some of them, such as British India,[133] adopted the gold-exchange standard, in which foreign exchange reserves substituted for actual gold reserves. A peripheral country that adopted this system, when it recorded a current account surplus at the expense of England or another core country, increased its liquidity balances in London (or in another financial centre) rather than withdraw gold from the reserve currency country. In this way, the core country could, substantially, maintain the quantity of money stable and pursue a smooth adjustment process.[134]

[132]See Triffin (1969).

[133]See Keynes (1913).

[134]See Officer (2008).

3.11 Conclusions

As has been seen, the adhesion of a country to the gold standard was accompanied by the definition of a set of domestic rules (through laws or statutory norms) aimed at guaranteeing the permanence of the national currency within the system. These mainly took the form of limits on the quantity of banknotes issued[135] and the imposition of a convertibility constraint.

This led to adherence to the gold standard becoming part of the process of formation and consolidation of nation states that characterized many European and non-European countries in the second half of the nineteenth century. This process, in the industrial countries, at the monetary level, manifested itself in the centralization of the money supply in the hands of the state. It was accompanied by a growing complexity and articulation of the bureaucratic apparatus of the states (consider for example, the role assumed by central banks and the development of an appropriate fiscal capacity).

The gold standard, by favouring the acceptance and diffusion of banknotes and bank money (to a greater degree than bi-metallism could have done), allowed industrial countries to better support the growth of the economy and the development of national financial systems.[136] Adherence to the gold standard, therefore, while associated with liberal and free trade policies, was functional to the power politics that the core countries of that system, namely Britain, Germany and France, pursued.

It is, therefore, not surprising that the gold standard was not based on agreements and cooperation between states. In fact, cooperation between central banks when it occurred, almost always, took the form of bilateral relations of an occasional nature, aimed at resolving moments of scarcity of liquid resources of a central bank.

The hegemonic role of Great Britain and the Bank of England deserves clarification. In particular, it seems possible to exclude the idea that Great Britain exercised political leadership, in other words, forms of coercion, pressure or persuasion on other countries and their central banks to adhere to the gold standard and respect its rules.[137]

The minutes of the parliamentary debates show that the British political class attached very little importance to international monetary issues. The Bank of England itself did not exercise any hegemonic role in the gold standard: it did not promote negotiations for the definition of the rules to be respected by the countries adhering to the system nor did it favour the launch of institutionalized forms of cooperation between central banks.

The payment technology on which the gold standard was based allows us to understand why the pound sterling assumed the role of international currency in this system. Two main factors contributed to this. The first was the high substitutability

[135]The most obvious example of this practice is represented by the Bank Charter Act of 1944, subsequently imitated by many other countries. See Giannini (2011).

[136]See Knafo (2013).

[137]See Gallarotti (1995).

between sterling and gold. The value of the British currency with respect to gold had remained unchanged since Newton's monetary reform of 1717, while, over time, the other currencies of advanced countries had shown a tendency to depreciate against gold. Even after World War I, Britain was the only one of these countries to return to its pre-war gold-exchange rate.

It is difficult to give a clear justification for the behaviour of the British authorities. However, the hypothesis put forward by Grossman (1988) seems plausible, according to which the British authorities maintained the value of the pound sterling fixed over time (with respect to gold) with the aim of more easily financing future wars.

A second factor that contributed to the adoption of the pound as an international currency is linked to the role that Britain had in international trade. In fact, in 1870 it was responsible for over 25% of international trade; while the degree of openness of this country was in excess of 50%. This aspect confirms the importance of the size and openness of a country for the acceptance of a commodity money (since sterling could be considered as such, given its high degree of substitutability with gold).

These two aspects lead us to believe that the emergence of the pound sterling as an international currency can be explained satisfactorily on the basis of the Mengerian theory.

Sterling's role as the international currency guaranteed Britain an indisputable financial primacy. This certainly allowed it to exploit the right of international seigniorage. The latter, however, was quantitatively limited by sterling's convertibility constraint. It was, therefore, in no way comparable to the seigniorage privilege enjoyed by a country that issues an international fiat currency. To this must be added the fact that in the last decades of the nineteenth century Great Britain was not perceived as a threat by the countries of continental Europe. The impact of its military spending on GDP was, in fact, very limited. Furthermore, it was mainly aimed at covering the expenses of the navy.[138] The combination of these factors contributed to reducing the concerns of other countries regarding the eventual repercussions of their adherence to the gold standard on their safety: the asymmetry of relative gains was not a concern for these countries at that time.

References

Alesina, A. (1988). The end of large public debts. In F. Giavazzi & L. Spaventa (Eds.), *High public debt: The Italian experience*. Cambridge University Press.

Aliber, R. Z. (2000). *International finance*. Edward Elgar.

Bagehot, W. (1873). *Lombard street: A description of the money market*. Henry S. King.

Bamberger, L. (1871). Rede Über das gesetz, betreffs die ausprägung von reichsgoldmünzen, gehalten im reichstag am 11. November 1871. In K. Helfferich (Ed.), *Ausgewählte reden und aufsätze über geld und bankwesen von ludwig Bamberger*. J. Guttentag Verlagsbuchhandlung.

[138]See Kennedy (1987).

Bergsten, C. F. (1975). *The dilemmas of the dollar: The economics and politics of United States international monetary policy*. New York University Press.
Beyen, J. W. (1949). *Money in a maelstrom*. Macmillan.
Bloomfield, A. (1959). *Monetary policy under the international gold Standard, 1880–1914*. Federal Reserve Bank of New York.
Bloomfield, A. (1963) *Short term capital movements under the pre-1914 gold standard*. Princeton Studies in International Finance, n. 11.
Bloomfield, A. (1968). Rules of the game of international adjustment? In C. R. Whittlesey & J. S. G. Wilson (Eds.), *Essays in money and banking in honor of RS Sayers*. Oxford University Press.
Bordo, M. (1981, May 2–17). *The classical gold standard: Some lessons for today*. Federal Reserve Bank of St. Louis Economic Research.
Bordo, M. (1993, March). *The gold standard, Bretton Woods and other monetary regimes: A historical appraisal* (pp. 123–191). Federal Reserve Bank of St. Louis Review.
Bordo, M., & Kydland, F. E. (1995). The gold standard as a rule: An essay in exploration. *Explorations in Economic History, 32*, 423–465.
Bordo, M. D., & Rockoff, H. (1996). The gold standard as a good housekeeping seal of approval. *Journal of Economic History, 56*, 389–428.
Bordo, M., & Schwartz, A. J. (1996). The operation of specie standard: Evidence for core and peripheral countries. In B. Eichengreen & J. Braga de Macedo (Eds.), *Historical perspectives on the gold standard: Portugal and the world* (pp. 1880–1890). Routledge.
Brown, W. (1940). *The international gold standard reinterpreted, 1914–1934*. NBER.
Bryan, S. (2010). *The gold standard at the turn of the twentieth century*. Columbia University Press.
Cain, P. J., & Hopkins, A. G. (2001). *British imperialism, 1688–2000*. Longman.
Calomiris, C., Flandreau, M., & Laeven, L. (2016). Political foundations of the lender of last resort: A global historical narrative. *Journal of Financial Intermediation, 28*, 1–66.
Cameron, R. (1967). *Banking in early stages of industrialization*. Oxford University Press.
Chevalier, M. (1859). *On the probable fall in the value of gold*. Appleton.
Clapham, J. (1944). *The Bank of England: A history*. Cambridge University Press.
Clapham, J. (1954). *The Bank of England*. Cambridge University Press.
van Cleveland, H. B. (1976). The international monetary system in the interwar period. In B. M. Rowland (Ed.), *Balance of power or hegemony: The interwar monetary system*. New York University Press.
Clough, S., & Cole, C. (1946). *Economic history of Europe*. Hat Heath.
Clower, R. W. (1969). *Monetary theory: Selected readings*. Penguin.
Cohen, B. (1977). *Organizing the world's money: The political economy of international monetary relations*. Basic Books.
Cooper, R. (1982). The gold standard: Historical facts and future prospects. *Brookings Papers on Economic Activities, 1*, 1–56.
Darwin, L. (1898). *Bimetallism: A summary and examination of the arguments for and against a bimetallic system of currency*. Appleton.
Davatyan, N., & Parke, W. R. (1995). The operations of the Bank of England, 1890-1908: A dynamic probit approach. *Journal of Money, Credit and Banking, 27*, 1099–1112.
De Cecco, M. (1974). *Money and empire: The international gold standard, 1890–1914*. Blackwell.
De Kock, M. H. (1974). *Central banking*. Crosby Lockwood Staples.
Della Paolera, G., & Taylor, A. M. (2001). *Straining the anchor. The argentine currency Board and the search for macroeconomic stability, 1880-1935*. The University of Chicago Press.
Diebolt, C., & Parent, A. (2008). Bimetallism: The 'rules of the game'. *Explorations in Economic History, 45*, 288–302.
Drake, L. S. (1985). Reconstruction of a bimetallic price level. *Explorations in Economic History, 22*, 194–219.

Dutton, J. (1984). The Bank of England and the rules of the game under the international gold standard: New evidence. In M. D. Bordo & A. J. Schwartz (Eds.), *A retrospective on the classical gold standard* (pp. 1821–1931). University of Chicago Press.
Eichengreen, B. (1985). Editor's introduction. In B. Eichengreen (Ed.), *The gold standard in theory and history*. Methuen.
Eichengreen, B. (1987). Conducting the international orchestra: Bank of England leadership under the classical gold standard. *Journal of International Money and Finance, 6*, 5–29.
Eichengreen, B. (1992). *Golden fetters: The gold standard and the great depression, 1919–1939*. Oxford University Press.
Eichengreen, B. (2004). *Capital flows and crises*. MIT.
Eichengreen, B., & Flandreau, M. (1998). The geography of the gold standard. In J. Braga de Macedo, B. Eichengreen, & J. Reis (Eds.), *Currency convertibility: The gold standard and beyond*. Routledge.
Einaudi, L. (2000). From the franc to the Europe: The attempted transformation of the Latin Monetary Union into a European Monetary Union, 1865-1873. *Economic History Review, 53*, 284–308.
Einaudi, L. (2001). *Money and politics, European monetary unification and the gold standard (1865–73)*. Oxford University Press.
Feis, H. (1930). *Europe, the World's Banker, 1870-1914* (Ed. 1965). Norton.
Ferguson, N., & Schularik, M. (2006). The empire effect: The determinant of country risk in the first age of globalization, 1880-1913. *Journal of Economic History, 66*, 283–312.
Ferguson, N., & Schularik, M. (2012). The thin film of gold: Monetary rules and policy credibility. *European Review of Economic History, 16*, 384–407.
Fetter, F. W. (1965). *Development of British monetary orthodoxy, 1797–1875*. Harvard University Press.
Fisher, I. (1911). *The purchasing power of money*. Macmillan.
Fishlow, A. (1985). Lessons from the past: Capital markets during the 19th century and the interwar period. *International Organization, 39*, 383–439.
Flandreau, M. (1996). The French crime of 1873: An essay in the emergence of the international gold standard, 1870-1880. *Journal of Economic History, 56*, 862–897.
Flandreau, M. (1997a). As good as gold? Bimetallism in equilibrium. In M. C. Marcuzzo, L. H. Officer, & A. Rosselli (Eds.), *Monetary standards and exchange rates* (pp. 1850–1870). Routledge.
Flandreau, M. (1997b). Central bank cooperation in historical perspective: A sceptical view. *Economic History Review, 50*, 735–763.
Flandreau, M. (2003). *The glitter of gold*. Oxford University Press.
Flandreau, M., & Oosterlinck, K. (2012). Was the emergence of the international gold standard expected? Evidence from Indian government securities. *Journal of Monetary Economics, 59*, 649–669.
Flandreau, M., & Zumer, F. (2004). *The making of global finance*. OECD.
Ford, A. G. (1960). Notes on the working of the gold standard before 1914. *Oxford Economic Papers, 12*, 52–76 (Reprinted in 1985 in B. Eichengreen & M. Flandreau (Eds.), The gold standard in theory and history. Routledge).
Ford, A. G. (1962). *The gold standard 1880–1914, Britain and Argentina*. Oxford University Press.
Ford, A. G. (1989). International financial policy and the gold standard. In P. Mathias & S. Pollard (Eds.), *The Cambridge economic history* (Vol. VIII, pp. 1870–1914). Cambridge University Press.
Frieden, J. (1991). Invested interests: The politics of national economic policies in a world of global finance. *International Organization, 45*, 425–451.
Frieden, J. (2015). *Currency politics*. Princeton University Press.
Friedman, M. (1951). Commodity reserve currency. *Journal of Political Economy, 59*, 203–232.
Friedman, M. (1990a). Bimetallism revisited. *Journal of Economic Perspectives, 4*, 85–104.
Friedman, M. (1990b). The crime of 1873. *Journal of Political Economy, 98*, 1159–1194.

Friedman, M., & Schwartz, A. (1963). *The monetary history of the United States*. Princeton University Press.
Gallarotti, G. (1995). *The anatomy of an international monetary regime*. Oxford University Press.
Gallarotti, G. (2005). Hegemons of a lesser god: The Bank of France and monetary leadership under the classical gold standard. *Review of International Political Economy, 12*, 624–646.
Gallarotti, G. (2010). *Cosmopolitan power in international relations: A synthesis of realism, neoliberalism, and constructivism*. Cambridge University Press.
Giannini, C. (1995). Money, trust and central banking. *Journal of Economics and Business, 47*, 217–237.
Giannini, C. (2011). *The age of central banks*. Edward Elgar.
Gilpin, R. (1981). *War and change in world politics*. Cambridge University Press.
Giovannini, A. (1986). Rules of the game during the international gold standard: England and Germany. *Journal of International Money and Finance, 5*, 467–483.
Goodhart, C. A. E. (1972). *The business of banking*. Weidenfeld and Nicolson.
Grossman, H. (1988). *The political economy of war debts and inflation*. NBER working paper n. 2743.
He, W. (2013). *Paths toward the modern fiscal state*. Harvard University Press.
Helfferich, K. T. (1898). *Die Reform des deutschen Geldwesens der Grundung des Reiches* (Vol. I). Duncker and Humblot.
Helleiner, E. (1999). Denationalizing money? Economic liberalism and the 'national question' in currency affairs. In E. Gilbert & E. Helleiner (Eds.), *Nation states and money*. Routledge.
Helleiner, E. (2003). *The making of national money*. Cornell University Press.
Hobson, C. K. (1914). *Export of capital*. Constable.
Hobson, J. (2002). Two hegemonies or one? In P. O'Brien & A. Clesse (Eds.), *Two hegemonies: Britain, 1846–1914 and the United States* (pp. 1941–2001). Ashgate.
Holsti, K. J. (1992). *International politics: A framework for analysis*. Prentice Hall.
Hume, D. (1752). On the balance of trade. Reprinted in 1987. In E. Miller & D. Hume (Eds.), *Essay, moral, political and literary* (Vol. 1, pp. 330–345). Liberty Fund.
Hunter, J. (2003). *Bankers, investors and risk: British capital and Japan during the years of the Anglo-Japanese alliance (1902–1913)*. International Studies 03/443. Suntory-Toyota International Centre in Economics and Related Disciplines.
Jeanne, O. (1995). Monetary policy in England, 1893-1914: A structural VAR analysis. *Explorations in Economic History, 32*, 302–326.
Jonung, L. (1984). Swedish experience under the classic gold standard, 1873-1914. In M. Bordo & A. J. Schwartz (Eds.), *A retrospective on the classical gold standard* (pp. 1821–1931). University of Chicago Press.
Kennedy, P. (1987). *The rise and fall of the great powers*. Random House.
Keynes, J. M. (1913). *Indian currency and finance*. Frankfurt am Main: Verlag (Ed. 2020).
Keynes, J. M. (1914). War and the financial system. *Economic Journal, 24*, 460–486.
Keynes, J. M. (1930). *A treatise on money* (Vol. II). Macmillan.
Kindleberger, C. (1973). *The world in depression, 1929–1939*. University of California Press.
Kindleberger, C. (1984). *A financial history of Western Europe*. George Allen & Unwin.
King, W. T. C. (1936). *History of the London discount market*. Routledge.
Kisch, C. H., & Elkin, W. A. (1928). *Central Banks*. Macmillan.
Knafo, S. (2006). The gold standard and the origins of the modern international monetary system. *Review of International Political Economy, 13*, 78–102.
Knafo, S. (2013). *The making of modern finance*. Routledge.
Krasner, S. (1976). State power and the structure of international trade. *World Politics, 28*, 317–347.
Kuznets, S. (1966). *Modern economic growth*. Yale University Press.
Laughlin, J. L. (1896). *The history of bimetallism in the United States*. Appleton.
Lewis, W. A. (1978). *The evolution of the international economic order*. Princeton University Press.

Lindert, P. (1969). *Key currencies and gold, 1900–1913*. Princeton Studies in International Finance n. 24. Princeton University Press.

Marichal, C. (1989). *A century of debt crises in Latin America, from independence to the great depression, 1820–1930*. Princeton University Press.

Matsukata, M. (1899). *Report on the adoption of the gold standard in Japan*. The Government Press.

Mauro, P., Sussman, N., & Yafeh, Y. (2006). *Emerging markets and financial globalization*. Oxford University Press.

Maxfield, S. (1997). *Gatekeepers of growth: The international political economy of central banking in developing countries*. Princeton University Press.

McGouldrick, P. (1984). Operations of the German central bank and the rules of the game, 1879–1913. In M. Bordo & A. J. Schwartz (Eds.), *A retrospective on the classical gold standard* (pp. 1821–1931). University of Chicago Press.

McKinnon, R. (1993). The rules of the game: International money in historical perspective. *Journal of Economic Literature, 31*, 1–44.

Meissner, C. M. (2005). A new world order: Explaining the emergence of the classical gold standard. *Journal of International Economics, 66*, 385–406.

Meissner, C. M. (2015). *The limits of bimetallism*. NBER working paper n. 20852.

Mertens, J. E. (1944). *La naissance et le development de l'etalon-or, 1696–1922*. Presses Universitaires de France.

Mill, J. S. (1848). *Principles of political economy, books III-IV* (ed. 1965). Routledge & Kegan Paul.

Milward, A. (1996). The origins of the gold standard. In J. Braga de Macedo, B. Eichengreen, & J. Reis (Eds.), *Currency convertibility: The gold standard and beyond*. Routledge.

Mitchener, K. J., & Weidener, M. (2015). Was the classical gold standard credible on the periphery? Evidence from currency risk. *Journal of Economic History, 75*, 479–511.

Morgan, E. (1943). *The theory and practice of central banking 1797-1913*. Cass. Reprinted in 1965.

Morys, M. (2006). *The classical gold standard in the European periphery: A case study of Austria-Hungary and Italy, 1870–1919*. Ph.D. thesis, London School of Economics.

Morys, M. (2012). *The emergence of the classical gold standard*. University of York, Economic History working paper.

O'Brien, P. (2002). The pax Britannica and American hegemony: Precedent, antecedent or just another history? In P. O'Brien & A. Clesse (Eds.), *Two hegemonies: Britain, 1846–1914 and the United States* (pp. 1941–2001). Ashgate.

Obstfeld, M., & Taylor, A. M. (2004). *Global capital markets: Integration, crisis and growth*. Cambridge University Press.

Officer, L. H. (2008). Gold standard. In *New Palgrave dictionary of economics*. Palgrave Macmillan.

Oppers, S. E. (1993). *A model of the bimetallic system*. University of Michigan Research Forum on International Economics, Discussion Paper n. 332.

Oppers, S. E. (1995). Recent developments in bimetallic theory. In J. Reis (Ed.), *International monetary systems in historical perspective*. St. Martin's Press.

Oppers, S. E. (1996). Was the worldwide shift to gold inevitable? An analysis of the end of bimetallism. *Journal of Monetary Economics, 37*, 143–162.

Oppers, S. E. (2000). A model of the bimetallic system. *Journal of Monetary Economics, 46*, 517–533.

Overstone, S. J. Lord. (1837a). Reflections suggested by a perusal of Mr. J. Horsley Palmer's pamphlet: On the causes and consequences of the pressure on the money market (Reprinted in Tracts, pp. 1–40).

Overstone, S. J. Lord. (1837b). *Further reflections on the state of the currency and the action of the Bank of England* (Reprinted in Annex to Tracts, pp. 41–158).

Overstone, S. J. Lord. (1840). *Remarks on the management of the circulation and the conduct of the Bank of England* (Reprinted in Tracts, pp. 1–52).

Panic, M. (1992). *European monetary union. Lessons from the classical gold standard*. St. Martin Press.
Pippenger, J. (1984). Bank of England operations 1893-1913. In M. Bordo & A. J. Schwartz (Eds.), *A retrospective on the classical gold standard*. University of Chicago Press.
Pittaluga, G. B., & Seghezza, E. (2016). How Japan remained on the gold standard despite unsustainable external debt. *Explorations in Economic History, 59*, 40–54.
Redish, A. (1990). The evolution of the gold standard in England. *Journal of Economic History, 50*, 789–805.
Redish, A. (1992). *The evolution of the classical gold standard: The case of France*. University of British Columbia, Dept. of Economics Discussion Paper n. 92-22.
Redish, A. (2000). *Bimetallism: An economic and historical analysis*. Cambridge University Press.
Reti, S. P. (1998). *Silver and gold: The political economy of international monetary conferences: 1867–1892*. Greenwood Press.
Russell, H. (1898). *International monetary conferences: Their purposes, character and results*. Harper and Brothers.
Sargent, D., & Velde, F. (2001). *The big problem of small change*. Princeton University Press.
Sayers, R. (1957). *Central banking after Bagehot*. Oxford University Press.
Sayers, R. (1976). *The Bank of England, 1891–1944*. Cambridge University Press.
Scammell, W. M. (1965). The working of the gold standard. *Bulletin of Economic Research, 17*, 32–45 (Reprinted in 1985 in B. Eichengreen (Ed.), *The gold standard in theory and history*. Methuen.
Schenk, C., & Straumann, T. (2016). Central banks and the stability of the international monetary regime. In M. D. Bordo, O. Eitrheim, M. Flandreau, & J. F. Quigstad (Eds.), *Central banks at a crossroads*. Cambridge University Press.
Schiltz, M. (2012). Money on the road to empire: Japan's adoption of gold monometallism: 1873–1897. *Economic History Review 65*, 1147–1168.
Schumpeter, J. A. (1954). *History of economic analysis*. Oxford University Press.
Selgin, G. (2008). *Good money: Birmingham Button makers, the Royal Mint and the beginnings of modern Coinage, 1775–1821*. University of Michigan Press.
Simmons, B. A. (2000). The legalization of international monetary affairs. *International Organization, 54*, 573–602.
Skidelsky, R. (1976). Retreat from leadership: The evolution of British economic policy. In B. M. Rowland (Ed.), *Balance of power or hegemony: The interwar monetary system* (pp. 1870–1939). New York University Press.
Sussman, N., & Yafeh, Y. (2001). Institutions, reforms, and country risk. *Lessons from Japanese government debt in the Meiji era. Journal of Economic History, 60*, 442–467.
Tamaki, N. (1995). *Japanese banking: A history 1859–1959*. Cambridge University Press.
Triffin, R. (1969). *The myth and realities of the so-called gold standard* (Reprinted in 1985 In B. Eichengreen & M. Flandreau (Eds.), *The gold standard in theory and history*. Routledge).
Velde, F. R., & Weber, W. E. (2000). A model of bimetallism. *Journal of Political Economy, 108*, 1210–1234.
Viner, J. (1937). *Studies in the theory of international trade*. Harper.
Viner, J. (1960). *Studies in the theory of international trade*. Harper & Brothers.
Vishwanathan, S. (1975). Paradox of Japan's nationalism: Relations with Asia. In T. Fusé (Ed.), *Modernization and stress in Japan*. Brill.
Walker, F. A. (1896). *International bimetallism*. Halt.
White, H. (1893). *The gold standard*. Evening Post Publ. Co.
Wiegand, J. (2019). *Destabilizing the global monetary system: Germany's adoption of the gold standard in the early 1870s*. IMF working paper n. WP/19/32.

Chapter 4
The Gold-Exchange Standard, Its Collapse and the Interwar Lack of an International Money

4.1 Introduction

The classical gold standard was a system based on commodity money, where the monetary sovereignty of the member countries was limited. In fact, there was an unwritten law that if a country, for some reason, suspended its convertibility, would have to re-establish it as soon as possible. This implied that, in the long run, governments could only expand the amount of money in line with the growth of their gold reserves. In fact, between 1870 and 1914, the total quantity of money worldwide increased to the same extent as did gold reserves.

When a country returned to the gold standard after a period of suspension of convertibility, the adjustment costs were primarily borne by the working class, that is to say by the interest group that, at that time, had the least political power.

With the First World War, convertibility was suspended by almost all the countries who participated in the war. In the immediate post-war period, most of these countries found themselves with price levels significantly higher than the pre-war period. In some countries, hit by hyperinflation, the value of the currency was zeroed.

It is in this scenario that governments reached the conclusion that only by stabilizing prices and exchange rates, could international trade and output return to growth. Based on this conviction the idea became widespread that it was necessary to rebuild an international monetary order by re-establishing the gold standard.

The lead role in the pursuit of this goal was taken by Great Britain, which promoted two international conferences. The first was held in Brussels in 1920 and the second in Genoa in 1922. In these conferences, in particular that in Genoa, the basis for the gold-exchange standard was laid.

The gold-exchange standard and the classic gold standard, despite many similarities, differed in several respects. First, while the classic gold standard was based on commodity money—gold—the gold-exchange standard was a two-tier system: the two key currencies, the sterling and the dollar were exclusively convertible into gold,

G. B. Pittaluga, E. Seghezza, *Building Trust in the International Monetary System*, Frontiers in Economic History, https://doi.org/10.1007/978-3-030-78491-1_4

while the other currencies were also convertible into the key currencies. The choice of a two-tier system was made necessary by the fact that, after the First World War, gold reserves were mainly concentrated in the USA. The other countries generally had insufficient gold reserves to defend the gold convertibility of their currencies.

The gold-exchange standard lasted only from 1925, when Britain joined it, followed by many other countries, to 1931, when, as the recession deepened, Britain and other countries abandoned the system.

Various explanations have been given for the short life and subsequent collapse of the gold-exchange standard. Some insist that underlying this failure was the behaviour of one or more states. Others point to changes in the political and economic balance within countries in the post-war period which made the adjustment of the imbalances imposed by the gold-exchange standard unsustainable.

As discussed in Chap. 2, the emergence of a convertible, or fiat, currency, as a means of payment can only be adequately understood taking into account the nature of the domestic socio-political balance and relations between states in the international arena. On the basis of this theoretical framework, we advance the hypothesis that the failure of the gold-exchange standard was not only due to the behaviour of one or more states, to policy errors or to the growing weight attributed by governments to internal objectives with respect to external ones, but also, to a large extent, to the state of international relations in the immediate post-war period.

For various reasons, but in particular because it was a two-tier monetary system, the gold-exchange standard was characterized by a higher elasticity of money supply than the gold standard. This exposed it to the risk of large variations in the international monetary multiplier and, therefore, with the same quantity of available gold reserves, to large fluctuations in the world money supply. The stabilization of the multiplier would therefore have required coordination between states, aimed at preventing the sterilization of capital inflows and re-composition of the official reserves in favour of gold. However, in the interwar period, the balance of international relations was incompatible with the creation of such an institutional framework.

As confirmed by the numerous international conferences held at that time and the activities of the League of Nations, in the monetary and financial field in the 1920s there existed a demand for an institutional architecture aimed at guaranteeing the stability of the gold-exchange standard. The lack of supply of mechanisms and institutions capable of creating the necessary trust is here traced to the prevailing multipolar equilibrium in the international arena. As already mentioned in Chap. 2, Kindleberger (1973) attributed the collapse of the gold-exchange standard to the refusal of the USA to exercise the functions of the leading country; those functions, in his view, which in the gold standard had been exercised by Britain. It has to be borne in mind, however, that the gold-exchange standard, because of its two-tier structure, offered greater scope for exploitation of seigniorage by the leading country than the gold standard did. In it, therefore, the problem of relative gains arose more forcefully. The so-called renunciation of monetary hegemony by the USA can therefore also be interpreted as an unwillingness of the other powers to accept it.

4.2 The Resolutions of the Genoa Conference and the Establishment of the Gold-Exchange Standard

The First World War had been much longer than expected. The effort to finance the war mainly through taxes proved impossible. Hence, varying in degree from country to country, a large part of war spending had been financed by money. Because of this, the currency in circulation of the countries who had participated in the war had increased considerably. The increase in the money supply was followed by significant increases in price levels. In the face of high and persistent inflation rates and accentuated exchange rate volatility, the authorities of the leading countries considered that the only way to stabilize prices and exchange rates was to return to the gold standard.

Commenting on the instability of the post-war exchange rates, Nurkse (1944, p. 137) stated: "If there is anything that interwar experience has clearly shown, it is that paper currency cannot be left free to fluctuate from day to day under the influence of the market supply and demand".

International monetary disorder, due to extreme exchange rate instability, helps to explain why governments were generally in favour of re-introducing the gold standard as early and as widely as possible. Temin (1989) traces this point of view back to an exclusively ideological basis,[1] Giannini (2011) to an inability to think of an alternative monetary system.

Whatever the reason, the decision to return to the gold standard, and to do so as soon as possible, left the governments of the industrialized countries facing a choice: pursue deflationary policies aimed at bringing prices back to their pre-war levels or accept all, or part, of the current price level and stabilize currency at parity with the new gold price.[2]

The country that urged most strongly for a prompt restoration of the gold standard was Britain, and in particular the governor of the central bank of that country, Montagu Norman. The commission chaired by Walter Cunliffe, tasked by parliament in 1918 to study the monetary question and to make proposals on the matter, had concluded that: "In our opinion it is imperative that after the war the conditions necessary to the maintenance of an effective gold standard should be restored without delay".[3]

Benjamin Strong, president of the main American Federal Reserve Bank, that of New York, believed that there were no alternatives to the return to the gold standard. He argued that had this system been permanently abandoned, governments would

[1] "Choices made by monetary and fiscal authorities in the years around 1930 were made according to a view of the world that maintenance of the gold standard ... was the primary requisite for prosperity". Temin (1989, pp. 7–8).

[2] See Eichengreen (1992).

[3] See Cunliffe Committee (1918, p. 114).

have been tempted to adopt monetary systems based solely on paper money. Inflation and disorder in the financial and currency markets would have resulted.[4]

Norman and Strong's position was shared by the governments of the other main European countries. Despite this shared view, however, there was a widespread belief that there was a worldwide lack of gold, that the available gold was distributed asymmetrically (as a result of the war), and that there were difficulties in implementing deflationary policies to restore the price level, and therefore the parities, at pre-war levels.

Various solutions were proposed to solve the problem of global gold scarcity. A first solution suggested by Cassel (1928) and von Mises (1928) foresaw the increase in the price of gold and, therefore, the depreciation of all currencies compared to the commodity money. In this way the demand for gold would have decreased, its relative scarcity eliminated, as would the risk of introducing deflationary policies.

A different position was that of those who believed that the problem of the lack of liquidity at the world level could be resolved by expanding the range of payment instruments. In 1913, in his book *Indian Currency and Finance*, Keynes proposed a reform of the Indian monetary system aimed at increasing the elasticity of the money supply. This reform foresaw the possibility of covering the currency in circulation not only with gold, but also with foreign currency reserves. In truth, this practice had already been followed by many governments before 1914.[5] According to Keynes in *A Tract on Monetary Reform*, the monetary authorities should have pursued the goal of stabilizing prices rather than the exchange rate. For this purpose they should have acted on both the demand and supply of money.

Of the two possible solutions the second was chosen. The gold-exchange standard, in fact, in contrast to the classic gold standard, was designed as a pyramidal scheme, divided into two levels: only the leading currencies (sterling and dollar) were convertible exclusively into gold, the other currencies could be converted, as well as into gold, into the lead currencies.

The person who committed himself most actively in the introduction of the gold-exchange standard was Norman, while, its principal theorist was Hawtrey, a long-time senior official of the British Treasury. Hawtrey, in particular, had in mind a system in which the quantity of money no longer depended on objective constraints, such as the amount of gold available, but could be managed by the government at its discretion.[6]

The context in which the conditions and methods of a return to the gold standard were established, albeit in the form of the gold-exchange standard, is represented by the Brussels Conference of 1920 and, above all, by that of Genoa in 1922. The latter

---

[4]This position is expressed by Strong in a memorandum of January 1925, quoted in Moggridge (1972, pp. 59–60).

[5]See Nurkse (1944).

[6]Hawtrey (1923, p. 136) writes: "If all the gold standard countries adhere to it, gold will nowhere be needed as a means of remittance, and gold will only be withdrawn from the reserve for use as a raw material of industry".

was strongly supported by the British Prime Minister Lloyd George. At a meeting of the Supreme Allied Council held in Cannes in January 1922, he succeeded in convincing the governments of the winning countries to hold an economic and financial conference for the reconstruction of Western and Eastern Europe as soon as possible.

The British immediately appointed an interdepartmental commission, presided over by Sir Sydney Chapman, secretary of the Board of Trade, with the task of organizing the conference. In March 1922, the Chapman Commission published a report detailing the main points to be discussed in the conference. Crucial importance was given to the reorganization of the international monetary system and cooperation between central banks.

Within the Conference, whose work opened in Genoa on April 10, 1922, various commissions were set up. One of the most important of these was the financial commission, presided over by Sir Robert Horne, the Chancellor of the Exchequer. This commission, in turn, was divided into three sub-commissions, covering debts, credits, exchange rates and currencies. A plan for the reform of the international monetary system, drawn up by Hawtrey, was presented to the Finance Committee which, based on this, then proposed 12 Resolutions for approval.[7] These Resolutions were approved by the Conference's General Assembly. They came to represent the basis of the monetary system of the 1920s, or the gold-exchange standard. It is therefore impossible to disagree with Rothbard (1998, p. 133), when he writes: "Many historians have written off the Genoa Conference as a 'failure' and dismiss its influence on the international money of the Twentieth century [...] But the critical point is that Genoa triumphed anyway ...".

The final goal of the Resolutions approved at the Genoa Conference was the restoration of the gold standard, albeit in a slightly different version from the classic gold standard. This restoration would inevitably require the adoption of strict fiscal and monetary policies. On the monetary front this implied a major strengthening of central banks and, in countries where they did not yet exist, their creation. It also implied the centralization of the conduct of monetary policy and the refusal of all forms of free banking in these countries.

At the same time, however, there was a widespread belief that the stabilization processes required the broad autonomy of central banks from political control.[8] This principle was vigorously adopted in the countries that, as part of the stabilization process, availed themselves of the assistance and advice of the League of Nations Financial Commission: in all these countries an autonomous central bank was established with a monopoly on issuing money. This happened in Poland (1923), Hungary (1924), Danzig (1924), Bulgaria (1926), Greece (1927) and Estonia

[7]See League of Nations (1922).

[8]Resolution 2, in fact, provided that "Banks, and especially banks of issue, should be free from political pressure, and should be conducted solely on lines of prudent finance. In countries where there is no central bank of issue, one should be established". See League of Nations (1922, p. 678).

(1926–27).[9] The emphasis placed by Resolution 2 on the autonomy of central banks underlies the need to prevent monetary and exchange policy from being influenced by political pressure in a period marked by profound change, such as the introduction of universal suffrage.[10]

The main proponent of this principle was Norman, who argued that "... a central bank should acquire by external help ... or by internal recognition ... a certain freedom or independence within ... its own state".[11] At the Brussels Conference in 1920 he reiterated this concept: "Banks and especially banks of issue should be free from political pressure and should be conducted only on line of prudent finance".[12] The determination with which Norman promoted the establishment of independent central banks came not only from the need to safeguard the functioning of the gold-exchange standard, but also from the intention to create, through these institutions, a channel of political and financial influence for their countries.[13]

It should be noted that in the 1920s, the independence of central banks, unlike the final decade of the last century, was never considered as a mechanism to create confidence in the stability of the value of money, but rather was seen as an instrument that would make re-integration and permanence in the gold-exchange standard and the integration of the country into international financial markets easier.[14] For the League of Nations itself, central bank independence was a means of exercising influence (through its officials included on the boards of these institutions) on the conduct of monetary policy in countries assisted by it rather than as a mechanism aimed at safeguarding the stability of domestic prices.

Giannini (2011, pp. 134–135) correctly writes that in countries whose stabilization had been supported by the League of Nations "the autonomy principle [had been regarded] more as something forced on them by international creditors bent upon keeping the monetary lever out of their debtors' hands than as an institutional advance".

In the Resolutions of the Genoa Conference the nature and functioning of the gold-exchange standard were defined. In particular, Resolution 9 established the ways in which demand for gold could be limited. This was achieved through an international convention, based on the gold-exchange standard. The Conference

---

[9]See Singleton (2011).

[10]With reference to these changes Strakosch, a British banker, wrote: "The trend of political evolution the world over ... is in a direction which makes it less safe to entrust governments with the management of currencies than it may have been in the pre-war days". Letter of Henry Strakosch to Basil Blackett, October 17, 1925, T176/25B, p. 3, PRO. Quoted in Helleiner (2003: 148).

[11]See Montagu Norman to J.P. Morgan, 19 November 1927, BE 41/307.

[12]See Jacobsson, Notes on a conversation with Sir Otto Niemeyer, 13 December 1933, BE OV50/6.

[13]With reference to the diffusion of central banks in English domains, Plumptre (1940, p. 193) wrote: "The desire in England for a chain of Empire central bank was a latter day expression of financial imperialism ... the essential purpose was the same: the maintenance and extension of London's influence and control".

[14]See, among others, James (2001, pp. 36–37).

Table 4.1 Reserve requirements against the issue of money (percentage values)

	Coverage required for:	In gold	In gold and foreign currency
Belgium	Notes and deposits on demand	30	40
France	Notes and deposits on demand	35	
Germany	Banknotes	30	40
Switzerland	Banknotes	40	
UK	Banknotes in excess of £ 280 million	100	
USA	Banknotes and deposits	40 35	

Source: Federal Reserve Board (1930, p. 502), Federal Reserve Bulletin, June 1930

established that the system had a pyramidal structure: a participating country could hold official reserves not only in gold but also in the principal currencies, sterling and the dollar.

In this way it sought to reduce the demand for gold. The achievement of this goal also contributed to the adoption of a cover ratio of between 30 and 40% (Table 4.1).

Furthermore, the possibility of changing cover ratios made money more elastic: central banks could, therefore, influence the money multiplier. These characteristics of the gold-exchange standard have led some scholars to consider it an inflationary monetary system.[15]

In fact, the gold-exchange standard given its pyramidal structure could, depending on the behaviour of central banks, be either inflationary or deflationary. The participants at the Genoa Conference were aware of this fact and believed that both inflation and deflation could be avoided if the countries cooperated. In particular, central banks had to centralize and coordinate the demand for gold in order to avoid large price fluctuations in this asset.

In addition, central banks were urged to cooperate constantly in order to allow the good functioning and preservation of the gold-exchange standard. This need for close cooperation between central banks was reiterated in Resolution 12, where the Bank of England was assigned the task of organizing, as soon as possible, a conference of central bankers so that they could propose the stipulation of an international monetary convention to their governments. This conference was originally scheduled for June 1922 but was postponed several times for the most varied reasons. Eventually the proposal for the meeting was forgotten.

Although no agreement or treaty was signed by the participants, the influence of the Resolutions approved at the Genoa Conference was considerable. Firstly, in the 1920s several new central banks were created. Secondly, the League of Nations Financial Commission contributed to the stabilization of a good number of countries, based on the Resolutions approved in 1922. And finally, what perhaps counts most, starting from 1925, after the return to the gold standard of the pound, most developed countries restored the convertibility of their own currencies. This process was accompanied by the dismantling of controls on capital movements. Thus a system

[15]See, among others, Fink (1984).

was fully constituted which, consistent with the macroeconomic trilemma, provided for fixed exchange rates and free movement of capital.

It seemed that the hands of time had been turned back, to the happy situation of the classical gold standard when Western economies had recorded a tumultuous increase in output. It was not to be. The gold-exchange standard lasted only 6 years. Its collapse occurs in September 1931 when the pound was declared non-convertible.

4.3 The Launch and Functioning of the Gold-Exchange Standard

The gold-exchange standard was established with the support of a large number of countries between 1924 and 1927 on the basis of the Resolutions of the Genoa Conference. After the hyperinflation of 1923, Germany stabilized its currency and returned to the gold standard in 1924, Sweden returned to gold the same year. However, the event that decisively marked the launch of the gold-exchange standard was the return to the pre-war gold standard of the pound sterling, a decision made by the then Chancellor of the Exchequer Winston Churchill at the end of April 1925 and approved by the British Parliament on May 13th of the same year.

Britain's adoption of the gold-exchange standard was immediately followed by many British colonies. By the end of 1925, 35 countries had re-established the gold standard (Fig. 4.1).

France joined the system with a slight delay. After overcoming the critical situation of mid-1926 and averting an inflationary process, the Poincaré government

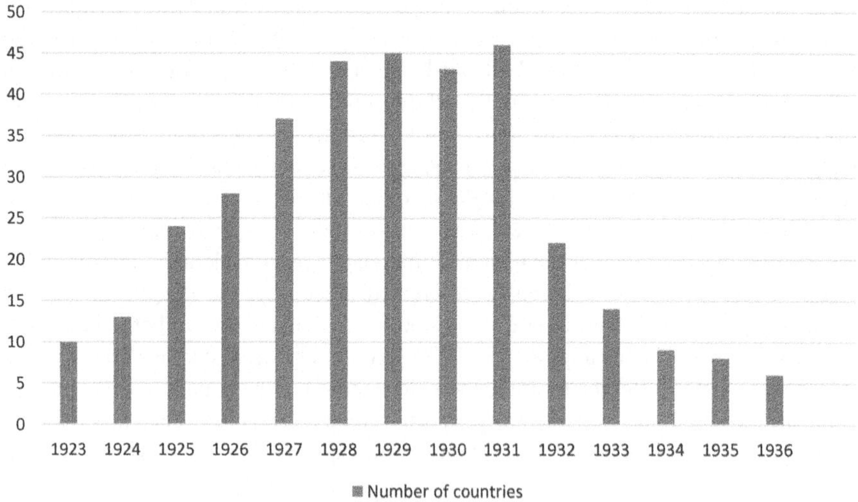

Fig. 4.1 Number of countries in the gold-exchange standard. Source: Eichengreen (1992)

Table 4.2 Values of manufacturing exports (1913 = 100)

	1929	1937
England	151	90
France	128	96
Germany	136	116
Italy	111	66
USA	120	93

Source: Dimsdale (1981)

managed to stabilize the franc at the end of that year. The official return of the French currency to the gold parity was, however, only in June 1928. With the new parity the French franc was devalued by about 80% compared to its pre-war level.

As Boyce, (2009, p. 165) writes: "France decision to rejoin the United States and Britain on the gold standard in 1928 ostensibly strengthened the global system. But since the decision was informed as much by nationalism as liberalism, it scarcely hampered well for global cooperation". The restoration of the gold standard in the gold-exchange standard version offered only the temporary illusion of stability. In fact, over its short duration the system was unstable. There were various reasons for the instability of the gold-exchange standard. Some of which, as will be seen, determined its collapse.

One of the main issues was the mismatch in exchange rates. As we have seen, Britain returned to the pre-war gold parity. Since the price levels in this country were still considerably higher in 1925 than in 1914, the real exchange rate of the pound had increased. By contrast, the real exchange rate of other currencies, starting with the French franc had depreciated. Exchange rate mismatches favoured the emergence of balance of payments imbalances and, therefore, inflows or outflows of gold reserves or high-value currencies.

This situation had a particular impact on Britain. Aiming to restore real exchange rate of the pound led to deflationary policies. Such policies impacted negatively on employment, giving rise to social tension and street demonstrations such as the Great Strike of 1926. Despite making this effort again in 1929, the real exchange rate of the pound was, nonetheless, overvalued (Table 4.2).

The overvaluation of the exchange rate of the pound penalized exports and, hence, the growth of the British economy. The negative effects of the sterling overvaluation were attacked by Keynes in *The Economic Consequences of Mr. Churchill.*[16]

Therefore, the weak link in the gold-exchange standard turned out to be the country that had most stubbornly sought it. As Kooker (1976, pp. 88–89) writes: "The marvellous network of financial institutions and the desire to remain bankers to the world were incompatible with the impoverishment of the nation, the stagnation of export industries, and a declining invisible surplus".

[16]Johnson (1975, p. 110) writes: "Had the exchange value of the pound been fixed realistically in the 1920s—a prescription fully in accord with orthodox economic theory—there would have been no need for mass unemployment".

Table 4.3 Gold holdings of central banks and Treasuries (in millions of US dollars)

	1926	1927	1928	1929
USA	838	818	770	802
France	175	202	258	336
Britain	151	152	153	146
World	1951	2001	2083	2143

Source: Strakosch (1930).

On the other hand, since the end of 1926, the country that most benefited from the system was France, a country that had joined with little enthusiasm. The French attitude was based on both political and economic concerns. From an economic point of view, France considered the gold-exchange standard intrinsically inflationary, since the same amount of gold supported the creation of liquidity both in the country that held gold reserves and in the country that held the principal currencies of the system as reserve. From a political point of view, France saw in the gold-exchange standard, and the consequent strengthening of the pound, a threat to its interests in Eastern Europe.

Despite these doubts regarding the gold-exchange standard France derived important benefits from the system. In fact, after the stabilization of the franc, it benefited not only from favourable balance of trade,[17] but also from large capital inflows. This was consisted largely of French capital which was being repatriated following renewed confidence in the national currency.[18]

The positive balance of payments, as Nurkse (1944, p. 77) notes, was sterilized with the reduction of the public debt held by the Bank of France. Consequently, between the end of 1926 and that of 1929, French gold reserves increased impressively (Table 4.3).

This process meant that the gold available worldwide was progressively concentrated in two countries: the USA and France. Compared to the first half of the 1920s, in Europe, the situations of France and Britain had been reversed. "Holding large short-term balances in London, the Bank of France, after so many years of weakness, found itself in a powerful bargaining position ... By the same token the position of the Bank of England was extremely weak, forcing Norman to fall back, ... on the warning that, if pressed too far, Britain might have no alternative to abandon the gold standard".[19]

The weakness of the pound was not only due to the weakness of the British economy, but also to the competitiveness of the other key currency in the system: the dollar. Confidence in the US currency was higher than in sterling as the USA held much higher levels of gold reserves than Britain (Table 4.3).

Contrary to the opinion of many supporters of international monetary systems based on multiple key currencies,[20] the presence of two key currencies contributed to

[17]See Kemp (1972).

[18]See Rist (1932), Eichengreen and Wyplosz (1988), and Sicsic (1993).

[19]See Clarke (1967, p. 116).

[20]See, for example, Angeloni et al. (2011).

the instability of the gold-exchange standard. This instability was mainly due to stress on the pound. In 1927 the British currency was affected by a first serious crisis. This was due to a number of factors, firstly the impact on gold reserves due to a fall in coal exports in 1926 and secondly, to capital outflows caused by a fall in the return on investments in London and the repatriation of funds to France following the stabilization of the franc.[21]

In a number of meetings between the central bankers of France (Moreau), Germany (Schacht), England (Montagu Norman) and USA (Strong), measures were agreed on to support the pound. The USA in particular, adopted an expansive monetary policy, reducing the discount rate. The result was an outflow of gold from the USA to England: the pound strengthened.

Cooperation between the central banks of the advanced countries, which reached its peak at the time of the 1927 sterling crisis, gradually diminished in the following years. In mid-1929 the British currency was affected by a new crisis. In this case the cause was speculation on the New York Stock Exchange that reached a frenzy and the tendency of France to replace foreign exchange reserves, primarily sterling, with gold. The reduction of its gold reserves forced the Bank of England to successively increase, between February and September 1929, the discount rate from 4.5 to 6.5%. This measure, however, was not sufficient to attract funds from abroad. The situation only improved in October with the collapse of the New York Stock Exchange, following which capital flowed from the USA and the pound strengthened.

The collapse of the gold-exchange standard can be dated to September 21, 1931, when the Bank of England, following the loss of large reserves of gold, found it impossible to defend the convertibility of the pound. However, this situation was itself preceded by a loss of confidence in the international monetary system. The crisis in fact began in May 1931 with the failure of the main Austrian bank, the Kreditanstalt. In June the crisis spread to Germany. Between May and September, the National Bank of Austria and the Reichsbank had lost a very substantial proportion of their gold reserves.

The result was a rush to turn their currency credits into gold. This, starting in July, also involved the Bank of England. Significant increases in bank rates had no effect. The suspension of sterling convertibility and the collapse of the gold-exchange standard were commented on by the *London Times*: "The international economic crisis has played a large part in the temporary abandonment of the gold standard. The responsibility for this partnership to those countries which have hoarded gold on an unprecedented scale".[22]

[21]See Eichengreen (1992, pp. 196–197).

[22]See New York Times (1931, p. 39).

4.4 The Different Assumptions of the Functioning of the Classical Gold Standard and the Gold-Exchange Standard

Significant differences between the classic gold standard and the gold-exchange standard concern above all changes to the internal political balance which had taken place in many countries since the First World War. In the period of the classic gold standard, limits to the right to vote, the absence of mass political parties and trade unions allowed governments to transfer the costs of adjusting macroeconomic imbalances onto the working class. These processes of transfer became much more difficult after the First World War, in a context in which workers had acquired a political role which could no longer be ignored.

Hence the need for a type of international currency offering a high level of elasticity, that is to say, to allow adjustment costs to be smoothed. A currency of this type, however, would have allowed the issuing country the privilege of exploiting seigniorage, a privilege inexistent in a monetary system based on commodity money, as the classic gold standard essentially was. The management of such a currency, however, also required a much more complex institutional architecture than the classic gold standard.

The higher elasticity of the money supply inherent in the gold-exchange standard derived mainly from its pyramidal nature. This structure implied that, at equal gold reserves, central banks, at least within certain limits, could vary the amount of money. In this way, the quantity of domestic and world currency was no longer exogenous.[23] Hence the importance of central banks' choices regarding the so-called cover ratio, i.e. the percentage of gold reserves of the issued currency.[24]

A lower cover ratio corresponded to a higher monetary multiplier and, therefore, greater liquidity. Confidence in the stability of the future value of the main currencies could only be maintained if the acceding countries respected the rules of the game that is to say if:

(i) they took decisive action in the presence of current account deficits;
(ii) they abstained from sterilizing any current account surpluses;
(iii) they accepted to consider gold and key currencies as perfect substitutes, avoiding to massively convert currency reserves into gold reserves.

Compliance with these rules was subject to two conditions. The first of these conditions implied that the participants gave greater importance to the functioning of the gold-exchange standard than to internal objectives, not only of an economic

[23]As James (2001, p. 16) writes: "The pleasing ambiguity of the gold exchange standard ... was that it provided at the same time a restraint... and also that no one could tell quite how restraining it would turn out to be".

[24]As Hawtrey (1927) argued, if central banks had cooperated, the value of gold would no longer have been an independent variable on which the value of each currency was based. Rather, it would have come to depend on the value of each national currency.

Table 4.4 Reserves in key currencies of the main countries (as a percentage of total reserves)

	1924	1926	1928	1930
Belgium	10.0	42.0[a]	39.0	41.0
Denmark	19.0	11.0	40.0[a]	37.0
France	2.0	14.0	51.0[a]	33.0
Germany	63.0[a]	35.0	16.0	26.0
Italy	9.0	41.0	54.0[a]	45.0
Netherlands	18.0	31.0[a]	33.0	37.0
Sweden	36.0[a]	48.0	48.0	62.0
Switzerland	27.0	32.0[a]	34.0	38.0
World's total	27.0	31.0	42.0	35.0

Source: Eichengreen (1992). [a]Year of return to convertibility or subsequent to this

nature, but also of national security. The second condition required a high level of cooperation between the central banks of the acceding countries. Respect for these conditions proved to be extremely difficult because the central banks, in substance, pursued objectives consistent with the policies of their national governments, lacking both an institutional architecture and a lead country capable of imposing the rules. However, until the central banks of the main countries cooperated, confidence in the functioning of the gold-exchange standard was solid. Between 1924 and 1928 the coverage of the currency in circulation with key currencies instead of gold increased significantly (Table 4.4).

The gold-exchange standard and the classic gold standard established themselves in periods marked by a radically different socio-political equilibrium within countries and geopolitical balance at the international level. In fact, the classic gold standard was established at a time when most European countries were undergoing a state capacity building process. In this context the problem of the consolidation of domestic power assumed great importance. In the context of this process of state capacity building, the reference model used, also as regards monetary institutions, was England.

The latter was thus able to exercise a sort of *soft-power* compared to the other main countries. The context in which the gold-exchange standard was established was different. The international context was characterized by increased instability in the balance between the great powers of continental Europe and the fact that security had become an obsessive concern for one of them, France.

Internally, with the emergence of mass parties and strong workers' unions, the adjustment of macroeconomic imbalances could no longer be easily passed on to the poorer classes, as had been the case in the past. This would have entailed high costs for the political elite.

The social and political changes in the advanced countries led to a demand for monetary reforms. To create a kind of club of central bankers free from political pressure who would cooperate with each other. This would have made it possible to overlook the considerable tensions in inter-state relations and to ensure that the gold-exchange standard functioned smoothly. The resulting resurgence of capital flows would have revitalized the City, restoring its centrality to international finance. This plan, after initial success, was shattered by the re-emergence of bitter disagreements between central bankers, particularly between Norman and Moreau, over the division of areas of financial, and therefore political, influence.

4.5 The Current Literature on the Failure of the Gold-Exchange Standard

The gold-exchange standard lasted only a relatively short period of time. As we have seen its duration is conventionally seen as being between two events: the return to the convertibility of the pound, that is to say 1925, and the suspension of the convertibility of this key currency 6 years later. Indeed, in the months following Britain's abandonment of gold-exchange standard in September 1931, more than 20 countries adopted the same policy.

There are various explanations for the final cause for the collapse of the gold-exchange standard. Some insist on objective factors, as the stock of gold reserves, others on the culpable behaviour of some countries and their central banks, others on the political and social changes after World War II.[25]

On the objectively fragile structure of the gold-exchange standard insisted at the time, those who, as Cassel (1928), von Mises (1928) and Rist (1932), referred to the fact that the high inflation during and after the war had determined, at the pre-war exchange rate, a decrease in the real value of gold reserves. In this context, a return to the gold standard would inevitably provoke worldwide deflation. On various occasions Mundell (1995, 2000), taking up Cassel (1923, 1936), emphasized that this vision was correct and that the expected deflation manifested itself with all its harshness with the Great Depression.

However, the view just outlined that in the 1920s the world economy suffered from a deep liquidity crisis has been subject to incisive criticism by Eichengreen (1992). He points out two facts. First, that gold had been eliminated from exchanges between individuals, inevitably reducing demand. Secondly, the monetary pyramid underlying the gold-exchange standard made international liquidity much more flexible than in the classic gold standard.

The same Eichengreen (1992) and Temin (1989) attribute the collapse of the gold-exchange standard principally to insufficient cooperation between central banks. According to this hypothesis, after the First World War the formation of powerful trade unions and the spread of universal suffrage significantly increased the political weight of the working class, who were no longer willing to accept the onerous adjustment processes that the gold standard involved.

---

[25]For Keynes (1923, ch. 3) the gold standard was a "barbarous relic". Its re-proposal was therefore unjustified.

Given the increasing unionization of this class, monetary wages had become less flexible. This downward rigidity caused negative shocks leading to widespread unemployment and social malaise. In summary, as Obstfeld and Taylor (2004) observe, in the 1920s, fundamental aspects of the macroeconomic trilemma collided: the need for governments to have wider margins of monetary autonomy conflicted with the maintenance of convertibility and free movement of international capital.

The need for governments to enjoy autonomy in the conduct of monetary policy inevitably clashed with the maintenance of the fixed exchange rate. The growing attention of the political class to internal objectives, such as the growth of output and employment, led to reduced willingness of central banks to cooperate to preserve gold parities. The credibility of the gold-exchange standard was seriously compromised. In this context, short-term capital movements would have turned from stabilizers to destabilizers. According to Eichengreen and Sussman (2000) and other scholars, such as Bernanke (1993), in the classic gold standard these movements were stabilizing, given the behaviour, almost automatic, of central banks: when a country identified a deficit in its accounts with foreign countries, the simple expectation of a tighter monetary policy approach favoured the inflow of capital that stabilized the exchange. By contrast, in the gold-exchange standard the credibility of gold parities was significantly weakened by the absence of effective international cooperation. Expectations of devaluation of currencies, in particular of key currencies such as the pound, meant that short-term speculative movements assumed a destabilizing character, exacerbating tensions on exchange rates.

Although widely shared, the hypothesis of insufficient cooperation between central banks as a cause of the collapse of the gold-exchange standard is not without its critics.[26] The main question is whether the assumption that cooperation was insufficient between central banks in the 1920s is actually supported by the facts. Historical evidence shows that, on the contrary, cooperation between central banks in the 1920s was intense. In fact some scholars argue that cooperation between central banks, also based on personal relations between governors, was more intense in the 1920s than in the pre-war period.[27] This is confirmed by empirical studies, such as those by Borio and Toniolo (2006). In their study they further point out that in the 1920s, compared to the period between 1870 and 1913, while cooperation between central banks increased, international relations between governments diminished. The hypothesis that the governments were responsible for the failure to comply with the rules is confirmed by the fact that, as shown by Eichengreen (1992), according to the then current legislation, the Bank of France could not carry out open market operations and, therefore, was forced to sterilize.[28] Legislation also required the Federal Reserve to hold very high levels of gold reserves, close to 50%, to cover the banknotes it issued.

[26]See, among others, Shucker (1988).

[27]See Clarke (1967) and Ahamed (2009).

[28]See also Bernanke and James (1991).

The anomalous behaviour of the Bank of France and the Fed had already been highlighted in 1931 by the MacMillan Report.[29] A similar point of view was expressed by Keynes (1931) and Hawtrey (1932). In recent years Johnson (1997) and Mouré (2002) have resumed this topic but focused mainly on the behaviour of France in the period of the gold-exchange standard. In fact, while the USA accumulated large reserves of gold during the First World War, France accumulated it during the years of the gold-exchange standard. It therefore violated one of the basic tenets of that system, namely that of sterilizing capital inflows from abroad. Considering this behaviour, France would have essentially determined the collapse of the gold-exchange standard and contributed to the crisis that led to the Great Depression.

The main limitation to the explanation just offered is that it fails to take into account the geopolitical balance prevailing after the Treaty of Versailles. As highlighted by Kissinger (1994, p. 228): "France alone knew just how weak it had become in comparison with Germany, though nobody else, especially not America, was prepared to believe it ... Like Israel in the modern period, France masked its vulnerability with prickliness, and incipient panic with intransigence".

A third explanation for the collapse of the gold-exchange standard is that of the hypothesis of hegemonic stability. With this in mind, Kindleberger (1973) and Carr (1939) highlighted the fact that after the First World War, Britain was no longer able to exercise the role of a hegemonic country, i.e. the role it had filled in the classic gold standard. At the same time no other power was able, or wanted, to replace Britain in this role. In particular, the USA, despite having adequate economic and military force to play the role of hegemon, had renounced the opportunity to do so. Even when applied to the gold-exchange standard the hypothesis of hegemonic stability has some limitations. On the one hand, it overlooks the fact that there are different tasks that the hegemonic country is called on to perform in the case of a commodity money and a quasi-fiat money and, on the other hand, it does not take into account the fact that there are different costs to be supported to ensure trust in the different forms of money. In light of this, we can put forward the hypothesis that the USA did not have the advantage of exercising the role of the leading country of the gold-exchange standard.

4.6 The Ultimate Reasons for the Collapse of the Gold-Exchange Standard

On the basis of the above, the hypothesis that the gold-exchange standard disintegrated, not so much due to a lack of cooperation between central banks, but rather to the failure of the participating states to comply with the "rules", is advanced

[29] See MacMillan Committee (1931).

here and that the USA had no interest in inducing the other countries to abide by these rules.[30] The collapse of this monetary regime was favoured by two factors[31]:

(i) the definition of unrealistic exchange rate parity. In particular, the return of England to the pre-war exchange rate implied a loss of competitiveness and balance of payments problems for this country. The pound was therefore structurally weak at a time when confidence in its convertibility was required. In fact, it affected both the negative balance of trade and the possibility of transferring funds to the other key currency, the dollar. This last aspect demonstrates that an international monetary system based on a plurality of currencies tends to be unstable.
(ii) The tendency of the USA and France to adopt sterilization policies. This behaviour determined a tendency to concentrate gold reserves in these two countries (Table 4.3).

As for point (i) it can be explained by the fact that after the First World War Britain wanted London to return to being the centre of world finance as it had been in the classic gold standard. This objective could only be achieved by demonstrating that investors in British securities would not be penalized by wartime inflation. This privileged treatment of the rentiers was strongly supported by the City, whose political weight was, at that time, much higher than that of the industrial working class. Once the pre-war parity was adopted, Britain found itself having to adopt a particularly costly deflationary path both in social and economic terms and one which was, therefore, difficult to achieve.

As for point (ii), it should be remembered that the sterilization policies of the USA and France were of different intensities and were based on different motives. Between 1925 and 1930 France increased its gold reserves by about 1.4 billion dollars, while the USA increased theirs by only 240 million dollars. What were the reasons for this apparently irrational behaviour by France?

Between 1926, the year of the stabilization of the franc, and 1930 the share of gold reserves held by France, as a percentage of that held by all European countries, increased from 27.7 to 48.7%.

A number of scholars have denounced the choice of the French authorities to accumulate gold. Some scholars refer to this policy as the ultimate cause for the collapse of the gold-exchange standard. Johnson (1997, p. 147) writes that "... while the United States did little to hinder the decline in world prices, especially after 1928, French policy can be charged with directly causing it". Likewise, Mouré (2002, p. 180) claims that: "The magnitude and timing of French gold absorption from mid-1928 to 1930 imposed a greater constraint on systemic monetary expansion than the gold accumulation in the United States during the same period". This position

[30] Due to this failure to comply with the rules, the credibility of the gold-exchange standard gradually weakened. See Simmons (1996).

[31] See Seghezza (2018, pp. 127–133).

tends to consider the behaviour of the state authorities as being totally irrational, if not irresponsible.

The fundamental flaw, however, lies in the fact that it limits itself to considering the economic aspects, ignoring the geopolitical context of the 1920s. Even Keynes underestimated the importance of this aspect when in *The Economic Consequences of Peace* he wrote: "To what a different future Europe might have looked forward if either Mr. Lloyd George or Mr. Wilson had apprehended that the most serious of the problems which claimed their attention were not political or territorial but financial and economic, and that the perils of the future lay not in frontiers or sovereignties but in food, coal and transport. Neither of them paid adequate attention to these problems at any stage of the Conference".[32]

The underlying issue is that the First World War had not favoured the emergence of a stable balance in international relations such as that which had prevailed since the Vienna Congress. In fact, unlike what happened in 1815, the Allies united front had broken down. The USA, after the war, had chosen isolationism, with no further interference in the issues of the old continent. Britain, with the neutralization of the German fleet, was back in charge of the seas.

> Paradoxically, France's vulnerability and Germany's strategic advantage were both magnified by the Treaty of Versailles despite its punitive provisions. Before the war Germany had faced strong neighbours in both the East and the West, ... But after the Treaty of Versailles, there was no longer a counterweight to Germany in the East. With France weakened, the Austro-Hungarian Empire dissolved, and Russia out of the picture for some time, there was simply no way of reconstructing the old balance of power, especially since the Anglo-Saxon refused to guarantee the Versailles settlement.[33]

In fact, the Anglo-Americans refused to guarantee the fulfilment of what had been defined in the Treaty of Versailles. The Authorities, and British public opinion (and the position of Keynes is witness to this), pressed for a lightening of the reparations which the Treaty obliged Germany to pay. This position was strongly supported by the governor of the Bank of England, Norman and basically shared by the Americans.

France realized that it could not count on Anglo-American support given President Wilson's irenic vision. In fact, he believed idealistically that, if a country had been attacked and its independence threatened, the international community would stand up for it. Under the conditions described above, the accumulation of foreign exchange reserves was the only instrument left to France to protect its national security.[34]

In international relations, the availability of reserves of goods and, in the monetary sphere, of currency, but above all of commodity money, is a strength. It makes it possible to increase the international power of a state in at least two respects. On the

[32]See Keynes (1919, p. 134).

[33]See Kissinger (1994, p. 242).

[34]As Carr (1947, p. 25) writes: "The most and persistent single factor in European affairs following 1919 was the French demand for security".

one hand, it increases its autonomy. As noted by Cohen (2015), a state that has reserves does not depend on others even in periods where for some reason it has negative trade balances.

Secondly, the holding of a large amount of reserves allows the country to exercise financial pressure on other countries. Having large foreign exchange reserves available, the Bank of France used them to induce Britain to conduct policies less hostile to France mainly regarding aspects that affected its security: the containment of Germany and the financial and political influence on the countries of Eastern Europe.[35]

This second aspect became an explicit element of friction between France and Britain in the spring of 1927 with regard to the stabilization of Poland. In fact, France wanted to gain influence on countries potentially hostile to Germany and, therefore, financially supported Poland against Lithuania, Czechoslovakia against Hungary, and Yugoslavia and Romania against Bulgaria.[36] This French interest was in conflict with that of Britain. In particular, the *City*, supported in this by the governor of the Bank of England, Norman, sought to play a prominent role in the financing of Eastern European countries.[37]

In order to play a political role in Eastern Europe, France wanted to be involved in the financing of countries it considered strategic. To achieve this goal, it was willing to put pressure on the British government, demanding the conversion of pounds into gold and thus forcing the Bank of England to either accept a reduction in its reserves or increase interest rates. This increase, on the one hand, made it more expensive for potential debtors to finance themselves in sterling and on the other hand, had a negative effect on the growth of GDP. The Bank of France resorted to this type of pressure, which had been repeatedly threatened, during the stabilization of Poland in May 1927.

A similar situation occurred at the beginning of 1928 concerning the stabilization of Romania. In February of that year, Moreau went to London to "offer Norman war or peace", convinced that Britain had chosen financially strategic points in Europe to strengthen its financial presence.[38] The meeting between the two could not take place due to the sudden indisposition of Norman. However, an agreement was reached between the delegations of the two central banks that involved France's

[35]The French attempt is illustrated in detail by Kirshner (1995, pp. 181–192).

[36]See Carr (1947, p. 43).

[37]The behaviour of the Bank of England is thus interpreted by the French Prime Minister Poincarè in a February 1928 letter to the Quai d'Orsay: "C'était un programme d'hégémonie financière, qui consistait à nous éliminer de la direction de tous les projets de réforme monétaire, à empêcher la Banque de France et les Ètablissements français d'obtenir avec des avantages moraux et matériels la possibilité d'exercer dans l'interêt français une influence sur le pays qui ne pouvent se passer du concours étrangers". See Archives of the Bank of France, Paris, *Mission financières françaises en Romanie*, No. 137020006/6: letter of the Prime Minister to the Foreign Minister, 24 February 1928.

[38]"Limpérialisme financier de M. Montagu Norman était une menace pour nos interêt le plus légitimes, notamment en Europe centrale, où l'influence anglaise risquait d'éclipser la nôtre, au préjudice grave de notre politique étrangére". See Moreau (1954, p. 452).

involvement in the stabilization processes of Eastern European countries, starting with Romania. However as soon as Norman returned to work he questioned the agreement. France, faced with what it considered a betrayal, provoked a massive sale of sterling. In 1928, gold exports from the United Kingdom to France were around 96 million pounds.[39] At this point Britain had to give in to the demands of France. The latter became the only country officially represented in the Finance Commission of the League of Nations, other countries being present in the Commission with experts and bankers.[40]

A second aspect on which France was exerting monetary pressure was due to its desire to contain Germany and to limit Britain's openness to the latter. An important phase of tension between Germany (supported by Britain) and France occurred between April and July 1929 and concerned German reparations, in particular the application of the Young Plan. In this period of time, perhaps not by chance, there was a significant decrease in the gold reserves of Germany, which corresponded to a notable increase in the same at the Bank of France. Because Germany bought gold in London,[41] France, speculating on the mark, also exerted pressure on Britain.

In the summer of 1931 another cause for tension arose between France and Britain in relation to the proposed customs union between Germany and Austria. The French government considered this union as a prelude to a political union and therefore was strongly opposed to it. Britain, on the other hand, considered the customs union as a purely economic matter. In July 1931, the sterling was the object of an intense speculative attack that fuelled doubts about the probable prospects of its convertibility. In August, Britain was forced to borrow from France, which was finally in a position to impose its political line on many Eastern European countries.[42]

On 20th September 1931 the sterling came out of the gold standard because it was too costly both economically and politically to defend its convertibility. There is no doubt that the behaviour of France, even more than that of the USA, contributed to making the quantity of gold available in the world scarce, and that this contributed significantly to the collapse of the gold-exchange standard. However, the behaviour of France, contrary to the opinion of scholars of the time, including Cassel (1932)[43] and Keynes,[44] reflected a clear logic: that of safeguarding its national security. Paradoxically, with the collapse of the gold-exchange standard and the advent of

[39]See Federal Reserve Bulletin (1930, September, p. 22).

[40]See Boyce (2009, p. 213).

[41]See Brown (1940, p. 767).

[42]See Brown (1940, p. 949).

[43]According to Cassel it was "... especially remarkable that the Bank of France has consistently and unnecessarily acquired enormous amounts of gold without troubling in the least about the consequences that such a procedure is bound to have on the rest of the world". Quoted in Irwin (2011, p. 17).

[44]In 1931 Keynes, considering France and the USA to be primarily responsible for the world price decline, argued that: "The whole world is heartily sick of the selfishness and folly with which the international gold standard is being worked". See Moggridge (1981, p. 600).

the Great Depression, France's network of alliances in Eastern Europe, built up with its operation of financial assistance, crumbled.[45]

4.7 The Gold-Exchange Standard and the Great Depression

For many years, the debate on the Great Depression focused on its internal causes. This was the case both in monetarist explanations of the Depression, first of all in *The Monetary History of the United States* by Friedman and Schwartz (1963), and also in Keynesian explanations, such as that in *Did Monetary Forces Cause the Great Depression?* by Temin (1976).

In a series of studies, Eichengreen[46] has shown that the international gold standard played a crucial role, if not in the initiation, then certainly in the spread and deepening of the worldwide recession.[47]

As a two-tier monetary system, the gold-exchange standard had a higher degree of flexibility than the gold standard. This flexibility stemmed from three main factors: the ability of countries to hold foreign exchange reserves (FX reserves), as well as gold, to cover the monetary base which they had issued; relatively low gold cover ratios; and a ratio of money in circulation (M1) to the monetary base.

The above three factors contributed to determining the value of the monetary multiplier, which could therefore be expressed as follows[48]:

$$\text{Money multiplier} = \frac{M1}{\text{Gold}} = \frac{M1}{\text{Money base}} * \frac{\text{Money base}}{\text{FX Reserves}} * \frac{\text{FX Reserves}}{\text{Gold}}$$

Between the end of the 1920s and the beginning of the 1930s, these three components of the monetary multiplier changed, leading to a decrease in the monetary multiplier.

The political instability that characterized that period fostered a loss of confidence in the stability of the gold-exchange standard. This loss of confidence, after 1930, resulted in a strong decline in some European countries—in particular France, Italy and Netherlands—in the share of foreign exchange reserves (Table 4.5).

In this context, when gold outflows occurred, countries were driven to raise their domestic interest rates in order to defend their gold reserves. This was the case even when they had a large amount of precious metal at their disposal. Emblematic is what happened in the USA in 1931, when Britain was forced to leave the gold-exchange

[45]As Carr (1939, p. 115) writes: "The rapid decline of French influence in Central Europe after 1931 was closely linked to the fact that, after the crisis, France was no longer able to carry out politics of financial support to those countries".

[46]See, among others, Eichengreen (1986, 1988, 1992).

[47]For an illustration of the different approaches to the Great Depression see Bernanke (2000).

[48]See Bernanke (1993).

Table 4.5 Foreign exchange reserves of central banks (as percentage of total)

Country	1928	1929	1930	1931	1932
Belgium	39	34	41	n.a	n.a
Denmark	40	34	37	n.a	n.a
Finland	70	68	75	67	70
France	51	38	33	24	5
Germany	16	26	26	n.a	n.a
Italy	54	50	45	28	18
Netherlands	33	33	37	9	7
Norway	22	32	33	13	17
Sweden	48	52	62	19	51

Source: Nurkse (1944)

standard and speculation turned its attention to the dollar. In that case the Fed, in order to stop the conversion of a substantial quantity of dollars to gold, raised the policy interest rate which then caused a further deterioration of the American economy. The policy rate hike in the USA inevitably had spillover effects: other countries threatened by gold losses were also forced to raise their policy rates if they wanted to preserve the convertibility of their currencies. The increase in the policy interest rate led to a decrease in the demand for loans, in bank money and thus in the M1/money base ratio. For this, in 1930 and even more in 1931, the ratio of M1 to money base decreased in many advanced countries. In fact, between 1929 and 1931 this ratio decreased by 8.5% in France, by 18.3% in Belgium and even by almost 25% in the USA.[49] The further deterioration of the economy as a result of the contraction of money supply and the higher interest rates led to a loss of confidence in the stability of the banks which led, as in the USA in 1931, to a massive increase in demands on banks to convert deposits into gold and other assets. This contributed in the early 1930s to a further decrease in the M1/money base ratio. In the presence of a stable quantity of gold, the decrease in the monetary multiplier for the reasons outlined above led to a contraction of world money. This, in turn, contributed to the recession of the early 1930s in the industrialized countries.[50]

Paradoxically, the gold-exchange standard's higher money supply elasticity, compared to the classical gold standard, proved to be gravely detrimental, when it provoked a de-multiplying process of the world's money supply.

In such an environment, the central banks of gold-exchange countries that wanted to preserve the convertibility of their currencies were forced to adopt restrictive monetary policies not for domestic reasons, but to defend their gold reserves. Resorting to restrictive monetary policies to defend the exchange rate inevitably had negative repercussions on the economic growth of these countries. It is not surprising, therefore, that, as some contributors have pointed out,[51] countries that had not joined the gold-exchange standard, such as China and Spain, or had left it

[49]Bee Bernanke (1995).

[50]See Hamilton (1987).

[51]See Eichengreen and Sachs (1985) and Choudri and Kochin (1980).

early, such as Britain and the Scandinavian countries, recorded higher GDP growth rates in the 1930s than those, such as France, which remained part of the system for longer.

4.8 The Demand for Institutions to Protect Trust in an Almost Fiat Money

We have seen in the previous sections how the equilibrium which prevailed at a world level after the First World War was of the multipolar type. A balance of this kind makes lasting forms of cooperation between states problematic. Moreover, in this context, it is difficult to see how a country could have emerged that had would gain advantage supporting the costs of producing trust in a quasi-*fiat* money and whose dominant position would have been accepted by the other Great Powers.

Despite the adverse geopolitical context, in the 1920s there were various institutional innovations aimed at encouraging cooperation between countries. These innovations had little success. However, they were at least partly taken up in the post-war period when it was decided to build a new international monetary order.[52]

In fact, while the classical gold standard arose spontaneously and its functioning did not require an ad hoc institutional architecture, the case of the gold-exchange standard was different, being based instead of on commodity money, on a quasi-*fiat* money. The convening in the 1920s of frequent international conferences, from that of Brussels in 1920, to that of Genoa in 1922, to that of London in 1927, shows that the authorities understood that cooperation between states played a crucial role in the maintenance of an international monetary order.

As Eichengreen (1992, p. 213) writes: “Starting in 1924, efforts to coordinate monetary and financial policies internationally had grown increasingly prevalent”. This cooperation contributed decisively to the stabilization of several countries, particularly in Central Europe. In fact, the central banks of the advanced countries exercised a sort of catalytic function towards the peripheral countries similar to that exercised by the IMF.[53] “In many cases the great international banking houses, such as Morgan’s, Rothschild’s, and Baring’s, refused to float stabilization loans if the nation’s borrowing did not at the same time receive a credit from foreign central banks”.[54] The will of the central banks of the advanced countries to cooperate, as we have seen, clearly emerged in the 1927 sterling crisis. However, from 1928 onwards, cooperation between central banks gradually diminished.[55]

---

[52]Pauly (1997, p. 44) writes: “Our textbooks in international relations and international economics leave the impression that the international organizations established after World War II were entirely new departures in history”.

[53]See Cottarelli and Giannini (2002).

[54]See Chandler (1958, pp. 285–286).

[55]Clarke (1967) attributes this flaw to the death of Benjamin Strong who had always mediated among the divergent positions of many European central bankers.

Recognition that the management of a monetary system such as the gold-exchange standard presupposed respect for certain rules by the member countries led to the establishment of international organizations that can be seen as the prototype of genuine supranational authorities. Among these the most important was the League of Nations Financial Commission. The role of the latter in the economic field began with the convening of the Brussels Conference. Furthermore, in the Genoa conference,[56] it was assigned the task of managing the financial crises of various European countries.[57] The League successfully coordinated the stabilization programs of five states (Austria, Hungary, Greece, Bulgaria and Danzig), in compliance with the Resolutions of the Genoa Conference.[58]

Its support for the states mentioned above took the form of financial aid and technical assistance. This assistance in turn, took various forms, among them was the appointment of a commissioner who had the task of controlling the use of loans granted to the country and the policy measures adopted by the governors, this commissioner was, in many cases, a member of the board of the central bank and thus monitored the setting of monetary policy.

The role played by the League of Nations in the management of the financial crises of some countries in the 1920s and the ways in which these crises were managed was a preview, in many respects, of the IMF's role in the management of numerous crises in the post-war period.[59]

However, the action of the League in the context just considered remained limited to smaller peripheral countries, often, newly established. This is explained not only by the restricted financial resources available to the League, but also by its limited international authority. As shown by the management of recent crises, starting with the Asian crisis of 1997–1998, the IMF is able, on the contrary, to place considerable limits on the fiscal and monetary sovereignty of even long-established medium-large states.

At the beginning of the 1930s, faced with increasing difficulties in the functioning of the gold-exchange standard, an attempt was made to institutionalize the coordination between central banks, wanting to ensure that this coordination was not simply the result of personal relations between the governors and therefore sporadic and discretional.

This choice resulted in the establishment in 1931 of the Bank for International Settlements (BIS). To which were assigned two tasks:

(i) provide a neutral solution to the problem of reparations;
(ii) encourage cooperation between central banks so as to make international capital movements less volatile.

[56]The work of the Genoa Conference was coordinated by the League of Nations Secretariat.

[57]See Santaella (1993).

[58]On stabilizations in these countries see Eichengreen (1992).

[59]See Pauly (1997).

The BIS, due to its limited financial resources and lack of authority, was unable to effectively fulfil either task. It was powerless in the face of the progressive deterioration of the international financial situation and its degeneration into the Great Depression.

The gradual reduction in cooperation between the central banks of the advanced countries towards the end of the 1920s and the limited successes of international institutions, such as the League of Nations and the BIS, show the limits of the functionalist hypothesis. A demand for monetary innovation is not enough to ensure that these are established and consolidated over time.

In the case of the introduction of a quasi-fiat or fiat money, it is necessary that the demand for this form of money be accompanied by the establishment of an adequate institutional architecture aimed at protecting the property rights of the holders of the type of money in question.

In addition to the multipolar equilibrium prevailing between the two wars, no great power had the strength and, therefore, a sufficient interest in producing confidence in the gold-exchange standard, i.e. in a system based on a quasi-fiat currency. There was only the possibility for each Great Power to exert monetary influence and to impose the use of its currency and monetary system in circumscribed areas, i.e. to establish monetary blocs with very limited trade relations between them.

4.9 The Emergence of Regional Monetary Blocs

We have seen in Chap. 2 that when multipolar equilibrium prevails in international relations, it is not only difficult for an international quasi-fiat or fiat currency to emerge, but on the contrary regional currencies tend to emerge. These currencies possess, in a limited area, the conditions that govern the widespread acceptance of a currency as an international fiat currency.

The conditions are essentially two. Firstly, the existence of a regional leader country that has an interest in generating confidence in its currency and, secondly, that between the leading country and the other countries of the regional monetary area there must be a significant imbalance of political and military power in favour of the former. In this context, other countries tend to attribute little weight to the relative gains that the leading country of the region derives from the possible exploitation of the right of seigniorage.

When regional monetary blocs are formed, at an international level there is a lack of money and international monetary system. This contributes to explaining the international monetary disorder that emerged after the collapse of the gold-exchange standard and which lasted until the Second World War. In this period, in fact, three regional monetary blocs emerged, whose composition is shown in Table 4.6.

Table 4.6 Member countries of the regional monetary blocs that prevailed after the collapse of the gold-exchange standard

Gold block	Sterling block	Block of the Reichsmark
Belgium, France, the Netherlands, Switzerland	United Kingdom, Ireland, Denmark, Norway, Sweden, Portugal, Australia, India, New Zealand, South Africa	Germany, Austria, Hungary, Yugoslavia, Poland

The three monetary blocks shown in Table 3.6 were characterized by homogeneous payment systems and intense commerce within them.[60] The Scandinavian countries abandoned the gold-exchange standard immediately following the abandonment of this system by Britain. Taking the pound as a reference monetary parameter, they intensified trade with the sterling area, decreasing their trade with Germany.[61]

Several countries tried to defend the gold parity of their currency. This block included the countries that had previously been part of the Latin Monetary Union.[62] These countries, as their currencies increasingly appreciated in real terms (compared to those of countries that had abandoned the gold-exchange standard), were forced to defend their exchange rates by limiting domestic demand through credit restrictions and by imposing quotas and duties on imports.[63] These measures, on the one hand, helped defend the parity of the currencies with respect to gold but, on the other, had a negative impact on economic growth in the countries that were part of the block.

The third monetary block was made up of numerous countries from central and south-eastern Europe that, after the collapse of the gold-exchange standard and the devaluation of the pound, were found without a valuable reference currency.[64] In November 1931, at a conference held in Prague between the Danube countries under the auspices of the BIS, multilateral clearing agreements were negotiated with the aim of facilitating trade within the block without there being a transfer of money from one country to another. The scarcity of reserves led the countries of this block to introduce administrative controls on currency transactions, rigid constraints on capital movements and on private individuals holding of currency.[65]

In the clearing agreements that developed in the 1930s in central and south-eastern Europe, Germany played a crucial role for two main reasons.[66] In the first place, after the economic and political collapse of Russia, it was the largest exporting country in the area. Secondly, especially after the rise to power of national-socialism, Germany adopted a trade policy that made neighbouring countries increasingly

[60]See Eichengreen and Irwin (1995), and Wolf and Ritschl (2011).

[61]See Meyer (1952).

[62]See Eichengreen (1992) and Feinstein et al. (2008).

[63]See Eichengreen (1992).

[64]See Gowa and Hicks (2013).

[65]See Ellis (1941), Milward (1981) and Mitchener and Wandshneider (2014).

[66]See Mitchener and Wandshneider (2014).

Table 4.7 Trade, GDP and unemployment in the interwar years in advanced countries

	Trade	Real GDP	Unemployment
1929	100	100	7.2
1930	94.8	95.2	14.1
1931	89.5	89.2	22.8
1932	76.5	83.3	31.4
1933	78.4	84.3	29.8
1934	79.6	89.0	23.9
1935	81.8	94.0	21.9

Source: Crafts and Fearon (2010)

dependent on it.[67] In this context, over time the latter adopted an exchange rate pegged to the Reichsmark.[68]

The formation of monetary blocs provoked a "... severe breakdown in the multilateral trade and payments system the world economy had enjoyed prior to World War I and had started to revive in the late 1920s".[69] While the subsequent fall in foreign trade was another factor that helped turn the recession of the early 1930s into the Great Depression (Table 4.7).

It has been observed that the interwar economic system and the formation of economic blocs exacerbated tensions between the great powers.[70] However, the causal chain seems to have been reversed. It was the growing conflicts between great powers that generated opposing monetary and economic blocs.[71]

4.10 Conclusions

In the Brussels Conference and, above all, in that of Genoa a new order was given to the international monetary system: it was here that the gold-exchange standard was defined and launched.

Thanks to its pyramidal nature, this system involved a significant increase in the elasticity of the money supply compared to the classical gold standard: the quantity of world money was dependent on the discretionary behaviour of central banks and states. In such a system the growth of money supply could have been consistent with that of the world economy only with adequate respect of the rules by the states. Such behaviour would have involved close cooperation between central banks. This, however, as noted above, cracked from the latter part of the 1920s.

[67] See Hirschman (1945).

[68] See Milward (1981).

[69] See Irwin et al. (2008, p. 7). This hypothesis is put forward by several scholars. See, in particular, Irwin et al. (2008) and Aldcroft (2001).

[70] See Findlay and O'Rourke (2007).

[71] See Eichengreen and Irwin (1995) and Gowa and Hicks (2013).

According to the prevailing interpretation of the collapse of the gold-exchange standard, the lack of cooperation between central banks could be attributed to the fact that, after the First World War, given the increased political weight of the working class and unionization, it was no longer possible to transfer onto this group the costs of macroeconomic adjustments for the maintenance of convertibility. In a word, the pursuit of internal objectives had taken priority over the defence of the exchange rate.

This inconsistency between the development of national monetary systems and the gold-exchange standard was at the root of the collapse of this international monetary system. This interpretation does not explain why the conditions, at an international level, for creating a monetary system compatible with the evolution of payment technologies at national levels were lacking. A plausible explanation for this can be found in the geopolitical equilibrium after the First World War and, even more, after the Treaty of Versailles.

This equilibrium can be defined as of a multipolar type and characterized by a high instability of alliances. In a context of this nature no leading country could emerge that had an interest in, and was allowed, to play the role necessary to favour the creation and existence of an institutional architecture that would guarantee confidence in an international monetary system based on a quasi-*fiat* currency.

In addition to this, the multipolar equilibrium prevailing in the immediate post-war period was extremely unstable, since the alliance between the winning countries had dissolved, each of them now sought their own national interests. Among the winning countries, France was in a weaker position when compared to the period before the war. In fact, Germany was no longer contained to the east by Russia nor in central Europe by the Austro-Hungarian Empire. In this context France was greatly concerned about its security. This concern led her to accumulate gold and sterling reserves.

Accumulating reserves could exercise forms of financial "statecraft" towards Germany and, more especially, towards Britain. In fact, on several occasions, France converted pounds into gold in order to induce Britain to adopt a foreign policy more in line with the interest of French security.

France's statecraft policy towards the pound was facilitated by the fact that sterling was fragile for objective reasons. On the one hand, Britain, having adopted the pre-war parity and, hence, having low competitivity often recorded balance of trade deficits; on the other hand, the difficult conditions of the British economy induced financial investors to prefer the other key currency, the dollar, confidence in whose convertibility was high given the huge gold reserves of the USA.

The absence of a leading country that could induce the member countries to respect the rules of the game, primarily not to sterilize capital inflows, the existence of two key currencies, one strong and the other weak, made the gold exchange an extremely fragile standard. It collapsed in 1931, when the loss of confidence in the gold convertibility of the currencies, starting from the peripheral ones to the pound, led to a currency run. The subsequent international monetary disorder resulted in the creation of three monetary blocs and the absence of an international currency, which contributed significantly to the reduction of international trade.

References

Ahamed, L. (2009). *Lords of finance*. Penguin.

Aldcroft, D. H. (2001). *The European economy 1914–2000*. Routledge.

Angeloni, I., Bénassy-Quéré, A., Carton, B., Darvas, Z., Destais, C., Pisany-Ferry, J., Sapir, A., & Vallée, S. (2011). *Global currencies for tomorrow: A European perspective*. Bruegel Blueprints Series, CEPII Research Reports.

Bernanke, B. (1993). The world on a cross of gold. *Journal of Monetary Economics, 31*, 251–267.

Bernanke, B. (1995). The macroeconomics of the Great depression: A comparative approach. *Journal of Money Credit and Banking, 27*, 1–28.

Bernanke, B. (2000). *Essays on the great depression*. Princeton University Press.

Bernanke, B., & James, H. (1991). The gold standard, deflation, and financial crisis in the great depression: An international comparison. In R. G. Hubbard (Ed.), *Financial markets and financial crises*. University of Chicago Press.

Borio, C., & Toniolo, G. (2006). *One hundred and thirty years of central bank cooperation: A BIS perspective*. BIS working paper n. 197.

Boyce, R. (2009). *The great interwar crisis*. Palgrave Macmillan.

Brown, W. (1940). *The international gold standard reinterpreted, 1914–1934*. NBER.

Carr, E. (1939). *The twenty years' crisis, 1919–1939: An introduction to the study of international relations* (Ed. 2016). Palgrave Macmillan.

Carr, E. (1947). *International relations between the two world wars*. Macmillan.

Cassel, G. (1923). The restoration of gold standard. *Economica, 9*, 171–185.

Cassel, G. (1928). *Post-war monetary stabilization*. Columbia University Press.

Cassel, G. (1932). *The crisis in the world's monetary system*. Clarendon.

Cassel, G. (1936). *The downfall of the gold standard*. Clarendon.

Chandler, L. (1958). *Benjamin Strong: central banker*. Columbia University Press.

Choudri, E. U., & Kochin, L. A. (1980). The exchange rate and the international transmission of business cycle disturbances: Some evidence from the great depression. *Journal of Money, Credit, and Banking, 12*, 565–574.

Clarke, S. (1967). *Central bank cooperation, 1924–31*. Federal Reserve Bank of New York.

Cohen, B. (2015). *Currency power: Understanding monetary rivalry*. Princeton University Press.

Cottarelli, C., & Giannini, C. (2002). *Bedfellows, hostages or perfect strangers?. Global capital markets and catalytic effect of IMF crisis lending*. IMF working paper n. WP/02/193.

Crafts, N., & Fearon, P. (2010). Lessons from the 1930s great depression. *Oxford Review of Economic Policy, 26*, 285–317.

Cunliffe Committee. (1918). Cunliffe Committee on currency and foreign exchange after the war: interim report. (Reprinted in 1997 in B. Eichengreen & M. Flandreau (Eds.), The gold standard in theory and history. Routledge).

Dimsdale, N. (1981). British monetary policy and the exchange rate 1920–1938. *Oxford Economic Papers, 33*, 306–349.

Eichengreen, B. (1986). The Bank of France and the sterilization of gold, 1926-1932. *Explorations in Economic History, 23*, 56–84.

Eichengreen, B. (1988). *The Gold-Exchange standard and the Great Depression*. NBER working paper n. 2198.

Eichengreen, B. (1992). *Golden fetters: The gold standard and the great depression, 1919–1939*. Oxford University Press.

Eichengreen, B., & Irwin, D. A. (1995). Trade blocs, currency blocs and the reorientation of world trade in the 1930s. *Journal of International Economics, 38*, 1–24.

Eichengreen, B., & Sachs, J. (1985). Exchange rates and economic recovery in the 1930s. *Journal of Economic History, 45*, 925–946.

Eichengreen, B. & Sussman N. (2000). *The international monetary system in the (very) long run*. IMF working paper n. 00-43.

Eichengreen, B., & Wyplosz, C. (1988). The economic consequence of the franc Poincaré. In E. Helpman, A. Razin, & E. Sadks (Eds.), *Economic effects of the government budget*. MIT.
Ellis, H. S. (1941). *Exchange control in Central Europe*. Harvard University Press.
Federal Reserve Board. (1930, June). Federal Reserve Bulletin.
Feinstein, C. F., Temin, P., & Toniolo, G. (2008). *The world economy between the world wars*. Oxford University Press.
Findlay, R., & O'Rourke, K. H. (2007). *Power and plenty: Trade, war and the world economy in the second millennium*. Princeton University Press.
Fink, C. (1984). *The Genoa conference, European diplomacy, 1921–1922*. University of North Carolina Press.
Friedman, M., & Schwartz, A. (1963). *The monetary history of the United States*. Princeton University Press.
Giannini, C. (2011). *The age of central banks*. Edward Elgar.
Gowa, J., & Hicks, R. (2013). Politics, institutions, and trade: Lessons of the interwar era. *International Organization, 67*, 439–467.
Hamilton, J. (1987). Monetary factors in the great depression. *Journal of Monetary Economics, 34*, 145–169.
Hawtrey, R. (1923). *Monetary reconstruction*. Longmans.
Hawtrey, R. (1927). *The gold standard in theory and practice*. Longmans.
Hawtrey, R. (1932). *The art of central banking*. Longmans.
Helleiner, E. (2003). *The making of national money*. Cornell University Press.
Hirschman, A. O. (1945). *National power and the structure of foreign trade*. University of California Press.
Irwin, D. (2011). *Anticipating the great depression? Gustav Cassel's analysis of the interwar gold standard*. NBER working paper n. 17597.
Irwin, D., Mavroidis, P. C., & Sykes, A. O. (2008). *The genesis of the GATT*. Cambridge University Press.
James, H. (2001). *The end of globalization, lessons from the great depression*. Harvard University Press.
Johnson, H. (1975). Keynes and British economics. In J. M. Keynes (Ed.), *Essays on John Maynard Keynes*. Cambridge University Press.
Johnson, H. (1997). *Gold, France, and the great depression, 1919–1932*. Yale University Press.
Kemp, T. (1972). *The French economy, 1913–39. The history of a decline*. St. Martins.
Keynes, J. M. (1919). *The economic consequences of the peace*. Harcourt.
Keynes, J. M. (1923). A tract on monetary reform. In D. Moggridge (Ed.), *The collected writings of John Maynard Keynes* (Vol. 4). Macmillan. (1971).
Keynes, J. M. (1931, September 12). A gold conference. *The New Statesman and Nations*.
Kindleberger, C. (1973). *The world in depression, 1929–1939*. University of California Press.
Kirshner, J. (1995). *Currency and coercion: The political economy of international monetary power*. Princeton University Press.
Kissinger, H. (1994). *Diplomacy*. Simon & Schuster.
Kooker, J. L. (1976). French financial diplomacy: The interwar years. In B. M. Rowland (Ed.), *Balance of power or hegemony: The interwar monetary system*. New York University Press.
League of Nations. (1922). Genoa financial commission report. In *Federal Reserve Board, Federal Reserve Bulletin*, June 1922.
Macmillan Committee. (1931). Report. Cmd. 3897. HMSO.
Meyer, F. V. (1952). The Reichsmark bloc and the international economy. In G. Hirschfel & L. Kettenacker (Eds.), *Der Fuhrerstat: Mythos un realitat*. Ernst Klett.
Milward, A. (1981). The Reichsmark bloc and the international economy. In G. Hirschfel & L. Kettenacker (Eds.), *Der Fuhrerstaat: mythos und realitat*. Klett.
von Mises. (1928). Monetary stabilization and cyclical policy. (Reprinted in 2006 in P. Greaves (Ed.), *On the manipulation of money and credit*. Dobbs Ferry: Free Market Books).

Mitchener, K. J., & Wandshneider, K. (2014). *Capital controls and recovery from the financial crisis of the 1930s*. NBER working paper n. 20220.
Moggridge, D. (1972). *British monetary policy, 1924-1931: The Norman conquest of $4.86*. Cambridge University Press.
Moggridge, D. (1981). *Collected works of John Maynard Keynes: Vol. 20, Activities, 1929-31: Rethinking employment and unemployment policies*. Cambridge University Press.
Moreau, E. (1954). *Souvenirs d'un gouverneur de la Banque de France. Histoire de la stabilization du franc (1926-1928)*. M-Genin Editor.
Mouré, K. (2002). *The gold standard illusion*. Oxford University Press.
Mundell, R.A. (1995). The International monetary system: The missing factor. *Journal of Policy Modeling, 17*, 479–92.
Mundell, R. (2000). The euro and the stability of the international monetary system. In R. Mundell & A. Cleese (Eds.), *The euro as a stabilizer in the international economic system*. Kluwer Academic.
New York Times. (1931, September 20). *The commercial and financial chronicle* (Vol. 133).
Nurkse, R. (1944). *International currency experience*. League of Nations.
Obstfeld, M., & Taylor, A. M. (2004). *Global capital markets: Integration, crisis and growth*. Cambridge University Press.
Pauly, L. W. (1997). *Who elected the bankers? Surveillance and control in the world economy*. Cornell University Press.
Plumptre, A. F. W. (1940). *Central banking in the British dominions*. University of Toronto Press.
Rist, C. (1932). The international consequences of the present distribution of gold holdings. (Reprinted in 2011 by Royal Institute for International Affairs, *The International Gold Problem*. Oxford University Press).
Rothbard, M. N. (1998). The gold exchange standard in the interwar years. In K. Dowd & R. H. Timberlake (Eds.), *Money and the nation state*. The Independent Institute.
Santaella, J. (1993). Stabilization programs and external enforcement. *IMF Staff Papers, 40*, 584–621.
Shucker, S.A. (1988). *American "Reparations" to Germany, 1919-33: implications for the third-world debt crisis*. Princeton Studies in International Finance n. 61.
Seghezza, E. (2018). *L'evoluzione del sistema monetario internazionale. Il ruolo della domanda di innovazioni e della produzione di fiducia*. Soveria Mannelli.
Sicsic, P. (1993). *The inflow of gold to France from 1928 to 1934*. Notes d'Etudes et de Recherches, Banque de France.
Simmons, B. A. (1996). Rulers of the game: Central bank independence during the inter-war years. *International Organization, 50*, 407–443.
Singleton, J. (2011). *Central banking in the twentieth century*. Cambridge University Press.
Strakosch, H. (1930, July 5). Gold and the price level: A memorandum on the economic consequences of changes in the value of gold. *The Economist*, Supplement.
Temin, P. (1976). *Did monetary forces cause the great depression?* Norton.
Temin, P. (1989). *Lessons from the great depression*. MIT.
Wolf, N., & Ritschl, A. (2011). Endogeneity of currency areas and trade blocs: Evidence from a natural experiment. *Kyklos, 64*, 291–312.

Chapter 5
The Bretton Woods System

5.1 Introduction

As the end of World War II approached, the Allies, and in particular the USA, were intent on creating a new international monetary order. Many believed that, in the 1930s, the worldwide transmission of deflation and the frequent recourse by countries to competitive devaluations had contributed to the Great Depression.

The goal of the USA and Great Britain was to develop a new international monetary system. To this end, in 1944, they convened an international conference in Bretton Woods. It was here that in July of that year the Agreements that took their name from the location of the conference were signed by 44 countries. These Agreements were the culmination of 3 years of negotiations.

They sought, on the one hand, to spur the growth of international trade by adopting a regime of fixed exchange rates, while, on the other, preserving individual states' margins of discretion in the conduct of monetary policy. These two objectives were rendered compatible by limiting international movements of capital.

Implementation of the Bretton Woods Agreements, as will be seen in Sect. 5.5, required a long period of preparation. The monetary system based on these Agreements only became operational in 1958, when 10 European countries made their currencies convertible. A number of obstacles stood in the way of a more rapid implementation of the Agreements.

First, many countries were anchored to the bilateralism that had prevailed in the interwar period, when such trade agreements were common. This made it difficult to accept an institutional framework that provided for a partial transfer of sovereignty to international institutions. Second, the lack of reserves made it necessary for many countries to resort to the use of restrictions on foreign trade, in addition to exchange rate controls. The lack of adequate foreign exchange reserves with which European countries and Japan emerged from the Second World War was aggravated by the scarcity of dollars in circulation. The Marshall Plan launched in 1948 combined with

G. B. Pittaluga, E. Seghezza, *Building Trust in the International Monetary System*,
Frontiers in Economic History, https://doi.org/10.1007/978-3-030-78491-1_5

the European Payments Union[1] (established in 1952 under the auspices of the Organization of European Economic Cooperation) contributed to solving this problem and eliminating its negative effects on trade.[2] Third, the International Monetary Fund was not initially equipped to support reconstruction and its authority suffered as a consequence.[3] This was evident in the French franc crisis of 1948 and in Canada's decision to let its currency float in 1950.

The influx of funds with the Marshall Plan[4] and the definition of realistic exchange parities, starting with the heavily devalued pound in 1949, finally allowed European countries to make their currencies convertible. The monetary system which was finally implemented from the end of the 1950s took the form of a fixed exchange rate system based on the dollar as the key currency.

The classic gold standard and the Bretton Woods international monetary system were both characterized by the existence of an international currency. They have many similarities, but also profound differences. The existence of an international means of payment favoured, in both regimes, a significant expansion of world trade. The latter was accompanied by a pronounced increase in the income of industrialized countries.

Despite the similarity of the two regimes, they had several different characteristics. The classic gold standard was, in fact, based on a commodity money, gold. In it, the pound had the role of international currency, both for the weight of Great Britain in international trade and for its high degree of substitutability with respect to gold. By contrast, the Bretton Woods system was based on a currency convertible into gold, the dollar, while other currencies were convertible into dollars. In this respect it was similar to the gold-exchange standard: both being two-tier systems. The absence of constraints on the cover ratio of the dollar and the double level of convertibility of currencies made the elasticity of supply of the world currency very high, but at the same time posed problems of confidence in the stability of currencies of member countries, and in particular of the key currency, since they tended to take the form of quasi-fiat currencies.

As noted in Chap. 2, commodity money, once adopted, is self-enforcing[5]: in fact, it has an intrinsic value that corresponds to its face value. Unlike commodity money, fiat or quasi-fiat type currencies require confidence in the stability of the future value of the currency. Such trust can only be produced at an international level by an adequate institutional framework.

The crucial aspect of the system based on the Bretton Woods Agreements lies in the fact that, for the first time, it was an attempt at a legalization of international monetary affairs: a set of rules and institutions, shared and accepted by a large

[1]It was a form of multilateral clearing. For a detailed illustration of the European Payments Union and its operating procedures, see Martinez-Oliva and Stefani (2001).

[2]Thanks to this Plan, between 1948 and 1952, about 13 billion dollars flowed into Europe.

[3]See Mundell (1969).

[4]For an examination of the reasons and effects of this Plan, see De Long and Eichengreen (1991).

[5]It, as highlighted by Menger (1892) and confirmed in the search-theoretic models, is the result of a market selection process of the various payment methods.

number of countries, that aimed at ensuring the functioning of an international payment system.

This made it possible to introduce, at the international level, innovative payment systems based, rather than on commodity money, as in the gold standard, on a fiat currency, the dollar. The maintenance of confidence in the stability of the international currency and the monetary system based on it was entrusted to the institutional architecture defined in the Bretton Woods Agreements.

There are various interpretations given to the Bretton Woods Agreements. Here we support the hypothesis that they were the result of a political exchange between the leading country, the USA, and follower countries, starting with England, that is, between partners who had substantially different objectives. From this exchange both sides drew important economic benefits.

The period in which the Bretton Woods system was in force was marked by high growth in trade and GDP for the adhering countries, as well as by price stability. Despite this, indeed precisely because the system was based on a political exchange, it had within itself the seeds of its eventual collapse, which occurred in 1971, by which time the prevailing balance of power after the Second World War had already changed. In particular, European countries, starting with France, questioned the exorbitant privilege that the USA was deriving from the exploitation of seigniorage and denouncing its inflationary effects on other advanced countries. For their part, the USA was no longer prepared to bear the costs of building trust in the system.

5.2 Its Origins

The desire to create a new international order arose from an awareness of the unsolved problems between the two wars and the mistakes made during that period. As was seen in the previous chapter, the gold-exchange standard collapsed for two main reasons. On the one hand, as noted by a large part of the literature, there was significant conflict, within states, between domestic objectives, that is the stability of output and full employment, and the external objective, that is the convertibility of the exchange rate. On the other hand, the international political equilibrium that had existed after the First World War was multipolar and characterized by heated rivalry. At the end of the Second World War, the need to build a new world monetary order, compatible with the pursuit of a stable domestic macroeconomic equilibrium, made the definitive abandonment not only of the classic gold standard, but also of the gold-exchange standard that had prevailed after the First World War.

After the breakdown of the latter, in 1931, a majority of countries adopted flexible exchange rates. This experience, however, proved to be wholly unsatisfactory. In fact, countries implemented competitive devaluations which, together with increases in tariffs formed the pillars of protectionist trade politics.[6]

[6]See Cesarano (2006).

In this context, in some countries short-term speculative capital flows provoked high levels of economic instability.[7] In 1944 Nurkse wrote: "If there is anything that the interwar experience has clearly demonstrated, it is that paper currency exchanges cannot be left free to fluctuate from day to day under the influence of market supply and demand" because speculation plays a role in determining their level.[8]

This view was shared by most economists of the period.[9] In his *Tract on Monetary Reform,* Keynes writes that he was "... entirely in favour of practical measures towards de facto stability so long as there are no fundamental grounds for a different policy".[10] Keynes's position was shared by Williams, a professor at Harvard University and an influential advisor to the Federal Reserve Bank of New York, according to whom, however, even in a regime of fixed exchange rates the possibility of reviewing parities should not be excluded: "... when other means of control have been exhausted".[11]

Given the broad consensus in government circles and central banks towards the compromise position just described, there was practically no debate on the exchange rate regime to be adopted after World War II.[12] Indeed, as will be seen, the plans proposed by Keynes and White at Bretton Woods assumed, albeit with different nuances, the establishment of fixed but adjustable exchange rates.

Maintaining a fixed exchange rate regime, however, presupposed the removal of what was believed to be the cause of the high volatility of exchange rates, namely large short-term capital flows. These flows, driven mostly by speculation, had affected not only the stability of exchange rates, but also the ability of states to implement appropriate monetary policies.[13] Therefore, the opinion that limits should be placed on international movements of capital was widespread.[14]

Furthermore, the adoption of a fixed exchange rate regime required the solution of two major problems that had emerged in the gold-exchange standard and that had undermined it.[15] The first of these problems was insufficient international liquidity.

---

[7]In Germany the instability of capital flows caused a sudden stop and, because of this, a hyperinflation. See Morelli and Seghezza (2020).

[8]See Nurkse (1944, p. 137-138).

[9]There were, however, albeit minority ones, expression of supports for the adoption of a system of flexible exchange rates, such as those of Graham and Whittlesey (1934).

[10]See Keynes (1923 [1980, vol. 21, p. 501]).

[11]See Williams (1936, p. 163). Critical of this compromise position was Hayek who argued that the adoption of fixed but adjustable rates would allow governments a discretionary management of the currency, or what he termed "monetary nationalism". Therefore, he held that "instead of flexible parities or a widening of the gold points, absolute fixity of the exchange rates should be secured by a system of international par clearance". See Hayek (1937, p. 84). Hayek's rigid position was shared by Robbins (1937, 1943).

[12]See Irwin (2017).

[13]See James (2012).

[14]See Horsefield (1969, vol. III, p. 31).

[15]In recent years, the belief in the preferability of fixed exchange rates to flexible ones has been questioned by several scholars. In particular, Friedman (1953) challenged the idea that speculation

As we saw in the previous chapter, especially towards the end of the 1920s, the quantity of world money was strongly linked to the quantity of gold available. This problem was compounded by the low elasticity of the money supply typical of gold standard systems.

The second serious problem that emerged in international monetary relations between the two wars concerned the methods of adjusting foreign trade imbalances. Since the central banks of the surplus countries tended to sterilize capital inflows, the central banks of the deficit countries were forced to contract domestic money supply. This behaviour led to a deflationary distortion worldwide.[16]

Experts and politicians involved in the negotiations for the creation of a new international monetary system were aware of the shortcomings of the international monetary order that had existed between the two wars. The negotiations lasted 3 years and concluded with the signing of the Bretton Woods Agreements.

The conference leading up to these Agreements was held in July 1944 at the Mount Washington hotel in Bretton Woods, New Hampshire, and was attended by delegates from 44 countries. The final text of the Agreements was signed on 23 July.

In the negotiations that preceded the Agreements, the USA's principal interlocutor was England. The American delegation was led by Dexter White, a Treasury official who was one of Morgenthau's senior advisors. The British delegation was led by Keynes. It also included other economists such as Robbins and Robertson.

The two delegations represented at least partly different interests and objectives. The Americans attributed two main objectives to the conference: the revitalization of international trade and the internationalization of the New Deal. The first objective stemmed from the American administration's fear that after the war the American economy would fall back into a recession similar to that of the 1930s. For the American Administration, in particular for the State Department, the main objective of the Bretton Woods conference was the definition of an institutional architecture that envisaged the removal of barriers and the creation of a monetary order aimed at reducing the transaction costs of international trade.[17] The consequent development of international trade would allow the USA to exploit the competitive advantage it enjoyed at the time. Growth in exports would therefore have helped keep the country's aggregate demand high.

The Secretary of State Cordell Hull was particularly conscious of this issue. The objective of reaching a multilateral agreement that envisaged the reduction of tariffs and the abolition of quotas had inspired his actions even in the years prior to 1944. In fact, it can already be traced as early as 1941 in the art. VII of the Land-Lease Agreement signed between the USA and England; here, given the huge American funding provided to Britain to support the war effort, it was envisaged that the two

has a destabilizing effects in flexible exchange rates, that is, that it tends to distance exchange rates from their equilibrium value. Eichengreen (1982), examining the case of the 1923–24 French franc crisis, found that speculative operation was extraneous to it.

[16]See Nurkse (1944).

[17]See James (2012).

signatory countries of the Agreement "... promote mutually advantageous economic relations between them and the betterment of world-wide economic relations: they shall provide against discrimination in either the United States of America or the United Kingdom against the importation of any product originating in the other country". This was an attempt to break the British Empire's foreign trade barriers.

The goal of internationalizing the New Deal is clear from the words of the US Treasury Secretary Henry Morgenthau, in his inaugural address of the Conference: "I hope that this Conference will focus its attention upon two elementary economic axioms. The first of these is this: that prosperity has no fixed limits... The second axiom is a corollary of the first. Prosperity, like peace, is indivisible. We cannot afford to have it scattered here or there among the fortunate or to enjoy it at the expense of others".

The British delegation had somewhat different objectives. England had emerged from World War II with a large foreign debt and an economy to rebuild. It was therefore essential for it to be in a position to proceed gradually with the repayment of the debt which it had incurred and to start the reconstruction of the country. This presupposed the availability of a high level of monetary and fiscal sovereignty. The English goals, albeit to different degrees, were shared by the other Allies, that is, by the follower countries. The differences between the objectives of the two sides are evident in the underlying plans used by the two countries to negotiate the text of the Bretton Woods Agreements: the Keynes Plan and the White Plan.

5.2.1 The Keynes Plan

In July 1940, that is, when Germany was the dominant power of continental Europe and the war seemed destined to end, in an important speech, the German Minister of Economy Walther Funk outlined the characteristics of the German proposals for a new international monetary order. This focused on the definitive abandonment of gold as the international money and foresaw the establishment of a bilateral clearing system between European countries.[18] This system would then gradually evolve into a multilateral clearing system. The prerequisites for the European clearing system were to have been the establishment of a fixed exchange rate regime and the maintenance by member countries of the current account balances in substantial balance.

The publication of the Funk Plan led the British government responding with an alternative proposal. This was more than anything a propaganda effort, aimed at communicating to the world that not only that Germany had not yet won the war, but rather, they would eventually lose it and hence post-war planning would be in other hands. The task of developing an alternative document was entrusted to Keynes.

The first version of the Keynes Plan was ready at the end of November 1940. A second version, much more complex than the first and entitled *Proposals for an*

[18]See Steil (2013).

International Monetary Union, was presented by Keynes in November 1941. It was followed by a third version published in 1942[19] and the final version published on April 7, 1943.[20]

The Keynes Plan took up some of the assumptions of the Funk Plan, in particular the de-monetization of gold. Countries' credit and debt adjustments would be compensated multilaterally through the establishment of an International Clearing Union (ICU) and an International Clearing Bank (ICB). The latter was to issue its own currency, the *bancor*, the price of which was fixed in terms of gold.

Each country was to adopt a fixed (albeit adjustable) exchange rate of its own currency with respect to the bancor, which thus formed the unit of account and with which credits and debts between countries were settled. For the working of this scheme each country was to be allocated a certain sum of bancor. This amount was commensurate with the average amount of its imports and exports over the preceding 3 years. The bancor, in addition to being a unit of account, was the reserve currency of the system. In this way, a system of multilateral compensation between countries could be established: a country could be a net debtor to another country, and this debt could be offset by its net credit towards a third country.

The member countries of the system could modify their amount of bancor reserves by buying or selling national currency to the ICB. They could deposit funds with this bank when their current account balances were positive and borrow from it in the event of negative current account balances.

With the establishment of the International Clearing Union, Keynes aimed to ensure that after World War II the problems that had arisen in the international monetary system in the interwar period would not recur. Firstly, in fact, it would have made it possible to ward off the global economy deflationary effects of the policy of accumulating reserves and sterilization practices implemented in the 1920s and 1930s by some countries with persistent current account surpluses. Those behaviours were inextricably linked to the gold-exchange standard, where not only the burden of adjustment rested exclusively on the debtor country, but the accumulation of reserves by creditor countries contributed to the emergence of deflation in the world economy.[21]

With the establishment of the ICB, Keynes sought to make adjustments to foreign imbalances symmetrical. Penalties could have been imposed on creditor countries, such as asking to revalue the exchange rate or applying high interest rates to their credits from the ICB, if these were greater than a quarter of their share of reserves. Debtor countries were to be allowed to devalue their exchange rate, prohibit capital exports and sell gold to or receive credits from the ICB. The ICB was to have $26

[19]See Keynes (1942).

[20]See Keynes (1943).

[21]In illustrating the advantages of his Plan, Keynes (1943 [1969, p. 27]) writes: "It should be much easier, and surely more satisfactory for all of us, to enter into a general and collective responsibility, applying to all countries alike, that a country finding itself in a creditor position against the rest of the world as a whole should enter into an arrangement not to allow this credit balance to exercise a contractionist pressure against world economy".

billion at its disposal for this purpose. Obviously, the country that had current account deficits was encouraged to correct the imbalance over time. In fact, in the case of persistent debt positions, the country could be expelled from the International Clearing Union.

The removal of the asymmetries in the processes of adjustment of current account imbalances would have made it possible to eliminate two factors considered by most scholars of the time to be the determining cause of the monetary disorder between the two wars, namely the competitive devaluations of the exchange rate and the extreme volatility of short-term capital movements.[22]

The task of the ICB was not only to provide for the multilateral compensation of debts and credits and to favour, through incentives and disincentives, a symmetrical adjustment of imbalances with foreign countries, but was also, if necessary, to operate as a real central bank.

The managers of this institution, in fact, had the power to regulate the total supply of bancor in an anti-cyclical sense "The governing body shall be entitled to reduce the quotas of members, all in the same specified proportion, if it seems necessary to correct in this manner an excess of world purchasing power".[23] The ICB could, if necessary, also create money and in doing so stimulate the world economy. In this way, the ICB would clearly have functions similar to a central bank, such as exercising the functions of lender of last resort.

Aware of the significant weakening of the UK as a result of the immense efforts made during World War II and eager to ensure his country a leading role on the world stage, Keynes proposed that the ICB was managed jointly by the USA and England.[24]

5.2.2 *The White Plan*

At the request of the Secretary of US Treasury Henry Morgenthau, Dexter White, a senior Treasury official,[25] was called upon to devise a plan to order the international

---

[22]For many of these scholars, generally British like Keynes, the great attention paid to the problem of asymmetric adjustments stemmed from their interpretation of the collapse of the gold-exchange standard. This collapse, according to this interpretation, was to be attributed exclusively to the behaviour of France and the USA, more specifically the abnormal accumulation of gold reserves of these countries and the sterilization policies implemented by them. Unlike these scholars, others, mainly American, traced the collapse of the gold-exchange standard to the inability of deficit countries to correct their foreign imbalances and, ultimately, to their lack of monetary discipline.

[23]See Keynes (1943 [1969, p. 25]).

[24]As Boughton (2002, p. 14) writes: "[Keynes] envisaged the Clearing Union primarily as an agreement between the two 'founder-states' with other countries joining it as they wished by complying with specified conditions". Also on this occasion Keynes confirmed himself as the defender of a declining England, which Skidelsky (2003) portrayed in the second volume of his monumental biography.

[25]With considerably experience in economics. See on this aspect Harrod (1951), Stein (1969) and Flanders (1990).

monetary system. In the spring of 1942, a document prepared by White entitled *Suggested Plan for a United and Associated Nations Stabilization Fund and a Bank for Reconstruction and Development of the United and Associated Nations* was made public.

In the letter addressed to Secretary of State Morgenthau, to which his Plan was attached, White wrote: "... we shall be faced with three inescapable problems: to prevent the disruption of the foreign exchanges and the collapse of monetary and credit system; to assure the restoration of foreign trade; and to supply the huge volume of capital which will be needed virtually throughout the world for reconstruction, for relief and for economic recovery".[26]

In the introduction to the document, White specified that the three problems he had highlighted could be addressed by the United Nations with two objectives: the creation of a fixed exchange rate system, whose stability was preserved through institutional means, and the provision of adequate resources to countries to support post-war reconstruction and foster the transition from war to peacetime economies.

To achieve these two objectives, White proposed establishing a Stabilization Fund and a Bank for Reconstruction and Development of the United Nations.

The White Plan devoted considerable space to the structure of the Fund and the ways in which it would operate. Initial exchange rates parity were to be determined by the Fund while changes in the exchange parity would have been possible "... only when essential to correct a fundamental disequilibrium, and only with the consent of four-fifths of member votes". In this way, White proposed to prevent the use of competitive devaluations, which in his view were one of the main causes of the monetary disorder between the wars. The Plan envisaged that countries could ask the Fund for currency to deal with negative current account balances. However, the amount that could be withdrawn by any country for this purpose could not exceed 100% of the amount—in terms of gold, foreign currencies and national currency—originally deposited with the Fund.

At its discretion, the Fund could lend additional resources to countries in difficulty. For this purpose, it would have total resources of 5 billion dollars, an amount significantly less than the 26 billion dollars, which Keynes said the ICB required. Furthermore, the Fund, unlike the ICB, could not create an international currency.

A country that received loans from the Fund had to put in place adequate measures to address the imbalance in its current account. The Fund's interventions were therefore to be considered limited to temporary imbalances in external accounts. Its resources could not, therefore, be directed to support post-war reconstruction or reconversion.

In the White Plan, support for reconstruction and productive reconversion through long-term financing would come, not from the Fund, but rather from the International Bank for Reconstruction and Development, which was to have at its disposal 10 billion dollars. In addition, this Bank could issue banknotes (the *Unitas*), covered by bonds and gold deposits of the member countries. This facility, however,

---

[26]See IMF Records Office, April 1942, quoted in Asher and Mason (1973, p. 15).

was eliminated in a later version of the White Plan following extreme opposition to it by the US Congress.

5.2.3 A Comparison Between the Two Plans

Both Plans aimed to create a multilateral payments system with the aim of revitalizing international trade. Both Plans, albeit differently, provided mechanisms that would favour smooth adjustment processes of any imbalances between countries, that is, so as to have the lowest possible costs in terms of falling output and employment. In both Plans, the achievement of these objectives depended on two conditions[27]:

(i) the provision of adequate international liquidity;
(ii) a mechanism that would allow the adjustment of any balance of payments imbalances, minimizing their costs.

Regarding the first point (point *i*), the provision of international liquidity, there were profound differences between the two Plans. A first difference was the amount of resources available to the Stabilization Fund and the ICB. A second difference was the way in which the two institutions procured these resources. In fact, those of the Stabilization Fund were conferred by the member countries. The maximum amount of funding that each of these could receive was represented by its Fund's quota. By contrast, the ICB loans were proposed to function as bank credit facilities. The access limit of a country was given only by the drawing rights of the other member countries.

A third important difference between the two Plans was that the resources of the Stabilization Fund were limited and predefined, while those of the ICB could vary in relation to demand. From this point of view, the ICB was configured as a genuine international central bank.

One final difference between the two Plans, again with regard to the first point, concerned the conditions under which countries could access funding. In the case of the ICB these conditions were unspecified. Conversely, the Stabilization Fund envisaged making resources available to members only in the presence of current account imbalances.

Regarding the adjustment process (point *ii*), in both Plans, not only was the possibility of exchange rate controls excluded, but the revision of parities was not considered as the preferred adjustment tool. It was not discretionary, but rather authorized by the Stabilization Fund in the White Plan and agreed by member countries through the International Clearing Union in the Keynes Plan.[28]

---

[27] See Gardner (1956).

[28] In particular, the Stabilization Fund was given the responsibility of determining the parities of the member countries: these parities could only be changed in the presence of a fundamental imbalance.

In both Plans, measures were proposed to favour a symmetrical adjustment process. However, in the White Plan, in the event of significant current account imbalances and requests for a loan exceeding half the country's quotas, the Stabilization Fund was expected to grant the loan only if the requesting country committed itself to taking adequate corrective measures. In the Keynes Plan, on the other hand, any external interference in internal policy choices was excluded "There should be the least possible interference with internal national policies ... the authority of the governing board of the proposed institution should be limited to recommendations ...".[29]

5.3 The Outcome of the Bretton Woods Negotiations

The basic negotiations between the Americans and the British on the basis of the two Plans outlined above were conducted before the Bretton Woods Conference. Other countries also participated in these negotiations, including the Canadians and the French, who presented their proposals. The outcome of these negotiations was the publication in April 1944 of the *Joint Statement of Experts on the Establishment of an International Monetary Fund.*

This document contained the articles of the International Monetary Fund Agreement adopted in July 1944 by the United Nations Conference at Bretton Woods. The compromise reached mainly concerned the two aspects mentioned above: the provision of liquidity and the mechanism for adjusting external imbalances.

5.3.1 The Provision of Liquidity

As previously mentioned, the Keynes Plan provided for international liquidity to be made available to countries that needed it by opening a line of credit and, therefore, to an almost unlimited extent. This seemed unacceptable to the US Congress, since it would have undermined the powers granted to it by the Constitution, in particular that of authorizing taxes and public spending. As a counter proposal, it agreed to raise the resources available to the Stabilization Fund from 5 to 8.8 billion dollars.

Having yielded on this point, the British tried to maintain the principle that access to liquidity was at the discretion of each individual country. This principle was explicit in article V, section 3(a) of the Agreement: "A member shall be entitled to buy the currency of another member from the Fund in exchange for its own

In the *International Clearing Union* the member countries agreed on the initial parity of their currency with the *Bancor*. They could change this parity only in the presence of a persistent current account deficit and up to a maximum of 5%.

[29]Preface to *Proposals for an International Clearing Union.*

currency". However, this possibility was subject to various conditions, including that the liquidity thus obtained could not be used in a way contrary to the objectives of the Fund. This implied a form of supervision by this institution over the ability of countries to obtain international liquidity.

5.3.2 The Adjustment Mechanism

Having seen the proposal for creating an international central bank rejected, Keynes and the British delegation proposed another mechanism that would give countries the possibility of gradual adjustment of any imbalances. This mechanism consisted in making it easier to adjust exchange rate parities. It was agreed that parity could only be varied "to correct a fundamental disequilibrium".[30] However, it is important to note that the Agreement lacked a definition of fundamental imbalance, a typical example of constructive ambiguity.

The American delegation demanded that the Fund, together with the supervision of the management of exchange rates, be granted the right to communicate to its members its point of view on the internal economic policies and conditions that could lead to account imbalances.[31]

The *Joint Statement of Experts on the Establishment of an International Monetary Fund* formed the basis for discussion and negotiation between the 44 countries that attended the Bretton Woods Conference in July. In this Conference while the existence of three commissions[32] and many committees[33] gave the impression of a management open to the contribution of all participant countries, in reality the outcome on the individual topics had been mostly predetermined by the US and UK delegations.

The Final Act of the Conference of Bretton Woods included the articles of the Agreement of the International Monetary Fund. This institution thus formed the fulcrum of the monetary system enshrined in the Bretton Woods Agreements.

The basic principles of the Bretton Woods system can be deduced from the IMF Agreement and were as follows.

(i) Art. 1 of the Agreement established that the IMF should: "promote international monetary cooperation through a permanent institution which provides the machinery for consultation and collaboration on international monetary

[30]See Article IV, section 5(a).

[31]See Article XII, section 8.

[32]Commission I was on the Fund, and was chaired by Harry Dexter White, Commission II was on the Bank and was chaired by John Maynard Keynes, Commission III was on the international financial cooperation and was chaired by Eduardo Suarez of Mexico.

[33]The work of the Commissions was carried out by Committee on specific topics.

problems".[34] IMF membership was open to all countries participating in the Conference and to those accepting the terms of the Agreements. A country became a member of the IMF by acquiring a quota of its capital. These quotas were established on the basis of several criteria, including the size of the country's economy. The quota in turn determines the voting rights of each member country in the IMF's governance as well as how much financing it can receive from this institution. A quarter of each country's quotas is paid in the form of Special Drawing Rights (SDRs) which are a claim issued by the IMF.

(ii) The exchange rates of the monetary system defined at Bretton Woods were fixed, although they could be varied in the presence of "structural imbalances". Changes in exchange rate parities were a matter of international concern and could take place only with the authorization of the IMF. Art. IV established that: "the par value of the currency of each member shall be expressed in terms of gold as a common denominator or in terms of United States dollar . . .", whose par value with respect to gold was fixed at 35 dollars an ounce. Since most of the gold reserves were held by the USA, the Bretton Woods system was configured—like the gold-exchange standard—as a monetary system on two levels: the dollar was convertible into gold, the other currencies into gold or dollars. To maintain the fixed exchange rate, countries could resort to controls on capital movements. By granting this possibility to the states, the aim was to prevent exchange rate stability from being compromised by the volatility of short-term capital movements as had occurred in the interwar period. In this way, the macroeconomic trilemma was respected, maintaining monetary sovereignty without compromising the convertibility of currencies at fixed parities. The latter was protected, as well as through the restrictions on capital movements, by providing for compliance with certain behavioural rules.

(iii) Each member country could have access to resources, in addition to its foreign exchange reserves, to deal with current account imbalances. In this way, the re-absorption of any imbalances could be done gradually, without requiring an immediate adjustment of the external accounts and hence without provoking seriously negative impact on GDP and employment. The additional resources consisted of an international pool of currencies held by the IMF and paid by member countries on the basis of their quotas in this international institution.

(iv) The objective of achieving non-conflicting trade policies and high economic well-being was pursued simultaneously through a system of multilateral exchanges, non-discriminatory international payments and convertible currencies. No country was allowed to maintain discriminatory exchange rates

[34]Thanks to the cooperation between states, the fund would have had the task "to facilitate the expansion and balanced growth of international trade, and to contribute thereby to the promotion and maintenance of high levels of employment and real income..." See Horsefield (1969, vol. III, p. 187).

arrangements and multiple exchange rates without the prior approval of the IMF.

(v) The adjustment of balance of payments imbalances had to be symmetrical, that is, to burden both the debtor and the creditor country. In this perspective, art. VII established the "scarce currency clause" by which the IMF, to replenish its holdings of the currency of a member country, could declare it "scarce" and impose "... limitations on the freedom of exchange operations ..." in this currency.

(vi) Since monetary tensions often originate from non-monetary causes, the IMF was tasked with cooperating with other international institutions responsible for "real" problems, such as the liberalization of international trade.

(vii) A substantial investment was needed to safeguard the stability of the international economy. For this purpose, private finance flows were to be flanked by loans from an international investment bank.

5.4 The Main Interpretations of the Bretton Woods Agreements

In the previous section it was stated that the crucial aspect of the Bretton Woods Agreements is the fact that a set of rules and institutions were established in support of a new monetary system aimed at ensuring confidence in its stability. At the same time, the rules and institutions that would allow the functioning of the international monetary system were also aimed to be compatible with the internal economic and political equilibrium of the adhering countries. Hence the question inevitably arises as to why, in the interwar period, it had not been possible to establish a monetary system that satisfied this need for compatibility.

Several answers have been given to this question. One explanation refers to the hegemonic stability hypothesis. In the neo-realist version of this approach, it is assumed that the USA after World War II was an ascending hegemonic power and imposed a monetary and economic system reflecting its interests on the allied countries. According to Gilpin (1987, p. 75), who can be considered the leading exponent of this interpretation, "the gold standard of the nineteenth century and the postwar Bretton Woods system are notable examples of an economic regime in which the hegemon establishes and enforces the rules of a liberal market regime and suppresses the ever-present tendencies toward economic nationalism". This explanation, apart from the drawbacks of the hegemonic stability hypothesis illustrated in Chap. 2, assuming an act of coercion by the hegemon on follower countries, does not explain why, as noted by Ruggie (1982), the Bretton Woods agreements can be considered a compromise between the need for monetary autonomy, to which Britain and the European countries were particularly sensitive, and the definition of an international monetary order (sought by the USA) which would provide for the stability of exchange rates and promote the development of trade. Ruggie called this compromise between the preservation of domestic stability and the pursuit of multilateralism in trade "embedded liberalism".

Neo-realists do not reject Ruggie's point of view nor the hypothesis of embedded liberalism, however they tend to distinguish between the content of the Bretton Woods Agreements and their implementation.[35]

The Agreements and their signing by numerous countries reflected the emotionally optimistic and cooperative climate that prevailed among the Allies at the end of the war. There was then, as perhaps always happens on such occasions, the conviction that this would be the last war and this view, at least in the immediate post-war period, induced them to behave highly cooperatively. The result of this behaviour was the Bretton Woods Agreements which were inspired by the logic of an embedded liberalism. However, the implementation of the Agreements took place long after their being signed.

In the long intervening period international relations changed radically. The watershed of these changes was 1947, with the start of the Cold War between the USA and the Soviet Union. With this change, albeit not a war, the world was divided into two blocs, on the one hand, the countries of Eastern Europe and on the other the US-led Atlantic bloc, including mostly Western Europe. Given the latter's economic weakness in the years immediately following WWII, the political hegemony of the USA was rapidly consolidated.

In this context, according to the neo-realists, the international monetary system was forged by the Americans prioritizing US interests[36] through, not few, variations from the contents of the Bretton Woods Agreements.[37]

In the first place, the international monetary system took the shape of a system of virtually fixed exchange rates rather than a system of frequently adjustable exchange rates, as foreseen in the Agreements. Secondly, the high demand for international liquidity, which accompanied the intense growth of industrial countries in the 1950s, highlighted the limits of the IMF as a supplier of international liquidity. In this context, the dollar took on greater importance compared to other forms of international money, starting with gold. Consequently, the USA assumed the role of issuing country of the international currency and thus acquired the privilege of international seigniorage.[38]

---

[35]On this aspect, see Block (1977).

[36]"The role of the dollar in the post-war monetary regime, in short, conferred upon the USA a greater degree of freedom in domestic and foreign security policy than was available to other states participating in the regime" See Gowa (1983, p. 44).

[37]See, among others Gilpin (2002, p. 167): "In subsequent years the original Bretton Woods system has been significantly modified in response to economic and political realities beginning immediately after the end of World War".

[38]See on this aspect Gowa (1983, p 37): "Over time, the member states of the Bretton Woods regime come to rely not only on the Fund and gold but also on a variety of ad hoc arrangements and, increasingly, on US payments deficits for supply of international liquidity. Thus, the system evolved into a full-fledged gold-dollar standard; the USA was its key currency country".

As already highlighted in Chap. 2, the neorealist version of the hegemonic stability theory, insisting exclusively on the role of the hegemonic country, neglects the demand factors underlying the creation and preservation of a given monetary system. Of these factors, at least in part, the neo-liberal version of hegemonic stability theory takes into account. In light of the latter, in fact, the USA, both in the Bretton Woods Agreements and in their implementation, thanks to their hegemonic power, have solved the problem of collective action and made cooperation between countries possible. From this perspective, the Bretton Woods Agreements, but more generally the monetary system derived from these agreements, were the product of the prevalence of cooperative behaviour on a global and monetary level.[39] As von Dormael (1978, p. 28) writes: "The Bretton Woods agreements were the first successful attempt consciously undertaken by a large group of Nations to shape and control their economic relations".

The states' willingness to cooperate originated in the awareness that the monetary disorder of the period between the two wars had been the result of errors in the behaviour and policy choices of governments, errors that should never be repeated.

By attaching predominant importance to the economic objective of the states and underestimating the goal of security, the neo-realists end up tracing the Bretton Woods system only to the demand for institutions that, guaranteeing trust in a fiat currency, allowed the domestic economic stability of the participating countries and, at the same time, the use of an international currency. The risk of this vision is functionalism: that the demand for certain institutions is sufficient for it to be supplied.

If countries aim to maximize the well-being of their citizens and cooperation between them guarantees higher levels of well-being, why did cooperative behaviour between countries not prevail between the two wars? An answer to this question can only be found in an analysis of the conditions for which the supply of an institutional framework, which would guarantee confidence in a currency without intrinsic value and be congruent with the demand of the individual states, could emerge in the international arena.

In fact, what happened between the two wars cannot be considered as the result of irrational behaviour. Such an explanation would, inevitably, lead to the question why do states behave irrationally.

An answer to the problem of why in Bretton Woods the compromise of embedded liberalism was finally found is provided by the constructivist approach. It is from this perspective, that Ikenberry argues that the Bretton Woods Agreements were the result of the work of economists and experts sharing a common ideological thread, the Keynesian one: "... a set of policy ideas inspired by Keynesianism and embraced by a group of well-placed British and American economists and policy specialists was crucial in defining government conceptions of postwar interests, building coalitions in support of the postwar settlement, and legitimating the exercise of American power".[40]

---

[39]See Keohane (1984).

[40]See Ikenberry (1993, p. 157).

In short, thanks to the spread and affirmation of the Keynesian economic view, American and British economists and practitioners found a common ideological denominator on which to base the negotiations and the Bretton Woods Agreements. As Odell (1993) observes, however, the emergence of certain economic views in most cases does not translate into policy choices. It is also plausible that, as Shepsle (1985) writes, the ideas, above all scientific ideas, are "hooks on which politicians hang their objectives and further their interests". Certain ideas can suggest to politicians solutions that favour the reconciliation of differing, at least partly non-conflicting, interests, as happened at Bretton Woods and in the subsequent implementation of those Agreements.

The limitations of the different interpretations of the Bretton Woods system are largely linked to the fact that they do not take into account that the different types of money require different institutional frameworks. The functioning of a monetary system based on commodity money, such as the classic gold standard, was based on the principle of respect for convertibility and therefore required an articulated domestic institutional framework, primarily the existence of a central bank, but, no international institutional framework was necessary. On the other hand, an international monetary system based on a fiat money, can exist only if there is an institutional framework that guarantees trust in it and in the system as a whole. In turn, the supply of a framework of this type can only exist if there is a country that finds it convenient to bear the costs of its creation and preservation.

On the basis of the theoretical framework proposed in Chap. 2, the hypothesis is put forward here that the Bretton Woods system is the result of a political exchange between a leader nation, the USA, and the follower countries.[41]

In this political exchange the parties pursued slightly differing interests. The USA certainly pursued the goal of expanding foreign trade, but it also aimed to strengthen its influence internationally.

As the leading country, the USA benefited from creating and sustaining the institutional architecture that guaranteed confidence in a monetary system based on a quasi-fiat currency, since the revenues derived from seigniorage exceeded the costs of these functions. Follower countries benefited from the public good represented by the international currency and the monetary and financial system based on it. At the same time, they wanted to have margins of autonomy in the conduct of their economic policy in order to achieve high levels of growth, being also able to count on the protective umbrella of the USA in foreign policy.

The kind of exchange just described was facilitated by the political alliance between the countries involved. As Mastanduno (2009, p. 129) writes: "The Bretton Woods was based on a tacit deal between the United States and its principal allies that spanned trade, finance and security".

[41]See Seghezza (2018, pp. 167–168).

5.5 The Slow Move to Currencies' Convertibility

Due to various obstacles that prevented the immediate operation of this system it eventually took 15 years for the Bretton Woods system to become operational.[42] A first obstacle was the scarcity of gold and dollars. In fact, at the end of the Second World War most of the world's gold reserves were held by the USA. The rest of the world, especially Europe, had a shortage of both gold and dollars. The process of reconstruction of the European countries that had fought the Second World War was, therefore, seriously hampered. Indeed, they did not have the resources to cover the substantial current account deficits caused by reduced capacity to produce and export goods and the need to import food and raw materials. The structural imbalances in the external accounts of the main European countries were further aggravated by the fact that the exchange rates set by these countries (under pressure from the IMF) were overvalued in real terms and their competitiveness on the world market was penalized as a result.[43]

The constraints just described hindered the start of a solid reconstruction process in Europe. The economic situation of the main countries of the old continent became critical in 1947. Britain was close to bankruptcy and managed to escape it only thanks to a loan from the USA that came with stringent conditions, including dismantling its trade barriers and those of the Commonwealth with the rest of the world. France and Italy were plagued by high inflation, social tension and the risk of starvation. With the start of the Cold War between the USA and the USSR it was possible that, given the precarious economic conditions of the population, communism could establish itself as the dominant political party in these countries and, hence, the Soviet Union's conquest of Western as well as Eastern Europe.

Faced with this situation, the USA chose to support the old continent with the Marshall Plan, through this Plan between 1948 and 1951 the USA paid 13.2 billion dollars to Europe for its reconstruction, divided as follows: 3.2 billion to the United Kingdom, 2.7 billion to France, 1.5 billion to Italy and 1.4 billion to West Germany.[44]

According to Milward (1984) and other scholars, the contribution of the Marshall Plan to the economic recovery of European countries was however not decisive. Rather, as pointed out by De Long and Eichengreen (1991), perhaps the most important aspect of this Plan was its "conditionality". In fact, it pushed the European governments that benefited from it towards a "mixed economy" more oriented to the market than to direct planning. In the absence of the Marshall Plan, European countries would almost certainly have had extensive recourse to administrative controls on the allocation of resources, they would have maintained levels of public spending incompatible with financial stability in an open economy, and this would have encouraged governments to close themselves off from foreign trade.

---

[42] See Bordo (2017).

[43] See Triffin (1957).

[44] See De Long and Eichengreen (1991).

With the contributions of the Plan, European countries were able to finance their trade deficits, importing raw materials and capital goods. This enabled them to restart production and grow at a more marked pace than would have been the case in the absence of such a plan.

In accordance with the Bretton Woods goal of fostering the growth of international trade, in the Geneva Round of the General Agreement on Tariffs and Trade (GATT) held in 1947 and in the Annecy Round of 1949 the USA and 20 other states agreed drastic tariff reductions.[45] In 1951 the United Kingdom and Germany and a few years later Japan joined GATT.

The reduction in tariffs stimulated the growth of foreign trade; however, the expansion of trade required countries to have adequate foreign exchange reserves. This was necessary so that any shocks to the current account balance did not require an immediate adjustment to correct the imbalance leading to countries resorting to restrictive monetary and fiscal policies, and over time inducing governments to resort to protectionist measures.

In European countries the problem of the shortage of foreign exchange reserves was initially solved with the creation, in September 1950, of the European Payments Union (EPU). This was formed by 18 members of the Organization for European Economic Cooperation (OEEC) and acted as an international clearing house (managed by the BIS) thanks to which the external accounts of each country with the other member countries were offset and balanced.[46] Within this Union, exchange parities were established between the currencies of the acceding countries and a unit of account established in gold. At the end of each month, the BIS cleared the balance items and calculated the net credit or debit balance for each country. The settlement of the balance was carried out partly in gold and partly through credits to the EPU. This clearing system lasted for 8 years and ended with the declaration of convertibility of the currencies of most of the member countries in 1958.[47]

The accumulation of foreign exchange reserves by European countries was gradually facilitated by the trend of the US balance of payments which was characterized by two different phases:

1. A surplus position averaging $2 billion per year between 1946 and 1949;
2. A deficit position averaging $1.5 billion between 1950 and 1958, with the sole exception of 1957, when a small surplus occurred.

This trend in the US balance of payments reflects that of the current account. In the immediate post-war period, the USA was almost the only source of supply of goods that the war-weary countries, especially Europe, needed.[48] During the 1950s, however, European countries gradually rebuilt their economies and consequently,

---

[45]See Finger (1979).

[46]See Kaplan and Schleimnger (1989).

[47]See Bordo (1993).

[48]Between 1946 and 1949 the US current account balance recorded positive balances between 6 and 11 billion of dollars.

Table 5.1 Gross reserves and percentage held in foreign exchange, Sterling area and continental EPU

	United Kingdom		Other sterling area		Continental EPU countries	
	Reserves ($bn)	In foreign exchange (%)	Reserves ($bn)	In foreign exchange (%)	Reserves ($bn)	In foreign exchange (%)
1948	2.0	20	7.3	92	5.9	40
1950	3.7	21	5.6	89	6.9	43
1954	2.8	0	5.0	86	11.4	51
1957	2.4	33	4.0	83	14.6	45

Source: IMF

albeit gradually, their overseas imports declined and as a result, the US current account surplus contracted to such an extent that it was no longer sufficient to offset capital outflows. During this period, therefore, the increase in the reserves of these countries was very pronounced (Table 5.1).

The accumulation of foreign exchange reserves enabled the major European countries, on the one hand, to cope with temporary current account imbalances and, on the other hand, to maintain a convertible exchange rate. Since the reserves held were considered adequate, the major European countries in 1958 decided for the convertibility of their currencies into dollar. This decision was favoured by the fact that these countries were linked to the USA not only economically, but also politically. This link made their economic and political stability of common interest and explains why the parities established in 1958 were credible even if the ratio between reserves and imports, while it had increased significantly for Germany, had remained substantially stable for the other main European countries.

5.6 The Decline of the Sterling

In 1947 the British currency represented 87.4% of international liquidity. However, at the end of the Second World War, England was the most indebted country in the world. Not only did it owe £3 trillion to its wartime creditors, but its balance of payments had large and persistent deficits. In addition to this, the Labour government headed by Clement Attlee was committed to maintaining full employment and creating an advanced welfare state. Given this, in the autumn of 1945 Britain attempted to obtain a $5 billion zero interest loan from the USA.

In the American Administration, with Truman's succession to Roosevelt, the position of the State Department had become pre-eminent: the growth of the USA was not to be the result of expansionary fiscal policies agreed at the national level, but rather by the elimination of trade barriers.[49] In the eyes of the American

[49]See Newton (1984).

administration, the sterling area was akin to a discriminatory economic bloc that hindered trade liberalization.

At the end of 1945 the Attlee government, given the country's difficult economic situation, was forced to ask for a loan from the USA. The USA agreed a more limited sum, $3750 million dollars at 2% interest under the Anglo-American Loan Agreement,[50] which included the following conditions[51]:

(a) the obligation of Britain to dissolve the Sterling area dollar pool, allowing the sterling receipts of this area's countries to be convertible in any other currency;
(b) its article X required the freeing of the blocked sterling balances accumulated by the sterling area countries in the face of Britain war debts;
(c) its article VIII provided for the establishment of the convertibility of the pound sterling.

The previous condition implied the removal of any discrimination against dollar imports in the Commonwealth countries. This agreement signalled the subordination of Britain to the USA in international relations,[52] but also meant the start of the decline of the pound as an international currency.

The commitment to making the pound convertible was risky for England because it had inadequate gold and dollar reserves to defend the convertibility of the pound. These two risk factors were certainly part of the causes of the outflow of capital from England which began as early as July 1947, became gradually more pronounced in August, until the British government was forced on 23 August 1947 to suspend the convertibility of the pound.

What also contributed to the huge outflow of capital, and in particular of dollars, from England was the fact that worldwide, faced with a dollar shortage, the only convertible currency was the pound on which the effects of the high demand for dollars in international payments fell.[53] The weakness and instability of the pound inevitably impacted on its role as an international currency (Table 5.2).

A further loss to sterling's credibility, in particular of the stability of its value over time, came from its devaluation by about 30 percent in 1949. This decision was urged by the American administration and favoured by the IMF.[54] James (1996, p. 117) argues that according to the IMF the devaluation was necessary to "clear the way for general European adjustment". The Bank of England, which has always been concerned about keeping the value of the pound sterling stable in order to protect the role of the City's as a leading international financial centre, was opposed to the devaluation.[55]

[50]The British delegation that concluded the negotiations with the American counterpart was led by Keynes.

[51]See, among others, Burnham (1992).

[52]See, among others, Brett (1985), Lipietz (1987) and Tomlinson (1990).

[53]Furthermore, the British government was under the impression that it would be possible to persuade some countries to cancel their sterling balances to offset their war debts.

[54]See Cairncross and Eichengreen (1983).

[55]See Cairncross and Eichengreen (1983).

Table 5.2 Composition of gross foreign exchange assets, 1947–57 (billions of dollars)

Year	Total	Dollars	Sterling	EPU liabilities	BIS deposits	Errors and omissions
1947	13,900	1850	12,147	–	8	−105
1950	13,600	4450	7775	402	250	723
1954	15,250	7000	6980	1108	465	−303
1957	16,050	8300	6833	1269	409	239

Source: Horsefield (1969, vol. II, p. 271)

Despite this, the devaluation of the pound was inevitable due to the structural trade deficit which became extremely large in the early part of 1949. This deficit was accompanied by a significant reduction in Britain's foreign exchange reserves.[56] The latter was further compounded by speculation through leads and lags in sterling payments.[57] The limited availability of reserves made the stability of the sterling fragile. This eroded its position in the international monetary system and the sterling's share in gross foreign exchange assets between 1947 and 1954 fell from 87.4 to 45.8%.

A further blow to the international credibility of the pound came from the handling of the Suez crisis of 1956. When it occurred, the USA, opposed to the military occupation of the canal by Britain, together with France and Israel, through the Fed, encouraged a speculative attack on the sterling. In defence of its currency, Britain lost £310 million in reserves between September and November and, in order to avoid another devaluation of the pound, the British government withdrew its troops from Egypt.[58]

By 1957, the sterling's share in gross foreign exchange assets had fallen further to 42.6%, this suggests that the decline of the pound sterling can be traced both to internal reasons, primarily the macroeconomic imbalances suffered by the British economy after the Second World War, and to international events, in particular, to the behaviour of the USA which favoured a weakening of the British currency and encouraged its replacement by the dollar as the international currency.

This replacement process, however, was not rapid. Even in the mid-1950s, the pound sterling remained the dominant reserve assets for various countries. Krugman (1984) and others[59] believe that this slow pace is mainly due to inertial factors deriving from network economies. Schenk (2002, 2010) traces the slow decline of the sterling to "colonial monetary systems and pre-war commonwealth links".[60]

The possession of colonies allowed Britain to form a so-called sterling area which had three main characteristics. Member countries "pegged their exchange rate to sterling, maintained a common exchange rate control against the rest of the world

---

[56]In 1949, the gold reserves of Britain fell from 318.2 million pounds to 190.2 million pounds.

[57]See Einzig (1968).

[58]This is an example of financial statecraft in international relations between states. See Kirshner (1995).

[59]See Strange (1971) and James (1996).

[60]See Schenk (2010, p. 36).

Table 5.3 Percentage share of sterling in total reserves, 1950–1958

	1950	1951	1952	1953	1954	1955	1956	1957	1958
Iraq	95	80	81	86	91	84	80	71	66
Ceylon	89	73	78	67	73	67	56	53	47
Australia	82	66	65	70	64	49	58	65	55
Pakistan	78	79	52	57	59	62	53	50	44
India	73	69	69	97	97	98	56	44	33
New Zealand	64	61	62	73	69	61	72	63	66
South Africa	24	22	23	8	19	7	8	n.a.	n.a.

Source: Schenk (2010)

while enjoying free current account and capital transactions with the UK and, thirdly, maintained national reserves in sterling which required pooling foreign exchange earnings".[61]

The decline of sterling as a reserve currency was blunted by the substantial stability of sterling balances held by the countries of the sterling area (Table 5.3). This partially compensated for the decreased holding of sterling by other countries.

From this premises, it can be concluded that the decline of a currency, such as the dollar, issued by a country without an empire, as was the British one, could be faster. This conclusion, however, does not take into account the differences between convertible international currencies, such as the pound sterling in the post-World War II period, and fiat type international currencies, such as the dollar today. Trust in the latter requires an institutional architecture whose costs only a leading country can bear.

5.7 Functioning of the Bretton Woods System

In the 15 years before the Bretton Woods Agreements could be implemented, the world's geopolitical balance had changed profoundly. It is not surprising, therefore, that the international monetary system that began in 1958 differed in many respects from the system outlined in the 1944 Agreements. In fact, instead of being configured as a system in which all currencies were equal, it assumed the structure of the gold-exchange standard. With the decline of the pound,[62] accelerated by the 1947 and 1949 devaluations, the key currency of the system became the dollar. So, the international monetary system became increasingly similar to that envisioned by Williams (1936, 1943), i.e. a monetary system based on a single key currency,[63] in which the issuing country was subject to different rules from other countries.

[61] See Schenk (2010, p. 36).

[62] The use of British currency in international trade decreased significantly, from about 50% in 1945 to 30% in 1967. See Dam (1982).

[63] See Johnson (1972).

As Box 5.1 shows, countries participating in the system other than the USA were first required to fix a par value for their national currency with the US dollar (point I). In order to safeguard the convertibility of their currencies, they could use controls on capital movements (point II) and had to hold official exchange reserves in US dollars (point III). They had to prevent tensions on the convertibility of their currencies by keeping under control money growth (point IV) and the size of their current account imbalances (point V). The lower part of Box 5.1 shows the rules that the USA had to follow. Of particular note among these rules is point VII, which summarizes the so-called redundancy problem. In the absence of an international commodity money, this problem could be solved only if among the *N* existing currencies, the currency of a certain country was designated as the Nth or "anchor" currency of the system.[64]

Box 5.1 The Fixed-Rate Dollar Standard, 1958–1971

Industrial countries other than the USA	
I	Fix a par value for the national currency with the US dollar as the numeraire, and keep exchange rate within one percent of this par value indefinitely.
II	Free currency convertibility for current account payments; use capital controls to insulate domestic financial markets, but begin liberalization.
III	Use the dollar as the intervention currency, and keep active official exchange reserves in US Treasury bonds.
IV	Subordinate long-run growth in the domestic money supply to the fixed exchange rate and to the prevailing rate of price inflation (in tradable goods) in the USA.
V	Offset substantial short-run losses in exchange reserves by having the central bank purchase domestic assets to partially restore the liquidity of domestic banks and the money supply (Bagehot's rule).
VI	Limit current account imbalances by adjusting national fiscal policy (government net saving) to offset any divergences between private saving and investment.
	The USA
VII	Remain passive in the foreign exchanges: practice free trade with neither a balance of payments nor an exchange rate target. Do not hold significant official reserves of foreign exchange.
VIII	Keep US capital markets open to foreign governments and private residents as borrowers or depositors.
IX	Maintain position as a net international creditor (in dollar-denominated assets) and limit fiscal deficits.
X	Anchor the dollar (world) price level for tradable goods by an independently chosen American monetary policy.

Source: McKinnon (1993)

In the fixed-rate dollar standard, as the Bretton Woods system in fact was, the USA had two main obligations. First, they had to comply with the formal obligation

[64]See Mundell (1968) and McKinnon (1993).

to maintain the dollar parity in terms of gold[65] as required by article IV of the Agreement of International Monetary Fund. Second, the US central bank, the Fed, was required not to intervene in the exchange rate market. The other central banks, based on art. IV of the Agreement, could buy and sell dollars to keep their exchange rate within a 1% range against the dollar.

Consequently, the American authorities had no control over their country's balance of payments.[66] Its balance was determined "... by the appetite of the rest of the world reserves, and its dollar-gold composition by its preferences for gold and dollars".[67] "... [T]his American passivity in allowing other countries to choose their exchange rates against the dollar was... an essential element in the harmonious working of the global monetary system".[68]

As far as exchange rate management is concerned, the system evolved from a flexible pegging system, as envisaged in both the White and Keynes plans, into a system of rigidly fixed exchange rates.[69] In fact, after most of the G-10 established de facto convertibility of their currencies in December 1958, there were few changes in exchange rates and were largely concentrated in the second half of the 1960s. With the evolution of the Bretton Woods system into a gold-exchange standard, some problems that characterized the international monetary system in the second half of the 1920s reemerged, in particular the shortage of international liquidity, to which the problem of adjustments was connected, and maintaining confidence in the convertibility of the key currency, the dollar.

The problem of the shortage of international liquidity was made acute by the fact that, contrary to the provisions of the Agreement of International Monetary Fund, the adjustment was not symmetrical as required by the *scarce currency clause*. It weighed entirely on the deficit countries. The latter found it difficult to implement immediate corrective measures given the growing rigidity of wages and the goal of full employment of Keynesian policies. The availability of international liquidity would have allowed forms of deferral and smoothing of the imbalance adjustment measures. However, the creation of international liquidity depended on America's balance of payments: ultimately, on this country's monetary policy and dollar issuance. This resulted in a wide debate and various proposals on how to create international liquidity.

Finally, there was the problem of confidence in the dollar's convertibility. This problem was well presented by Triffin (1947, 1960), according to whom the USA was faced with a dilemma (later known as *Triffin's dilemma*) deriving from the fact that trade between countries grew to a greater extent than their gold reserves. They could accommodate the growth of foreign trade by adjusting the issue of dollars to it:

---

[65]$ 35 for an ounce of gold.

[66]See McKinnon (2013).

[67]See Mundell (2003).

[68]See McKinnon (2013, p. 39).

[69]There were very few exchange adjustments between 1958 and 1967: two devaluations of France in 1957 and 1958 and the revaluations of Germany and Holland in 1961.

in this case, however, the amount of the latter in circulation would gradually exceed the gold reserves of the USA. This would result in a loss of confidence in the dollar's convertibility and ultimately abandoning it as a key currency.

Alternatively, the USA could decide not to accommodate the world's demand for liquidity, curb economic growth, but preserve confidence in the dollar's gold convertibility. The USA chose the first alternative: they satisfied the demand for liquidity, stimulating world economic growth with the concomitant increase in trade.

5.7.1 The Debate on the Creation of International Liquidity

Special attention was paid to this issue by scholars and politicians in the 1960s. In 1961 ten countries,[70] which were later called the G-10, stipulated the General Arrangements to Borrow (GAB) thanks to which these countries could lend funds to the IMF so that it, in turn, could, if required, support one of the countries adhering to the agreement. The importance of the GAB lay in the fact that the USA, thanks to it, could borrow currencies from third countries via the IMF and buy dollars from the IMF if it was necessary to support the exchange rate of the American currency. Furthermore, the constitution of the G-10 expressed the goal of the adhering countries to a multilateral management of the international monetary system. The G-10 supported, in this task, the IMF, considered (at least by the European countries) to be excessively under the influence of the USA.

GAB was an important support for foreign exchange market interventions in order to preserve parities. However, it did not solve the problem of how to satisfy the growing demand for international liquidity.

For various reasons, the European countries, primarily France, agreed on the need to create a reserve instrument other than the dollar. Britain was in favour of creating another reserve instrument in addition to the dollar which would have offered it additional liquidity to prevent the balance of payments crises that the country periodically encountered. Germany was aware that if the creation of international liquidity depended solely on the creation of dollars, the USA could be inclined to run persistent overall balance of payments deficits, thus exporting inflation to countries with trade surpluses.[71]

France, longing to restore its role as a great power in the international arena, showed itself increasingly intolerant of the fact that the USA could exploit the right of seigniorage as it pleased. In a press conference in February 1965, President De Gaulle remarked "the fact that many states accept dollars as equivalent to gold... has enabled the United States to be indebted to foreign countries free of charge. Indeed, what they owe these countries, they pay... in dollars that they themselves can issue

---

[70]Belgium, Canada, France, Germany, Italy, Japan, the Netherlands, the United Kingdom, the USA, Sweden and Switzerland.

[71]See Bird (1998).

as they wish".[72] This view, which emphasized the undesirable international hegemony of the dollar was summarized by the Minister of Finance of the time, Giscard d'Estaing, with the expression *exorbitant privilege*.[73]

France's position reflected the new balance of power that was being defined in the international arena. In the early 1960s, in fact, the Common Market was consolidating and, within it, France wanted to exercise a sort of primacy, helped in this by having an independent nuclear capability. In De Gaulle's vision, France could aspire to be independent of the USA and to present itself as the political leader of Europe.[74] France was, therefore, in the position of a follower country which, after its post-war reconstruction, no longer recognized itself in the political exchange signed at Bretton Woods nor in the way in which those Agreements had been implemented in practice.

Taking into account the pressures of European countries, albeit for different reasons, in mid-1963 the then Secretary of the Treasury of the USA, Henry H. Fowler, agreed on the need to start a discussion on how to improve the international monetary arrangements.[75] In 1968, the creation of the Special Drawing Rights (SDRs) was approved at the 23rd IMF Annual Meeting and were first allocated by the IMF in 1969. They were (and are) distributed on the basis of member countries shares in the IMF. Through this instrument, member countries can increase their available international liquidity. The fact that SDRs can only be used between states, and not between individuals, but above all the fact that they are issued in limited quantities, excludes the possibility that they can be considered as money or that the IMF can be considered a central bank.[76]

If the intent of issuing SDRs was to save the Bretton Woods system, it failed, since in 1971 the USA suspended dollar convertibility. With the advent of a flexible exchange rate system in 1973, the demand for reserves to deal with balance of payments imbalances eased. In this context, the USA played their hand well in holding back the development of an instrument that would have undermined the seigniorage privilege associated with creating externally held dollars. Hence the rapid decline of SDRs (Table 5.4).

5.7.2 Mechanisms to Preserve Confidence in the Dollar

As mentioned earlier, Triffin had found that any growth in dollar issues higher than that of the USA's gold reserves would gradually undermine the credibility of the American currency or the confidence in its convertibility. Indeed, as Fig. 5.1 shows, the gold coverage of the dollars in circulation gradually decreased.

[72]See Lacouture (1992, p. 381).

[73]See Eichengreen (2011).

[74]See Kissinger (1994).

[75]See Bordo and James (2012).

[76]For an illustration of the characteristics of the SDRs, see Williamson (2009).

Table 5.4 Holdings of SDRs among participating countries (as a percentage of non-gold reserves)

	All participants	Industrial countries	Developing countries
1971	8.9	9.9	6.1
1975	6.0	8.9	2.4
1980	5.6	7.1	3.5
1985	4.4	6.3	1.7
1990	3.9	4.6	1.5
1995	2.6	3.5	1.1

Source: IMF, Annual Report 1995

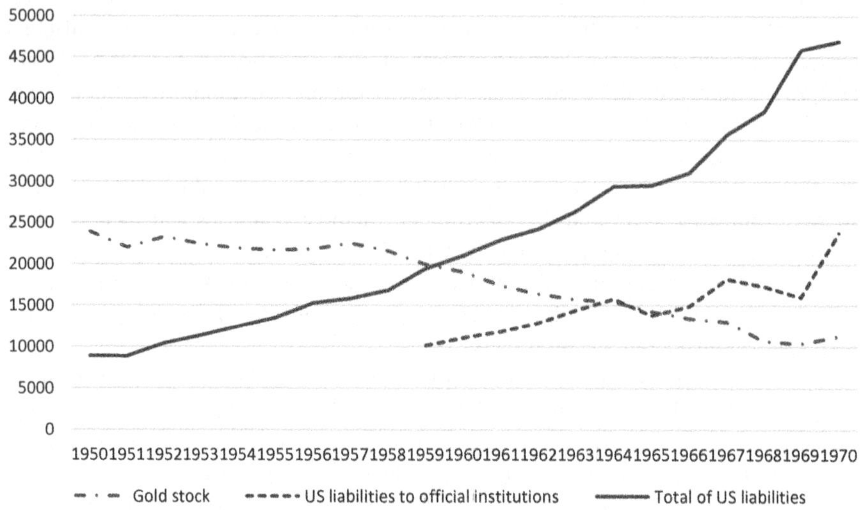

Fig. 5.1 US monetary gold stock and external liabilities. Source: Board of Governors of the Federal Reserve System Banking and Monetary Statistics, 1941–1976, September 1976

An obvious symptom of the gradual erosion of confidence in the dollar's convertibility was France's 1965 decision to convert dollar reserves into gold, at the same time presenting a proposal to replace the dollar-based monetary system with one more directly tied to gold. This proposal reflected the historical position of France, which had opposed the attribution of a special status to any national currency from as early as the Genoa Conference of 1922.[77] This proposal evidently did not take into account that the restoration of a system based on commodity money was by now anachronistic.

To cauterize the progressive diminishing credibility of the dollar, the Fed and the central banks of the other advanced countries resorted primarily to two instruments: the Gold Pool and swap lines contracts.[78]

[77]See Eichengreen (2019).

[78]See Bordo et al. (2014).

The London Gold market, closed in 1939, was reopened in 1954 as part of the British government's strategic decision to strengthen the capital's financial role.[79] It became a barometer of the credibility of dollar convertibility. In the autumn of 1960, shortly after the currencies of the main countries had become convertible into dollars, the London Gold market price of gold went beyond the gold-dollar parity, set at $35 an ounce, touching $40 an ounce. To bring the gold price back to the official level, the Bank of England sold gold on behalf of the USA. Subsequently, to avoid deviations between the market price of gold and the official gold-dollar parity, the group of central banks which formed part of the Bank of International Settlements undertook not to buy gold on the London market when its price was higher than gold-dollar parity.[80]

The London Gold Pool was subsequently established with the task of buying and selling gold in order to stabilize its price at $35 an ounce. This body, which included the central banks of the USA and seven European countries[81] became operational in November 1961 and proved effective in stabilizing the price of gold over the following 6 years.

During this period however, cracks appeared in the cooperation of the central banks. In 1965, as already mentioned, the Bank of France converted large amounts of dollars into gold.[82] It was, however, at the time of the 1967 devaluation of the pound that speculative pressures on the dollar became disruptive.[83] These pressures stemmed from a loss of confidence in the stability of the dollar's value, as the gold coverage of US monetary base had fallen significantly, the latter being driven by financing the Vietnam War.[84]

In March 1968, due to the losses that the central banks suffered to support the gold-dollar parity, the Gold Pool was disbanded. This resulted in two gold markets: in the first, operated by central banks, gold was bought and sold at $35 an ounce while in the second, operated by private individuals, the price of gold was free.

The collapse of the London Gold Pool suggested that the conditions for the suspension of the dollar's convertibility were imminent. The result was that "as Gresham had foreseen, gold was diverted out of the international monetary circuit to be used for private purposes (industry, jewelry, dentistry, etc.). At the same time, dollars were taking the place of gold in central bank coffers".[85] The key currency

[79]See Strange (1976), Harvey (2013) and Schenk (2013).

[80]See Toniolo and Clement (2005) and Bordo et al. (2019).

[81]Germany, the United Kingdom, France, Italy, Belgium, the Netherlands and Switzerland.

[82]From the empirical evidence it would seem, however, that this choice did not have a noticeable impact on the gold market (see Bordo et al., 2019). Meltzer (1991) has a different opinion.

[83]Gavin (2007) and Schenk (2010) showed that the USA, fearing the repercussions of a devaluation of the pound on gold-dollar parity, had given financial support to Britain and its currency between 1961 and 1967. This had ended up creating a close link between the pound and the dollar. See Strange (1976).

[84]See Bordo et al. (2019), Bordo (1993), Schenk (2010), Toniolo and Clement (2005) and Eichengreen (2010).

[85]See De Grauwe (1989).

was now convertible into a commodity, gold, at a conventional price, rather than at its market price.

The second instrument used by the central banks of advanced countries to support gold-dollar parity was swap lines contracts. Under these contracts, the Federal Reserve sold spot dollars to another central bank for the latter's currency, while, at the same time, sold back future to them (at the same exchange rate) the foreign currency that had been acquired. The liquidity in dollars thus provided by the Fed to the other central banks allowed them to face temporary tensions on gold-dollar parity. The amount of swap lines contracts gradually increased from $900 million in 1962 to $30 billion in 1978.[86]

Although both the Gold Pool and the use of swap lines indicate the existence of a good level of cooperation at the international level,[87] one cannot disagree with Gilbert (1985, p. 247) when he writes: "It must be recognized, however, that every country gives priority to its own basic interests and that the demands on cooperation cannot violate those interests". According to several scholars, the pursuit of national interests by states explains the so-called *gold puzzle*, or the fact that between 1950 and 1970 the total amount of gold held by the USA decreased significantly, while that held by other countries increased markedly and their dollar reserves decreased correspondingly (Fig. 5.2). From this perspective, the restructuring of reserves in favour of gold by the industrialized countries could be traced to growing expectations of a devaluation of the American currency.

However, this explanation clashes with the fact that, in the main continental European countries at least, the share of gold in official reserves has been consistently high (Table 5.5): the trend of this share is not associated with the decreased gold coverage of dollars issued by the Fed.

The hypothesis that the accumulation of gold reserves by continental European countries can be traced, in addition to a diminished confidence in the dollar's convertibility, to political reasons, in particular to the desire for that form of power that Cohen (2012, 2013) calls autonomy, cannot be excluded. "An actor is also powerful to the extent that it is able to exercise operational independence—to act freely, … insulated from outside pressures … In this sense, power does not mean influencing others; rather it means not allowing others to influence you".[88] While the use of the dollar required the acquiescence of the behaviour of the USA, the holding of gold was completely in the hands of the holding country and allowed greater margins of autonomy in domestic economic policy choices.[89]

In the view just outlined, the accumulation of gold reserves by continental European countries over time affected the functioning of the Bretton Woods System.[90] This despite the fact that it was fully consistent with one of the objectives of

[86]See James (1996) and Bordo et al. (2012).

[87]See James (1990).

[88]See Cohen (2008, p. 456).

[89]See Machlup (1966).

[90]See Monnet and Puy (2019).

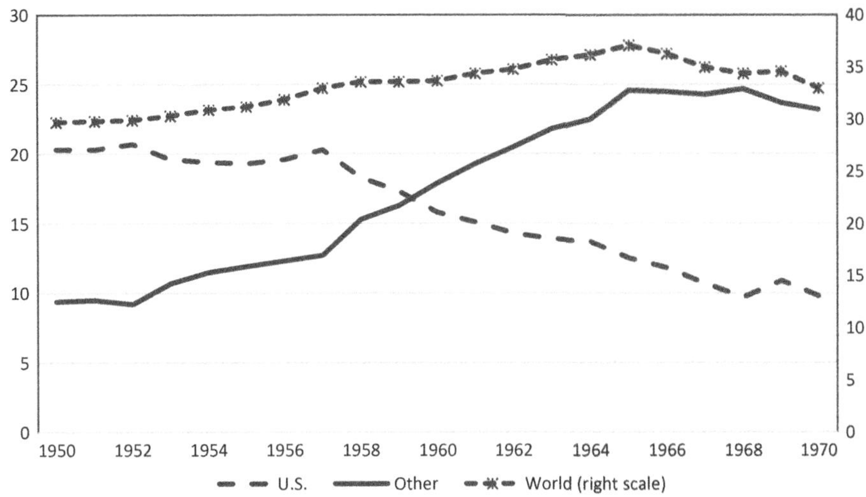

Fig. 5.2 Share of gold on international reserves (percentages). Source: Green (1999)

Table 5.5 Share of gold on countries' official reserves (percentage)

Country	1965	1967	1971
USA	91.0	81.4	77.8
United Kingdom	75.4	47.9	33.9
France	67.6	74.8	69.4
Germany	74.2	51.9	64.2
Italy	59.4	43.9	68.5
Canada	38.0	37.5	16.3
Japan	15.2	16.7	9.1

Source: IMF, Annual Report, several years

the 1944 Agreements, namely that of leaving the acceding countries margins of freedom in the management of domestic economic policy.

5.8 The Eurodollar Market

It is a generally accepted fact that in 1957 a new international money market began: the eurodollar market. This market consisted, and still consists, of US dollar-denominated deposits with banks outside the USA, mainly those in the City of London.

The development of this market was rapid. As Table 5.6 shows, over the course of the 1960s the eurodollar market grew significantly. The growth of this market was also driven by speculative investments whose intensity was particularly high between 1971 and 1973.

Table 5.6 Estimated size of the Eurodollar market in 13 countries[a] (billions of dollars)

Year	Gross	Net
1964	20	14
1969	85	50
1971	145	80
1973	295	105

Source: Whitman et al. (1974)

[a]West-Germany, France, Italy, United Kingdom, Belgium, Luxembourg, Netherlands, Switzerland, Sweden, Bahamas, Canada, Japan and Singapore

It is inevitable to ask what were the factors that favoured such rapid and impressive growth of this market. Traditional explanations point to the emergence of the eurodollar market as a regulation-induced monetary innovation.[91] Indeed, in correspondence with yet another sterling crisis in 1957 the Bank of England once again imposed restrictions on granting external sterling credits, in particular on the sterling financing of non-UK trade.[92] This would have encouraged British banks to use dollars for their foreign operations. At the same time, the possibility of being able to deposit funds in an off-shore and, therefore, deregulated market, allowed American banks to escape the regulatory constraints of their domestic market, in particular reserve constraints and regulation Q.

According to Schenk (1998) this explanation of the origin of the eurodollar market is not fully satisfactory. In her opinion, in fact, the regulatory restrictions may have favoured the development of this market, but they were certainly not the main determinant. In fact, the first dollar transactions by British banks, in particular Midland Bank, date to 1955, before the restrictions introduced by the Bank of England in 1957. They initially consisted of a response to the liquidity preferences by the Midland Bank, which exploited the opportunities for interest arbitrage by the spread between British Treasury Bills and the comparable rate in New York.

The eurodollar market has often been described as a financial market created by operators outside any government intervention.[93] In fact, the development of this market was not only allowed, but also facilitated, by both the British and American governments.[94]

British support for the eurodollar market was crucial. It consisted mainly in allowing it to operate in the City without being subject to regulation. In Britain financial officials and the Bank of England were strongly committed to maintaining and, if possible, strengthening the role of the City as a leading international financial centre. This objective would be facilitated if bankers were allowed to operate without constraints in foreign currencies, especially in US dollars.[95] On the other

[91]See Silber (1983), Llewellyn (1992) and Helleiner (1994).

[92]See Strange (1976).

[93]See Wriston (1988) and von Dormael (1997).

[94]See Frieden (1987), Strange (1971) and Helleiner (1994).

[95]See Burn (1999).

hand, the inflows of capital would allow Britain to better address its balance of payments imbalances.

The possibility for American banks to exercise an off-shore activity in the eurodollar market was not discouraged by the US authorities for two main reasons. In the first place, this was a way of easing the aversion of large American banks to the restrictive Bretton Woods financial order, in particular to the possibility of countries to introduce controls and restrictions on the movement of capital. As Block (1977, p. 53) writes: "They [the American international bankers] feared that extensive national or international governmental intervention would eliminate the role that private international bankers had historically played". This concern made them favour the *key currency plan* proposed by Williams. This plan envisaged a return to the gold standard, and therefore to a system based on the perfect mobility of capital, whose key currency was, however, the dollar. "With the creation of the euromarket, bankers in both countries stumbled on a solution to the problem of how to reconstruct the London-New York financial axis that had been prominent in the 1920s".[96]

In the second place, the American authorities benign neglect of the formation of the eurodollar market is attributable to their objective of increasing the attractiveness of the dollar.[97] This was initially a way to help the American currency rise to the rank of international currency, but later, when the USA incurred persistent current account deficits, it was a way to prevent dollar holders from demanding their conversion into gold. De Cecco (1987, p. 187) opportunely recalls that in 1960 Douglas Dillon, under-secretary of state for economic affairs, speaking to the US Congress, enthused that the eurodollar market represented "quite a good way of convincing foreigners to keep their deposits in dollars".

Indeed, holders of US currency, holding deposits in the Eurozone, could receive significantly higher interest rates on their deposits than in the USA, where interest rates on bank deposits were limited by Regulation Q.

The gradual development of the eurodollar market laid the foundations for the return of global finance, which the restrictions on capital mobility put in place by the advanced countries in the 1950s and 1960s were intended to prevent or, in any case, to reduce to a marginal role.

5.9 The Consolidation of the International Monetary Fund

The consolidation of the international institutions created in Bretton Woods, particularly of the International Monetary Fund, was slow and tortuous. At its inception, it appeared, on one hand, untimely in urging countries to declare par values of their

[96]See Helleiner (1994, p. 89).

[97]See Helleiner (1994).

currencies too soon, and on the other, unable to offer assistance to countries with large external deficits in the years immediately following the Second World War.

Between 1944 and 1947 the scenario of international relations changed profoundly. With the start of the Cold War, the USA paid increased attention to geopolitical security. In this new context, it was the World Bank that was initially used to support those countries that were in conflict with the Soviet Union, as in the case of Yugoslavia in 1948,[98] those that could "contain" Soviet expansionism, such as Iran[99] or operations to overthrow communist sympathizer regimes, as in 1953 that of Guatemalan President Jacobo Arbenz.[100]

The political influence of the USA on the IMF was less pervasive and immediate in its initial phase. In large part this was due to the informal agreement between the participants that the appointment of the President of the World Bank would go to the USA, while that of the managing director of the IMF would not.

Nevertheless, the USA exercised some influence over IMF decisions through its right of veto. In fact, having 17% of the votes, they could block any decision of the Board that required a special majority of 85% of votes.[101] This majority was required for a country to acquire a share in the IMF or to increase it. Consequently, US control grew by the process of increasing the institution's resources.[102]

In its first years of existence, the activity of the IMF was modest. It was limited both by the prevalence of bilateral agreements between the USA and countries in need of financial support, and by the so-called *ERP Decision* according to which countries receiving assistance under the European Recovery Programme could buy dollars from the IMF only in exceptional cases. Finally, its activity was also contained by the insistence of the US Executive Director that the use of IMF resources should be subject to close scrutiny, a condition opposed by European countries who demanded automaticity of requests to access IMF resources".[103]

In November 1950 the IMF's Managing Director Camille Gutt put forward the proposal to link drawings to the commitment of the members to implement measures to adjust the balance of payments imbalances. This proposal was in fact accepted by European countries and hence the USA, thanks to its economic and political power, succeeded in enshrining the principle of conditionality in the IMF's lending business.[104] As the General Counsel of the Fund of that time, Joseph Gold, wrote, "The [Executive Board's] decision of February 13, 1952 [adopting the principle of

[98]See Woods (2006).

[99]See Kapur et al. (1997).

[100]See O'Rourke (2018).

[101]The importance of this power increased as the number of decisions requiring a special majority increased. See Gold (1977) and Lister (1984).

[102]See Woods (2006, p. 29).

[103]See Dell (1981, pp. 9–10).

[104]See De Vries (1976, pp. 256–257).

conditionality] was intended to reinvigorate the Fund by encouraging members to believe that they would be able to use its resources".[105]

In its first years of life, in exercising conditionality, the IMF adhered to the *Polak model*.[106] The basic principle of this model was the *absorption approach* to the balance of payments. According to this approach, a country with a balance of payments deficit should have corrected the public budget, reducing spending or increasing taxes, and reducing domestic credit creation. The Polak model therefore implied clear policy prescriptions. In fact, it contradicted the provisions of art. VII of the Agreement of the International Monetary Fund which, referring to the clause of *scarce currencies*, provided that the adjustments to the balance of payments imbalances were symmetrical.

The definition of the principle of conditionality finally allowed the IMF to become operational and, with the full operation of this institution, the Bretton Woods system began. The system, although based on the 1944 Agreements, differed from them in many respects. However, it acknowledged the basic principle, namely giving rise to an "international monetary law". In this perspective, "the international monetary system... can be taken to be the international monetary relations that are regulated by the body of rules and practices that monetary authorities... consider themselves legally or morally bound to observe or engage in".[107] The existence of an "international monetary law" allowed the use of fiat money at an international level: the stability of the monetary system based on it being guaranteed by an articulated institutional architecture. This architecture has been adapted over time to changes in the international payment system; the Amendments to the Agreement of the International Monetary Fund which were approved over time are emblematic of this.

5.10 The Effects of the Bretton Woods System on the Real Economy

It has already been said that the architects of the post-war international economic order set out to design institutions and promote policies that favoured the expansion of international trade. To this end they, on the one hand, defined an international monetary system based on the stability of exchange rates and, on the other hand, envisaged the launch of negotiations with the aim of reducing tariff barriers and more generally eliminating obstacles to international trade.

In 1945 the USA promoted negotiations to reach a multilateral agreement for the constitution of an International Trade Organization (ITO), to be placed alongside the IMF and IBRD. Although for various reasons this plan failed, the goal of liberalizing trade was not abandoned. It found its concrete realization in the General Agreement

[105]See Gold (1969, vol. 2, p. 524).

[106]See Polak (1957), De Vries (1987) and Frenkel and Goldstein (1991).

[107]See Gold (1982, p. 156).

Table 5.7 Average tariff levels in selected countries (in percent)

	1913	1925	1931	1952
Belgium	6	7	17	na
France	14	9	38	19
Germany	12	15	40	16
Italy	17	16	48	24
Netherlands	2	4	na	na
United Kingdom	na	4	17	17
USA	32	26	na	16

Source: Irwin (1994)

on Tariff and Trade (GATT) signed by 23 countries[108] in Geneva in October 1947 and, following the Annecy negotiations of 1948, the member countries increased to 34. The GATT agreements and subsequent rounds led to a significant decrease in tariffs[109] (Table 5.7).

The stability guaranteed by the monetary system based on the Bretton Woods principles and the removal of tariff barriers favoured a marked expansion of trade and hence the world economy avoided falling into a phase of stagnation as had happened after the First World War. Between 1946 and 1957 world exports increased eightfold, while between 1918 and 1929 they had increased only threefold. The increase in trade was accompanied by a significant increase in world GDP (Fig. 5.3).

From Table 5.8 it appears that, in the period in which the Bretton Woods system was effectively in force, the growth of per capita GDP in the G7 was on average 4.5% per year, significantly higher than in the period between the two wars (1.2%) and in the period of the gold standard between 1881 and 1913 (1.5%). The higher growth of the G7 economies in the Bretton Woods years was accompanied by lower GDP volatility, the values of which are shown in parentheses in part 2 of the table.

We must ask ourselves whether it was the Bretton Woods system that favoured high growth and low volatility of output or whether it was the latter that favoured the stability of the monetary system established after World War II.[110] An indication in favour of the fact that it was the Bretton Woods system which encouraged reduced volatility of output is given by the lower volatility of money supply in this system than in the period between the wars (Part 3 of Table 5.8). In addition to this it is plausible that in the Bretton Woods system growth was less volatile than in the gold standard and in the interwar period due to the greater degrees of freedom left in that system to domestic economic policy.

[108]Australia, Belgium, Brazil, Burma, Canada, Ceylon, Chile, China, Cuba, Czechoslovakia, France, India, Lebanon, Luxembourg, the Netherlands, New Zealand, Norway, Pakistan, South Africa, Southern Rhodesia, Syria, the United Kingdom, the USA. With the Annecy negotiations of 1949, these first countries were joined by: Colombia, Denmark, Dominican Republic, Finland, Greece, Haiti, Italy, Liberia, Nicaragua, Sweden and Uruguay.

[109]See Irwin (1994).

[110]For a detailed examination of this aspect, see Eichengreen (1993).

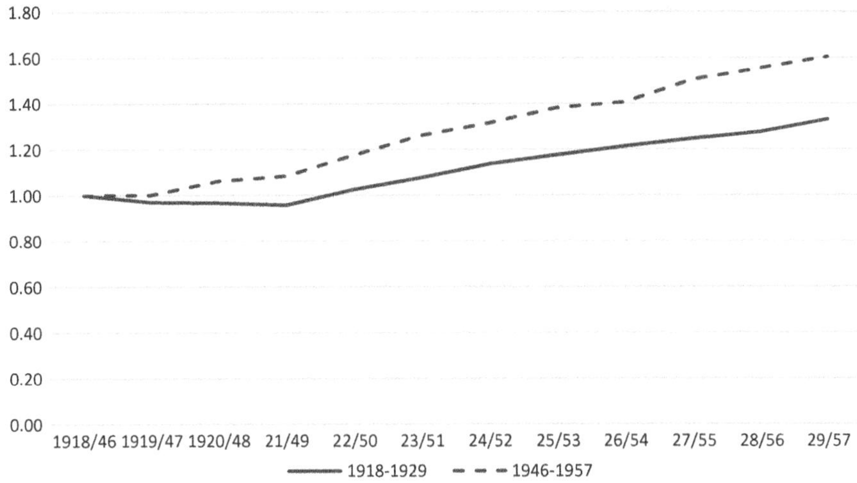

Fig. 5.3 GDP growth after World War I and II (in five advanced economies). Legenda: 1918 and 1946 = 1.00. List of countries: Germany, France, Japan, United Kingdom, the USA. Source: Maddison Project Database 2020

In addition to a lower volatility of output growth, the Bretton Woods years were characterized by a lower volatility of the inflation rate compared to the gold standard, the previous system based on fixed exchange rates. In the classical gold standard, the accumulation of gold reserves by some countries inevitably led to a worldwide shortage of money and therefore deflation. Under the Bretton Woods system, the accumulation of dollar reserves was predominantly through the holding of US Treasury securities. Therefore, there was no subtraction of money from world trade. Consequently, the volatility of money growth was lower.

5.11 The Collapse of the Bretton Woods System

On August 15, 1971, the President of the USA Richard Nixon announced on television a series of measures that were supposed to increase the country's competitiveness and economic growth. The most important of these measures was the temporary suspension of dollar convertibility.[111] With this decision Nixon put an end to the Bretton Woods monetary system.

Various explanations have been given for the end of the system; they can roughly be divided into two streams of thought: those strictly economic and those that also

[111]The other measures consisted of a 10% surcharge on imports and freezing prices and wages for 90 days.

Table 5.8 A comparison of the gold standard (1881–1913), the interwar period (1919–1938) and the Bretton Woods system (1959–1970)

	(1) Inflation			(2) Real per capita growth			(3) Money growth		
	1881–1913	1919–1938	1959–1970	1881–1913	1919–1938	1959–1970	1881–1913	1919–1938	1959–1970
Canada	0.4 (1.4)	−1.9 (6.0)	3.5 (1.1)	2.3 (2.8)	0.2 (8.8)	3.8 (1.1)	7.4 (5.3)	1.1 (4.7)	9.4 (4.3)
France	−0.0 (5.0)	−2.2 (9.1)	5.5 (3.6)	1.5 (4.6)	1.3 (7.2)	3.9 (1.3)	2.2 (3.5)	6.4 (8.5)	8.6 (6.6)
Germany	0.6 (2.6)	−2.1 (4.7)	3.2 (1.8)	1.7 (2.9)	2.6 (8.5)	3.6 (2.6)	5.7 (4.7)	1.3 (10.1)	10.9 (4.7)
Japan	4.6 (5.5)	−1.7 (7.3)	5.5 (1.0)	1.4 (3.8)	2.0 (6.1)	8.9 (2.4)	5.8 (10.8)	0.5 (9.7)	14.6 (2.5)
Italy	0.6 (3.2)	−1.1 (11.7)	3.8 (2.1)	1.0 (4.1)	0.8 (4.7)	5.8 (1.9)	3.2 (3.1)	3.6 (6.2)	12.4 (2.0)
UK	0.3 (3.1)	−1.5 (7.8)	3.4 (1.5)	1.1 (2.4)	1.2 (4.5)	2.3 (1.4)	2.1 (1.7)	0.8 (4.7)	5.5 (2.9)
United States	0.3 (3.1)	−1.8 (7.6)	2.6 (1.5)	1.8 (5.0)	0.2 (8.1)	2.9 (1.9)	6.1 (5.9)	0.6 (8.6)	7.0 (1.5)
Average	1.0 (3.4)	−1.1 (7.7)	3.9 (1.8)	1.5 (3.7)	1.2 (6.8)	4.5 (1.8)	4.6 (5.0)	2.0 (7.5)	9.8 (3.5)

The standard deviation of the variable in parentheses. Source: Bordo (1993)

take into account aspects of politics and are therefore to be considered political economy explanations.

5.11.1 *The Strictly Economic Explanations*

In the context of these explanations, a dominant one traces the collapse of the Bretton Woods system to the loss of confidence in the convertibility of the dollar, as predicted by the Triffin dilemma, because of the USA provided the amount of dollars required by the growth of trade, and consequently the cover ratio of the dollar declined, as the confidence in its convertibility.

Although tempting, the hypothesis of the loss of trust clashes with the fact that, as shown in Fig. 5.1, the USA gold reserves decreased gradually.

There was no run on American gold reserves nor was there a reduction in the amount of US dollars in circulation, a precondition for world deflation. As Triffin stated, "the decline in the US liquidity ratio would have led to large-scale conversions of dollars into gold by central banks. These conversions would, in fact, have induced a tendency to reduce existing liabilities in dollars".[112] By contrast the dollars

[112]Garber (1993) and De Grauwe (1989) have shown the drawbacks of this explanation.

in circulation worldwide increased. Added to this is the paradoxical fact that, after the suspension of convertibility, countries and individuals accumulated a quantity of dollars vastly higher than during the fixed exchange rate system.

A second economic explanation insists that the main reason for the breakdown of the fixed exchange rate system lies in the excessive growth of money supply in the USA in the late 1960s. This, it is argued, encouraged an acceleration of the domestic inflation rate, which, however, was transmitted to other advanced economies through capital flows.[113] This monetary policy stance, despite involving significant losses in gold reserves, did not appear to be corrected by the Federal Reserve. Cooper (1993) criticized this explanation by arguing that at that time, particularly in 1970, the difference between money growth and output growth in the USA was no greater than that which emerged in other recessions. Meltzer (2009), in turn, countered this objection arguing that, since the high growth of money supply in the late 1960s was associated with a persistent worsening of current accounts "... the rest of the world had ample reason to believe that exchange rate stability ranked far below higher employment as an administration objective, so inflationary policies would continue".[114] In a nutshell, there was a widespread perception that the leading country placed internal economic problems before the stability of the international monetary system[115] and under these conditions the Bretton Woods system could not survive.

A third explanation for the Bretton Woods collapse relates to the structural changes that had taken place in the international financial system. The development of the eurodollar market and the return to convertibility of the currencies of the major countries favoured a significant growth in the international mobility of capital, making the capital controls adopted by European countries gradually less effective.[116] Financial openness therefore undermined the monetary autonomy of these countries. In particular, the artificially low interest rates and credit rationing policy which many of them had resorted to in their economic planning risked losing its effectiveness.[117] In short, there was a violation of the so-called macroeconomic trilemma: the international mobility of capital had become incompatible with fixed exchange rates and the autonomy of monetary policy.[118]

---

[113]See Bordo (1993) and Darby et al. (1983).

[114]See Meltzer (2009, p. 756).

[115]See Meltzer (2009, p. 757).

[116]See Helleiner (1994).

[117]See Zysman (1983). In this context, an irremediable rift arose between, on the one hand, Britain and the USA, in favour of increasing financial openness, and the countries of continental Europe, which wanted an international agreement on capital controls. See Kloss (1972).

[118]See Mundell (1963) and Padoa-Schioppa (1982).

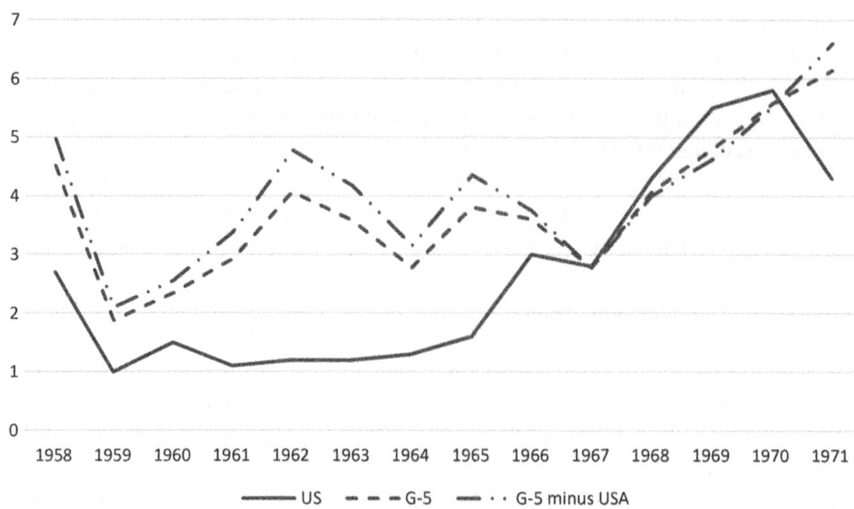

Fig. 5.4 Inflation in the USA, G-5 and G-5 without the USA. Source: OECD database

5.11.2 The Political Economy Explanations

It has already been highlighted that the US current account balance had deteriorated during the 1960s. This deterioration was due to the relative loss of competitiveness of American manufactured goods. This inevitably led to disputes between the USA and other countries over whether exchange rate adjustments should be made and how to implement these adjustments.

As we saw in the previous subsection, some economists argued that in the late 1960s the growth of the US money supply had been excessive. The acceleration of the inflation rate was then exported to the other advanced countries due to the flows of capital in a regime of fixed exchange rates. This was the viewpoint of the European countries who, therefore, asked for a correction of the US monetary policy stance or a devaluation of the dollar.

The American administration, on the other hand, argued, as shown by Fig. 5.4, that American inflation in the second half of the 1960s was similar to, if not lower than, the weighted one of the G-7 net of American inflation[119] and that the dynamics of inflation reflected that of money supply.

This evidence allowed the Americans to propose alternative explanations for the acceleration of inflation in European countries and Japan after 1965. A first argument was based on the Balassa and Samuelson theorem and referred to the different types of growth of the USA and that of Japan and the European countries. With the growth of the latter being driven by a *catching-up process*. Consequently, productivity in the

[119]Similar evidence was found when comparing American inflation with Japanese inflation. Compared to Germany, however, American inflation was higher starting from 1968.

tradable goods sector increased more pronouncedly in them than in the USA. In these countries, therefore, wages also increased in non-tradable sectors characterized by low productivity gains resulting in an increase in domestic inflation. This process, however, did not affect their competitiveness.

The second argument put forward by the Americans to explain the inflationary acceleration of Europe and Japan referred to the changes in domestic industrial relations resulting from the intense economic growth they had enjoyed. This growth had enabled them to reach full employment and to drain employment from the agricultural sector. This process had led to an increase in the bargaining power of workers, who in this way were able to achieve substantial wage increases. These increases were inevitably reflected in price dynamics.[120]

To these strictly economic arguments, the Americans added political arguments, reminding Europeans and Japanese that the US's high military spending and its, partial, financing through issuing dollars offered them a protective umbrella for their national security.

The discussion about responsibility for accelerating price growth led to contrasting conclusions about who should adjust the exchange rate parity.[121] European countries, primarily France and Germany, argued that it was up to the USA to devalue the dollar. The USA argued that it was up to Germany and Japan to correct large trade balance surpluses with a revaluation of their currencies.

The USA was unwilling to devalue the dollar, not only because it did not consider itself responsible for the inflationary acceleration in Europe and Japan, but also for at least three other reasons. First, devaluing the dollar against gold would have meant increasing the wealth of the main producers of this metal, namely South Africa and the USSR, the latter the principal enemy of the USA at that time. Secondly, a devaluation of the dollar would have punished the USA's closest allies, that is, the countries that held most of their reserves in dollars to support the exchange rate of the American currency. Thirdly, as argued in a report by a group of experts known as the *Volcker Group*, the dollar was the key currency of the Bretton Woods system and as such all other currencies were related to the dollar. Therefore, it was up to the other currencies to make parity adjustments.

The American position was strongly opposed by the European countries, in particular Germany, who on the one hand, exerted pressure on the IMF to induce the USA to change its economic policy and, on the other, urged the member countries of the European Economic Community to stand together and demand for this area a larger fluctuation in exchange rates than the 1% foreseen by the Bretton Woods Agreements.

The resulting stalemate can be explained in three ways. One explanation is that, starting in the late 1960s, both in the USA and in the other advanced countries, domestic policy goals were given precedence over those of a monetary policy aimed at preserving the public good of the Bretton Woods monetary system. Referring to

[120] See James (1996).

[121] See James (1996).

Olson (1982) it can be assumed that, especially in the defeated countries, at the end of WWII the power of certain interest groups to put pressure on the governments had been profoundly weakened. However, the rapid economic growth of the European countries and Japan in the 1950s and 1960s was associated with the re-emergence of these, now, powerful interest groups. Their pressure then made compliance with the rules of a fixed exchange rate regime politically more problematic, in particular as within the Bretton Woods system it had become difficult to adjust parities without political costs.

In such a context, the fixed exchange rate regime outlined in the 1944 Agreements was no longer sustainable. This aspect was pertinent not only to the European countries, but also to the USA where, according to some scholars,[122] awareness of the domestic economic and political situation was the main reason for Nixon's decision to suspend dollar convertibility.

The second explanation of the different views of US and European countries focuses on the evolution of the political power of the leading country in the international arena rather than on the evolution of the political priorities of the countries adhering to the system. According to the economic stability hypothesis, the survival of the Bretton Woods system depended on the ability of the USA to enforce compliance with the underlying agreements. They, as long as they had a high level of power at the international level, acted in such a way that the ambiguities of the Bretton Woods Agreements could be overcome, imposing on the other countries to behave in a cooperative way.[123] However, as the USA's position weakened in comparative terms, it was no longer able to perform this function.[124]

Faced with this new context, the European countries and Japan placed the protection of their interests ahead of that of the international public good and made proposals for the solution of the problems congruent with this priority.

A third explanation focuses on the tensions between US domestic and international goals.[125] These tensions primarily concerned relations between the USA and the European countries, not only regarding the method for reviewing exchange rates, but also on the division of the military spending in defence of Europe. These expenses, in fact, according to the Americans were one of the causes of their trade deficit. For the USA, the costs of being the fulcrum of the Bretton Woods system were not limited, however, to the accumulation of external deficits and a narrowing of margins in the conduct of domestic economic policy. They were also linked to the share of American economy in world economy, and to the economic structure of the US economy. In fact, following the loss of competitiveness of its exports, in the 1950s and 1960s, the share of the American manufacturing industry in the total output of the main countries had fallen significantly (Table 5.9).

[122]See Gowa (1983) and Odell (1982).

[123]See Best (2005).

[124]See Block (1977), Gilpin (1987) and Keohane and Nye (1977).

[125]See Bergsten (1975) and Calleo (1982).

Table 5.9 Shares of total manufacturing output of the main industrial countries (percentage values)

	1950	1955	1960	1965	1970	1975
USA	61.9	58.1	50.5	50.1	43.6	42.5
Canada	3.5	3.4	3.3	3.5	3.4	3.7
Japan	2.1	3.5	6.3	8.0	13.1	13.2
Denmark	0.7	0.5	0.6	0.6	0.7	0.7
France	7.6	7.1	8.1	8.1	8.9	9.8
Germany	10.1	14.1	17.2	16.7	17.2	16.5
Italy	2.2	2.5	3.1	3.1	3.7	4.3
Netherlands	1.8	1.9	2.2	2.1	2.3	2.3
Sweden	2.0	1.7	1.9	1.9	1.9	2.0
UK	8.2	7.2	6.9	5.9	5.3	4.9

Source: Branson (1980)

The decline of the manufacturing industry had already manifested itself in the 1950s, even when American monetary policy was absolutely virtuous, but nonetheless was tolerable in the most acute phase of confrontation with the USSR, when Europe was facing the dramatic problems of reconstruction and its levels of poverty might expose it to the risk of communist takeover.

It was no longer tolerable when Europe and Japan were now presenting themselves as world economic powers and their per capita income level was not far from the American one. By suspending the convertibility of the dollar, and effectively bringing about the end of the Bretton Woods system, the USA, aware that a hegemonic power could not give up a strong manufacturing industry, would be able, if not arrest, at least slow down its industrial decline. They, therefore chose to "... throw off the regime's constraints on the exercise of American economic power to influence international monetary politics"[126] by suspending the convertibility of the dollar.

The various political economy hypotheses just illustrated, ultimately, propose different reasons for the fact that the costs of exercising leadership in the Bretton Woods system had become excessively high for the USA. Hence, as we will see in the next chapter, their lack of enthusiasm for re-establishing a system of fixed exchange rates, albeit adjustable, as advocated by European countries.

5.12 Conclusions

The Bretton Woods System, although it only partially reflects the international monetary system outlined in the Bretton Woods Agreements, reflects its underlying objectives. These objectives can be summarized in the promotion of international trade and in the possibility for member countries to manage their domestic economic policy with significant margins of discretion.

[126] See Keohane and Nye (1977, p. 140).

The unique nature of the Bretton Woods system compared to previous international monetary systems, such as the gold standard and the gold-exchange standard, was that it amounts to an agreement between states and that its operation is ensured by rules and institutions established on the basis of this mutual agreement.

This was in contrast to both the gold standard and the gold-exchange standard neither of which were supported by a specific institutional architecture and individual countries adopted them unilaterally, declaring their currency convertible.

The interpretations of the Bretton Woods system are in fact explanations of how the participating states arrived at the Agreements that are its basis. According to the neo-realists, this system is the result of a coercive act exercised by the hegemonic country, the USA, on countries subject to its political influence, its creation was, therefore, for the exclusive interest of the hegemon. Other scholars, on the other hand, have traced the Bretton Woods Agreements and the system based on them to the prevailing cultural climate in the immediate post-war period. In particular, the emergence of the Keynesian approach and, more generally, the desirability of an embedded liberalism had constituted the common ground between the experts and politicians coming from different countries, but in particular from the USA and England, and who formed part of the Bretton Woods negotiations even more so in their preparatory phase.

Finally, liberal neo-realists have traced the Bretton Woods Agreements, and the monetary system that emerged from them, to a cooperative agreement between states. This Agreement allowed for what has been called a "legalisation of monetary affairs".

Chapter 2 explained why cooperation between states, even in the monetary sphere, is problematic. This is especially true in the case of a quasi-flat currency such as the dollar in the Bretton Woods system. In this system, in fact, the key currency—the dollar—was anchored to gold, but the degree of gold coverage of that currency was not predefined. The same was true for currencies convertible into the key currency. This made it possible to significantly increase the elasticity of international liquidity supply.

At the same time, however, two problems arose. The first concerned how confidence in the stability of the value of the key currency and the monetary system based on it would be safeguarded. The second problem concerned the privilege of international seigniorage and who would enjoy it.

These two problems were settled through a political agreement between the lead country and the follower countries, from which the two sides derived partly overlapping and partly different net benefits. The lead country, for its part, bore the costs of ensuring the stability of the value of its currency and of the monetary system as a whole. In return for these costs, it has been able to exploit the right of international seigniorage, establishing the dominance of the dollar in real and financial exchanges. The follower countries, on the one hand, accepted that the USA could exploit international seigniorage, believing that the relative asymmetric gains from it would not alter the balance of power between them and the leading country, and on the other hand, benefited from the fixed exchange rate regime and the existence of an international currency, being able to expand their exports and enjoy high growth rates in their domestic income as well as the protective umbrella of the USA.

Over time, the different dynamics of inflation and productivity made the Bretton Woods system less attractive for the countries who had agreed to the political agreement on which the Bretton Woods system was founded. European countries, primarily France and Germany, complained that in the second half of the 1960s American monetary policy had become excessively lax, spreading inflation in Europe and undermining confidence in the dollar's convertibility, as had been predicted by Triffin. The USA countered these accusations, arguing that the acceleration of inflation in Europe in the late 1960s stemmed from domestic wage dynamics and that the exchange parity of certain currencies, primarily that of the German mark, should be revised upwards in order to correct the competitive advantage of these countries in the international market. As a result of the real appreciation of the dollar and its lower productivity growth, the USA suffered a pronounced reduction in its manufacturing industry, leading the USA to want to regain its discretionary leeway in the conduct of monetary policy for domestic reasons, not least the goal of re-electing the incumbent president. It is presumable, however, that the US administration may also have been concerned that their economic downsizing would be associated with a geopolitical decline of the USA. For this country, in the conditions that had arisen, letting the dollar continue to act as the system's N^{th} currency had become too expensive.

From this perspective, Nixon's decision to suspend the convertibility of the dollar adopted on August 15, 1971 does seem clearly rooted in domestic objectives, in particular the upcoming elections, but also for strategic reasons. Since the preconditions for the political exchange that had been the basis of the Bretton Woods Agreement had disappeared, the system collapsed.

The collapse of this system did not, however, mean abandoning the underlying objectives of those Agreements. In the first place, if, as stated in Art. 1 of the Agreement of International Monetary Fund, the objective of that system was to promote free trade and the financing of imbalances, we can say that it continued working in later years and, indeed, is still working today.[127] Secondly, the idea that the international monetary system is a public good and that its production, in the case of a fiat money, can be achieved through the legalization of international monetary affairs is still a view shared by the international community.[128] As Dornbusch (1993, p. 100) writes: "It represents a set of rules that are implicitly or explicitly accepted and followed, and this in return creates a presumption of stability on trade and payments relations". Thirdly, the legalization of international monetary affairs has proved to be a flexible instrument. In fact, it has been able, through incremental changes to cope with shocks by making possible monetary reforms aimed at improving the stability of the system.[129] In this context, innovations have been

---

[127] See Dornbusch (1993).

[128] See Simmons (2000).

[129] See Chwieroth (2009), Pauly (2008) and Fioretos and Heldt (2019).

possible, such as the regional monetary agreements, including, the European Monetary System (EMS) and the European Monetary Union (EMU).

References

Asher, R. E., & Mason, E. S. (1973). *The World Bank since Bretton woods*. Brookings Institution.

Bergsten, C. F. (1975). *The dilemmas of the dollar: The economics and politics of United States international monetary policy*. New York University Press.

Best, J. (2005). *The limits of transparency*. Cornell University Press.

Bird, G. (1998). The political economy of the SDR: The rise and fall of an international reserve asset. *Global Governance, 4*, 355–379.

Block, F. (1977). *The origins of international economic disorder. A study of United States international monetary policy from World War II to present*. University of California Press.

Bordo, M. (1993). The Bretton Woods international monetary system: A historical overview. In M. Bordo & B. Eichengreen (Eds.), *A retrospective on the Bretton Woods system*. University of Chicago Press.

Bordo, M. (2017). *The operation and demise of the Bretton Woods system: 1958 to 1971*. NBER working paper n. 23189.

Bordo, M., & James, H. (2012). Reserves and baskets. *Open Economies Review, 23*, 113–127.

Bordo, M., Humpage, O. F., & Schwartz, A. J. (2012). *Bretton Woods, swap lines, and the Federal Reserve's return to intervention*. Federal Reserve Bank of Cleveland working paper n. 12–32.

Bordo, M., Humpage, O. F., & Schwartz, A. (2014). *The evolution of the Federal Reserve swap lines since 1962*. NBER working paper n. 20755.

Bordo, M., Monnet, E., & Naef, A. (2019). The Gold Pool (1961-1968) and the fall of the Bretton Woods system: Lessons for central bank cooperation. *Journal of Economic History, 79*, 1027–1059.

Boughton, J. M. (2002). *Why White, not Keynes? Inventing the postwar international monetary system*. IMF working paper n. WP/02/52.

Branson, W. H. (1980). *Trends in U.S. international trade and investment since World War II*. NBER working paper n. 0469.

Brett, E. (1985). *The world economy since the war*. Blackwell.

Burn, G. (1999). The state, the City and the Euromarkets. *Review of International Political Economy, 6*, 225–261.

Burnham, P. (1992). Re-evaluating the Washington loan agreement: A revisionist view of the limits of post-war American power. *Review of International Studies, 18*, 241–259.

Cairncross, A., & Eichengreen, B. (1983). *Sterling in decline: The devaluations of 1931, 1949 and 1967*. Basil Blackwell.

Calleo, D. P. (1982). *The imperious economy*. Harvard University Press.

Cesarano, F. (2006). *Monetary theory and Bretton Woods*. Cambridge University Press.

Chwieroth, J. M. (2009). *Capital ideas: The IMF and the rise of financial liberalization*. Princeton University Press.

Cohen, B. (2008). The international monetary system: Diffusion and ambiguity. *International Affairs, 84*, 455–470.

Cohen, B. (2012). The benefits and costs of an international currency: Getting the calculus right. *Open Economies Review, 23*, 13–31.

Cohen, B. (2013). Currency and state power. In M. Finnemore & J. Goldstein (Eds.), *Back to the basics: State power in a contemporary world*. Oxford University Press.

Cooper, R. (1993). Comment. In M. Bordo & B. Eichengreen (Eds.), *A retrospective on the Bretton Woods system*. University of Chicago Press.

Dam, K. (1982). *The rules of the game: Reform and evolution in the international monetary system.* University of Chicago Press.
Darby, M., Lothian, J., Gandolfi, A., Schwartz, A., & Stockman, A. (1983). *The international transmission of inflation*. University of Chicago Press.
De Cecco, M. (1987). Inflation and the structural change in the Eurodollar market. In M. De Cecco & J. P. Fitoussi (Eds.), *Monetary theory and economic institutions*. Macmillan.
De Grauwe, P. (1989). *International money*. Oxford University Press.
De Long, J., & Eichengreen, B. (1991). *The Marshall plan: History's most successful structural adjustment program*. NBER working paper n. 3899.
De Vries, M. G. (1976). *The international monetary fund 1966–1971: The system under stress*. IMF.
De Vries, M. G. (1987). *Balance of payments adjustment, 1945–1986: The IMF experience*. IMF.
Dell, S. (1981). *On being grandmotherly: The evolution of IMF conditionality*. Essays in International Finance, n. 144. International Finance Section. Princeton University.
von Dormael, A. (1978). *Bretton Woods: Birth of a monetary system*. Palgrave Macmillan.
von Dormael, A. (1997). *The power of money*. Macmillan.
Dornbusch, R. (1993). Comment on Bordo M, The Bretton Woods international monetary system: A historical overview. In M. Bordo & B. Eichengreeen (Eds.), *A retrospective on the Bretton Woods system*. University of Chicago Press.
Eichengreen, B. (1982). The Bank of France and the sterilization of gold, 1926–1932. *Explorations in Economic History, 19*, 71–100.
Eichengreen, B. (1993). Epilogue: Three perspectives on the Bretton Woods system. In M. Bordo & B. Eichengreen (Eds.), *A retrospective on the Bretton Woods system: Lessons for international monetary reform*. Chicago University Press.
Eichengreen, B. (2010). *Global imbalances and the lessons of Bretton Woods*. MIT.
Eichengreen, B. (2011). *Exorbitant privilege: The rise and fall of the dollar and the future of the international monetary system*. Oxford University Press.
Eichengreen, B. (2019). *Globalizing capital*. Princeton University Press.
Einzig, P. (1968). *Leads and lags. The main cause of devaluation*. Macmillan.
Finger, J. M. (1979). Trade liberalization: A public choice perspective. In R. C. Amacher, G. Haberler, & T. D. Willett (Eds.), *Challenges to a liberal international economic order*. American Enterprise Institute.
Flanders, M. (1990). *International monetary economics, 1870–1960*. Cambridge University Press.
Frenkel, J. A., & Goldstein, M. (1991). Monetary policy in an emerging European economic and monetary union – Key issues. *IMF Staff Paper, 38*, 356–373.
Frieden, J. (1987). *Banking on the world: The politics of American international finance*. Harper & Row.
Friedman, M. (1953). The case for flexible exchange rates. In M. Friedman (Ed.), *Essays in positive economics*. University of Chicago Press.
Garber, P. M. (1993). The collapse of the Bretton Woods fixed exchange rate system. In M. Bordo & B. Eichengreen (Eds.), *A retrospective on the Bretton Woods system: Lessons for international monetary reform*. Chicago University Press.
Gardner, R. (1956). *Sterling-dollar diplomacy*. Clarendon.
Gavin, F. J. (2007). *Gold, dollars, and power: The politics of international monetary relations, 1958–1971*. The University of North Carolina Press.
Gilbert, M. (1985). The gold-dollar system: Conditions of equilibrium and the price of gold. In B. Eichengreen (Ed.), *The gold standard in theory and history*. Methuen.
Gilpin, R. (1987). *The political economy of international relations*. Princeton University Press.
Gilpin, R. (2002). The rise of American hegemony. In P. O'Brien & A. Clesse (Eds.), *Two hegemonies: Britain 1846–1914 and the United States 1941–2001*. Ashgate.
Gold, J. (1969). Use of the Fund's resources. In J. K. Horsefield (Ed.), *The international Monetary Fund* (pp. 1945–1965). IMF.
Gold, J. (1977). *Voting majorities in the fund: Effects of second amendment of the articles*. IMF.

Gold, J. (1982). *Developments in the international monetary system*. The International Monetary Fund, and international monetary law since 1971. Receuil des Courses, n. 107.
Gowa, J. (1983). *Closing the gold window: Domestic politics and the end of Bretton Woods*. Cornell University Press.
Graham, F. D., & Whittlesey, C. R. (1934). Fluctuating exchange rates, foreign trade, and the price level. *American Economic Review, 24*, 401–416.
Green, T. (1999). *Central bank gold reserves*. World Gold Council Research Study n. 23.
Harrod, R. (1951). *The life of John Maynard Keynes*. Macmillan.
Harvey, R. (2013). Market status/status markets: The London gold fixing in the Bretton Woods era. In S. Bott (Ed.), *The global gold market and the international monetary system from the late 19th century to the present: Actors, networks, power*. Palgrave Macmillan.
Hayek, F. (1937). *Monetary nationalism and international stability*. Longman.
Helleiner, E. (1994). *States and the reemergence of global finance: From Bretton Woods to the 1990s*. Cornell university Press.
Horsefield, J. K. (1969). *The International Monetary Fund, 1945–1965: Twenty years of international monetary cooperation*. IMF.
Ikenberry, G. J. (1993). The political origins of Bretton Woods. In M. Bordo & B. Eichengreen (Eds.), *A retrospective on the Bretton Woods system: Lessons for international monetary reform*. University of Chicago Press.
Irwin, D. (1994). *The GATT's contribution to economic recovery in postwar Western Europe*. NBER working paper n. 4944.
Irwin, D. (2017). *The missing Bretton Woods debate over flexible exchange rates*. NBER working paper n. 23037.
James, H. (1990). Enduring international preeminence of dollar. In E. Helleiner & J. Kirshner (Eds.), *The future of dollar*. Cornell University Press.
James, H. (1996). *International monetary cooperation since Bretton Woods*. Oxford University Press.
James, H. (2012). The multiple context of Bretton Woods. *Oxford Review of Economic Policy, 28*, 411–430.
Johnson, H. (1972). The Bretton Woods system, key currencies and the dollar crisis of 1971. *Three Banks Review, 94*, 3–22.
Kaplan, J., & Schleimnger, G. (1989). *The European Payments Union: Financial diplomacy in the 1950s*. Clarendon.
Kapur, D., Lewis, J., & Webb, R. (1997). *The World Bank: Its first half century* (Vol. I). Brookings Institution.
Keohane, R. O. (1984). *After hegemony: Cooperation and discord in the world political economy*. Princeton University Press.
Keohane, R. O., & Nye, J. (1977). *Power and interdependence*. Little Brown.
Keynes, J. M. (1923). A tract on monetary reform. In D. Moggridge (Ed.), *The collected writings of John Maynard Keynes* (Vol. 4). Macmillan. (1971).
Keynes, J. M. (1942). Proposals for an international currency (or clearing) union (Reprinted in 1969, in J. K. Horsefield, *The International Monetary Fund, 1945–1965* (Vol. III: Documents). IMF).
Keynes, J. M. (1943). Proposals for an international clearing union (Reprinted in 1969 in J. K. Horsefield, *The International Monetary Fund* (Vol. III: Documents). IMF).
Kirshner, J. (1995). *Currency and coercion: The political economy of international monetary power*. Princeton University Press.
Kissinger, H. (1994). *Diplomacy*. Simon & Schuster.
Kloss, H. (1972). Monetary policy and liberalization of capital markets. In W. Schmitz (Ed.), *Convertibility, multilateralism, and freedom: World economic policy in the seventies*. Springer.
Krugman, P. (1984). The international role of the dollar: Theory and prospect. In J. F. O. Bilson & R. C. Marston (Eds.), *Exchange rate theory and practice*. University of Chicago Press.
Lacouture, J. (1992). *De Gaulle: The ruler 1945–1970*. Norton.

Lipietz, A. (1987). *Mirages and miracles*. Editions La Decouverte.
Lister, F. (1984). *Decision-making strategies for international organizations: The IMF model*. Graduate School of International Studies, University of Denver.
Llewellyn, D. (1992). Financial innovation: A basic analysis. In A. Cavanna (Ed.), *Financial innovation*. Routledge.
Machlup, F. (1966). The need for monetary reserves. *PSL Quarterly Review, 61*, 818–832.
Martinez-Oliva, J., & Stefani, M. (2001). *Dal Piano Marshall all'Unione europea dei pagamenti. Alle origini dell'integrazione economica europea*. In F. Cotula (Ed.), *Stabilità e sviluppo negli anni Cinquanta. L'Italia nel contesto internazionale*. Ricerche per la Storia della Banca d'Italia, Laterza.
Mastanduno, M. (2009). System maker and privilege taker: US power and the international political economy. *World Politics, 61*, 121–154.
McKinnon, R. (1993). The rules of the game: International money in historical perspective. *Journal of Economic Literature, 31*, 1–44.
McKinnon, R. (2013). *The unloved dollar standard*. Oxford University Press.
Meltzer, A. (1991). US polity in the Bretton Woods era. *Federal Reserve Bank of St. Louis Review, 73*, 54–83.
Meltzer, A. (2009). *A history of the federal reserve, Vol. II, 1970-1986*. University of Chicago Press.
Menger, K. (1892). On the origin of money. *Economic Journal, 2*, 239–255.
Milward, A. (1984). *The reconstruction of Western Europe 1945–51*. Routledge.
Monnet, E., & Puy, D. (2019). *Do old habits die hard? Central bank and the Bretton Woods gold puzzle*. IMF working paper n. WP/19/161.
Morelli, P., & Seghezza, E. (2020). Was a sudden stop at the origin of German hyperinflation? *Financial History Review, 27*, 161–186.
Mundell, R. (1963). Capital mobility and stabilization policy under fixed and flexible exchange rates. *Canadian Journal of Economics and Political Science, 29*, 475–485.
Mundell, R. (1968). The redundancy problem and the world price level. In R. Mundell (Ed.), *International economics*. Macmillan.
Mundell, R. (1969). The International Monetary Fund. *Journal of World Trade Law, 3*, 455–497.
Mundell, R. (2003). *The international monetary system and the case for a world currency*. Leon Kozminski Academy of Entrepreneurship and Management (WSPiZ) and TIGER Distinguished Lectures Series n. 12. Warsaw, October 23.
Newton, C. C. S. (1984). The sterling crisis of 1947 and the British response to the Marshall plan. *Economic History Review, 37*, 391–408.
Nurkse, R. (1944). *International currency experience*. League of Nations.
O'Rourke, L. (2018). *Covert regime change*. Cornell University Press.
Odell, J. (1982). *International monetary policy: Markets, power and ideas as sources of change*. Princeton University Press.
Odell, J. (1993). Comment. In M. Bordo & B. Eichengreen (Eds.), *A retrospective on the Bretton Woods system: Lessons for international monetary reform*. University of Chicago Press.
Olson, M. (1982). *The rise and decline of nations: Economic growth, stagflation and social rigidities*. Yale University Press.
Padoa-Schioppa, T. (1982). Capital mobility: Why is the treaty not implemented? In T. Padoa-Schioppa (Ed.), *The road to monetary union in Europe*. Clarendon.
Pauly, L. W. (2008). The institutional legacy of Bretton Woods: IMF surveillance. In D. Andrews (Ed.), *Orderly change: International monetary relations since Bretton Woods* (pp. 1973–2007). Cornell University Press.
Polak, J. J. (1957). Monetary analysis of income formation and payment problems. *IMF Staff Papers, 6*, 1–50.
Robbins, L. (1937). *Economic planning and international order*. Macmillan.
Ruggie, J. (1982). International regimes, transactions, and change: Embedded liberalism in the postwar economic order. *International Organization, 36*, 379–415.

Schenk, C. (1998). The origins of the eurodollar market in London: 1955–1963. *Explorations in Economic History, 35*, 221–238.
Schenk, C. (2002). Sterling, international monetary reform and Britain's application to the EEC in the 1960s. *Contemporary European History, 11*, 345–359.
Schenk, C. (2010). *The decline of sterling. Managing the retreat of an international currency, 1945 to 1992*. Cambridge University Press.
Schenk, C. (2013). The global gold market and the international monetary system. In S. Bott (Ed.), *The global gold market and the international monetary system from the late 19th century to the present: Actors, networks, power*. Palgrave Macmillan.
Seghezza, E. (2018). *L'evoluzione del sistema monetario internazionale. Il ruolo della domanda di innovazioni e della produzione di fiducia*. Soveria Mannelli.
Shepsle, K. (1985). Comment of why the regulators chose to deregulate. In R. Noll (Ed.), *Regulatory policy and the social sciences*. University of California Press.
Silber, W. L. (1983). The process of financial innovation. *American Economic Review Papers and Proceedings, 73*, 89–94.
Simmons, B. A. (2000). The legalization of international monetary affairs. *International Organization, 54*, 573–602.
Skidelsky, R. (2003). *John Maynard Keynes, 1883-1946. Economist, philosopher, statesman*. Macmillan.
Steil, B. (2013). *The battle of Bretton Woods*. Princeton University Press.
Stein, H. (1969). *The fiscal revolution in America*. University of Chicago Press.
Strange, S. (1971). *Sterling and British policy: A political study of an international currency in decline*. Oxford University Press.
Strange, S. (1976). International monetary relations. In A. Shonfield (Ed.), *International economic relations of the Western world* (pp. 1959–1971). Oxford University Press.
Tomlinson, J. (1990). *Public policy and the economy since 1900*. Clarendon.
Toniolo, G., & Clement, P. (2005). *Central Bank Cooperation at the Bank for International Settlements, 1930–1973*. Cambridge University Press.
Triffin, R. (1947). National central banking and the international economy. *Postwar Economic Studies, 7*, 46–81.
Triffin, R. (1957). *Europe and the money muddle*. Yale University Press.
Triffin, R. (1960). *Gold and the dollar crisis: The future of convertibility*. Yale University Press.
Whitman, M. V. N., Cooper, R. N., & Solomon, R. (1974). The current and future role of the dollar: How much symmetry? *Brookings Papers on Economic Activity, 3*, 539–591.
Williams, J. H. (1936). The adequacy of existing currency mechanisms under varying circumstances. *American Economic Review, 27*, 151–168.
Williams, J. H. (1943). Currency stabilization: The Keynes and White plans. In J. K. Horsefield (Ed.), *The International Monetary Fund* (pp. 1945–1965). IMF.
Williamson, J. (2009). *Understanding special drawing rights (SDRs)*. Peterson Institute for International Economics, Policy Brief: P809-11.
Woods. (2006). *The globalizers: The IMF, the World Bank and their borrowers*. Cornell University Press.
Wriston, W. (1988). Technology and sovereignty. *Foreign Affairs, 67*, 63–75.
Zysman, J. (1983). *Government, markets, and growth: Financial systems and politics of industrial change*. Cornell University Press.

Chapter 6
The Dollar Standard

6.1 Introduction

In August 1971, without informing either the partner countries nor the IMF in advance, President Nixon suspended convertibility of the US dollar, marking the end of the Bretton Woods system. Initially, the European countries were relieved at the news of the suspension of dollar convertibility, believing that this decision would lead to negotiations on a redefinition of new parities and thus to the restoration of the Bretton Woods system of fixed exchange rates on a new basis.

Nixon's objectives were to regain margins of flexibility in the conduct of US domestic economic policy and, at the same time, safeguard American manufacturing, and through this the economic power of the USA. These objectives could only be achieved by a significant devaluation of the dollar and a rebalancing of external accounts.

Subsequent attempts to return, to some form of fixed exchange rate system proved futile. In particular, the revision of exchange rate parities agreed by the G-10[1] at the Smithsonian Institute in December 1971 and the simultaneous establishment of an exchange rate band did not survive the speculative attacks of the following months.

As previously mentioned, with the collapse of the Bretton Woods system, the objectives of the 1944 Agreements, namely the pursuit of foreign trade development and the simultaneous preservation of domestic monetary autonomy did not fail.[2] From this perspective, Andrews (2006, p. 10) writes: "The breakdown of the Bretton Woods system and the shift to flexible exchange rates did not result in reversion to these prewar practices; far from it. Instead, this change in monetary regime simply provided a different means for realizing the continuing commitments of the Bretton Woods order".

---

[1]Belgium, Canada, France, Germany, Italy, Japan, the Netherlands, Sweden, Switzerland, the United Kingdom and the USA.

[2]See, in particular Dornbusch (1993a).

G. B. Pittaluga, E. Seghezza, *Building Trust in the International Monetary System*, Frontiers in Economic History, https://doi.org/10.1007/978-3-030-78491-1_6

In contrast to this view, other scholars, such as Helleiner (1994) and Best (2005), have argued that the collapse of Bretton Woods entailed a change of objectives and the end of the ideology underlying the Bretton Woods system, namely embedded liberalism. They argue that this was the result of an ideological change in the American administration. In fact, unlike previous administrations, "during the Nixon and Ford administrations, the making of international financial policy was largely influenced by advocates of neo-liberal thought".[3]

There is no doubt that ideological factors influenced the US administration's decision to suspend the convertibility of the dollar and abandon the fixed exchange rate system. However, it is also true that, despite the neo-liberal policies by Margaret Thatcher in England and Ronald Reagan in the USA, it cannot be said that in the advanced countries, primarily in Europe, the principles of embedded liberalism were abandoned. With the end of the fixed exchange rate regime and the definitive abandonment of an anchor, the international monetary system became a system based exclusively on fiat money. In this context, governments' discretion in managing monetary policy expanded significantly. The result in the 1970s was a high degree of monetary disorder, characterized by excessive monetary expansion and high exchange rate volatility. The stability of the international monetary system was recovered through institutional reforms and changes in the conduct of individual countries' monetary policy. These reforms and changes led to a reduction in domestic inflation rates and, consequently, to a drastic reduction in exchange rate volatility.

At the same time, the increase in international trade, technological innovations and the liberalization of capital movements led to a growing financial interdependence of the various economies. As a result, currency and financial crises, especially in emerging countries, became more frequent. They mainly affected countries that had adopted exchange rate pegging. This led to a polarization towards the extremes in exchange rate arrangements. Many countries, especially emerging and developing countries, abandoned pegging choosing to adopt flexible or managed floating exchange rates. In other cases, as in Europe, monetary integration began, with the adoption of a single country.

6.2 The Failure of Attempts to Restore a System of Fixed Exchange Rates: 1971–1974

After the announcement of the suspension of the convertibility of the dollar, Nixon sent the Secretary of the Treasury, Connally, and the Under Secretary of the Treasury, Volcker, to the capitals of the major countries of the world to convince their leaders of the need for an adjustment of their parities.[4]

[3]See Helleiner (1994, p. 115).

[4]See Volcker and Gyohten (1992).

Table 6.1 Bretton Woods System and Smithsonian Agreements

Bretton Woods system	Smithsonian Agreements
The dollar was linked to gold. Its value was 35 dollars per ounce of gold The dollar was convertible into gold	The dollar was linked to gold. Its value was $38 per ounce of gold The dollar was not convertible into gold
Each member of the system set the parity of its currency against the dollar	Each member of the system set the parity of its currency against the dollar
Exchange rates could fluctuate by 1% above and below parity	Exchange rates could fluctuate 2.25% above and below parity
The central bank of each country had to intervene to ensure that the fluctuation bands were respected	The central bank of each country had to intervene to ensure that the fluctuation bands were respected

At a meeting in November 1971, French President Pompidou reiterated to Nixon that it was appropriate for the USA to devalue its currency and, at a meeting on 11 December of the major countries at the Smithsonian Institute in Washington, D.C., a compromise was reached whereby the dollar was devalued by 8.5% (raising the price of gold from $35 to $38), European currencies were revalued by the same amount and the Japanese yen by 16.9%.[5] Moreover, it was decided that the band of fluctuation around the new parities should be 2.25% and not, as in the Bretton Woods System, 1% (Table 6.1).

The signatories to the Smithsonian Agreement considered it to be a temporary measure. In April 1972, in order to safeguard the Common Agricultural Policy (CAP) a number of European countries,[6] with the aim of limiting the exchange rate fluctuations of their currencies, made an agreement, known as the *snake*. According to the agreement, the exchange rates of the participating countries were to be kept within a 2.25% spread and could move jointly within the 4.5% band established by the Smithsonian Agreement. This band was called the *tunnel*, the agreement between the European countries became known as *snake in the tunnel*.

In the Smithsonian agreement, two points were established that clearly represented a break with the past[7]:

(a) It was recognized that the US current account deficit was a problem for the international monetary system. This implied the need to find alternative international liquidity instruments to the dollar;
(b) The USA would henceforth pursue its own balance of payments objectives. In this way, it would abandon its role as the Nth country and regain a degree of freedom in managing its domestic economic policy.

The Smithsonian agreement demonstrates that none of the parties involved—that is the authorities in the USA, those in the G10 and the remaining European countries,

[5]See Bordo (2018).

[6]West Germany, France, Italy, Netherlands, Belgium, Luxembourg.

[7]See Whitman et al. (1974).

the senior officials of international institutions such as the IMF and the IDB—saw Nixon's decision to suspend convertibility as the definitive end of an international monetary system based on fixed exchange rates. There was a prevailing desire in all advanced countries for reform that would re-establish, albeit on a new basis, a system of fixed exchange rates similar to that which had just collapsed.

Further confirmation of this comes from the fact that within the Smithsonian Agreement the G-10 declared that the reform should identify the appropriate monetary means and define the division of responsibilities "... for [1] defending stable exchange rates and for [2] insuring a proper degree of convertibility of the system; [3] to the proper role of gold, reserve currencies, and of the Special Drawing Rights in the operation of the system; [4] to the appropriate volume of liquidity; [5] to the re-examination of the permissible margins of fluctuation around established exchange rates and other means of establishing a suitable degree of flexibility; and [6] other measures of dealing with movements of liquid capital".[8]

In the meetings prior to the start of the reform discussions, the first point of negotiation was the question of the composition of the committee responsible for drafting the international monetary system reform proposal. The management of the IMF and the countries that were part of the IMF's executive board, but not part of the G-10, made a strong case for inclusion in the reform discussions. The USA supported this request in the belief that the involvement of a larger number of players would weaken the European/G-10 front.

At the beginning of 1972, the Governors of the IMF established the Committee of Twenty (C-20), composed of the 20 members of its Executive board.[9] In September of that year, the new US Treasury Secretary, George P. Shultz, presented a proposal at the IMF Annual Meeting proposing to correct the imbalances through the establishment of a quasi-flexible exchange rate system.[10] This was consistent with Shultz's background as a student of Friedman, who favoured a monetary system based on flexible exchange rates.[11]

The US proposal stressed the need for symmetry in the solution of imbalances,[12] proposing that the contribution of surplus and deficit countries to the adjustment processes should be symmetrical. The US position on this point was the opposite to that which it had held during the Bretton Woods negotiations. It also reaffirmed the

[8]See Solomon (1982, p. 209).

[9]At the same time, all member countries were allowed to participate in the discussion. See Truman (2017).

[10]See Shultz (1972).

[11]See Friedman (1951). This position contrasted with that of Fed Chairman Burns, who was in favour of re-establishing fixed exchange rates. There were therefore different positions within the US administration on the type of international monetary system that should be established.

[12]The effectiveness of the adjustment mechanisms should have been ensured, in addition to symmetry, by the so-called reserve indicator mechanism. This indicator, by signalling disproportionate gains or losses in reserves, would have signalled the need for adjustment. For a discussion of this point see Schenk (2017).

oil-importing countries. This deterioration implied a decrease or slowdown in income growth in these countries. In many cases, this led to social conflict in which interest groups tended to pass on the costs of the deteriorating terms of trade to others. High inflation favoured forms of income redistribution between the various interest groups, so that the consequences of the deterioration in the terms of trade were passed on to the politically weaker groups.[23]

Attempts to resist pressure from the political class to pursue accommodative monetary policies were useless. In particular, in 1974, the governor of the Bank of France, Olivier Wormser, who in an article published in *Le Figaro*[24] had urged the government to redouble the effort in the fight against inflation through a restriction and a reduction in public spending, was fired by President Giscard d'Estaing.[25] The Governor of the Bank of Italy, Guido Carli, realized that it was impossible to oppose the will of the political class to use monetary policy to support the growth of output. "We ask ourselves then, and continue to do so, whether the Bank of Italy could have refused, or could still refuse, to finance the public sector's deficit by abstaining from exercising the faculty, granted by law, to purchase government securities. Refusal ... would give the appearance of being a monetary policy act; in substance it would be a seditious act which would be followed by a paralysis of the public administration".[26]

Burns, President of the Fed, writing in 1979 about those years said: "What is unique about our inflation is its stubborn persistence, not the behaviour of central bankers. This persistence. . . reflects the philosophic and political currents of thought that have impinged on economic life since the Great Depression and particularly since the mid-1960s".[27]

Regardless of its various explanations, the fact remains that the Great Inflation was associated with high domestic inflation volatility, large inflation differentials between countries, high exchange rate instability and absolute uncertainty about their future development.

The Great Inflation prompted governments to adopt measures to limit exchange rate volatility through central bank intervention in foreign exchange market and forms of macroeconomic policy coordination. These measures had only a limited and time-bound effect.

The effectiveness of the monetary reforms prompted by the high inflation of the 1970s was different. These reforms concerned both the institutional framework for the conduct of monetary policy and the way monetary policy was conducted. The implementation of these monetary reforms allowed advanced countries to disinflate their economies and drastically reduce exchange rate volatility.

---

[23]See Pittaluga and Seghezza (2012). On the political origin of the Great Inflation of the 1970s, see also Meltzer (2005).

[24]Quoted in Prate (1987, pp. 210–211).

[25]See Goodman (1992).

[26]See Carli (1974), quoted in Giannini (2011, p. 148).

[27]See Burns (1979, p. 21).

6.5 The Contrasting Outcomes of Central Banks' Interventions in the Foreign Exchange Market

In the 1970s and for a large part of the 1980s the US economy was characterized by high volatility not only of output but also of the inflation and nominal interest rates (Fig. 6.1).

In this context, the dollar saw its function as anchor of the international monetary system diminished, exchange rate volatility was very high because of this and the inflation differentials between countries. Despite high domestic inflation, the dollar soared in the first half of the 1980s.[28] Its effective exchange rate at the end of February 1985 had appreciated by 81% compared to the 1980 average.

While this appreciation of the dollar could be explained by the short-term interest rate differential,[29] it seems in notable contrast with the development of trade balances, given the widening trade deficit of the USA and the trade surplus of Germany and Japan. The most plausible explanation for the dollar's appreciation is that the USA, in the presence of high economic and foreign exchange market disorder and increasing global financial integration, was becoming a *safe haven*.[30]

The high volatility of exchange rates not only adversely affected the growth of international trade, but also hampered adjustment processes. The dollar, in fact, despite growing US trade deficits, was appreciating in real terms against the currencies of its trading partners.

The states tried to remedy this monetary disorder by intervening in the foreign exchange market in order to influence the exchange rate, and by means of cooperative agreements to coordinate these interventions and economic policies.

Interventions in the US foreign exchange market were limited in extent. Between April 1981 and the end of 1984, amounting to some 754 million dollars in purchases of marks and yen.[31] In essence, the USA behaved with benign neglect. This is explicit in the words of Treasury Secretary Sprinkel: "Significant and frequent intervention by governments assumes that a relatively few officials know better where exchange rates should (or shouldn't) be than a large number of decision makers in the market, and that public funds should be put at risk on the basis of that assumption".[32] These statements aroused surprise and disappointment in Europe. It is not surprising, then, that the level of intervention by other countries, particularly some European countries, was substantial. Between 1981 and 1984, the monetary authorities of the 13 major countries sold more than 50 billion dollars. Of these, about half were sold by the Bundesbank.

[28]The weighted-average value of the dollar in terms of 10 countries as measured by the Federal Reserve Board Staff.

[29]Due to the restrictive monetary policy conducted by Volcker in the USA.

[30]See Solomon (1982, p. 12).

[31]See Solomon (1982, p. 15).

[32]Statement of the Honorable Beryl W. Sprinkle, Under Secretary of the Treasury for Monetary Affairs, before the Joint Economic Committee, May 4, 1981, Department of the Treasury News.

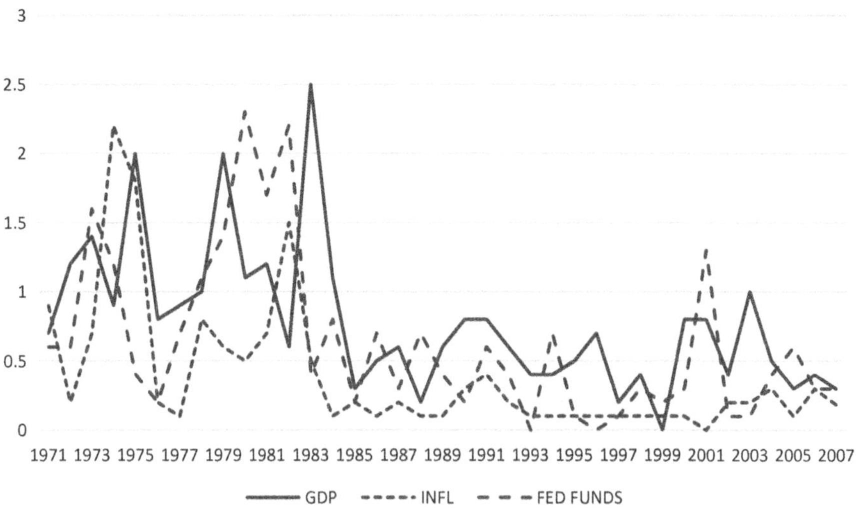

Fig. 6.1 Volatility of US GDP growth, inflation and Federal funds interest rates (standard deviation). Source: FRED, Federal Reserve Bank of St. Louis database

The effectiveness of these central bank interventions in the currency markets is doubtful. On this point, the *Jurgensen Report* published in 1983[33] expressed itself as follows: "... Effectiveness was found to have been greater when intervention was unsterilized than when its monetary effect were offset ... There was broad agreement that sterilized intervention did not generally have a lasting effect, but that intervention in conjunction with domestic policy changes did have a more durable impact." The recognition of the limited effectiveness of foreign exchange interventions,[34] particularly sterilized interventions, prompted the major countries to move towards coordinated interventions.

After 1983, as the country's current account deficit increased markedly, the USA began to argue that the advanced countries needed to coordinate their macroeconomic policies. In September 1985 the G-5 assembled at the Plaza Hotel in New York and after some hours of discussion they reached an agreement:

(a) The USA ended their policy of benign neglect and undertook to intervene in the foreign exchange market with the aim of encouraging a devaluation of the dollar;
(b) The governments of the other countries, for their part, undertook to intervene in the foreign exchange market in a coordinated manner with the Fed.

[33]Report for the working group on exchange market intervention, Paris, La Documentation Francaise, March 1983.

[34]For a survey of the literature on foreign exchange market interventions of the early 1980s see Edison (1993).

Table 6.5 Breakdown of foreign exchange reserves by currency, 1970–1984

	Dollar	Mark	Yen	Pound	Swiss Franc	French Franc	Other
Composition							
—at the end of 1972	78.6	4.6	0.1	7.1	1.0	0.9	7.7
—at the end of 1984	65.8	12.1	5.4	2.8	2.0	1.0	10.9
Gross changes	−12.8	7.5	5.3	−4.3	1.0	0.1	3.2
Net changes[a]							
1972–1976	3.4	4.8	2.6	−10.0	1.4	0.3	−2.5
1976–1979	−2.6	3.5	0.8	–	–	−0.3	−1.4
1979–1984	−3.5	−1.2	2.4	1.1	–	−0.2	1.4

Source: Horii (1986)
[a]Net of exchange rate changes

In the period following the Plaza Accords the dollar depreciated significantly. Despite this, the US current account deficit did not improve appreciably.

At the urging of the USA, finance ministers and central bank governors of G-5 countries convened in early 1987 at the Palais du Louvre. The agreements that emerged from this meeting, on the one hand, underlined the success of the Plaza Accords, and, on the other, stipulated that coordination between countries would extend from exchange rate interventions to economic policies: Germany would carry out a tax reduction and Japan would relax its monetary policy stance. These measures would facilitate, if not an adjustment, a reduction in the large external imbalances of some countries.

Despite the coordination of exchange rate interventions and economic policies, in the late 1980s exchange rate volatility remained high (Fig. 6.1). Given the uncertain perspectives of the dollar's value its share in the foreign exchange reserves held by central banks tended to decline. This decline, net of exchange rate changes, was particularly pronounced between 1976 and 1984 (Table 6.5).

As pointed out in Chap. 2, the country issuing the international money can exploit seigniorage only within certain limits, beyond those limits, it undermines the acceptability of its currency in foreign exchanges.[35]

The volatility of the US dollar and advanced countries' exchange rate declined during the 1980s as inflation and output in these countries became less volatile, largely as a result of monetary reforms during that period. These reforms consisted of institutional changes, primarily the increased independence of central banks, and the adoption of rules, such as inflation targeting, in the conduct of monetary policy. The adoption of these reforms corresponded to a drastic fall in the inflation rate, accompanied by a long period of output stability.

[35]As Walter (2006, p. 69) writes: "... monetary leadership requires a relatively (but not excessively) conservative macroeconomic policy from the leader".

6.6 Institutional Reforms in the Conduct of Monetary Policy and Price Stabilization

The Great Inflation and the concomitant disorder in the foreign exchange markets fostered an intense debate that led to a number of proposals for reforming the international monetary system. A first type of proposal suggested a return to some form of convertibility into real assets. In this context, the Parliamentary Commission set up in the USA by President Reagan in 1981 proposed a return to gold convertibility.[36] A return of currency convertibility into a commodity money would have entailed a reduction in the elasticity of the money supply, which would have entailed risks of deflation.

A second type of proposal focused on the institutional framework of money creation. On this issue, some scholars proposed to take the power to conduct monetary policy away from central banks, whose mismanagement was blamed for the Great Inflation. The *free bankers* were main part of this view.[37] According to this theory the production of money should be left to the free market, thus breaking up the monopoly of the central banks.[38] The limits of this solution lay in the fact that, especially in the case of fiat money, given the existence of information asymmetries between producer and user, the risk of fraudulent behaviour was high. In this context, therefore, the problem of the over-issuance of money reemerged, no longer because of the behaviour of the government and elected bodies, but because of the behaviour of producers.

The limits of free banking raised again the problem of how the monopoly production of money was conditioned by policymakers and how this conditioning could be mitigated or, even, eliminated. This issue was addressed very clearly in a seminal paper by Kydland and Prescott (1977) in which they illustrated the so-called *time inconsistency* problem in public policy. This paradigm was extended to monetary policy by Barro and Gordon (1983a) who, in accordance with the Kydland and Prescott approach, assume that a policymaker, when not constrained by institutional mechanisms, has an incentive to resort to an inflationary surprise in order to achieve a lower than natural rate of unemployment. Individuals, because they have rational expectations, expect the policymaker to behave in this way and anticipate the likely inflationary surprise by behaving as if it actually occurred. Because of this the central bank, if it wants to prevent the unemployment rate from rising, is forced to accommodate the behaviour of individuals. This being the case, the economy is characterized by an inflationary bias.

This bias tends to undermine the stability of the value of fiat money and, hence, its acceptability. This, in turn, creates the need to introduce an institutional mechanism that, by eliminating or mitigating the problem of inflationary bias, would restore

[36]See Cagan (1984).

[37]See Dowd (1996) and White (1984).

[38]On this aspect see Hayek (1976).

confidence in fiat money. The time inconsistency framework called for two institutional changes in the conduct of monetary policy: an increase in the de jure and/or de facto independence of central banks and the adoption of transparent rules in the conduct of monetary policy.

6.6.1 Central Bank Reform

Because of the Great Inflation, monetary policy credibility has attracted most attention in the literature. On this aspect, in order to regain the credibility of monetary policy, four proposals have been made: the use of *non-contingent rules*, such as Friedman's (1959) *k* percent rule[39]; the establishment of Rogoff's (1985) *conservative* central banker; the introduction of *optimal performance contract* such as Walsh (1995) and Persson and Tabellini (1993); and the strengthening of the central bank *reputation*, such as Barro and Gordon (1983b).[40]

For Friedman's *k percent rule*, money growth is fixed a priori at a constant level. In this way, the conduct of monetary policy is removed from the discretion of central bankers who, eager to be confirmed in office, tend to comply with the demands of policymakers, who are structurally inclined to resort to inflationary surprises in order to stimulate economic growth and gain electoral support. The main drawback of the *k percent rule* is that it sterilizes the money supply elasticity of fiat money. In a nutshell, its adoption would mean a return to past gold standard rigidities. This is perhaps the main reason why it has not been applied in practice. More fortunate were the proposals to strengthen the independence of central banks from politics.[41]

In a well-known article in 1985, Rogoff showed how the inflationary bias could be eliminated by assigning the task of managing fiat money to a *conservative* central banker, i.e. a central banker who, while having the same output and inflation objectives as the general public, attached greater weight to the latter than the general public and government did.

Rogoff's *conservative* central banker is independent of the political class both with respect to the objectives to be pursued[42] and the instruments to be used for this purpose.[43] It has been observed that the Rogoff scheme is flawed by a trade-off between anti-inflationary credibility and flexibility. In a nutshell, in this scheme the pursuit of price stability can be at the expense of output stability, since the latter is given less weight. Excessive output volatility, however, may undermine social support for the central bank and signal the end of its independence.

[39]See also Friedman (1961).

[40]See also Backus and Driffil (1985), and Barro (1986).

[41]See Cukierman (1992).

[42]For example, in choosing the desired inflation rate.

[43]That is, whether to use the control of the monetary base, the policy interest rate or something else.

Table 6.6 Central bank independence reforms in main industrial countries

Country	Year of Reform	Country	Year of Reform
Austria	1991	Italy	1998
Australia	None	Netherlands	1998
Belgium	1993	New Zealand	1990
Canada	None	Norway	2001
Denmark	None	Portugal	1998
Finland	1998	Spain	1994
France	1994	Sweden	1999
Greece	1997	Switzerland	2000
Germany	None	United Kingdom	1998
Japan	1996	USA	None

This problem is, however, solved in the *performance contract* approach,[44] here it is the government or parliament that sets the monetary policy objective to be pursued and delegates the task to the central banker, ensuring that the latter has incentives to comply with the task delegated to him.

The patterns outlined above are the basis for many of the central bank reforms in recent decades (Table 6.6).

These reforms generally contain rules of competence, which relate to the functions and activities of central banks, and rules of procedure, which aim to regulate the relationship between these institutions and elected bodies.

The rules of competence almost always include a ban on central banks buying public bonds on the primary market, so that governments do not find it easy to cover public deficits. Procedural rules, however, are genuine institutional mechanisms aimed at preserving central banks autonomy by politics. They mainly concern the definition of the monetary authority governance and its requirements, the procedures for appointing and removing members from office and the ownership structure of the central bank.

Some, few in fact, central banks enjoy high anti-inflationary credibility due to the reputation they have acquired over time. They are de facto independent.[45] This is the case of the Bundesbank which consolidated its reputation after the first oil crisis, when its president Klasen refused to accommodate, with an expansive monetary policy, the demands for large wage increases made by the trade unions and supported by the social-democratic government.[46] As a result of this decision by its central banker, Germany was one of the few countries not to experience an acceleration in the inflation rate after the tripling of oil prices in 1973.

It is inevitable to ask what factors have led governments and elected bodies to grant a high degree of independence to central banks and, more generally, to accept a

[44]See Walsh (1995) and Persson and Tabellini (1993).

[45]See Barro and Gordon (1983b).

[46]See Goodman (1992).

Table 6.7 Industrial countries: distribution by monetary frameworks

	1970	1975	1980	1990	1995
Exchange rate pegging	18	11	10	11	6
Inflation targeting	0	0	0	1	5
Intermediate target	0	8	7	6	5
Discretion	4	3	5	4	6

Source: Giannini and Cottarelli (1997)

drastic reduction in their domestic monetary power. Two factors seem to be the most important drivers behind this behaviour.

The first factor is linked to a significant increase in the strata of the population holding financial assets. Since holders of these assets are traditionally inflation-averse, this has inevitably led to a decline in acceptance of inflationary policies and forms of income redistribution resulting from inflation.[47]

The second factor that has helped reduce the reluctance of elected bodies to relinquish monetary power is the increasing international mobility of capital.[48] In the presence of high international financial interdependence, the autonomy of governments in conducting monetary policy has diminished significantly. A case in point is President Mitterrand when, at the start of his term in 1981, he embarked on an expansionary economic policy that differed from that of other advanced economies. As a result of this policy, France experienced a pronounced outflow of capital. Faced with the risk of a depreciation of the franc, Mitterrand was forced to revise his economic policy to be more restrictive.

6.6.2 *Changes in the Conduct of Monetary Policy*

The literature on time inconsistency, in showing the importance of individuals' expectations, called not only for reforms in the statutes of central banks but also for changes in the way these institutions conduct monetary policy.

The announcement of targets made credible by institutional reforms affected people's expectations and thus the effectiveness of monetary stimuli. From this perspective, the use of rules became preferable to activist monetary policies. In the 1980s and 1990s,[49] a heated debate on the advantages and disadvantages of rule-based and discretion-based monetary frameworks began.[50] As a result, more and more countries adopted monetary policy targets (Table 6.7).

[47] See Posen (1993).

[48] The changing theoretical attitude towards competition as an instrument for allocating financial resources also contributed to this process. See McKinnon (1973) and Shaw (1973).

[49] See Lindberg and Maier (1985).

[50] See Fischer (1990).

At present, most countries follow some form of inflation targeting. In many cases the adoption of this scheme is formally defined, while in others, as in the case of the Fed and the ECB, an inflation target is pursued, but is not set by elected bodies. However, central banks that explicitly or implicitly follow inflation targeting seek to stabilize output and employment as long as it is possible to keep the inflation rate low and stable. This type of approach to monetary policy, common to most central banks in industrialized countries, has been called *constrained discretion* by Bernanke (2003). The latter involves adherence to two principles: "First, … the central bank must establish a strong commitment to keeping inflation low and stable. Second, subject to the condition that inflation be kept low and stable, … monetary policy should strive to limit cyclical swings in resource utilization".[51]

Following this approach, a large proportion of central banks have adopted the so-called Taylor rule in the conduct of monetary policy. According to this rule, the central bank must raise (lower) the policy interest rate when the actual or expected inflation rate is higher (lower) than the target rate and when the output gap is positive (negative). In this context, the central bank's behaviour is predictable, which helps to keep prices and output stable.

The adoption of rules in the conduct of monetary policy not only improves the effectiveness of the transmission of monetary impulses, but also enables elected bodies and the community to monitor the behaviour of central banks, i.e. an unelected body. The accountability and transparency of these institutions make their independence from elected bodies compatible with democracy.

6.7 The Disinflation Process in the USA and Advanced Economies

During the 1980s, the increased *de jure* and *de facto* independence of central banks and changes in the conduct of monetary policy enabled advanced countries to achieve success in the pursuit of price and output stability.

The disinflation of the US economy by Fed Chairman Volcker was emblematic. He was convinced that the tumultuous price growth was due to a price-wage spiral caused by the consolidation of inflationary expectations. These expectations had become entrenched as a result of inflation targeting policies which were not credible.[52] Hence the need to adopt new procedures in the conduct of monetary policy. According to Volcker, therefore, in order to dampen inflationary expectations "we

[51]See Bernanke (2003).

[52]"After years of failed or prematurely truncated efforts to deal with inflation, markets had developed a high degree of cynism about the willingness of what they dismissed as "Washington" in general, or the Federal Reserve in particular, to stand firm". See Volcker and Gyohten (1992, p. 165–166).

must have a credible and disciplined monetary policy".[53] He therefore persuaded the Federal Open Market Committee (FOMC) in October 1979 to change its monetary policy procedures from using the policy interest rate to controlling the monetary base.[54]

There were several reasons for this decision. Firstly, Volcker believed that setting the policy interest rate at a level that would encourage disinflation in the US economy would entail significant political costs and, therefore, more pronounced resistance to restrictive policy on the part of elected bodies. Secondly, the setting of a quantitative target would have given a visible signal to the public of the genuine intention to disinflate the economy and would thus have affected their inflation expectations: "More focus on the money supply also would be a way of telling the public that we meant business people don't need an advanced course in economics to understand that inflation has something to do with too much money".[55]

By persisting with his restrictive monetary policy, despite much resistance and many obstacles, but with the support of President Reagan, Volcker eventually succeeded in drastically reducing the US inflation rate and stabilising domestic prices.[56]

The US disinflation process contributed significantly to the return to an orderly functioning of the international monetary system. Firstly, by stabilizing domestic prices, the USA reduced uncertainty about the future purchasing power of the dollar and increased its acceptance as a key currency. From the second half of the 1980s, the share of the US currency in the official reserves of the rest of the world rose again. Second, the completion of the disinflation process in the US economy had spillover effects on other countries, primarily the advanced ones. On the one hand, in the context of increasing financial integration, other advanced countries were induced to raise policy interest rates to avoid or contain capital outflows. On the other hand, in the context of a significant appreciation of the dollar, European countries, especially those belonging to the European Monetary System (EMS), were forced to revise their monetary policy in a restrictive direction. For these countries, the appreciation of the dollar implied an increase in the price of raw materials in national currency and, therefore, a rise in the inflation rate[57] and as a result the process of disinflation in the industrialized countries, primarily in the EMS countries, accelerated (Table 6.3). During the 1980s and 1990s in most advanced countries the inflation rate fell significantly (Table 6.8).

[53]Quoted in Bernanke (2013, p. 35).

[54]In particular, it was decided to adopt a quantitative target for non-borrowed reserves. By pursuing such a target, the FOMC changed the Federal Funds interest rate to reach the market equilibrium point for bank reserves. See Lindley et al. (2005).

[55]See Volcker and Gyohten (1992, p. 167).

[56]See Meltzer (2005).

[57]See Meltzer (2009, p. 1089).

Table 6.8 Consumer inflation (percent)

	1980–1984	1985–1989	1990–1994	1995–1999	2000–2003
World	14.1	15.5	30.4	8.4	4.1
Industrialized economies	8.7	3.9	3.8	2.0	2.0
Developing countries	31.4	48.0	53.2	13.1	5.7
Economies in transition	6.2	7.7	363.2	53.9	14.5

Source: IMF, World Economic Outlook

Table 6.9 Volatility of U.S. real GDP (standard deviation)

Time period	Real GDP	Consumer inflation
1930–1954	69.7	34.4
1955–1969	5.4	2.3
1970–1984	7.5	11.4
1985–2006	1.5	1.3

Source: Bureau of Economic Analysis

The disinflation process was followed by a phase called Great Moderation. This phase, characterized by low volatility in the inflation rate and output, lasted until 2006–2007 (Table 6.9).[58]

It was not simply a U.S. phenomenon but occurred around the same time in many other advanced economies. The stabilization of prices in the advanced countries and the dampening of the magnitude of the economic cycle in these countries helped to stabilize exchange rates and the functioning of the international monetary system.

6.8 The European Monetary System (EMS)

The stabilization of exchange rates and the smooth functioning of the international monetary system were not only helped by the reduced volatility of inflation and output in the advanced countries, but also by the conclusion of the exchange rate agreement between European countries, that is, the EMS. This exchange rate agreement was an important step in the process of European monetary integration.

As early as December 1969, the Conference of Heads of State and Government of the European Economic Community countries gave Pierre Werner, Minister of Finance of Luxembourg, the task of drawing up a draft for an Economic and Monetary Union of the member states that would develop the proposals of the Barre Plan which had been presented to the Commission only shortly before.

The Werner Plan was presented to the European Council in June 1970. It envisaged that European monetary integration would take place in two stages. In the first stage, economic policy coordination was to be strengthened. In the second, it was envisaged that cooperation would become closer and eventually allow the

[58]On the causes of the latter, see Summers (2005) and Bernanke (2004).

establishment of irreversible exchange rate parity between member countries and the complete liberalization of capital movements between them. The transition to monetary union was expected to last a decade. During this period, the parity fluctuations band would be progressively reduced.

The idea of the EMS was supported primarily by France and Germany. France was concerned about the effects of exchange rate instability on the CAP (Common Agricultural Policy) which provided very substantial benefits to French farmers. German Chancellor Brandt, showing his support for the EMS, wanted to alleviate French misgivings about his *Ostpolitik* and the risk of Germany loosening its ties with the West.

In the run-up to the report, despite the common goal of EMU, different views emerged from Germany and France as to how EMS should be achieved. For the French, it would have to be achieved quickly, economic and monetary convergence would have followed.[59] This position was termed *monetarist* and reflected the domestic objective of preserving the CAP by initiating an intra-European fixed exchange rate regime. It was countered by the German view, the so-called *economist position*, according to which the integration process should only start when the member countries had demonstrated that they were absolutely committed to monetary stability and their domestic economic situation converged to that of Germany.

The conditions set by Germany on how monetary integration should take place were also the product of domestic interests, more precisely the pressure of banks and industrial organizations, which were concerned that monetary integration would import inflation into Germany.[60]

After the conclusion of the Smithsonian Agreement the EC's member states, in order to facilitate the process of creating the EMU, implemented, as already discussed, the *snake*, i.e. an exchange rate regime with small margins of fluctuation. Within the snake, the mark played the role of anchor currency. This meant that monetary policy for the EC's member states was determined by the Bundesbank.

The monetary disorder that followed the first oil crisis and the inflation differentials between European countries marked the failure of the snake. In the absence of adequate exchange rate stability, intra-EC trade was heavily penalized and the CAP was threatened with disruption. It was in this context that the conditions for an exchange rate agreement between European countries matured.

The first impetus to the establishment of this agreement came from Roy Jenkins, President of the European Commission from 1977 to 1981. In a Jean Monnet lecture delivered in October 1977, called for a new Community initiative in the monetary sphere. This proposal was endorsed by the French President Giscard d'Estaing and German Chancellor Helmut Schmidt who started contacts and negotiations in order to initiate the project.[61] The EMS became operational on March 13, 1979. Eight

---

[59] See Dyson (1994).

[60] See Goodman (1992).

[61] See Ludlow (1982).

countries (France, Denmark, Belgium, Luxembourg, Ireland, the Netherlands, Germany and Italy) initially joined the exchange rate agreement.

The EMS has been interpreted in various ways. A first type of explanation focuses on the need of EU countries to reduce exchange rate volatility in order to smooth the operation of the complicated mechanism of the Common Agricultural Policy (CAP).[62] The collapse of the CAP was of particular concern to France, given the high bargaining power farmers enjoyed in it. France's interests were supported by Germany, which felt the need to be supported by its powerful neighbour in its complex relations with the Soviet bloc. A second type of explanation traces the creation of the EMS to the tensions with the USA that emerged in the late 1960s and became acute after the suspension of dollar convertibility. The exchange rate agreement was an attempt to restore monetary autonomy to the EU.[63]

These explanations attribute crucial importance in the construction of the EMS, and ultimately in the process of European monetary integration, to the hegemony of the Franco-German axis. A different type of explanation refers, instead of inter-state relations, to the lobbying of different interest groups within the EU. From this perspective, the impetus to create the EMS came mainly from different interest groups, such as multinationals, international investors, producers of high-tech products, producers of non-tradable goods, workers and consumers.[64] In the 1980s, thanks to changes in the balance of power among French and Italian parties, the interests of these groups became prevalent. At the same time, German industry pressed for the adoption of a fixed exchange rate regime in the EU in order to gain advantages over its competitors in inflationary Southern European countries.[65]

Another interpretation of the EMS attributes a primary role to political factors, in primis to international relations. In a period of substantial US retreat compared to the growing influence of the USSR in various world theatres, the need was felt by the major European powers to make progress towards greater European political union. The exchange rate agreement was promoted by Germany and France not so much with the intention of encouraging the emergence of a third power, an alternative to the USA and Soviet Union, but rather to strengthen the Atlantic Alliance's role in Europe at a time of a weakening USA.

The decision to set up the EMS, taken at a European Council meeting in Brussels in December 1978, foresaw a system of fixed, but adjustable, exchange rates. The main components of the Exchange Rate Mechanism (ERM) were four pillars[66]:

---

[62]See Tsoukalis (1977), Story and De Cecco (1993) and McNamara (1998).

[63]See Ludlow (1982) and Story (1988).

[64]See Frieden (1998, 2000).

[65]See Hefeker (1997). Some studies consider these various explanations to show that the creation of the EMS, and, more generally, the start of the process of European monetary integration, depended on a combination of domestic distribution issues and inter-state bargaining. See, among others, Eichengreen and Frieden (1993).

[66]For a description of the structure and functioning of the EMS, see Gros and Thygesen (1998).

parity grid, mutual support, joint management of exchange rate realignments, the European currency unit (ECU).[67]

The parity grid was a matrix-like table collecting all pairwise central parities and their associated fluctuation margins. All currencies were fixed to each other, with a band of fluctuation of ±2.25 around the central parity against the ECU. The responsibility of maintaining bilateral parity was equally divided between the two countries concerned. With mutual support, it was expected that when the bilateral parity of a currency was threatened the central banks of both countries would undertake unlimited interventions to defend the fixed parity. In order to avoid beggar-thy-neighbour behaviour, EMS member countries committed to a joint management of exchange rate realignments. In this way the risk of unilateral realignments was categorically excluded. The last pillar was represented by the creation of a unit of account, the ECU.

The operation of the EMS can be divided into two distinct phases. In the first phase, from 1979 to 1986, called by Giavazzi and Spaventa (1990) the *flexible* EMS, member countries, given the existence of restrictions on capital movements and frequent realignments of exchange rates (Table 6.10), enjoyed a certain degree of autonomy in monetary policy.

Despite this, between 1978 and 1987, the inflation rate for most of the member countries fell. That reduction was particularly marked for those countries that, at the time of their adhesion to the EMS, were suffering from high inflation rates. By joining the EMS these countries could adopt an exchange-rate-based disinflation process.[68] They could, therefore, benefit from the advantages that a disinflation process of this type involves, in particular, of the gradualism with which it works.[69]

The approval of the Single Market Agreement in 1986 was a step towards building a single European capital market. That agreement provided, among other things for the removal of controls on capital movements.

In the late 1980s and early 1990s all member countries liberalized their capital markets. In this new situation, it was difficult to reach multilateral agreements on parity realignments without arousing currency speculation and generating tensions in the financial markets. This helps to explain why, between 1987 and 1992, during the *rigid* EMS phase,[70] it was decided not to conduct realignments despite significant changes in the real exchange rates of some countries.

In this context, EMS member countries saw a gradual shrinking of their discretion in monetary policy and the emergence of a leader country, Germany, which, enjoying lower inflation than the others, was able to impose its monetary policy.

In a nutshell, the so-called *n-1 problem* inherent in fixed exchange rate regimes arose. This problem implies that, since there are only *n-1* exchange rates among the

[67]This was a basket of the currencies of all countries participating in the ERM. Each currency was weighted with the GDP and the share of trade of the country.

[68]See Giavazzi and Pagano (1988).

[69]See among others Calvo and Végh (1994).

[70]According to the definition given by Giavazzi and Spaventa (1990).

Table 6.10 ERM realignments

	Mar 79	Sept 79	Nov 79	Mar 81	Oct 81	Feb 82	Jun 82	Mar 83	Jul 85	Apr 86	Aug 86	Jan 87	Jun 89	Jan 90	Oct 90
Belgium	En 2.25%					−8.5		+1.5	+2.0	+1.0		+2.0			
Denmark	En 2.25%	−2.9	−4.8			−3.0		+2.5	+2.0	+1.0					
Germany	En 2.25%	+2.0			+5.5		+4.25	+5.5	+2.0	+3.0		+3.0			
France	En 2.25%				−3.0		−5.75	−2.5	+2.0	−3.0					
Ireland	En 2.25%							−3.5	+2.0		−8.0				
Italy	En 2.25%			−6.0	−3.0			−2.5	−6.0					B 2.25%	
Netherland	En 2.25%				+5.5			+3.5	+2.0	+3.0		+3.0			
UK															En2.25%
Spain												En 6%			

− = %devaluation; + = %revaluation; B% = new band; En% = entry band

Table 6.11 Current account balances (billions of dollars)

	1983	1984	1985	1986	1987	1988	1989	1990	1991	1992
France	−5.2	−0.9	–	2.4	−4.4	−4.8	−5.6	−13.8	−6.1	2.4
Germany	5.4	9.6	17.0	40.1	46.3	50.6	57.6	46.3	−19.5	−25.1
Italy	1.5	−2.4	−3.4	2.8	−1.5	−5.9	−10.9	−14.4	−21.4	−25.4
UK	5.5	2.1	3.9	–	−7.6	−28.8	−35.6	−29.4	−11.4	−20.9

Source: Bank of Italy (1993), Annual Report, Rome

n countries participating in an exchange rate agreement, either a country becomes the leader and sets monetary policy for all, or monetary policy is set by all countries together, in a cooperative way. The formation and consolidation of the leadership of the mark meant the disappearance of monetary sovereignty margins in the other countries.[71]

Since the convergence process of inflation rates was incomplete, it encouraged the emergence of macroeconomic imbalances and the final collapse of the system. The first turbulence within the EMS appeared in June 1992, when Denmark in a referendum decided not to join the EMU project. The outcome of this referendum created a public perception that the project to complete the monetary union of Europe had stalled. The exchange rate of the currencies of the weaker countries of EMS,[72] in primis the Italian lira, reached the lower limit of the oscillation band.

A meeting of the Economic and Financial Affairs Council (ECOFIN) was held in Bath in early September to agree a coordinated response to these tensions. The meeting, however, ended in failure, since, during the meeting, it became clear that member countries had very different positions. In particular, Germany refused to reduce its domestic interest rate, raised after 1989 to counter the acceleration of the inflation rate due to unification. In most other countries, given the economic slowdown, an adjustment of the interest rate to the German one was unsustainable.

The stalemate of the negotiations, together with the event just described, led to a change in investor expectations. Between 1987 and 1992 the Italian real exchange rate[73] rose by 8.5%. A similar increase occurred in the UK (8.1%). Both countries had persistent and sizeable current account deficits (Table 6.11).

Despite the German central bank reducing the official interest rate in early September, the weaker countries of the system, in particular the UK and Italy, were affected by large capital outflows.

On September 16, the UK decided to abandon the exchange rate arrangement. Following this decision, Italy decided to suspend interventions to defend the lira. Such interventions, since the beginning of the crisis, had depleted the country's foreign reserves to the tune of 29 billion liras.

[71] See Fratianni and Von Hagen (1990) and De Grauwe et al. (1994).

[72] That is the Italian lira, sterling, the peseta and the escudo.

[73] Measured with respect to unit labour costs.

Various explanations have been given for the EMS crisis.[74] The most plausible of them suggests that it was due to the deterioration of the fundamentals of some countries, which then resulted in a large capital outflow.[75]

On 2 August 1993, the countries which were still part of the EMS decided to widen the allowed fluctuation range of the exchange rate from ±2.25 to ±15%, leaving central parities unchanged, in practise marking the end of the EMS.

The 1992 crisis once again demonstrated the impossibility of violating the macroeconomic trilemma: in a regime of fixed exchange rates and high capital mobility it is not possible for countries to enjoy monetary autonomy. It also highlighted the limits of fixed exchange rate regimes. In particular, it showed that when adopting the policy of "tie one's hands" the persistence of institutional and economic differences between countries determines real appreciation of exchange rates and, consequently, current account imbalances. This point helps to explain many of the currency crises that have affected emerging and developing countries since the second half of the 1990s.

6.9 Financial Globalization

As we have just seen, in addition to macroeconomic imbalances in some countries, the high international mobility of capital contributed to the collapse of the EMS. The removal of constraints on capital movements, first, by the advanced countries and then by the emerging and developing ones fostered a growing financial interdependence of the world economy.

This process had started in the 1960s with the formation of the Eurodollar market, and then accelerated in the early 1970s, after the first oil crisis, when oil-rich countries, following the rise in the price of this commodity, had accumulated large current account surpluses and thus considerable financial wealth. A second pronounced acceleration of the process of global financial integration occurred in the 1990s. Between 1995 and 2015, the average de facto financial globalization (measured by global gross external assets as a share of world GDP) increased almost threefold (Fig. 6.2).

This increase remained very pronounced until 2007, but essentially stopped after the 2008 financial crisis. As shown in Fig. 6.2, the process of financial integration has mainly involved advanced countries and financial centres.[76] The share of global external assets on world GDP accounted for by emerging and developing countries,

---

[74]See Eichengreen and Wyplosz (1993).

[75]See Dornbusch (1993a, 1993b). Some scholars, however, have traced the EMS collapse to a change in expectations regarding the prospective stability of the exchange rate arrangement. See, among others, Eichengreen and Wyplosz (1993).

[76]These economies comprise both advanced economies such as Ireland, Luxembourg, Netherlands, Switzerland and the UK and small off-shore centres such as Bermuda and the Cayman Islands.

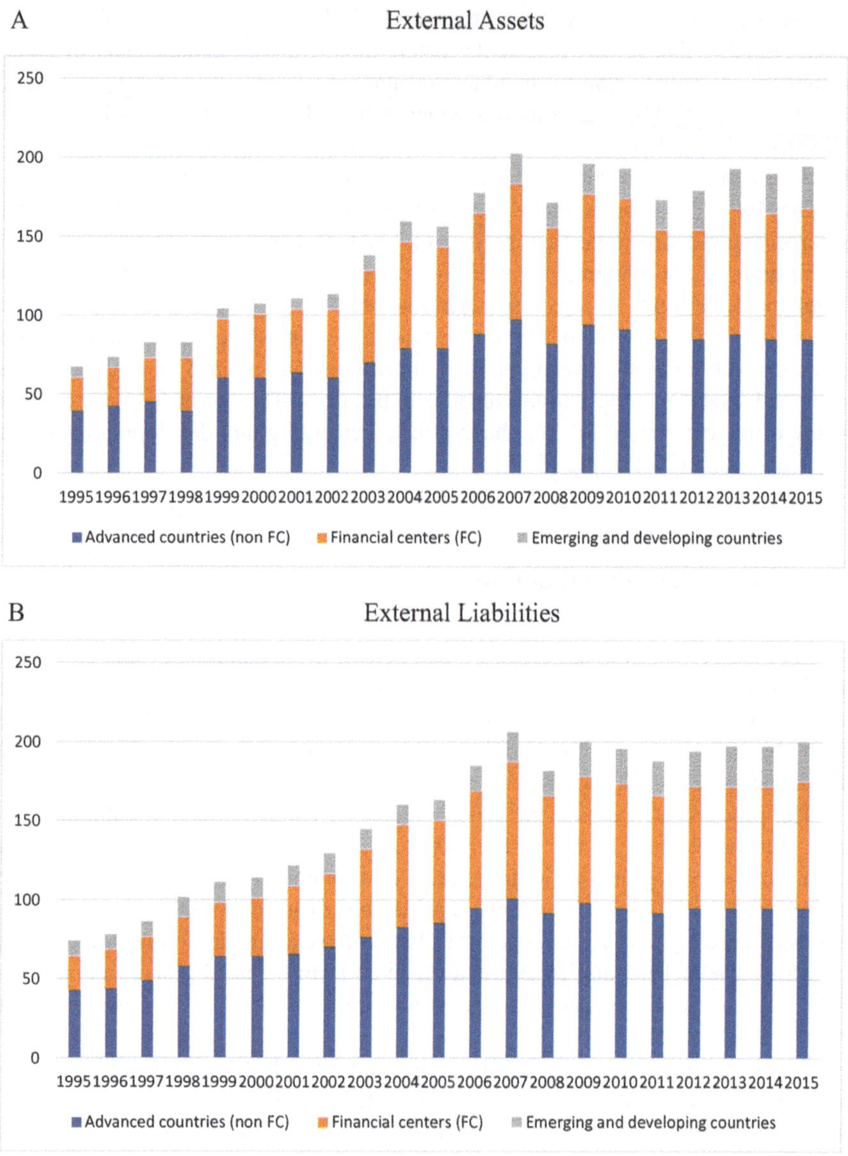

Fig. 6.2 Global external assets and liabilities (percent of GDP). (**a**) External Assets. (**b**) External Liabilities. Source: Lane and Milesi-Ferretti (2018)

although on the rise, remains a minority, despite these countries having seen a significant increase in their share of World GDP (Fig. 6.3).

This discrepancy is explained by the fact that financial integration among advanced countries has been characterized by two-way (i.e. by large gross holdings

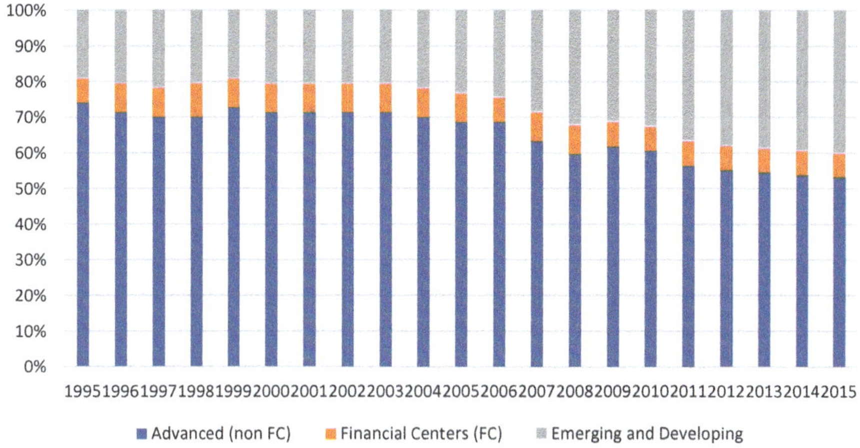

Fig. 6.3 The composition of World GDP. Source: Lane and Milesi-Ferretti (2018)

of assets and liabilities, but relatively small net external positions), whereas that of emerging and developing countries is characterized by relatively large net positions.

A large body of literature has highlighted the economic factors that have fostered the process of financial globalization.[77] Among these, the most important are undoubtedly the following:

1. The significant growth in trade. Trade integration inevitably generates financial links. Closer financial integration is evident in Europe where the introduction of the euro has encouraged the growth of cross-border transactions[78];
2. Technological development, in particular the growth of global telecommunications networks, has significantly reduced the cost of transferring funds from one country to another;
3. The development of domestic financial systems has encouraged both foreign investment in these markets and the acquisition of foreign assets by savers.[79]

The growing global financial integration of recent decades has been driven not only by economic factors but also by policy choices.[80] We have already seen how important the attitude of the British and American governments were in the birth and development of the Eurodollar market. The emergence of this market represented the first breach of the closed financial order, one of the main principles of Bretton Woods.

[77]See, among others, Obstfeld and Rogoff (2004), Lane and Milesi-Ferretti (2003, 2007, 2008, 2018).

[78]See Obstfeld and Rogoff (2000) and Obstfeld (2007).

[79]See Martin and Rey (2006).

[80]See Helleiner (1995).

In the course of the 1980s, however, this principle was completely overwhelmed by the gradual removal of controls on capital movements. By the end of that decade, all advanced countries had adopted full financial liberalization.

This process was led by the USA and Britain, partly, for different reasons. The American administration's favourable attitude towards financial openness was fuelled by the conviction that a more open international financial order would make it easier to cover the large public and current account deficits generated since 1982 by Reagan's expansionary fiscal policy.[81] These concerns of the American political class were compounded by pressure from multinational companies and the financial sector, which saw capital controls as an obstacle to the development of their business.[82] In the UK, the abolition of exchange controls and capital movements was supported by the City of London, which argued that otherwise London would not be able to compete with New York.

Added to these aspects was the fact that both US President Reagan and British Prime Minister Thatcher subscribed to a neo-liberal ideology, which, placing faith in market adjustment mechanisms, rejected all forms of regulation. The spread of this ideology and the fear that the USA and Britain, by removing constraints on capital movements, might discourage the inflow of foreign capital into them led the other advanced countries to liberalize and deregulate their financial sectors (Table 6.12).[83]

The importance of political choices in financial globalization leads us to revise, at least in part, the widespread opinion that this process was something that the states "suffered" and drastically reduced their power. The fact remains, however, that it affected the distribution of power at an international level.

As will be seen in the next section, financial globalization has helped strengthen the position of the dollar as an international currency and the influence of US monetary and financial policy on the rest of the world. However, while the process of international financial integration has fostered a more efficient allocation of savings at the global level, it has exposed the international monetary system to new factors of fragility and instability.

6.10 The Dollar's Dominance in the International Monetary System

From the perspective of hegemonic stability theory, the collapse of the Bretton Woods system was traced to the supposed political and military decline of the USA. It was inevitable that this decline would correspond to a re-dimensioning of the dollar in the international monetary system. A confirmation of this was seen in

[81] See Destler and Henning (1989).

[82] See Friedman (1991) and Goodman and Pauly (1993).

[83] See Strange (1990).

Table 6.12 The IMF Financial Reform Index, 1973–2005

	1973–1989	1990–1994	1995–2000	2001–2005
Austria	0.31	0.59	0.81	0.91
Belgium	0.52	0.84	0.94	0.97
Denmark	0.48	0.92	0.96	1.00
Finland	0.46	0.76	0.81	0.81
France	0.42	0.87	0.98	1.00
Germany	0.73	0.85	0.90	0.90
Greece	0.21	0.55	0.80	0.84
Ireland	0.61	0.92	1.00	1.00
Italy	0.34	0.64	0.88	0.91
Netherlands	0.76	0.93	0.95	0.99
Portugal	0.19	0.67	0.79	0.83
Spain	0.50	0.83	0.98	1.00
Sweden	0.49	0.93	0.95	0.95
UK	0.70	0.95	0.98	1.00
Norway	0.46	0.77	0.85	0.87
Switzerland	0.84	0.87	0.92	0.95
Australia	0.31	0.80	0.98	1.00
Canada	0.71	0.92	1.00	1.00
Japan	0.44	0.72	0.83	0.86
New Zealand	0.46	0.93	0.95	0.95
USA	0.75	0.90	0.96	1.00

Source: Abiad et al. (2008). Legenda: Financial liberalization outcomes range from 0 to 1, with 1 resembling full liberalization

the marked depreciation of the US currency. Between 1971 and 1974, the dollar depreciated by between 20% and 40% against the yen and the mark.

In the early 1970s, there were many who argued that, given the declining weight of the USA in the world economy, the high volatility of the dollar and its pronounced depreciation, confidence in the stability of the value of the US currency had weakened and inevitably its use as a medium of exchange in the world economy would decline.[84]

None of this happened. In the years after 1971 the dominance of the dollar increased significantly. This prompted Mundell (1973, p. 390) to write: "... the dollar assumed greater monetary importance than gold". In fact, the transition from fixed exchange rates to floating exchange rates had little impact on the use of the dollar as an international currency.[85]

In the years following the collapse of the Bretton Woods system, thanks to the centrality of the dollar in the international payments system, the USA exercised the functions attributed to a hegemonic country by Kindleberger (1973, 1981), namely

[84]See Aliber (1973) and McKinnon (1973).

[85]See Mundell (1973), Whitman et al. (1974) and Kenen (1983).

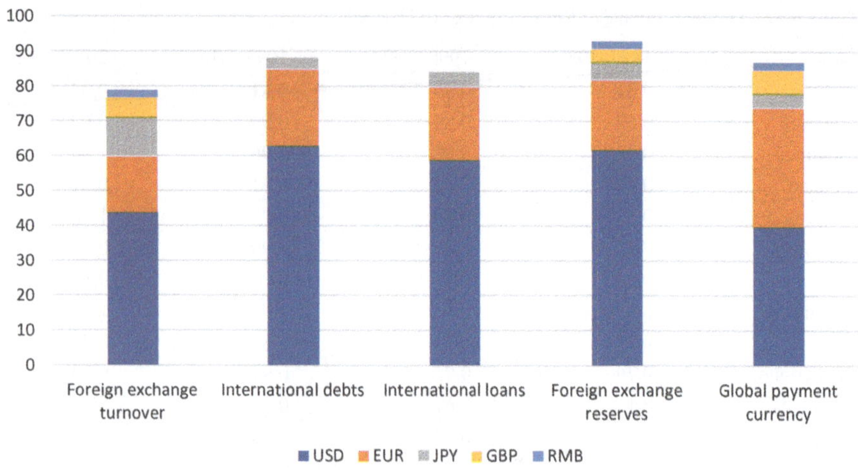

Fig. 6.4 The dominance of the dollar. Source: Eichengreen and Xia (2019). Data are referred to 2016.

to promote free trade and capital mobility, to stabilize financial markets, to promote the coordination of macroeconomic and financial policies and in crisis situations to act as an international lender of last resort.

The dollar has continued to play a dominant role both as a medium of exchange, as a unit of account and, finally, as a store of value (Fig. 6.4).

6.10.1 The Dollar as a Means of Payment

The high level of turnover of the dollar is primarily due to the extensive use of this currency as international means of exchange. Figure 6.5 highlights the dominance of dollar invoicing in world trade. In fact, the dollar's share as an invoicing currency has been estimated to be, on average, in the period 1999–2014, around 4.7 (3.1) times its share in world imports (exports). Instead, the euro's share is only slightly higher than that for imports and exports.[86]

6.10.2 The Dollar as a Unit of Account

After the collapse of the Bretton Woods system various countries anchored their currency to the dollar.[87] "When the United States suspended convertibility, the

[86]Goldberg and Tille (2009) and Ito and Chinn (2013) reach similar conclusions on the dominant role of the dollar as international means of exchange.

[87]See Ilzetzki et al. (2017).

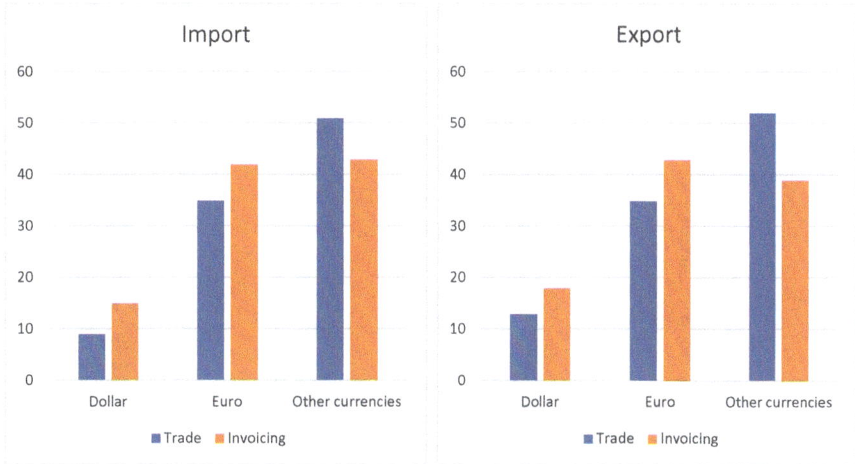

Fig. 6.5 The dominance of dollar invoicing in world trade. Source: Gopinath (2015)

Table 6.13 Exchange rate anchors, 2009–2017

	US dollar	Euro	Composite	Other currencies	Total
2009	52.4	26.3	13.5	7.8	100.0
2010	50.1	28.0	14.9	7.0	100.0
2011	49.5	27.8	14.5	8.2	100.0
2012	47.3	29.7	14.2	8.8	100.0
2013	47.8	29.3	14.1	8.7	100.0
2014	48.3	29.2	13.5	9.0	100.0
2015	48.3	28.7	13.8	9.2	100.0
2016	47.5	30.4	11.1	11.0	100.0
2017	47.5	30.4	11.1	11.0	100.0
2018	46.9	30.8	11.2	11.1	100.0
2019	47.5	31.2	10.1	11.3	100.0

Source: Areaer database

dollar was still the world unit of account. That is why the system did not collapse in 1971 or, to be more exact, why countries went back to the dollar. There was no alternative ready".[88]

Even after the global financial crisis (GFC), among the countries that adopt exchange rate anchors, the number of those that refer to the dollar remains high (Table 6.13).

[88]See Mundell (1973, p. 390).

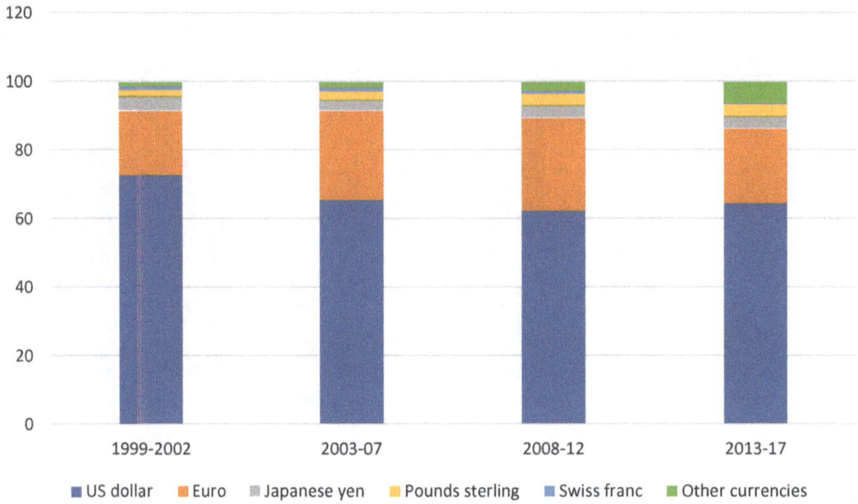

Fig. 6.6 Currency composition of official foreign exchange reserves. Source: IMF Cofer

6.10.3 The Dollar as a Store of Value

The dollar accounts for more than half of all external debts: more than double of the euro. The share of international loans in U.S. currency is almost 60% (Fig. 6.4). Figure 6.6 shows that the dollar still plays the key role as the main currency in which foreign exchange reserves held by central banks are denominated.[89]

There are several explanations for the high global demand for dollar-denominated assets. According to the *Bretton Woods II* (BWII) hypothesis,[90] it is associated with a mutual beneficial equilibrium between two groups of countries. On the one hand, emerging countries, following an export-led development strategy, try to prevent an appreciation of the real exchange rate of their currency, enjoy persistent current account surpluses and accumulate growing stocks of dollar-denominated securities. On the other hand, the USA benefits from the fact that its high consumption demand and resulting current account deficits are financed by large capital inflows from abroad. This situation could be characterized as a stable equilibrium, as the two groups of countries become mutually dependent.

An alternative explanation to the BWII hypothesis is the *Asset shortage theory*.[91] According to this theory, both payment imbalances and asset bubbles can be traced back to asymmetries in financial development. More precisely, the world economy would be characterized by a high demand for liquid and riskless assets. Given the asymmetrical development of financial markets, a large part of this demand would be

[89]According to Jeanne (2012) the US dollar has fulfilled this role quite well.

[90]See Dooley et al. (2003, 2009).

[91]See Caballero (2006).

met by the USA. This would result in large capital inflows into the USA at the cost of greatly increased financial fragility.

The two hypotheses just outlined regarding the reasons for the demand for US dollar-denominated financial assets are based on the assumption that these assets are liquid and riskless. Their liquidity depends on the fact that the US financial market is large and deep, while their lack of risk depends on the fact that the dollar is the key currency in the international monetary system. The American currency can fulfil this role because of the complementarity between the different functions it performs. Thus, the fact that most imports and exports are invoiced in dollars favours the use of the American currency as an anchor.[92] This use of the US currency reduces the volatility of countries' exchange rate and encourages funding through liabilities and holding of assets denominated in dollars. In turn, dollar funding and dollar holding[93] make dollar invoicing more desirable[94] and so the virtuous circle closes.

Establishing the initial link in this circle is problematic. It is plausible that in the Bretton Woods system this link was the significant weight of the American economy in the world economy. At present, given the significant decline in this weight, the initial link in the virtuous circle described above would seem to be represented by dollar funding and holding, i.e. the role assumed by the dollar in world finance following the process of financial globalization.

The dominance of the dollar in global finance has led to changes in the transmission of shocks and macroeconomic policies, undermining the monetary autonomy of the rest of the world, that is undermining one of the cornerstones of the Bretton Woods Agreement.[95]

As noted by Calvo et al. (1996): "... global factors affecting foreign investment tend to have an important cyclical component, which have given rise to repeated booms and busts in capital inflows". One of the main drivers of these global financial cycles is the monetary policy of the USA.[96]

For example, when the Fed lowers the policy interest rate, there are immediate effects on the rest of the world, since in other countries there are sectors (banks, households and corporates) that hold dollar-denominated assets and dollar-linked assets. The increase in the market price of these assets affects the net worth of these sectors and their ability to obtain credit. During this "risk-on" period abundant capital flows across boundaries. This results in a positive global financial cycle. This process is reversed in "risk-off" periods, in many cases triggered by a restrictive monetary policy introduced by the Fed.[97]

---

[92]See Egorov and Mukhin (2019).

[93]According to Maggioni et al. (2018), holding reserves in dollars encourages borrowing in dollars.

[94]See Gopinath and Stein (2018).

[95]See Rey (2019).

[96]See Miranda-Agrippino and Rey (2015).

[97]See Rey (2013) and Gerko and Rey (2017).

6.11 Financial Globalization and Currency Crises

Financial globalization has increased the possibility for many emerging and developing countries to draw on an international pool of financial capital. The inflow of foreign capital can help these countries achieve higher rates of accumulation and growth.[98]

In establishing what determines the capital flows to emerging and developing economies, the literature highlights "push" and "pull" factors. The push factors are external conditions, such as U.S. economic growth, U.S. interest rates, global commodity prices and the prevailing level of global risk aversion. The pull factors are the domestic characteristics of the potential destination country of the capital flows. These include domestic macroeconomic fundamentals, the degree of political stability, domestic policies and the domestic real and monetary cycle.

The debate on the relative importance of these two factors is wide-ranging. In the 1990s the pull factors probably played a dominant role as many emerging and developing countries pegged their exchange rate on the US dollar and attracted a large amount of capital from abroad. However, Calvo et al. (1996) have shown that international political and economic conditions play a significant role in determining foreign capital inflows and outflows. A change in these conditions can lead to a *sudden stop* and the onset of a currency and financial crisis in the developing or emerging country.[99]

There may be several sources for a sudden stop. A first source of risk stems from the denomination of debt in a foreign currency. A depreciation of the national currency against the currency in which the debt is denominated makes it more costly and difficult for the debtor country to repay its debt.[100] A second source of risk for foreign-indebted countries arises from the volatility of capital inflows. Calvo and Reinhart (2000) have shown that many financial crises in emerging countries have resulted from sudden stops. The risk of such events is particularly high when the country's foreign exposure is in the form of portfolio flows, i.e. short-term capital movements rather than direct foreign investment. Therefore, financial liberalization, by allowing this last type of capital flows, increases the likelihood of crises.[101] Table 6.14 shows that, during the phase of pronounced growth in foreign capital inflows to emerging countries, the volatility of capital flows and, hence, the likelihood of sudden stops, was higher for emerging than for industrialized countries.

The fact is that as financial systems have become increasingly integrated, crises have become more frequent, especially in emerging countries (Table 6.15).

In the 1990s, when capital inflows to emerging countries were at their strongest, a number of major crises occurred. The main causes of these crises seem to have been a combination of factors. The main one, which triggered both the 1994 Mexican and

---

[98]See Bosworth et al. (1999).

[99]See Calvo and Reinhart (2000).

[100]See Calomiris (2005).

[101]See Tornell and Westerman (2002) and Kaminsky and Reinhart (1999).

Table 6.14 Capital inflows (in percent of GDP) and their volatility (1975–1997)

	Average value	Relative standard deviation
Industrialized countries	4.53	1.40
Emerging countries	1.68	7.19
Africa	1.84	9.79
Asia	2.40	2.19
Eastern Europe	1.48	2.39
Middle East	1.71	2.54
Latin America	1.17	4.81

Source: Edwards (2001). Legenda: the coefficient of variation is the ration of the standard deviation to the mean

Table 6.15 Number of crises and their distribution

Markets	Banking crises	Currency crises	Double crises	Total
Industrialized countries				
1919–1939	11	13	12	36
1945–1971	0	21	0	21
1973–1997	9	29	6	44
Emerging and developing countries				
1919–1939	7	3	3	13
1945–1971	0	16	1	17
1973–1997	17	57	21	95

Source: Eichengreen and Bordo (2002)

the 1997 Thai crises, was the adoption of a fixed exchange rate regime and the inability to keep domestic price growth at the same pace as that of the country to which the exchange rate was pegged.

The crisis in Thailand was exacerbated by a second factor: the weakness of the domestic banking system and its inefficient regulation. Thai banks borrowed in dollars and lent this money, also in dollars, to businesses. When the Thai baht depreciated against the dollar, businesses were no longer able to repay their loans. Similar fragility led to the spread of the crisis to other Asian countries, starting with Korea.[102]

This crisis can be considered a benchmark.[103] Firstly, since unsustainable exchange rate regimes were widely perceived to be one of the main causes of the currency crises of the 1990s, including the EMS crisis in 1992, various economists[104] have suggested that, in a world of high international capital mobility, only the two extreme exchange rate regimes—a permanently fixed exchange rate regime

[102]The literature has identified several channels through which crises can spread between countries. The main ones are "real links", i.e. trade links between countries (See Gerlach & Smets, 1995) and "financial links", i.e. financial links between countries (see Calvo, 1998; Calvo & Mendoza, 2000).

[103]See Obstfeld and Rogoff (2009).

[104]See, among others, Obstfeld and Rogoff (1995) and Fischer (2001).

Table 6.16 Evolution of exchange rate regimes

	1990	2000	2010	2019
Hard peg	15.7	24.7	13.2	12.5
Soft peg	64.2	30.1	39.7	46.4
Floating	15.1	33.5	36.0	34.4
Residual	5.0	11.7	11.1	6.7
Total	100.0	100.0	100.0	100.0

Source: Areaer database

(such as a currency board or a monetary union) or a free floating exchange rate regime—are sustainable.[105] From Table 6.16 it appears that in the 2000s there has been a certain polarization of the exchange rate regimes. It should, however, be noted that often the countries officially classified as operating under a floating exchange rate regime in effect intervened to stabilize their exchange rate because of "fear of floating"[106]; however, the number of countries following a soft peg of the exchange rate seem to be increasing.

Secondly, the harsh conditions imposed by the IMF on South-East Asian countries in return for its financial support had a significant influence on their subsequent behaviour. The stigma suffered due to the significant reduction of their sovereignty is one of the reasons why, in the subsequent years, these countries accumulated a large amount of foreign exchange reserves in order to prevent future financial crises. Thirdly, since the 2000s, the importance of push factors has increased. The global financial cycle has become the determining factor of the waves of financial flows to and from emerging and developing countries. This cycle, however, given the dominant role of the dollar in the international payments system, depends to a large extent on the Fed's monetary policy. Financial instability in advanced countries also influences the capital flows to emerging and developing countries. In the 2008 financial crisis, under-capitalized banks in advanced countries contracted lending to emerging economies. The risk of these economies increased and investors diverted their capital from them to "safe havens".

The high frequency of crises in emerging countries, as a result of financial globalization, raises the question of how they can be prevented and, when they occur, cauterized while minimizing their costs. In the past, scholars and practitioners have focused mainly on the pull factors affecting flows to emerging and developing countries. From this perspective, some scholars[107] have argued that emerging countries should restrict capital flows through capital controls, others propose

[105]A different view in favour of intermediate exchange rate regimes can be found in Williamson (2000) and Masson (2001).

[106]Because depreciations in these countries often tend to be associated with economic contractions rather than expansions. See Calvo and Reinhart (2002).

[107]See Krugman (1998, 2000), Stiglitz (2002) and Tobin (2000). Empirical evidence, however, shows that capital controls are only effective for a short period of time. See Kaminsky and Schmukler (2001).

that,[108] in order to prevent currency and financial crises, emerging countries should proceed, at the same time, with financial liberalization and the strengthening of their domestic financial markets.

However, these measures risk having limited effect in a phase where push factors have become prevalent. In such a phase, advanced countries are called upon to monitor the international financial cycle more closely. The implementation of policy measures aimed at influencing both the push and pull factors of capital flows may be coordinated by international institutions, in particular the IMF, which in this way is called upon to play as important a role in crisis prevention as it does in crisis resolution.

6.12 The Evolution of the International Monetary Fund's Responsibilities

As seen in Chap. 5, the IMF was established by the Bretton Woods Agreement. The first article of the Agreement establishing the IMF defined its key functions: (*i*) Promoting international monetary cooperation; (*ii*) facilitating a balanced growth of international trade; (*iii*) Promoting exchange stability and orderly exchange arrangements and impeding competitive exchange rate depreciation; (*iv*) making members able to correct payment imbalances without using measures of trade protection; (*v*) reducing the duration and the size of payments imbalances.

The IMF became active in the mid-1950s[109] and in addition to monitoring the exchange rate policies of its member countries, it specialized in short-term loans of limited amounts to advanced countries. With the collapse of Bretton Woods and the introduction of a flexible exchange rate regime, the IMF no longer seemed to have any reason to exist. Nonetheless, it survived, though its role in the post-Bretton Woods international monetary system changed.[110]

Starting in the late 1970s, IMF programmes increasingly focused on providing financial support to emerging or developing countries hit by banking or sovereign debt crises. Particularly after the first oil crisis, the IMF became an important advisor to developing countries on the adjustment policies to be followed. Along with advice, it granted loans to these countries to make the adjustment of macroeconomic imbalances less costly.[111] IMF programmes generally allowed these countries to balance their external accounts by reducing output and imports.

In the 1980s, the IMF provided substantial loans to Latin American countries hit by a severe financial crisis. These loans were provided on condition that the involved governments agreed to follow macroeconomic stabilization policies. As Meltzer

[108]See Areta et al. (2001) and Edwards (2001).

[109]See James (1996).

[110]See Reinhart and Trebesch (2015).

[111]See Meltzer (1999).

(1999, p. 8) writes "IMF programmes postponed recognition of losses by U.S. and other international banks at the expense of living standards in Latin America".

It was after the Mexican crisis in 1994 that the IMF extended its surveillance on its member countries' financial sectors, in the belief that financial stability is a prerequisite for macroeconomic stability.[112] This is the context in which the IMF intervened to support Asian countries during the 1997–98 crisis. In return for its financial support, the IMF asked these countries to adopt not only macroeconomic adjustment measures,[113] but also far-reaching institutional reforms.[114]

The conditions imposed on the South-East Asian countries were considered by several observers to be excessively strict.[115] Following the debate on this intervention, various criticisms were levelled at the IMF's capital crisis management. In particular, some opponents of the IMF argued that its existence and its support operations for countries in default created moral hazard both in debtors, when they ask for loans, and in creditors, when they decide to grant them. In short, the IMF, by granting loans to countries facing a financial crisis, bails out their creditors.[116] From this perspective, the critics of the IMF believe that, rather than preventing, fosters financial crises. This view is shared by those according to whom in an era of internationally mobile private capital, countries with trade deficits, if they are worth financing, can obtain the funds they need on the international financial market. In reality, at the international level, as at the national level, the capital market is imperfect both because of the existence of information asymmetries and because of collective action problems.[117] The latter appears particularly relevant to the international arena, where anarchy reigns and there is, therefore, neither a legislative framework nor a supranational authority to regulate bankruptcy and to discourage it.[118] Hence the need for an institution, such as the IMF, to guarantee the stability of the current international monetary system based on fiat money. The authoritativeness of the IMF is guaranteed by the USA, which in this way induces follower countries to respect its decisions and advice regarding the policies and reforms to be implemented.

In return for this support, the USA derives various advantages from having the IMF prevent and manage capital crises.[119] First, they can share the burden of fighting crises across the members of the IMF. Otherwise, this would fall largely on them. Second, conditions on borrowers are more easily accepted if they are imposed by a multilateral institution than by an individual country. In the latter case, such

[112]See Moschella (2010).

[113]Considered by some scholars, such as Stiglitz (2002), as worsening the crisis.

[114]The imposition of the latter type of measures has been sharply criticised by Feldstein (1998).

[115]See Stiglitz (2002).

[116]Roubini and Setser (2004) find no evidence of moral hazard in IMF lending.

[117]This can lead to herd behaviour and creditor panic. See Masson and Mussa (1997).

[118]See the wide-ranging debate on the reasons why a debtor state should repay its debt, notably Eaton and Gersovitz (1981) and Bulow and Rogoff (1989).

[119]See Henning (2009).

conditions would be perceived as a severe loss of national sovereignty. Third, the maintenance of an international institution in crisis resolution avoids the emergence of regional and decentralized solutions to crises. In this way, the central position of the dollar in the current international monetary system is more easily maintained.

6.13 The European Monetary Union (EMU)

The currency crises that hit many emerging economies in the 1990s confirmed the idea that even stringent exchange rate constraints—from exchange rate pegging to currency boards—were not entirely credible. It can be argued, therefore, that in the *Delors Report* the establishment of the EMU was a strategy to prevent both exchange rate volatility and possible currency crises associated with a fixed exchange rate regime.[120]

The creation of the EMU was a unique event.[121] Never before had a number of states, on the one hand, formed a monetary union based on a new currency and managed by a common monetary authority and, on the other hand, retained their political independence in all other respects. This experiment is unprecedented in modern history. In the past, the creation of a domestic fiat money was always preceded by the formation of a state. The EMU, however, emerged as an important step towards finally achieving the political unification of Europe.[122] Indeed, in 1950 Jacques Rueff stated that Europe would be unified through the creation of a single currency or not at all.[123] This view was shared by some politicians[124] and scholars.[125] The Maastricht Treaty itself states that the aim of creating the EMU is "... an ever closer union among the peoples of Europe".

The impetus for the concrete implementation of European monetary integration came, however, due to particular circumstances that have arisen shortly after the European Council had entrusted a Committee chaired by Jacques Delors with the task of drawing up a blueprint for Economic and Monetary Union (EMU). As Padoa-Schioppa (2004, p. 7) writes: "During the crucial phase in which the blueprint prepared by the Delors Committee was at the junction of either being shelved or becoming a concrete political commitment, the Berlin wall fell (November 1989) and the course of post-world war II European history suddenly changed".

The unification of Germany reawakened fears of the re-emergence of German hegemony over Europe. It is not surprising that the impetus for the EMU as a first

[120] See Eichengreen (1997).

[121] For a history of the process of the European monetary integration see Preda (2017).

[122] See Jonung (2002).

[123] See Issing (2016).

[124] See Schauble and Lamers (1994).

[125] See Wallace (1997).

step towards the political union of Europe came from France, the country that had suffered most from German expansionism in the past. This push was strongly supported by Italy. Both Prime Minister Andreotti[126] and the Bank of Italy Governor Ciampi[127] played decisive roles in the preparation and stipulation of the Maastricht Treaty.

Kohl would have preferred monetary union to be preceded by political union. He was deeply concerned, a view supported by the Bundesbank, that monetary union could jeopardise German's "stability culture". However, not wishing to jeopardise the unification of the two Germanys, Kohl agreed to monetary union, but demanded that the Maastricht Treaty includes conditions for EMU participation so that his country's monetary stability would not be compromised.

In general, the creation of a monetary union entails certain costs for the participating states. The main ones are the loss of monetary sovereignty and the privilege of seigniorage. However, at the time of the EMU's establishment, these costs were relatively small. In the context of near-zero inflation rates, state seigniorage revenues were modest. While the scope for pursuing autonomous monetary policies had been severely curtailed by financial globalization. If a government reduced its policy interest rate to support the economy, it had to reckon with a depreciation of the exchange rate and an increase in imported inflation.[128]

At the root of the EMU there lay primarily political reasons confirming the belief of De Grauwe (1993, p. 656) that: "Not a single monetary union in the past came about because of a recognition of economic benefits of the union. In all cases the integration was driven by political objectives".

However, the creation of the EMU was not so much the result of the imposition of a hegemon, Germany, as might be assumed according to the hegemonic stability theory, but rather an alliance to prevent Germany, after unification, from loosening its ties with Western Europe and presenting itself in the international arena as an independent power. In addition, the creation of the single currency and its management by a common central bank was a counterweight to the monetary hegemony exercised by Germany in a fixed exchange rate system such as the EMS.

During the first years of the EMU, Germany was "the sick man of Europe", with GDP growth rates below the euro area average.[129] However, over time, thanks to important reforms in the labour market and the development of the high-quality manufacturing sector, the German economy gradually consolidated. Thus, after the 2008 crisis, Germany became the new European economic hegemon. This does not mean that this hegemony has also turned into political hegemony. On many

---

[126]Padoa-Schioppa explains how it was Andreotti himself who proposed an ultimate date for the establishment of the EMU (1 January 1999). See Carli (2014, p. 428).

[127]According to Krugman (1994, p. 192), the intention of Governor Ciampi was to put an external constraint on Italy, more precisely on the fiscal irresponsibility of its political class. However, it is to be believed that both Ciampi and Padoa-Schioppa, his close collaborator, firmly believed in the project of a federated Europe.

[128]See Helleiner (1995).

[129]See Scharpf (2011).

occasions, in fact, Germany has shown that it has renounced this role, putting its internal interests as an export-led country first. However, since GFC German authorities have demanded the pursuit of virtuous fiscal policies by the other EMU member countries and the adoption of severe fiscal austerity measures by the countries of the union affected by financial crises in 2010–2011.

These economic policy directions and low GDP growth in the euro area countries fostered the emergence of a crisis of confidence in the EMU in the countries of Southern Europe in the mid-2010s. The emergence of such crises inevitably raises the question of the sustainability of the EMU.[130] However, the collapse of the EMU would probably represent the end of the project of a political union of Europe: the political costs of this failure would perhaps be greater than the economic instability that would result.

Several studies have shown that the euro area is not an optimal currency area as defined by Mundell in 1961.[131] However, as Goodhart (1995, p. 452) writes: "The evidence ... suggests that the theory of optimal currency area has relatively little predictive value", the reason for this is that this theory is strikingly apolitical, neglecting in particular the fact that nation states still exist. In the case of the euro area, in particular, these states still enjoy considerable fiscal independence, have different institutional arrangements and sometimes different foreign policy.

On the basis of this theory, as is well known, a monetary union between countries is only sustainable if at least one of the following conditions is met: wage flexibility, centralization of public finance or perfect labour mobility.

History shows us that while monetary unions have emerged for political reasons, they have always failed because of political conflicts. Economic factors, in particular the benefits that a monetary union brings in terms of trade growth and monetary stability, while important, are not sufficient to ensure the sustainability of EMU over time.[132] Cohen (1998) argues that, on the basis of historical experience, the sustainability of a monetary alliance can result from two factors. The first of these is the existence of a hegemonic country which renders the monetary agreement on terms agreeable to all. The second factor consists in a set of institutional constraints which are respected due to a sense of belonging to a community. In the case of the EMU, given the differences that still exist between the member countries, it is plausible that a decisive factor for its sustainability is Germany's exercise of the role of a hegemonic country. Thanks to its economic power, it can convince the countries in the area to cede further forms of sovereignty to a common shared government. This is a path fraught with difficulties, but which, if accomplished, would make Europe a global political player.

---

[130]For a discussion of this aspect see, among others, Cohen (1998, 2003) McNamara and Jones (1996).

[131]This is the main reason why a large part of American economists have always looked with scepticism at the chances of success of EMU. See Dornbusch (1993b), Feldstein (1998) and Jonung and Drea (2009).

[132]See Cohen (2000) and Sadeh (2009).

6.13.1 The Path to EMU

In the second half of the 1980s, the enactment of the Single European Act of 1986 (which foresaw the removal of all barriers to the movement of people, goods, services and capital between European Community member countries by the end of 1992) and the smooth functioning of the EMS encouraged renewed interest in monetary integration among European countries. More precisely, it was believed that monetary integration would reinforce the benefits of economic integration by forcing member countries to adopt a common anti-inflationary monetary policy. The costs associated with exchange rate fluctuations would decrease and competitive devaluations would become unfeasible. In 1988, at the urging of the French and German foreign ministers, the European Commission was given the task of examining the feasibility of the project to unify Europe's currency.[133]

In April 1989 the Commission presented its "Report on Economic and Monetary Union in the European Community", a document better known as the *Delors Report*. This report defined the various stages in which the creation of the European economic and monetary union was to be articulated. The economic union would be completed with the implementation of the Single Act and the coordination of macroeconomic policies. Monetary union, however, was to be achieved when the member countries of the European Community had established a common monetary policy, managed by a European Central Bank and a single currency to replace the various national currencies.

Two years later, in 1990, the European Commission published an in-depth study on the advantages and costs of a possible monetary union entitled *One Money, One Market*. In the period that followed, the scientific and political debate was intense.

The Maastricht Treaty of 1991 between the EMS countries adopted most of the guidelines of the *Delors Report*. The latter tended to regard monetary union as a natural and almost obligatory outcome of the Single Act. This conclusion was essentially based on two considerations, namely that exchange rate volatility harms trade integration[134] and that the adoption of a fixed exchange rate does not allow for the proper conduct of monetary policy in the long run.[135]

In the Maastricht Treaty it was established that the monetary policy of the EMU was to be managed by the European System of Central Banks (ESCB). This is made up of the European Central Bank (ECB) and the national central banks of the countries that participate in EMU.

There was a shared conviction among the treaty negotiators that a single monetary policy would be possible without generating conflicts if EMU countries had low

---

[133]See Eichengreen (1993).

[134]For a long time this assumption was accepted without being supported by empirical evidence. In the more recent period, however, several contributions have shown that monetary unions promote significant growth in trade. See, in particular, Frankel and Rose (1998) and Baldwin et al. (2005).

[135]This assumption concealed the conviction that many EMS countries would not be able to "import" Germany's strict monetary policy in the medium to long term.

inflation rates and balanced public finances. Based on this belief, the adoption of a single currency would be sustainable over time if the participating countries had similar macroeconomic parameters. The Maastricht Treaty therefore laid down certain requirements for countries wishing to participate in EMU at its inception. In this context, these four so-called convergence criteria were specified:

(i) Achievement of a high degree of price stability, as evidenced by an average rate of inflation no more than 1.5 percentage points above that of the three best performing member states;
(ii) Sustainability of the government financial position, defined to mean both a fiscal deficit no higher than 3% of GDP and a level of public debt no higher than 60% of GDP;
(iii) Observance of the normal fluctuation margins provided for by the ERM, meaning no severe tensions and no devaluation for at least 2 years;
(iv) Durability of convergence in long-term interest rate levels, interpreted as an average rate over 1 year that is no more than 2 percentage points above that of the three best performing member states.

In 1998, the process of convergence towards the above parameters was completed successfully for all countries wishing to adopt the single currency. However, this process was not without its costs: between 1992 and 1998, the GDP growth rate of the euro area countries slowed markedly compared with the previous period and was significantly lower than that of the OECD countries.

6.13.2 EMU's Macroeconomic Outcomes

The institutional architecture of EMU, as defined in the Maastricht Treaty, was designed to achieve two basic objectives: price stability and fiscal discipline. Price stability was defined as the primary objective of the ECB. To this end, this institution was given a high degree of independence with respect to both instruments and objectives. The ECB, also because it has no defined political counterpart (given the limited power of the European Parliament), is perhaps the closest central banker to the figure of the "conservative" central banker proposed by Rogoff (1985). With reference to this institution, article 105 of the Maastricht Treaty provides as follows: "The primary objective of the ESCB shall be to maintain price stability". In this, the ECB differs from the Fed which has a dual mandate. It pursues not only price stability but also output stability.

In order to impose fiscal discipline on member countries, the *Stability and Growth Pact* was established in 1997. This Pact was subsequently revised, especially after the 2007–2008 financial crisis, to make it more flexible. The main objective of the Pact is to prevent undisciplined fiscal behaviour in one country from having spillover effects on the rest of the Union. In order to discourage undisciplined fiscal behaviour, at the beginning the ECB was not allowed to act as lender of last resort, so that it cannot be used for fiscal purposes, i.e. it is not called upon to buy sovereign debt

Table 6.17 Real GDP growth

	1999–2007	2008–2019	1999–2019
USA	3.0	1.7	2.2
Euro area	2.3	0.8	1.4
United Kingdom	2.8	1.2	1.9
Japan	1.3	0.5	0.8

Source*:* Federal Reserve economic data

securities in order to support their prices. These institutional mechanisms would have contributed to keeping fiscal responsibility confined to the national level.

When the EMU was established in 1999, it was widely believed that it would enable the euro area countries to achieve price stability and high economic growth. A little more than 20 years after the introduction of the euro, the objective of price stability seems to have been largely achieved: in fact, during this period the average inflation rate in the euro area has been very low, for long periods below 2%, i.e. the ECB's target for price stability. At the same time, the level of long-term interest rates has also fallen significantly, showing that inflation expectations in the area have declined significantly. These processes have favoured a decrease in the dispersion of inflation rates and long-term interest rates across member countries. All this shows that the ECB's monetary policy has been credible as well as effective.

The adoption of a single currency and efforts to harmonize institutions and regulations have fostered the formation of a large and deep European financial market. This not only improves the allocation of savings in the area but also makes the transmission of monetary impulses more effective.

While it is true that the euro has enabled the area to achieve solid price stability, contributed to a growth in trade, fostered the integration of financial markets and made the economic cycle of the member countries synchronous, it is also true that in these first two decades of the common currency the economic growth of the countries in the area has been modest, lower than that of the USA and the United Kingdom[136] (Table 6.17).

There are various explanations for the low growth in the euro area. Some economists attribute it to insufficient aggregate demand, blaming the ECB for an overly cautious monetary policy or seeing fiscal austerity as a brake on the adoption of adequate countercyclical fiscal measures.[137] Other economists and the ECB itself explain the low growth of the euro area by the existence of rigidities on the aggregate supply side, calling, therefore, for an extensive liberalization process in the markets for goods and production factors.[138] These two opposing visions have been taken up by Southern European and Northern European countries, respectively.

[136]A documented review of the early years of the euro can be found in ECB (2019) and Hartmann and Smets (2018).

[137]See Krugman (2012), Stiglitz (2017) and Mody (2018).

[138]See Gomes et al. (2013) and Masuch et al. (2018).

6.14 Conclusions

The collapse of the Bretton Woods system led to the emergence of a system of flexible exchange rates, in which the key currency and other currencies were no longer directly (in the case of the dollar) or indirectly (in the case of other currencies) anchored to a commodity. The use of a fiat currency, i.e. one whose supply elasticity was infinite, significantly expanded the scope for governments to exploit seigniorage rights. This helps to explain why the years after the abandonment of the Bretton Woods system were characterized by high inflation in almost all industrialized countries. Inflation accelerated after the 1973 oil crisis, resulting in what came to be known as the Great Inflation, the highest peacetime inflation phase ever.

In this phase, large inflation differentials between countries and high volatility in price growth favoured the emergence of extreme exchange rate instability. In particular, the dollar depreciated significantly on several occasions. This led to a decline in confidence in the stability of the value of the key currency and in the functioning of the international monetary system. Attempts to reduce exchange rate volatility were made by central banks through sterilized and unsterilized interventions in foreign exchange markets and arrangements involving the coordination of macroeconomic policies. These attempts were only partially successful.

There was strong demand for far-reaching monetary reform aimed at restoring confidence in the stability of the value of domestic and international money. The debate on what kind of reforms should be adopted saw two opposing views on how a monetary system based on a fiat money could be compatible with price stability. Some economists, the so-called *free bankers*, put forward the idea of abandoning monopoly money supply in favour of competitive money supply. International money would also emerge through a competitive process. The implementation of such a reform would, on the one hand, strip governments of all monetary power and, on the other hand, pose the problem of how to guarantee citizens against fraudulent behaviour by money producers.

Other scholars pointed out the problem of time inconsistency, which in the monetary sphere makes discretionary policy biased towards inflation. This bias could be, if not eliminated, at least mitigated by a commitment to make central banks independent of government and parliament. The use of rules in the conduct of monetary policy would have made it possible to monitor the behaviour of central bankers and verify the outcome of their actions.

During the 1980s, many countries reformed their central banks. Even more countries adopted rules, primarily either explicit or implicit forms of inflation targeting, in the conduct of their monetary policy.

The reorganization of the conduct of domestic policy in the advanced countries, the disinflation and stabilization of price levels led to a decrease in exchange rate volatility. From the second half of the 1980s onwards, a phase of low output volatility began. This phase, which lasted until 2007, is referred to as the Great Moderation.

De Long, J. (1997). America's peacetime inflation: The 1970s. In C. D. Romer & D. H. Romer (Eds.), *Reducing inflation: Motivation and strategy*. University of Chicago Press.
Destler, I., & Henning, C. R. (1989). *Dollar politics: Exchange rate policymaking in the US*. Institute for International Economics.
Dooley, M., Folkerts-Landau, D., & Garber, P. (2003). *An essay on the revived Bretton Woods system*. NBER working paper n. 9971.
Dooley, M., Folkerts-Landau, D., & Garber, P. (2009). *Bretton Woods II still defines the international monetary system*. NBER working paper n. 14731.
Dornbusch, R. (1993a). Comment on Bordo M, The Bretton Woods international monetary system: A historical overview. In M. Bordo & B. Eichengreeen (Eds.), *A retrospective on the Bretton Woods system*. University of Chicago Press.
Dornbusch, R. (1993b). Comment on Eichengreen B, Wyplosz C, The unstable EMS. *Brookings Papers on Economic Activity, 1*, 130–136.
Dowd, K. (1996). *Competition and finance. A reinterpretation of financial and monetary economics*. Macmillan.
Dyson, E. (1994). *Elusive union: The process of economic and monetary union in Europe*. Longman.
Eaton, J., & Gersovitz, M. (1981). Debt with potential repudiation: Theoretical and empirical analysis. *Review of Economic Studies, 48*, 289–309.
ECB. (2010, May). The great inflation: Lessons for monetary policy. *Monthly Bulletin*, 99–110.
ECB (2018). *The international role of the euro*. ECB.
ECB. (2019). *Twenty years of European economic and monetary union*. Conference Proceeding, 17–19 June.
Edison, H. J. (1993). *The effectiveness of central bank intervention: A survey of the literature after 1982*. Special Papers in International Economics n. 18. Department of Economics, Princeton University.
Edwards, S. (2001). *Capital mobility and economic performance: Are emerging economies different?*. NBER working paper n. 8076.
Egorov, K., & Mukhin, D. (2019). *Optimal monetary policy under dollar pricing*. Yale University.
Eichengreen, B. (1993). Epilogue: Three perspectives on the Bretton Woods system. In M. Bordo & B. Eichengreen (Eds.), *A retrospective on the Bretton Woods system: Lessons for international monetary reform*. Chicago University Press.
Eichengreen, B. (1997). *European monetary unification: Theory, practice and analysis*. MIT.
Eichengreen, B., & Bordo, M. (2002). *Crises now and then: What lessons from the last era of financial globalization*. NBER working paper n. 8716.
Eichengreen, B., & Frieden, J. (1993). The political economy of European monetary unification: An analytical introduction. *Economics and Politics, 5*, 85–105.
Eichengreen, B., & Xia, G. (2019). China and the SDR: Financial liberalization through the back door. *Quarterly Journal of Finance, 9*, 1–36.
Eichengreen, B., & Wyplosz, C. (1993). The unstable EMS. *Brookings Papers on Economic Activity, 24*, 51–144.
Feldstein, M. (1998, March/April). Refocusing the IMF. *Foreign Affairs 77*.
Fischer, S. (1990). Rules versus discretion in monetary policy. In B. Friedman & F. Hahn (Eds.), *Handbook of monetary economics* (Vol. 2). Elsevier.
Fischer, S. (2001). Exchange rate regimes: Is the bipolar view correct. *Journal of Economic Perspectives, 15*, 3–24.
Frankel, A., & Rose, A. K. (1998). The endogeneity of the optimum currency area criteria. *Economic Journal, 108*, 1009–1025.
Fratianni, M., & von Hagen, J. (1990). German dominance in the EMS. *Open Economies Review, 1*, 67–87.
Frieden, J. (1998). The euro: Who wins? Who loses? *Foreign Policy, 112*, 25–40.

Frieden, J. (2000). Making commitments: France and Italy in the European monetary system. In B. Eichengreen & J. Frieden (Eds.), *The political economy of European monetary unification* (pp. 1979–1985). Routledge.

Friedman, M. (1951). Commodity reserve currency. *Journal of Political Economy, 59*, 203–232.

Friedman, M. (1959). *A program for monetary stability*. Fordham University Press.

Friedman, M. (1961). The lag in effect of monetary policy. *Journal of Political Economy, 69*, 447–466.

Friedman, M. (1991). *Monetarist economics*. Basil Blackwell.

Gerko, H., & Rey, H. (2017). Monetary policy in the capitals of capital. *Journal of the European Economic Association, 4*, 721–745.

Gerlach, S., & Smets, F. (1995). Contagious speculative attack. *European Journal of Political Economy, 11*, 45–63.

Giannini, C. (2011). *The age of central banks*. Edward Elgar.

Giannini, C., & Cottarelli, C. (1997). *Credibility without rules*. IMF Occasional Papers n.1540.

Giavazzi, F., & Pagano, M. (1988). The advantage of tying one's hands: EMS discipline and central bank credibility. *European Economic Review, 32*, 1055–1075.

Giavazzi, F., & Spaventa, L. (1990). *The new EMS*. CEPR Discussion Paper n. 369.

Goldberg, L. S., & Tille, C. (2009). Macroeconomic interdependence and international role of the dollar. *Journal of Monetary Economics, 56*, 990–1003.

Gomes, S., Mohr, J. P., & Pisani, M. (2013). Structural reforms and macroeconomic performance in the euro area countries: A model-based assessment. *International Finance, 16*, 23–44.

Goodhart, C. A. E. (1995). The political economy of monetary union. In P. Kenen (Ed.), *Understanding interdependence: The macroeconomics of the open economy*. Princeton University Press.

Goodman, J. (1992). *Monetary policy. The politics of central banking in Western Europe*. Cornell University Press.

Goodman, J., & Pauly, L. (1993). The obsolescence of capital controls? Economic management in an age of global markets. *World Politics, 46*, 50–82.

Gopinath, G. (2015). *The international price system*. NBER working paper n. 21646.

Gopinath, G., & Stein, J. (2018). Trade invoicing, bank funding, and central bank reserve holding. *American Economic Review Papers and Proceedings, 108*, 342–346.

Gordon, R. J. (1975). Alternative responses of policy to external supply shocks. *Brookings Papers on Economic Activity, 6*, 183–206.

Gros, D., & Thygesen, N. (1998). *European monetary integration*. Longman.

Hartmann, P., & Smets, F. (2018). *The first twenty years of the European Central Bank: Monetary policy*. ECB working paper n. 2219.

Hayek, F. (1976). *The denationalisation of money*. Hobart Paper Special. Institute of Economic Affairs.

Hefeker, C. (1997). *Interest groups and monetary integration. The political economy of exchange rate regime*. Boulder.

Helleiner, E. (1994). *States and the reemergence of global finance: From Bretton Woods to the 1990s*. Cornell university Press.

Helleiner, E. (1995). Explaining the globalization of financial markets: Bringing states back. *Review of International Political Economy, 2*, 315–341.

Henning, C. R. (2009). *US interests and the International Monetary Fund*. Peterson Institute for International Economics Policy Brief n. PB 09-12.

Hetzel, R. L. (1998, winter). Arthur Burns and inflation. *Federal Reserve Bank of Richmond Economic Quarterly*, 21–44.

Horii, A. (1986). *The evolution of reserve currency diversification*. BIS Economic Papers n. 18.

Ilzetzki, E., Reinhart, C. M., & Rogoff, K. S. (2017). *Exchange arrangements entering the 21st century: which anchor will hold?*. NBER working paper n. 23134.

IMF. (1974). Outline of reform. In *IMF, International monetary reform: Documents of the Committee of Twenty*. IMF.
Issing, O. (2016). On the relation of monetary and political union. *Intereconomics, 51*, 16–20.
Ito, H., & Chinn, M. (2013). *The rise of the 'redback' and China's capital account liberalization: An empirical analysis on the determinants of invoicing currencies*. Asian Development Bank Institute working papers n. 473.
James, H. (1996). *International monetary cooperation since Bretton Woods*. Oxford University Press.
Jeanne, O. (2012). *The dollar and its discontents*. NBER working paper n. 18143.
Jonung, L. (2002). EMU – the first 10 years: Challenges to the sustainability and price stability of the euro area – what does history tell us? In M. Buti & A. Sapir (Eds.), *EMU and economic policy in Europe. The challenge of the early years*. Edward Elgar.
Jonung, L., & Drea, E. (2009). *The euro: It can't happen, it's a bad idea, it won't last. US economists on the EMU, 1989–2002*. European Economy, Economic Papers n. 395, Directorate General Economic and Financial Affairs (DG ECFIN), European Commission.
Kaminsky, G., & Reinhart, C. (1999). The twin crises: Causes of banking and balance of payments problems. *American Economic Review, 89*, 473–500.
Kaminsky, G., & Schmukler, S. (2001). Short and long run integration: Do capital controls matter? In S. Collins & D. Rodrik (Eds.), *Brookings trade forum 2000*. Brookings Institution.
Kenen, P. (1983). *The role of the dollar as an international currency*. New York Group of Thirty, Occasional Papers n. 13.
Kindleberger, C. (1973). *The world in depression, 1929–1939*. University of California Press.
Kindleberger, C. P. (1981). Dominance and leadership in the international economy. *International Studies, 25*, 242–254.
Krugman, P. (1994). *Peddling prosperity*. Norton.
Krugman, P. (1998, September, 7). Saving Asia: It's time to get radical. *Fortune*.
Krugman, P. (2000). Crises: The price of globalization?. In *Federal Reserve Bank of Kansas City, Conference on 'Global Economic Integration: Opportunities and Challenge'*. August 24–26.
Krugman, P. (2012, September 27). Euro austerity madness. *The New York Times*.
Kydland, F., & Prescott, E. (1977). Rules rather than discretion: The inconsistency of optimal plans. *Journal of Political Economy, 85*, 473–491.
Lane, P., & Milesi-Ferretti, G. (2003). International financial integration. *IMF Staff Papers, 50*, 82–113.
Lane, P., & Milesi-Ferretti, G. (2007). The external wealth of nations mark II: Revised and extended estimates of foreign assets and liabilities, 1970–2004. *Journal of International Economics, 73*, 223–250.
Lane, P., & Milesi-Ferretti, G. (2008). The drivers of financial globalization. *American Economic Review Papers & Proceeding, 98*, 327–332.
Lane, P., & Milesi-Ferretti, G. (2018). The external wealth of nations revisited: International financial integration in the aftermath of the global financial crisis. *IMF Economic Review, 66*, 189–222.
Lindberg, L. N., & Maier, C. S. (1985). *The politics of inflation and economic stagnation: Theoretical approaches and international case studies*. Brooking Institution Press.
Lindley, D., Orphanides, A., & Rasche, R. (2005). *The reform of October 1979: How it happened and why*. Federal Reserve Board, Finance and Economic Discussion Series working paper n. 2005-02.
Ludlow, L. (1982). *The making of the European monetary system. A case study of the politics of the European community*. Butterworth Scientific.
Maggioni, M., Neiman, B., & Schreger, J. (2018). *International currencies and capital allocation*. NBER working paper n. 24673.
Martin, P., & Rey, H. (2006). Globalization and emerging markets: With or without crash? *American Economic Review, 96*, 1631–1651.

Masson, P. R. (2001). Exchange rate regime transitions. *Journal of Development Economics, 64*, 571–586.
Masson, P. R., & Mussa, M. (1997). *The role of the IMF: Financing and its interactions with adjustments and surveillance*. IMF Pamphlet Series n. 50. IMF.
Masuch, K., Anderton, R., Setzer, R., & Benala, N. (2018). *Structural policies in the euro area*. ECB Occasional Papers n. 210.
McKinnon, R. (1973). *Money and capital in economic development*. Brookings Institution.
McNamara, K. R. (1998). *The currency of monetary politics in the European Union*. Cornell University Press.
McNamara, K. R., & Jones, E. (1996). The clash of institutions: Germany in European monetary affairs. *German Politics and Society, 14*, 5–30.
Meltzer, A. (1999). What's wrong with the IMF? What would be better? *Independent Review, 4*, 201–215.
Meltzer, A. (2005). Origins of the great inflation. *Federal Reserve Bank of St. Louis Review, 87*, 145–175.
Meltzer, A. (2009). *A history of the federal reserve, Vol. II, 1970-1986*. University of Chicago Press.
Miranda-Agrippino, S., & Rey, H. (2015). *US monetary policy and the global financial cycle*. NBER working paper n. 21722.
Mody, A. (2018). *Euro tragedy. A drama in nine acts*. Oxford University Press.
Moschella, M. (2010). *Governing risk. The IMF and global financial crises*. Palgrave Macmillan.
Mundell, R. (1973). The monetary consequences of Jacques Ruff. *Journal of Business, 46*, 384–395.
Nelson, E. (2004). *The great inflation of the seventies: What really happened?*. Federal Reserve Bank of St. Louis working paper n. 2004-001.
Nelson, E., & Nikolov, K. (2004). Monetary policy and stagflation in the UK. *Journal of Money, Credit and Banking, 36*, 293–318.
Obstfeld, M. (2007). *International risk sharing and the costs of trade*. Ohlin Lectures, Stockholm School of Economics.
Obstfeld, M., & Rogoff, K. (1995). The mirage of fixed exchange rates. *Journal of Economic Perspectives, 9*, 73–96.
Obstfeld, M., & Rogoff, K. (2000). *Perspectives on OECD capital market integration: Implications for the US current account adjustments*. Federal Reserve Bank of Kansas City symposium on 'Global Economic Integration: opportunities and challenges'. Jackson Hole, August 24–26.
Obstfeld, M., & Rogoff, K. (2004). *The unsustainable US current account position revisited*. NBER working paper n. 10869.
Obstfeld, M., & Rogoff, K. (2009). *Global imbalances and the financial crisis: Products of common causes*. Asia and the Global Financial Crisis. Asia Economic Policy Conference, Santa Barbara, October 18–20, Federal Reserve Bank of San Francisco.
Orphanides, A. (2002). *Monetary policy rules and the great inflation*. Federal Reserve Board, Finance and Economics Discussion Series n. 2002-8.
Orphanides, A. (2003). The quest for prosperity without inflation. *Journal of Monetary Economics, 50*, 633–663.
Padoa-Schioppa, T. (2004). *The Euro and its Central Bank*. MIT.
Persson, T., & Tabellini, G. (1993). Designing institutions for monetary stability. *Carnegie Rochester Conference Series on Public Policy, 39*, 59–84.
Pittaluga, G. B., & Seghezza, E. (2012). *La Grande inflazione in Italia*. ECIG.
Posen, A. (1993). Why central bank independence does not cause low inflation: There is no institutional fix for politics. In R. O'Brien (Ed.), *Finance and international economy*. Oxford University Press.
Prate, A. (1987). *La France et sa monnaie: essai sur la relation entre la Banque de France et le gouvernment*. Julliard.
Preda, D. (2017). *The history of the European monetary union*. Peter Lang.

Reinhart, C., & Trebesch, C. (2015). *The International Monetary Fund: 70 years of reinvention*. Harvard Kennedy School, RWP15-077.
Rey, H. (2013). *Dilemma not trilemma: The global financial cycle and monetary policy independence*. Federal Reserve Bank of Kansas City Economic Policy Symposium.
Rey, H. (2019). *International monetary system and global financial cycles*. Banca d'Italia, Lezioni Paolo Baffi di Moneta e Finanza. Rome, November 22.
Rogoff, K. (1985). The optimal degree of commitment to a monetary target. *Quarterly Journal of Economics, 100*, 1169–1190.
Romer, C. D., & Romer, D. H. (2002). Rehabilitation of monetary policy in the 1950s. *American Economic Review, 92*, 121–127.
Roubini, N., & Setser, B. (2004). *Bailouts or bain-in? Responding to financial crises in emerging economies*. Institution for International Economics.
Sadeh, T. (2009). EMU's diverging micro foundations: A study of governments' preferences and the sustainability of EMU. *Journal of European Public Policy, 16*, 545–563.
Scharpf, F. W. (2011). Monetary union, fiscal crisis and the pre-emption of democracy. *Zeitschrift für Staats - und Europawissenschaften/Journal for Comparative Government and European Policy, 9*, 163–198.
Schauble, W., & Lamers, K. (1994). *Überlegungen zur Europäishen politik*. CDU/CSU fraction, working paper.
Schenk, C. (2017). Coordination failures during Bretton Woods. In A. Ghosh & M. Quereshi (Eds.), *From great depression to great recession: The elusive quest for international policy coordination*. IMF.
Shaw, E. (1973). *Financial deepening in economic development*. Oxford University Press.
Shultz, G. P. (1972). *Statement by the Governor of the Fund and Bank for the United States*. In IMF Summary Proceedings of the Twenty-seventh Annual Meeting of the Board of Governors. September.
Solomon, R. (1982). *The international monetary system, 1945-1981*. Harper & Row.
Stiglitz, J. E. (2002). *Globalization and its discontents*. Norton.
Stiglitz, J. E. (2017). *The euro and its threat to the future of Europe*. Penguin books.
Story, J. (1988). The launching of the EMS: An analysis of change in foreign economic policy. *Political Studies, 36*, 397–412.
Story, J., & De Cecco, M. (1993). The politics and diplomacy of monetary union: 1985-1991. In J. Story (Ed.), *The new Europe: Politics, government and economy since 1945*. Blackwell.
Strange, S. (1990). Finance, information and power. *Review of International Studies, 16*, 259–274.
Summers, P. (2005). What caused the great moderation? Some cross-country evidence. *Federal Reserve Bank of Kansas City Economic Review, 90*, 5–32.
Tobin, J. (2000). Financial globalization. *World Development, 28*, 1101–1104.
Tornell, A., & Westerman, F. (2002). *Boom-bust cycles in middle-income countries: Facts and explanation*. NBER working paper n. 9219.
Truman, E. (2017). *The end of the Bretton Woods international monetary system*. Peterson Institute for International Economics, working paper, n. 17-11.
Tsoukalis, L. (1977). *The politics and economics of European monetary integration*. Allen & Unwin.
Volcker, P., & Gyohten, T. (1992). *Changing fortunes: The World's money and the threat to American leadership*. Times Books.
Wallace, H. (1997). At odds with Europe. *Political Studies, 45*, 677–688.
Walsh, C. (1995). Optimal contracts for central bankers. *American Economic Review, 85*, 150–167.
Walter, A. (2006). Domestic sources of international monetary leadership. In D. Andrews (Ed.), *International monetary power*. Cornell University Press.
White, L. (1984). *Free banking in Britain: Theory, experience and debate, 1800–1845*. Cambridge University Press.

Whitman, M. V. N., Cooper, R. N., & Solomon, R. (1974). The current and future role of the dollar: How much symmetry? *Brookings Papers on Economic Activity, 3*, 539–591.

Williamson, J. (2000). *Exchange rate regimes for emerging markets: Reviving the intermediate option*. Peterson Institute for International Economics.

Chapter 7
Critical Issues in the Current International Monetary System and Future Prospects

7.1 Introduction

Although the dollar, in the post-Bretton Woods period, has maintained, if not strengthened, its dominant role in the international monetary system, the system stability has been and is threatened by several factors.

A first threat to the stability of the current monetary system is the large and persistent current account imbalances. On the one hand, China and emerging countries, but also more recently the euro area, tend to run large and persistent current account surpluses. While, on the other hand, other countries, primarily the USA, are running large and persistent deficits.

Some scholars have argued that such imbalances do not undermine the stability of the existing international monetary system, reasoning that a kind of international division of labour takes place. Emerging countries specializing in the production of real goods, while the USA produces financial instruments in which the citizens of emerging countries can invest their savings.[1]

The 2008 global financial crisis (GFC) showed that this approach, the so-called *Bretton Woods II* hypothesis, is not plausible. Indeed, according to some scholars, large current account imbalances were at the origin of that crisis. China and the emerging countries invested their current account surpluses in US government securities, which led to a decline in long-term interest rates in these countries and thus to abnormal growth in bank lending.

This view, known as the saving glut hypothesis, refers to net capital flows. It has been challenged by those who believe that the GFC resulted from the massive increase in gross capital flows. Hence the hypothesis that this crisis was due to a credit boom caused by the banks' ability to raise resources on the international market, in particular on the US money market. Confirmation of this hypothesis is the

[1]See, for example, Dooley et al. (2003).

G. B. Pittaluga, E. Seghezza, *Building Trust in the International Monetary System*, Frontiers in Economic History, https://doi.org/10.1007/978-3-030-78491-1_7

fact that, in addition to American banks, several European banks were involved in the GFC, while the banks of emerging countries were not.

Current account imbalances, even if they cannot be considered the decisive cause of the GFC, are nevertheless a cause of instability for the international monetary system. A first area where they tend to create instability relates to the supply and demand for international liquidity. In this respect, given the tendency of emerging countries to accumulate foreign exchange reserves for prudential reasons or as an effect of export-led growth models, the demand for international liquidity grew significantly. Furthermore, as the economic size of the USA in relative terms is shrinking, its supply of liquidity is also shrinking: Triffin's dilemma re-emerges in new versions. In this context, the world economy may find itself in a liquidity shortage and spiral into a deflationary crisis, as happened in the early 1930s.

A second example of how current account imbalances can threaten the stability of the international monetary system is the sovereign debt crisis that occurred in the euro area between 2010 and 2011. This crisis stemmed, mainly, from the external imbalances accumulated by the "PIIGS"[2] countries in the first 10 years of existence of the single currency. These imbalances again resulted from a credit boom driven by low real interest rates in these countries. High levels of credit expansion fostered rising domestic demand and an excess of imports over exports covered by external debt. In 2010, the perception of its imminent default led to a sudden stop for Greece, which then spread to the more fragile Eurozone countries, precisely the PIIGS. The return to financial stability in this area was pursued asymmetrically. The adjustment measures were, in fact, borne entirely by the PIIGS which, especially at the insistence of Germany, adopted severe fiscal austerity measures. However, at that time, also the ECB seemed to share the "expansionary austerity" view.[3] In fact, its president Trichet in an interview to the newspaper *Liberation*, on July 8, 2010 observed that: "it is an error to think that fiscal austerity is a threat to growth and job creation. At present, a major problem is the lack of confidence on the part of households, firms, savers and investors who feel that fiscal policies are not sound and sustainable."

Between 2014 and 2015, the euro area risked entering a deflationary phase typical of a stagnant economy. During this period, especially in the PIIGS, political movements adverse to the EMU emerged and the EMU risked breaking up. To a large extent, these trends have been reversed thanks to the ECB's expansionary policy and the behaviour of the ECB and the EU during the COVID-19 crisis.

It is inevitable to ask whether the factors of instability in the international monetary system just mentioned are likely to contribute to weakening the dollar's position as the international currency.

[2]This acronym refers to Portugal, Ireland, Italy, Greece and Spain.

[3]On this view see Alesina and Ardagna (2009).

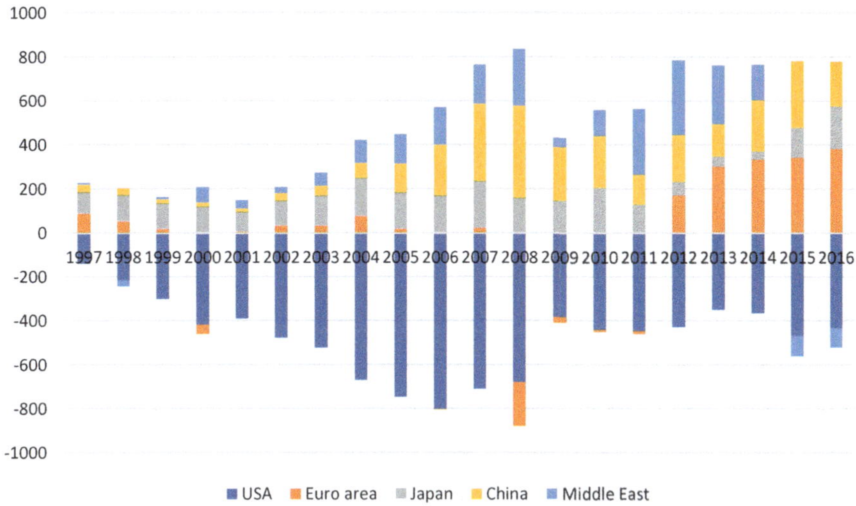

Fig. 7.1 Current account balances (billions of US dollars). Source: IMF, World Economic Outlook, several years

7.2 Current Account Imbalances: the Case of the USA as a World's Banker

Figure 7.1 shows that in the world, since the early 2000s, current account imbalances have significantly expanded.[4] In this process, different components can be identified which also have a different trend over time:

(i) A gradual increase in the U.S. current account deficit until 2006–2007 followed, in the subsequent period, by a slight decrease;
(ii) An increase in the surpluses of Middle East countries, in particular oil exporting nations until 2013, when oil prices were rising;
(iii) Since the 1990s a significant increase in China's surplus, which has broadly stabilized after 2008;
(iv) Persistent surpluses in advanced countries other than the US, in particular Japan and, in more recent years, the euro area.

In many cases current account imbalances are appropriate. This is the case, for example, of countries whose population are ageing rapidly, such as Japan and the Euro area, and which need to accumulate funds to draw down when their workers retire. In other cases, current account imbalances derive from incorrect macroeconomic policies, which lead to the accumulation of a high amount of external liabilities and make the country vulnerable to sudden stops. The reduction of this second type of imbalances contributes to decreasing the probability of a crisis and,

[4]See Eichengreen (2010).

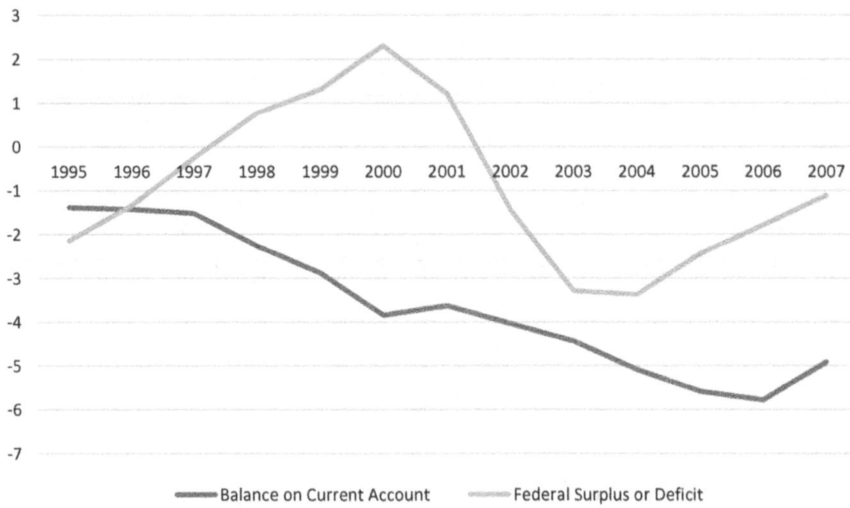

Fig. 7.2 Twin deficits. Source: Federal Reserve Economic Data (FRED) database. Note: Case-Shiller seasonally adjusted purchase price index

therefore, to the stability of the international monetary system. Figure 7.1 shows that a large part of the current account deficits detectable in the world economy concern the USA.[5] This country, compared to the others, is in a special position since its currency is the international fiat money. A sudden stop to this country is therefore unlikely.

Several explanations have been given to the widening current account deficits in the USA. In a first explanation, the growing imbalances of this country have been traced to domestic factors, in particular the decline in both public and private savings rates. In particular, the expansion of the public deficit has, according to this view, created the conditions for a twin deficit.

However, as Fig. 7.2 shows, in the years leading up to the GFC, the USA current account imbalances worsened significantly just as their public deficit was dramatically shrinking.

While the explanation of global imbalances just described holds that the U.S. current account deficit is "made in the USA" and is independent of what happens in other parts of the world, another explanation of these imbalances insists on external factors.

According to this explanation, the so-called *global saving glut*, the widening of global imbalances can be traced to an increase in the supply of net saving from emerging countries. Two factors contributed to the excess savings in these countries. First, the financial crisis of 1997–1998 led the South-East Asian countries involved

[5]See Obstfeld (2018).

Table 7.1 Foreign exchange reserves (billions of dollars)

	South Korea	Thailand	Malaysia	Singapore	Philippines	Indonesia
1997	20.5	26.9	21.5	71.4	8.7	17.5
2000	96.3	32.7	28.7	81.1	15.1	29.4
2003	155.5	42.2	44.3	97.7	17.1	36.3
2007	262.5	87.5	102.0	166.2	33.7	57.0

Source: World Bank database

in the crisis, primarily Korea and Thailand, to pursue large current account surpluses and thus to accumulate large foreign exchange reserves (Table 7.1).

China behaved similarly, although it was not involved in that crisis, as it was concerned about a potential future crisis similar to those which had hit other South-East Asian countries. These emerging countries used the proceeds of their balance of payments surpluses primarily to buy US Treasury bonds. Between 2003 and 2013, as oil prices rose, oil exporters also recorded large current account surpluses, which they invested largely in US government bonds.

Consequently, the long-term interest rate in the United States fell. Correspondingly, the prices of financial assets held by American savers rose. The result was an increase in their financial wealth, which led to an increase in domestic demand for goods and services, including high levels of imports. This, in turn, led to rising current account imbalances.

The global saving glut hypothesis does not offer an explanation as to why emerging and developing countries did not mobilize their savings internally, therefore not providing an explanation for the so-called *Lucas puzzle* according to which, under perfect foresight, capital flows should flow from countries with low returns to countries with high returns due to capital scarcity and favourable long-run prospects. In reality, as we have seen, capital flows mainly proceeded from emerging and developing countries to developed countries, in particular to the USA.

Several studies have tried to explain this paradox by the fact that the advanced economies exhibit higher autarky real returns than the rest of the world. Several reasons have been given for this.[6] Among these the fact that emerging and developing countries, because their financial markets are underdeveloped, have a shortage of financial assets, i.e. a shortage of means of storing value.[7]

Nonetheless, most of the studies just mentioned refer to net capital flows, i.e. to the inter-temporal transfer of resources between countries. In fact, a country's gross foreign asset position generally does not coincide with its current account, since it depends on changes in the market value of claims and liabilities.[8] Taking this aspect into account, some economists, in particular Kindleberger (1965), Despres et al. (1966) and, more recently, Gourinchas and Rey (2007) highlighted the different

[6]See Caballero et al. (2008), Mendoza et al. (2009), Angeletos and Parroux (2011), Antras and Caballero (2009), and Caballero and Krishnamurty (2009).

[7]See Caballero et al. (2008).

[8]See Lane and Milesi-Ferretti (2001).

typology of gross assets and gross liabilities held by the USA. This country, lending mostly at long term and borrowing short term, exercises the functions of "banker of the world".[9] In this way, the USA, on the one hand, provides liquidity to the rest of the world through a process of liquidity and maturity transformation and, on the other hand, profits from the seigniorage derived from the yield differential between its foreign assets and its foreign liabilities, i.e. exploits the exorbitant privilege it derives from issuing international currency.[10]

The liquidity creation described above is a routine activity. It should therefore be distinguished from the creation of liquidity by the USA in periods of crisis.[11] Nevertheless, it constitutes a form of countercyclical flow of capital in the sense of Kindleberger (1973). In fact, maturity transformation, while allowing the USA to take advantage of its exorbitant privilege, makes the USA responsible, in a global crisis, for acting as a global insurer.[12] In fact, during global crises, the value of long-term risky assets held by the USA goes down dramatically while the value of their short-term liabilities, mostly government debt, remains substantially stable. As a global insurer, the US acts as a shock absorber and thus contributes to the stability of the international monetary system.

7.3 The Global Financial Crisis (GFC)

The crises that struck emerging economies in the 1990s prompted scholars to focus their attention primarily on the risks of financial globalization for these countries.[13] Instead, optimism prevailed about the effects of globalization on advanced economies, in particular the fact that it allowed for greater risk sharing and an improvement in macroeconomic performance in these countries.[14] The risk of a large scale financial crisis was, with a few rare exceptions,[15] generally neglected.

---

[9]See Kindleberger (1965) and Despres et al. (1966).

[10]Various estimates, see in particular Lane and Milesi-Ferretti (2009) and Curcuru et al. (2008), show that the excess returns on the net foreign asset position of the USA have increased significantly in the period since the collapse of Bretton Woods. For which various explanations have been proposed. First, it may be that the foreign assets held by this country have become riskier over time and the foreign liabilities more liquid. Second, the excess returns on the US net asset position may have increased due to the trend depreciation of the dollar. As a result, the dollar value of foreign currency assets increases. The resulting capital gain leads to an increase in US excess returns on its net asset position. See Gourinchas and Rey (2014).

[11]Regarding this aspect see Norrlof and Reich (2015).

[12]See Gourinchas et al. (2010).

[13]See Rodrik (1998, 2000) and Obstfeld et al. (2009).

[14]See for example, Kose et al. (2009, 2009).

[15]See Rajan (2005) and Stulz (2005).

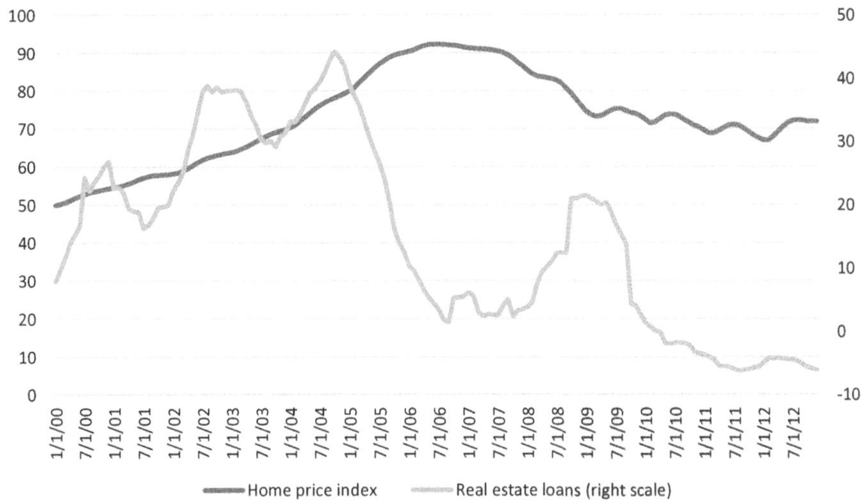

Fig. 7.3 US house price index and real estate loans. Source: Federal Reserve Economic Data (FRED) database. Note: Case-Shiller seasonally adjusted purchase price index. The data referring to real estate loans are annual percent change

7.3.1 Its Origin and Development

The financial crisis of 2007–2008 originated from a credit boom and was essentially a debt crisis.[16] In the previous years, the US and major industrialized countries had seen a particularly pronounced growth in bank debt. Between 1995 and 2007, the share of GDP of this type of credit increased from 123% to 179% in the US, from 128% to 213% in the UK, from 77% to 214% in Spain and from 69% to 129% in Italy.

The abnormal expansion of credit favoured the emergence of a real estate bubble between 2000 and 2006. The increase in real estate prices was particularly high in the USA (Fig. 7.3) and in countries where the increase of private sector's credit on GDP was highest.

While real estate prices rose to an unprecedented extent, the inflation rate for goods and services remained low. The anti-inflationary monetary policies pursued by the industrialized countries thus appeared to be successful.

In concomitance with loose monetary policies, there was a pronounced expansion of lending to the private sector. Such expansion, in addition to low policy interest rates, was facilitated by the introduction of unregulated financial innovations. In the USA, credit growth was largely driven by the spread of sub-prime mortgages, i.e. mortgages to borrowers with a high risk of default (Table 7.2). The diffusion of sub-prime mortgages was facilitated by the massive use of securitization through

[16]See, among others, Allen and Carletti (2010).

Table 7.2 Sub-prime mortgage lending and securitization (in billions of dollars)

	Emissions (a)	Securitization (b)	Ratio (b)/(a) (%)
2001	190	87	46
2002	231	123	53
2003	335	195	58
2004	540	363	67
2005	625	465	74
2006	600	449	75

Source: Ashcraft and Schuermann (2007)

derivative products, such as asset-backed securities (ABS). This allowed banks to significantly increase leverage.

The upward phase of real estate prices in the US peaked in 2005 and the following year house prices began to fall, and this decline became more and more pronounced. Correspondingly, the delinquency rate on sub-prime mortgages increased significantly. This resulted in large losses for shadow banks (mainly hedge funds, money market funds and special purpose vehicles), i.e. institutions that held asset-backed securities (ABS) and lacked the cash flows associated with repayments on securitized sub-prime mortgages.

The difficulties of the shadow banks were immediately reflected in the investment banks, which used these institutions to conduct off-balance sheet operations, primarily securitization transactions, which were not subject to regulation or supervision by the authorities.

In this situation, investment banks and shadow banks found themselves short of liquidity, but had difficulty obtaining it on the interbank market. In fact, the supply of funds in the interbank market became scarce: when confidence in the solvency of the counterparty declined, commercial banks resorted to "haircuts", i.e. demanding collateral from the debtor institution that was worth more than the value of the loan.

In March 2008, one of the largest US investment banks, Bear Stearns, found itself practically insolvent. In order to obtain liquidity, it was forced to sell assets at below-market prices and thus incurred substantial capital losses. Following the intervention of the Federal Reserve, the company was acquired by J.P. Morgan/Chase.

In the summer of 2008, there was a widespread belief that the crisis had been overcome. This belief was based on the fact that the sub-prime mortgage sector represented only a modest part of the capital market. However, within a few weeks, in the autumn of 2008, the situation came to a head. On 15 September, Lehman Brothers, the fourth-largest US investment bank with 25,000 employees and 600 billion dollars in assets, was declared bankrupt.

Following the collapse of Lehman Brothers, the crisis became global, hence its name Global Financial Crisis. In the wake of this event, not only in the US, but also in other industrialized countries, banks began to hoard liquidity reserves. This led to an increase in the amount of base money held in the form of free reserves. This had two effects. On the one hand, the functioning of the interbank market was severely impaired, as evidenced by the unusual increase of its interest rate, and, on the other, the money multiplier fell dramatically (Fig. 7.4).

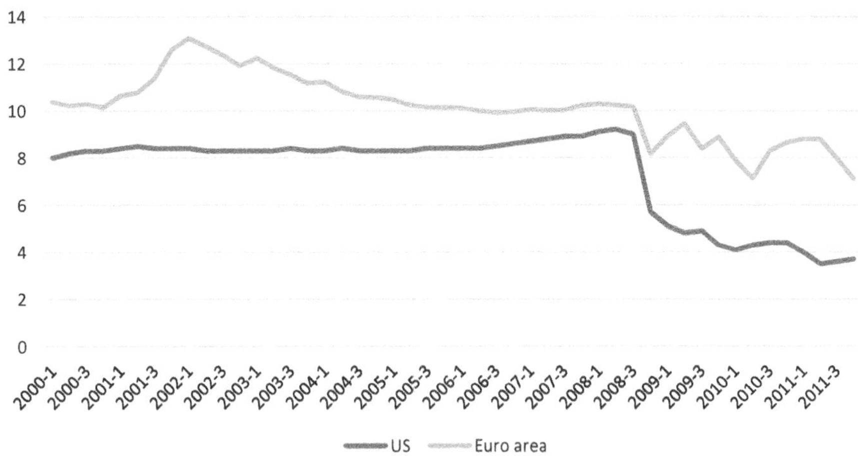

Fig. 7.4 Money multiplier in the USA and Euro area. Source: ECB dataset and FRED, Federal Reserve Bank of St. Louis database

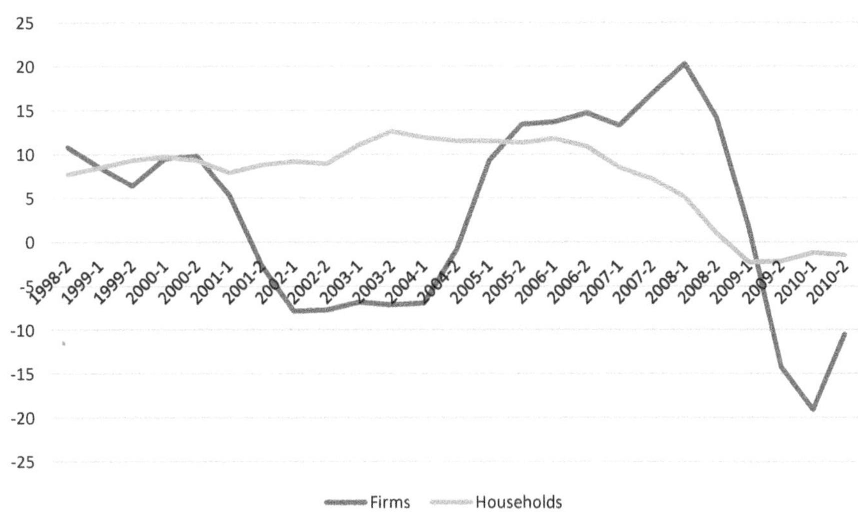

Fig. 7.5 US banks' loans to firms and households (annual percentage change). Source: FRED, Federal Reserve Bank of St. Louis database

In addition to the banks' liquidity hoarding, the fall in demand for credit from the private sector contributed to the decline in the money multiplier. In the USA, as in other advanced countries, companies and households had accumulated unsustainable debt positions over time. They therefore needed to regain normal levels of indebtedness. This could only be achieved through a deleveraging process (Fig. 7.5).

Table 7.3 GDP annual growth of main advanced countries

	USA	Euro area	Japan	England
2003	2.9	0.7	1.6	3.5
2004	3.8	2.0	2.2	2.3
2005	3.5	1.8	1.8	3.3
2006	2.9	3.3	1.3	2.5
2007	1.9	3.0	1.5	2.5
2008	−0.1	0.3	−1.2	−0.4
2009	−2.5	−4.5	−6.7	−4.6
2010	2.6	2.1	4.1	2.0

Source: OECD database

The fall in demand for investment and consumption in the US and other advanced countries led to a pronounced fall in GDP in 2009 and, in the following years, a slowdown in its growth rate. As shown in Table 7.3 GDP fell significantly in 2008–2009 in the major advanced countries. It remained below the long-term trend in the following years.

This prolonged recession, which came to be known as the Great Recession,[17] was different from normal cyclical crises. It was not caused by a temporary drop in aggregate demand, but by a financial crisis that, fuelled by disorderly credit growth, destroyed parts of the financial system and left large amounts of private sector debt and public debt. It took time to reabsorb these imbalances, which explains its persistence.[18]

As shown in Table 7.3 GDP fell significantly in 2008–2009 in the major advanced countries. It remained below the long-term trend in the following years.

7.3.2 *The Main Explanations of the GFC*

Two main explanations have been given for the GFC. The first of these is the *global saving glut*[19] hypothesis discussed in Sect. 6.1. This hypothesis is based on the assumption that in the years leading up to the crisis:

[17]On the Great Recession and its causes see Christiano et al. (2015), Eggertsson and Krugman (2012) and Guerrieri and Lorenzoni (2012).

[18]See on this point Blinder (2014).

[19]See Bernanke (2009), Eichengreen (2009), Kohn (2010), Krugman (2009) and Portes (2009).

(i) An excess of saving over investment in emerging countries flowed into advanced economies,[20] financing their current account deficits, easing financial conditions and reducing long-term interest rates there[21];
(ii) Net capital flows from current account surplus countries to deficit ones fuelled a credit boom in the latter.

Indeed, low interest rates led to a large increase in demand for mortgages and real estate purchases. Rising house prices in turn generated wealth effects and a reduction in domestic savings in the USA, this exacerbated current account imbalances. The vicious circle just described was aggravated by the accommodative monetary policy implemented by the Fed to counteract the negative effects of the collapse of the high-tech industry on the economy.[22] Emerging from the macroeconomic imbalances just described, the housing bubble was amplified, as previously stated, by the ABS. These innovations, not only allowed banks to increase leverage, but contributed to a global bubble, thanks to the high financial interdependence of advanced countries.

The hypothesis of excess saving as the main cause of the GFC is open to some objections. First, in the 2000s, credit booms also affected countries with current account surpluses, such as Brazil between 2003 and 2007, China between 1997 and 2000 and India between 2001 and 2004. Second, between 2004 and 2007 the US long-term interest rate tended to increase while the US current account deficit tended to widen (Fig. 7.6).

Third, the link between the US current account deficit and capital inflows into this country appears to be weak. In fact, as Table 7.4 shows, in 2007, the year before the onset of the crisis, gross capital inflows to the USA were about 2 trillion dollars, several times their current account deficit of about 730 billion dollars. Moreover, the private component of these flows was more than 75% (equivalent to 1648.5 billion dollars): banks' liabilities accounted for just under a third of this amount (509.3 billion dollars). The importance of gross capital flows becomes even more apparent when, instead of the annual flows in 2007, their change between 2003 and 2007 is considered. Table 7.4 shows that between 2003 and 2007, while the US current account deficit increased by just over 200 billion dollars, total gross flows to the US increased by about 1.3 trillion dollars.

The large amount of gross flows to and from the USA seems to be explained by acquisitions and disposals of financial assets rather than by trade in goods and services. In this type of activity, the role of financial institutions is crucial. Hence the hypothesis that these institutions by their behaviour had expanded the financial

[20]This excess saving is attributed to a variety of causes, such as the low levels of financial development in emerging countries (Mendoza et al., 2009), the lack of investment opportunities in these countries (Caballero et al., 2008; IMF, 2005) and the pursuit of export-led policies by many of them, particularly those in Asia (Bernanke, 2005).

[21]Obstfeld and Rogoff (2009) believe that the perception that the increase in productivity due to high-tech innovations was over also contributed to the decline in these interest rates.

[22]See Obstfeld and Rogoff (2009).

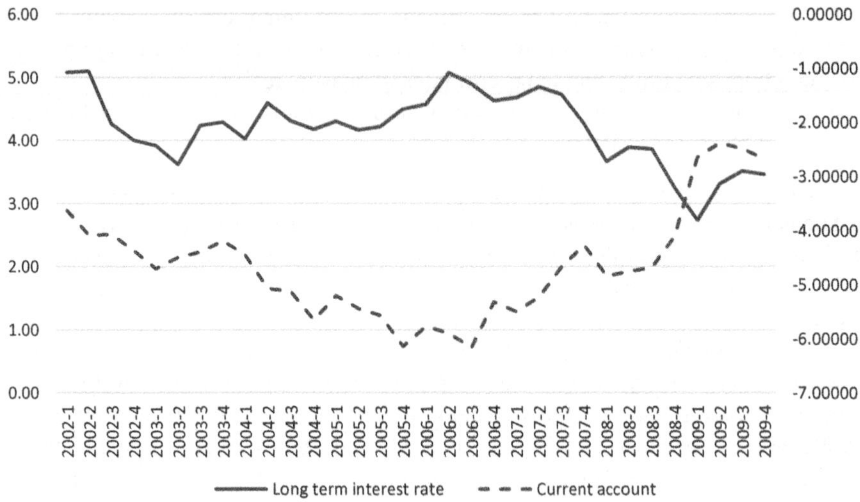

Fig. 7.6 US long-term interest rate and current account balance. Source: FRED, Federal Reserve Bank of St. Louis database

Table 7.4 Capital inflows in the USA (billions of dollars)

	2003	2007	Variations
Total	858.3	2129.5	1271.2
– Private sector	580.2	1648.5	1068.3
Securities	312.2	672.5	360.1
Banking liabilities	97.2	509.3	412.1
For memory:			
Current account deficit	521.5	726.6	205.1

Source: Johnson (2009)

cycle in the way predicted by Minsky (1982).[23] According to this scholar, a market economy can become more fragile in expansionary phases of the cycle. In these phases, firms, seeing high profit prospects, are inclined to take on more and more debt. Some of them become so indebted that they are unable to repay the borrowed capital but only the interest on it (Ponzi finance). The expansionary phase of the financial cycle ends when companies, due to their overexposure to debt, are forced to sell assets to meet their payment obligations. This is the so-called *Minsky moment*, when panic sets in: asset prices plummet, banks' willingness to lend contracts and the economy enters a recession.

Minsky's theory of the financial cycle suggests considering gross capital flows instead of net flows in the explanation of the GFC.[24] The indication that gross flows have been a key determinant of the GFC comes not only from the discrepancy

[23]See also Kindleberger (2000).

[24]See Borio and Disyatat (2011, p. 8).

Table 7.5 Capital inflows and outflows to and from the USA by country or region (thousands of billions of dollars, in 2007)

	Inflows	Outflows
Total	2129.5	1472.1
Europe	1015.9	1014.0
– Eurozone	360.3	477.2
– United Kingdom	561.0	422.4
Asia and the Pacific	450.0	26.8
– China	260.3	−2.0
– Japan	65.9	−50.0
– Taiwan	5.8	−2.8
– Singapore	20.9	14.0
– Australia	−0.2	27.3
Canada	83.5	67.9
Middle East	39.8	13.6
OPEC	52.1	19.2

Source: Johnson (2009)

between the US current account balance and capital inflows into the US, but also from the fact that, in the case of advanced economies such as the euro area, Japan and the UK, the levels of capital inflows and outflows to and from the US in 2007 were very similar (Table 7.5).

In these countries, a number of financial institutions were borrowing short term in US dollars in order to buy derivatives in that currency and profit from the yield spread. By doing so, they were exposing themselves to the risk of a maturity mismatch.

Taking into account gross flows rather than net flows leads to the conclusion that the crisis of 2008 was caused first and foremost by the non-virtuous behaviour of financial institutions in advanced countries. These institutions abnormally expanded their credit and financial portfolios.[25]

7.3.3 *Monetary and Financial Responses to the GFC*

Taking into account the lessons learned from the Great Depression, the 2007–2008 crisis was countered with markedly expansionary fiscal and monetary policy measures. Regarding monetary policy, the role of the major central banks, primarily the Federal Reserve and the ECB, was decisive.

In the initial phase of the crisis, the Fed was more willing than the ECB to cut interest rates. In fact, from September 2008, it reduced the interest rate on Federal Funds several times, bringing it almost to zero. The ECB acted with some delay.

[25] As a result of this crisis, there was a pronounced fall in foreign trade for the first time since the Second World War. See Baldwin (2009).

Table 7.6 Interest rate on interbank loans

	Jun 2007	Dec 2007	Jun 2008	Sept 2008	Dec 2008	Dec 2009	Dec 2010	Dec 2011
Federal Funds	5.26	4.24	2.00	1.54	0.16	0.11	0.19	0.07
EONIA	3.96	3.88	4.01	4.27	2.49	0.35	0.50	0.79

Source: Fed and ECB

Table 7.7 Total Fed and ECB assets (USD billion)

	Jun 2007	Dec 2007	Jun 2008	Sept 2008	Dec 2008	Dec 2009	Dec 2010	Dec 2011
Fed	847	874	875	1134	2207	2220	2407	2920
ECB	900	1037	941	1056	1519	1267	1516	1796

Source: Fed and ECB

However, it also reduced its interbank interest rate significantly from the end of 2008 and during 2009 (Table 7.6).

The decrease in the money market interest rate occurred as a result of a large injection of liquidity into the money market. This liquidity made it possible to counteract the fall in the monetary multiplier and to prevent it from being accompanied by a substantial fall in the growth rate of money and its inevitable negative impact on output. In short, policymakers avoided the mistake made by central banks in the 1930s, when they allowed the dramatic fall in the monetary multiplier to translate into a dramatic reduction in the money supply.[26]

Until September 2008, this policy was pursued mainly through changes in the structure of central banks' balance sheets. In this first phase, they significantly extended the range of eligible collateral and lengthened the maturity of refinancing operations. After the collapse of Lehman Brothers, however, as the interbank market broke down, the Fed and the ECB were forced to expand their assets. Between September 2008 and January 2009, the assets of the Fed and the ECB increased by 150% and 45% respectively (Table 7.7).

In the case of the Fed, a large part of this increase was due to lending of last resort to non-US banks. Between the end of 2008 and the beginning of 2009, as the severity of the crisis persisted, the actions of the Fed and the ECB took on different characteristics. The US central bank implemented initiatives to support private sector securities and non-bank markets. To this end, it used several rounds of Quantitative Easing (QE) to promote economic recovery. With these operations it started growing its balance by purchasing government bonds and mortgage-backed securities. The first round of QE, later called QE1, was launched in November 2008. It resulted in the purchase of 100 billion dollars of agency debt and 500 billion dollars of mortgage-backed securities. This first round was extended in March 2009 with the purchase of another 850 billion dollars of mortgage-backed securities and debt. In

[26]See Friedman and Schwartz (1963).

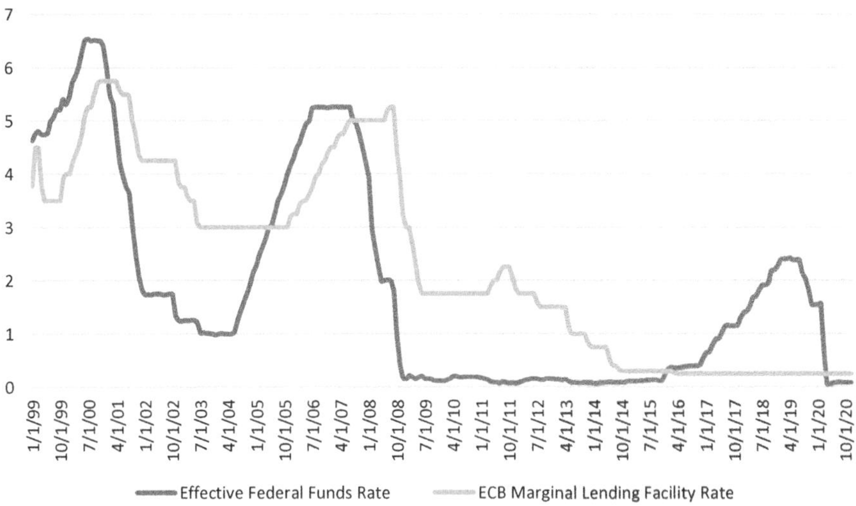

Fig. 7.7 Policy rates: the U.S. Federal Reserve and the European Central Bank. Source: FRED, Federal Reserve Bank of St. Louis database

addition, the Fed invested another 300 billion dollars in longer-dated treasuries. Other large QE operations were conducted by the Fed in 2010.

The ECB's response to the GFC was slower than the Fed's, more limited and less persistent. First, as shown in Fig. 7.7, this central bank in the years 2007–2008 changed the direction of its monetary policy with considerable delay compared to the Fed. In July 2008, in fact, when tensions were already being felt in the monetary and financial markets of the eurozone, it nonetheless raised the policy rate by 25 basis points. Second, in order to counteract this situation, the ECB intervened with a programme of purchasing public securities on the secondary market, the so-called Securities Markets Program (SMP). Overall, however, the liquidity created through these operations was sterilized.[27]

The adoption of the SMP was accompanied by a series of measures to facilitate liquidity provision. This was done by providing unlimited liquidity at a fixed interest rate to banks against collateral, by extending the maximum maturity of refinancing operations from 3 months to 1 year, by extending the list of assets accepted as collateral to include Asset-Backed Securities (ABS) and by providing liquidity to banks in foreign currencies, mainly dollars.

The ECB's interventions helped to restore orderly functioning in the euro area money and interbank markets. However, several European banks, because had taken out short-term dollar debts and had bought long-term assets in US dollars, given the malfunctioning of the federal funds market, encountered significant difficulties in

[27]The concern of the ECB President Trichet was that the monetary policy might become too accommodative. See Trichet and Papademos (2008). On this aspect see Mody (2018, p. 212).

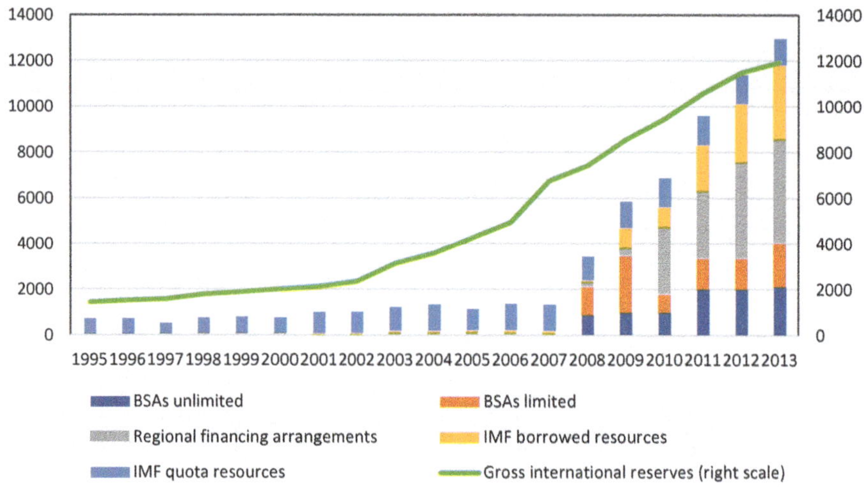

Fig. 7.8 Trend in the global financial safety net, 1995–2014 (USD billions). Source: IMF (2016)

rolling-over their short-term liabilities. This led to a significant increase in the Credit Default Swap prices of the banks concerned.

To address the dollar liquidity shortage, the Fed resorted to a liquidity creation instrument previously used in the 1920s[28]: the Bilateral Swap Arrangements (BSA). These arrangements imply a bilateral agreement whereby the two parties exchange currencies at fixed terms and for a fixed or unlimited amount, at the prevailing market exchange rate. In most cases, these BSAs involve a borrower (that is, the country requesting liquidity) and a creditor (the country that meets the request).

In December 2007 the Fed set up BSAs with the ECB and the Swiss National Bank (SNB). This enabled these two central banks to provide dollar funding to the commercial banks of their countries. Between December 2007 and February 2010 Fed set up a series of temporary swap lines with up to 14 central banks in advanced and emerging countries. Between September 15, 2008, the date of the collapse of Lehmann Brothers, and October 12, the Fed signed new BSAs with the central banks of Japan, UK, Canada, Australia, Sweden, Norway, New Zealand and Denmark. The new operations led to a remarkable increase in dollar liquidity supplied by the Fed: from 67 to 620 billion of dollar,[29] becoming one of the more important items of the world safety net (Fig. 7.8).

In the following period, in correspondence with a worsening of market conditions, the Fed eliminated value limits on BSAs with the ECB, the Bank of England, the

[28]Essentially, these instruments were first occasionally used in the 1920s (see Moessner & Allen, 2010, p. 25). With these operations, a central bank provided its own currency or gold to another central bank. See also Toniolo (2005), Coombs (1976), and Sayers (1976).

[29]See Obstfeld et al. (2009).

Swiss National Bank and the Bank of Japan. At the same time, it set up BSAs with some emerging countries: Brazil, Mexico, South Korea, New Zealand and Singapore. Figure 7.8 highlights the growing importance that this liquidity creation tool has had during the GFC. The swap lines programme launched to counter the liquidity shortage determined by the GFC was terminated on 1 February 2010.[30]

Some studies consider the recent widespread use of BSAs as part of a process leading toward a multilateral monetary system.[31] The main characteristic of this process would be the tendency to deepen regional arrangements, such as both the stipulation of local BSAs and agreements to pool currency reserves. However, this hypothesis presupposes that the stipulation of BSAs has been configured as a horizontal network. On the contrary, the system of BSAs that has emerged since the GFC has taken on a hierarchical structure. Indeed, excluding the Asian countries' swap lines with China, attributable to the Chiang Mai Initiative,[32] two types of these arrangements can be identified. The first-level network has the Fed as the creditor and the central banks of other advanced countries as the debtors. With respect to these countries, the American central bank acted as an international lender of last resort.[33] On the second level, we find the BSAs stipulated by some of these last countries (this time as creditors) with central banks of peripheral countries (as debtors), where they injected liquidity in their own currency (in particular euro and Swiss franc).

Therefore, the BSA network has assumed a hierarchical structure. It is indeed possible to identify at least two different swap networks: the euro network and the Swiss franc network. The euro network faced euro liquidity shortages developed in European countries outside the euro area. The ECB set up swap lines with the Danish, Hungarian, Polish and Swedish central banks. The Swiss National Bank supported Poland and Hungary because their large Swiss franc shortages.

The success of central banks in countering the GFC and its possible degeneration into a crisis similar to that of the 1930s has often been attributed to the fact that this crisis pushed the major economies to a high degree of policy coordination. However, similar crises after WWII, such as the Bretton Woods crisis, the oil crisis of the 1970s or the breakdown of the EMS, did not lead to meaningful Great Powers cooperation.[34]

At the time of the GFC, cooperation among advanced countries was led by the USA[35] which was concerned about the impact the crisis could have on the stability

[30]See McDowell (2011).

[31]See Duran (2015) and Henning (2015).

[32]This was implemented in 2000, but remained unused in the sub-prime mortgage crisis. Initially, the Chiang Mai Initiative was primarily aimed at promoting the use of the dollar in Asian countries. This initiative was subsequently revisited, shifting from bilateral lines to a multilateral network.

[33]See Broz (2015) and McDowell (2011, 2017).

[34]See Lake (2009).

[35]See Drezner (2014). According to other scholars, the cooperative behaviour of the major economies during this crisis was the result of pressure from special interest groups, mainly large financial firms, with a strong interest in an open global economy. However, these financial interest

of the monetary system. This concern was fuelled by the high financial interdependence of the advanced economies and the possible domino effects of the crisis. This interdependence, moreover, gave (and gives) the USA a high level of influence, given the dominant role of the dollar in the international monetary system.[36] They used their structural power to promote improvements in bank regulation.

Because GFC seems to have resulted from an over-elasticity of the banks' lending function, there was need to place limits on the capacity of these institutions to create credit, just as in the 1980s limits were placed on the elasticity of money supply by increasing the independence of central banks and resorting to rules in the management of monetary policy.

In December 2010, the Basel Committee on Banking Supervision (BCBS) adopted reforms aimed at strengthening the regulatory framework. The principal points of these reforms were:

(i) Higher mandatory capital adequacy ratios;
(ii) Improvements of capital quality;
(iii) The Introduction of minimum liquidity requirements;
(iv) The introduction of macro-prudential tools.

Points (*i*)–(*iii*) are part of the reform to the global regulatory standards dubbed Basel III.[37] The introduction of macro-prudential policies (point *iv*) stems from the realization that in some cases action taken by individual financial institutions to comply with microprudential regulations and safeguard their solvency could fuel, rather than mitigate, systemic risk in the financial system[38] A macro-prudential approach to financial regulation implies, among other things, the use of instruments designed to reduce procyclicality in the financial system and to "... calibrate prudential tools to individual institutions' contribution to system-wide risk, regardless of the institution's legal form, ...".[39]

7.4 New Versions of the Triffin Dilemma

After the crisis of 1997–1998, the demand for foreign exchange reserves by emerging countries have increased significantly (Fig. 7.8). According to some scholars this increase could be traced back to neo-mercantilist policies followed by many

groups were harmed by the micro- and macro-prudential measures taken after the GFC and, therefore, by the coordination between major powers. See McGuire and von Peter (2009), Helleiner (2014).

[36]See Ikenberry (2011), Beckley (2011) and Norrlof (2010).

[37]Basel Committee on Banking Supervision (2010).

[38]See Claessens (2015).

[39]See Caruana (2010).

emerging countries which, by maintaining uncompetitive real exchange rates, achieve large current account surplus and consequently accumulate large reserves.[40]

The increased demand for liquidity from emerging countries and the relative decline of the USA in the world economy, i.e. the main provider of international liquidity, has led several scholars to formulate new versions of the Triffin dilemma.[41] Underlying them is the concern that in the future the supply of international liquidity is insufficient to meet the growing demand for safe and liquid assets by emerging countries. Should this situation occur, it could result in severe global deflation.

The possibility of such an outcome is mainly prefigured in two new versions of the Triffin dilemma.[42] The first version maintains that the USA create international liquidity by covering their large and persistent current account deficits.[43] In this hypothesis, the so-called *current account hypothesis*, the shortage of international liquidity may derive from the fact that over time the persistence of the current account deficits of the USA tends to undermine confidence in the solvency of this country and, therefore, in the securities and currency issued by it.

There have been several criticisms of the current account hypothesis. First, it was noted that the USA' creation of international liquidity does not depend exclusively on its current account deficits. Indeed, as observed by Swoboda (2012) and Portes (2012), between the end of WWII up to the early 1970s, this country supplied liquidity to the world although its economy at that time featured large current account surpluses. Second, the current account hypothesis is part of the interpretations that lead the GFC to balance of payments imbalances and net capital flows. However, as we have seen in Sect. 7.2, this crisis is more plausible to have been caused by gross capital flows rather than net capital flows.[44]

These criticisms are taken into account in a second new version of the Triffin dilemma.[45] In this version, the so-called *fiscal hypothesis*, the source of international liquidity is represented by government securities of highly creditworthy countries, in particular by government securities issued by the USA to cover their fiscal deficits. Hence, the dilemma between two objectives: on the one hand, the need to satisfy the demand for international liquidity would require a significant increase in the ratio of public debt to GDP in the USA, on the other hand, trust in the prospective value of

---

[40]See Dooley et al. (2003) and Levy-Yeyati et al. (2013). Other scholars, on the other hand, believe that the accumulation of huge reserves by emerging countries is attributable to "precautionary motives". In particular, especially in the case of the Asian countries, this behaviour would be a consequence of the stigma left by the 1997–98 crisis and the loss of sovereignty imposed by the IMF in the face of financial support granted to these countries. On this debate see Aizenman and Lee (2007).

[41]See Seghezza (2018b).

[42]See Bordo and McCauley (2016).

[43]See Fratianni (2012) and Steiner (2014).

[44]See Johnson (2009), Borio and Disyatat (2015) and James (2018).

[45]See Obstfeld (2011, 2013) and Farhi et al. (2011).

these securities it would require the USA to pursue a sound fiscal policy and reduce this ratio.[46]

The new versions of the Triffin dilemma, both the *current account* and the *fiscal hypothesis*, express a strong concern that in the future the supply of low-risk assets in the international market may be insufficient to satisfy the demand for it.[47] However, Fig. 7.8 shows that after the GFC new liquidity instruments were created, others, already existing, were enhanced. Among the new instruments, the BSAs should be mentioned in the first place. We have already mentioned their contribution to solving the liquidity shortage problem that emerged after the 2008 crisis. However, since the GFC the network of swap arrangements has evolved. In 2011, the central banks of core advanced countries formalized their network of swap lines, announcing in 2013 that it would remain in place indefinitely in order to counter future strains in financial markets.

Since the GFC the possibility of countries to access to IMF funding has been significantly enhanced. Notably, the SDRs were increased nearly ten-fold. Since their allocation is based on quota size, most of the liquidity associated with this instrument has been allocated to larger economies. In addition, the 14th General Review of IMF's quotas has doubled the permanent resources of this institution, bringing them to 60 billion dollars.

In addition to the innovations just mentioned, other innovations have been introduced in the supply of international liquidity with the aim of reducing the demand for it on the international market. As Fig. 7.7 shows, since the GFC, new facilities have been introduced under existing Regional Financial Arrangements. As we have seen, in the euro area, the European Stability mechanism was created with the aim of safeguarding the financial stability of this area. In 2009, the Eurasian Fund for Stabilization and Development was established with the task of providing financial assistance to member countries. The BRICS have established a multilateral Contingent Reserve Arrangement which provide liquidity support against balance of payments pressures. The Chiang Mai Initiative, reformed in 2010 and become a multilateral currency swap arrangement (the Chiang Mai Initiative Multilateralization, CMIM) provides regional short-term liquidity.

7.5 The Sovereign Debt Crisis in the Euro Area

In its early years, the euro area experienced a credit boom. As shown in Table 7.8, credit to GDP ratios increased considerably in the peripheral countries, particularly in the so-called PIIGS.[48]

---

[46]See Obstfeld (2011).

[47]See Farhi et al. (2011). What makes an asset perceived as safe is the existence of a high rule of law. See Morelli and Seghezza (2018).

[48]Portugal, Ireland, Italy, Greece and Spain.

Table 7.8 Private credit dynamics

	1998	2002	2007
Greece	31.8	56.5	84.4
Ireland	81.2	104.4	184.3
Portugal	92.1	136.5	159.8
Spain	80.5	100.1	168.5
Italy	55.7	77.3	96.5
Germany	112.2	116.7	105.1
France	81.0	85.6	99.3

Source: World Bank Financial Database

Table 7.9 Current account imbalances (percent of GDP)

	1993–1997	1998–2002	2003–2007	2008–2011
Greece	−2.0	−5.9	−9.1	−11.1
Ireland	3.4	−0.2	−2.6	−1.6
Italy	2.1	0.2	−1.8	−2.9
Portugal	−2.4	−9.0	−9.2	−10.5
Spain	−0.6	−3.1	−7.0	−5.8
France	1.1	2.0	−0.2	−1.9
Germany	−0.9	−0.3	5.1	5.7

Source: International Monetary Fund database

The reason for this credit boom is that the peripheral countries benefited from a significant reduction in nominal and real interest rates with the launch of the euro.[49] This reduction stimulated the demand for credit, which was satisfied by large capital inflows from abroad. However, low interest rates and ample credit availability stimulated consumption-related and real estate related borrowing. It, therefore, had little effect on the productivity of the economy. In this context, the high domestic demand underpinned by the credit boom led to an increase in their domestic prices higher than the euro area average and, thus, to an appreciation of their real exchange rate, resulting in a loss of competitiveness and the emergence of large and growing current account deficits in the PIIGS (Table 7.9).

Also the stance of the fiscal policy contributed to the persistence of their external imbalances. In these countries in the years before 2007 it remained permissive or pro-cyclical, rather than anti-cyclical. The coverage of the current account deficits of the PIIGS was left to a growing indebtedness towards foreign financial institutions, attracted by the higher monetary interest rates prevailing in these countries on long-term securities.

The situation suddenly changed with the GFC. The GFC put an end to credit booms and encouraged capital outflows from the euro area. This led to a liquidity constraint in the funding market. Where the credit boom was associated with a bubble in construction, such as in Spain and Ireland, falling real estate prices caused huge loan losses in the banking sector.

[49] See Lane (2012).

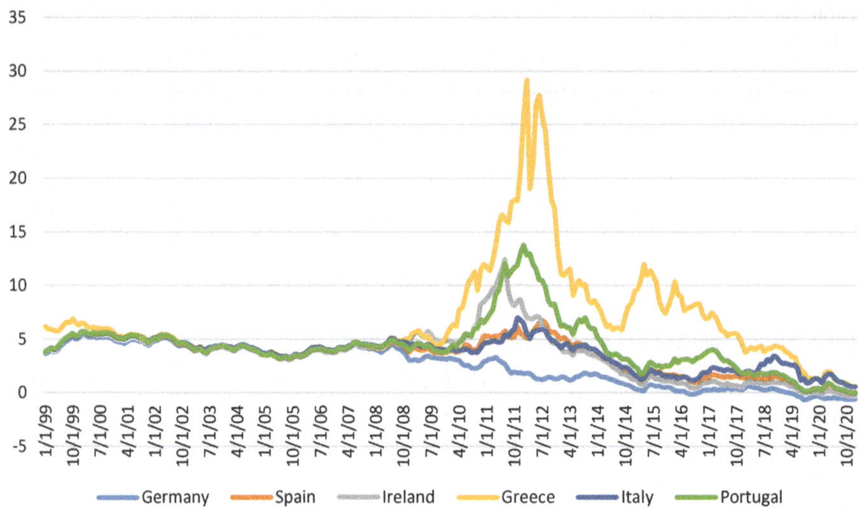

Fig. 7.9 Long-term interest rates. Source: FRED, Federal Reserve Bank of St. Louis database

The fall in GDP following the Great Recession, the expansionary fiscal policies to counteract the fall in productive activity and, in some countries, to prevent the banking distress from degenerating into a serious crisis of the system, contributed to increasing the public debt to GDP ratios in the peripheral countries.

Nevertheless, as shown by the development of long-term interest rates in Fig. 7.9, during 2008 and most of 2009 the euro area sovereign debt market remained relatively calm.

At the end of 2009, however, the fiscal situation of several euro area countries, in particular the PIIGS, deteriorated markedly. In particular, Greece revised its budget deficit forecast after the general elections in October 2009 up from the previous estimate of 6% to 12.7% and, at the same time, the Greek government also corrected the deficit figures for previous years, showing that they were higher than officially declared. Greece's blatant violation of the Maastricht rules contributed to the emergence of an interpretation of the crisis that started in Greece, and then spread to the periphery of the euro area, as being due to the fiscal irresponsibility of these countries.

In early 2010, Greece's long-term interest rate began to rise, highlighting a significant increase in the risk premium on bonds issued by this country. The situation worsened in spring, it was aggravated by the fact that when the EMU was established, no institutional mechanisms were foreseen to deal with the financial crisis of one or more member countries. This was also because Germany, together with the Netherlands and Austria, had misgivings about the creation of such mechanisms since they believed they might encourage irresponsible behaviour to the detriment of other members of the EMU. France and Italy had a different view, favouring forms of financial risk sharing within the euro area.

These two different visions contributed to the eurozone's slow reaction to the Greek crisis, underestimating the economic and political costs of a Greek exit from EMU and the EU. In this context, it is not surprising that in May 2010 speculation against the country was rife.[50]

In early May Greece and the EC entered into a Memorandum of Understanding (MOU) agreeing on a programme of fiscal adjustment. The financing of this programme was covered by the euro area member states (EAMS) and the IMF to the sum of 110 billion euros.[51]

This form of support was not sufficient to cauterize the Greek crisis and prevents it from spreading through contagion[52] to the weak euro area. The interest rate spread continued to widen and, at an extraordinary ECOFIN council meeting, it was decided to launch a series of measures to preserve financial stability in Europe.[53]

One of these measures was the creation of the European Financial Stability Facility (EFSF), a temporary credit-enhancement special purpose vehicle which could raise funds of up to 440 billion euros from capital markets. Complementing the EFSF was the simultaneous establishment of the European Financial Stability Mechanism (EFSM), which consisted in an intergovernmental agreement to provide assistance of up to 60 billion euros subject to stringent conditions. In addition to the funds made available by the EFSF and EFSM, the IMF also contributed 250 billion euros. This created a safety net of up to 750 billion euros. Part of these resources was used in bailouts for Ireland, Portugal and Greece. The details of the funding plans for these countries largely reflected standard IMF practices, i.e. commitments to strict fiscal adjustments.

The institutional architecture just described turned out to be poorly suited to solving the crisis that hit the euro area.[54] There were several limitations.[55] First, a predefined availability of funds, such as the amount of resources of the EFSF and EFSM, could not substitute a lender of last resort. Second, the fiscal adjustments required to the crisis countries were asymmetrical. There was a lack of effort on the part of the surplus countries, first and foremost Germany, which again showed itself to be a reluctant leader, to smooth these adjustment processes. Third, while the austerity measures adopted by the PIIGS improved the fiscal situation of these countries, they also negatively affected their aggregate demand, thus penalizing growth.

In 2013 GDP growth in the euro area became negative and the inflation rate fell to well below the ECB's target of 2%. Between 2014 and 2016 this area risked entering a phase of deflation. In that period the EMU risked break up. This was averted thanks

[50]See Chang and Leblond (2015).

[51]The EAMS contributed 80 billion euros and the IMF 30 billion euros.

[52]On the role of contagion in the sovereign debt crisis see Constancio (2012).

[53]See Council of European Union, extraordinary Council meeting, 9–10 March, 2010, Press Release No 9596/10 (Press 108).

[54]See De Grauwe (2013a, 2013b).

[55]See, among others, Lane (2012) and De Grauwe (2013a).

to the ECB's particularly expansionary monetary policy and its massive recourse to Quantitative Easing (QE) from March 2015 onwards. It is therefore not surprising that several scholars have criticized the austerity policies, believing that they were based on a misinterpretation of the causes of the sovereign debt crisis, which in their view was not due to the fiscal indiscipline of the PIIGS, but rather to the credit boom that affected them in the pre-GFC period, the resulting current account deficits, the coverage of these with foreign debt and, eventually, a sudden stop, similar to those recurring in Latin America.[56]

In this context, further adjustments to the euro safety net were necessary. In March 2011 the European Council decided to establish a permanent stability mechanism, the European Stability Mechanism (ESM). The lending capacity of this mechanism was set to 500 billion euros. With the EMS a guarantee-based approach was maintained, but unlike the EFSF the principle of private sector involvement was introduced. According to this principle, the country receiving assistance was obliged to reschedule its debts with private creditors. The first use of the EMS was made by Spain in 2012 to recapitalize its banks.

As the euro institutional mechanism for dealing with crises was refined over time, the ECB, on the one hand, changed its monetary policy stance, albeit belatedly, and, on the other hand, gradually took over the functions of lender of last resort. At the same time, the ECB started to support countries in crisis by launching unconventional operations, such as the longer-term refinancing operations (LTRO) in December 2011. With this additional liquidity, the commercial banks of the crisis countries increased their purchases of domestic government bonds and thus helped to support their prices. Draghi's statement in July 2012 that the ECB would do whatever was necessary to defend the euro calmed the financial markets: long-term interest rates in the PIIGS fell sharply.

The sovereign debt crisis finally came to an end in September 2012 with the announcement by the ECB of a new intervention instrument: the outright monetary transactions (OTM).[57] With this instrument, the ECB finally acquired the possibility of acting as a lender of last resort. In January 2015 this function was further consolidated with the adoption of a quantitative easing policy.

The sovereign debt crisis, therefore, not only favoured the creation of an institutional architecture in the euro area that would preserve financial stability, but also allowed the ECB to be equipped with a function essential to a central bank, namely that of lender of last resort, considered obsolete with the development of well-functioning financial markets by some scholars.[58]

---

[56]See Kopf (2011), Krugman (2011) and De Grauwe (2013b).

[57]This instrument consists of the direct purchase by the ECB of short-term government bonds issued by countries in severe and overt macroeconomic difficulties.

[58]See Goodfriend and King (1988). For a discussion on this aspect see Freixas and Parigi (2012) and Eichengreen and Wyplosz (2016).

7.6 The Covid-19 Crisis' Effects on the International Monetary System

In 2020, the world was hit by a severe Covid-19 pandemic. As a result of total or partial lockdowns to counter its spread and limit the number of deaths, in 2020 global GDP fell significantly; according to IMF estimates by 4.9%, while in the advanced countries, GDP fell even more sharply (by 8.0%). Despite this dramatic slowdown in growth, exchange rate volatility has been very low, confirming the long-term downward trend. This seems to be due primarily to the low inflation rates still prevailing worldwide. These low inflation rates are matched by very narrow long-term interest rate spreads.[59]

A second factor that helped to keep exchange rate volatility low was the provision of US dollar liquidity through swap lines when market tensions arose in March 2020 due to dollar liquidity shortages. Fed swap lines with foreign central banks grew to nearly 450 billion dollars in April. At the same time, it initiated a "repo" facility for central banks holding US treasury securities on deposit with the New York Fed. This measure allowed these central banks to receive US dollar liquidity in exchange for Treasury collateral.[60]

The dominant role of the dollar in the international monetary system and the high financial interdependence of advanced economies provided incentives for the central banks of these countries to stabilize their dollar exchange rates.[61]

Concerns, however, are mounting over the post-Covid-19 crisis period, in particular over the stability of the global economic and financial system and how the recovery may be undermined by local or systemic crises. As mentioned above, to cope with the Covid-19 crisis, governments and central banks have deployed all the tools at their disposal to support the economic system.

In contrast to the GFC, money has increased significantly in all advanced countries. This growth is primarily attributable to high demand for corporate loans and the extremely expansionary monetary policies of central banks.

Governments seem willing to take risks on inflation to promote growth and overcome the Covid-19 crisis. Another stimulus to inflation could come from a fall in foreign trade and a tightening of the global supply chain. In essence, the Covid-19 crisis could reverse the process that, according to several scholars, has contributed to keeping inflation rates low in the recent past.[62]

An increase in the world inflation rate and in inflation differentials between countries would break the long trend in falling exchange rate volatility and risk creating a situation similar to that of the years immediately following the suspension of dollar convertibility in 1971.

---

[59]See Ilzetzki et al. (2020).

[60]See Avdjiev et al. (2020), Eren et al. (2020) and Cetorelli et al. (2020).

[61]See Rey (2013) and Gopinath (2015).

[62]See Rogoff (2003) and Kose et al. (2018).

In order to support the income of their citizens, and to limit the fall in output caused by the Covid-19 crisis, governments have expanded their deficits and significantly increased public debt. Central banks facilitated the massive placement of government bonds through Quantitative Easing operations, preventing it from leading to increases in market interest rates.

In the post-Covid period, however, there may be misalignments in objectives and preferences between governments and central banks and between countries. For example, governments may wish to keep their borrowing costs low, while central banks, concerned about accelerating inflation, may wish to raise policy interest rates. The independence of central banks, which has stabilized economies and helped ensure the orderly functioning of the international monetary system, could be at risk.[63]

Finally, in the post-Covid period, it should be a priority for most countries, especially those whose debt-to-GDP ratio has reached particularly high levels, to rebuild policy buffers. Failure to do so could jeopardize the economic and financial stability of one or more countries and favours the emergence of systemic crisis situations.

7.7 The Possible Threat of Euro and Renminbi for the US Dollar

Since WWII the U.S. dollar has played a dominant role in the international monetary system.[64] The debate on the prospects for the dollar began as early as the early 1980s in connection with the international monetary disorder that emerged after the collapse of the Bretton Woods system. Since then several studies have argued that the decline of the dollar as an international currency is imminent.[65]

Many followers of the hegemonic stability theory attributed the monetary disorder post-Bretton Woods to the decline in power of the hegemonic country.[66] The reasons for the economic and political decline of the USA put forward by these scholars varied,[67] but the consensus was on the inevitable decline of the dollar as an international currency.[68] The hypothesis that the dollar's decline is imminent has

[63]See Borio (2020).

[64]See Chap. 5.

[65]See Cohen (2015).

[66]See Krasner (1983), Gilpin (1981), Smith (1981), Olson (1982) and Keohane (1984).

[67]Gilpin (1975) attributes this decline to US capital outflows abroad and the fact that this penalises domestic investment and US growth. Olson (1982), on the other hand, argues that the benefits enjoyed by the hegemonic country favour the emergence of powerful interest groups that over time undermine the efficient allocation of resources and growth in this country.

[68]This thesis is contested by Strange (1987) who refers to the concept of structural power instead of the neo-realists' concept of relational power.

been revived in recent times during periods of shocks, such as the GFC, or, before that, on the creation of the euro.

In the context of this debate, more than a few scholars have shown their belief that the decline of the dollar is not only inevitable, but imminent. As Eichengreen (2011a, p. 150) states: "The shift away from a dollar-denominated international system towards this more multipolar successor was accelerated, no doubt, by the 2008 crisis". This view is shared by other scholars[69] and international institutions. Indeed, according to the World Bank: "... the most likely scenario for the international monetary system is a multicurrency system centered around the U.S. dollar, the euro, and renminbi".[70] A similar position is held by the European Central Bank, according to whom "... the international monetary system is already on the verge of becoming tripolar".[71] According to these scholars and practitioners, significant benefits would accrue from the prevalence of a multipolar monetary system. Indeed, "a multipolar monetary system would alleviate the Triffin dilemma by diversifying the sources of international liquidity. Furthermore, multipolarity could act as a disciplinary device, international investors being offered a choice between several currencies ...".[72]

This widely held view is contested by Cohen and Benney (2013), who, using the Herfindahl–Hirschman index, find that the international monetary system is characterized by a high degree of concentration; thus the degree of competition is very low: "Even today there appears to be only one true pole in the system—namely the U.S. dollar."[73]

The hypothesis that the dollar is headed for a rapid decline is based on arguments that refer to the main theories of the origin of money discussed in Chap. 2, the Mengerian theory and the hegemonic stability theory.[74] Mengerian theory is used by those who argue that the declining share of US GDP and exports in world GDP and exports will make it less likely that the dollar will be accepted as a means of payment.[75] The view that the dollar is less likely to be accepted as a means of payment, given its large and persistent current account deficits and the consequent reduced confidence in the US currency, is also linked to this theory.[76]

On the other hand, those who believe that the military-political decline of the USA means that it is less able to impose the dollar or to induce other countries to behave cooperatively in the monetary sphere refer to the hegemonic stability theory.[77]

---

[69]See, in particular, Bénassy-Quéré and Pisani-Ferry (2011), Bergsten (2011) and Desai and Vreeland (2011).

[70]See World Bank (2011, p. 125–126).

[71]See ECB (2012, p. 11).

[72]See Bénassy-Quéré (2015, p. 4).

[73]See Cohen and Benney (2013, p. 22). See also Cohen (2017).

[74]See Helleiner and Kirshner (2009).

[75]See among others, Subramanian (2011).

[76]See Bergsten and Williamson (2003).

[77]See among others, Calleo (2009).

The two types of argument above both suffer from the limitations of the underlying theories. They overlook the fact that, as pointed out in Chap. 2, an international fiat money can only exist if there is a leading country that can guarantee confidence in the stability of its value and of the international monetary system based on it. At present, only the USA can offer these two public goods. The dominant position of the dollar, therefore, does not seem threatened by either the euro or the renminbi, though for different reasons.

At the start of the EMU, some economists, mainly Bergstein and Mundell, predicted that, with the euro area being similar in size to the USA, the new currency would challenge the dollar as the key currency.[78] The spread of the euro would reinforce the stability of the international monetary system, both because it would encourage diversification in the composition of countries' official reserves and because it would reduce the concentration of seigniorage privileges in one country.[79]

The hypothesis put forward by Bergstein and Mundell has been taken up by other scholars in recent times.[80] Indeed, according to some econometric studies by Chinn and Frankel (2007, 2008) the euro was predicted to supplant the dollar as an international currency between 2015 and 2022.

The scholars of hegemonic stability theory and of international political economy have, from the outset, been pessimistic about the potential of the euro to stand alongside or replace the dollar as an international currency. This view was based on the observation that the euro area had little political-military power in the international arena.

Considering the geopolitical premises for an international currency, the geopolitical weakness of the Eurozone has led, for example, Posen (2008, p. 1996) to write: "... economic factors alone, such as countries' relative size and inflation rates and then trade patterns, are insufficient to explain the pattern of reserve currency or exchange rate peg choices seen in the world—if these were together sufficient, the euro would already be a truly global currency in every sense". Therefore, according to Posen, given the low capacity of the Eurozone to acquire an adequate level of political-military influence on neighbouring countries, it was very unlikely that the euro would rise to the rank of an international currency.

The importance of the geopolitical aspects is also emphasized by Helleiner (2008), according to whom trust in an international currency depends, in addition to economic factors, on the international security power of the issuing country. The Eurozone has a very limited amount of this type of power, therefore, the euro, today, according to the classification given by Strange (1971a, 1971b),[81] would be a

---

[78]See Bergsten (1997), Mundell (1998) and Portes and Rey (1998).

[79]See Mundell (1998, 2000) and Eichengreen (1998).

[80]Other scholars, like Kenen (2002) and McKinnon (1998), while accepting the Mengerian theory on the origin of money, were skeptical about the possibility that the euro would compete against the dollar as an international currency due to the existence of network economies.

[81]According to this classification there are four types of international currencies: top currencies, master currencies, neutral currencies and negotiated currencies. "Master currency is distinguished from the others because the causative factor is primarily political..." (Strange, 1971b, p. 217). "The

Table 7.10 Turnover of OTC foreign exchange instruments (percent share)[a]

	2001	2004	2007	2010	2013	2016	2019
US dollar	90	88	86	85	87	86	88
Euro	38	37	37	39	33	31	32

Source: BIS (2019)
[a]Total percentage = 200

"neutral currency", that is to say a currency which, like the Swiss franc, is attractive for the stability of its value, but does not have the prerequisites to become a "top currency".

As part of the international political economy studies, Cohen (2010) highlights the difficulties of the euro to compete with the dollar—even more than to the geopolitical role of the eurozone in the international scenario—as having two internal weaknesses: the fragmentation of the European financial markets and the anti-growth bias entrenched in the Maastricht Treaty. These two factors are due to the absence of a true and recognizable governance in the euro area.

In the first two decades of the euro's existence, its international use grew markedly at first, but then, after the GFC, began to decline significantly. As shown in Fig. 6.6, after the sovereign debt crisis the share of foreign exchange reserves held in euro has decreased significantly. In the same period, as shown by the turnover of OTC foreign exchange instruments, the use of the euro as an international means of exchange also decreased (Table 7.10).

The main reason for the decreased international use of the euro seems to be due to the fact that after the recent financial crises the degree of integration of the eurozone financial market fell significantly.[82] Therefore, the degree of liquidity of assets denominated in euros became precarious. In the absence of a political union, due to differences in the economic structure and institutional framework of the various countries, the volatility of the price of euro securities varies depending on the country that issued them. Furthermore, given the absence of political unity, the euro area not only lacks a large and deep integrated financial market, but also the political and military capacity to create and maintain confidence in the stability of an international monetary system based on a fiat currency.

top currency may be defined as the currency of the state that has world economic leadership..." (Strange, 1971b, p. 221). The negotiated currency is, instead, a type of international currency ". . . so that holders had to be bribed with a variety of inducements ranging from the financial ones . . . through the promise of military protection . . ." (Strange, 1971b, p. 220). Lastly, the neutral currencies are currencies that preserve their value stable over time.

[82]The problem of low financial integration in the euro area was already raised by Dornbusch (1996) before the EMU was established.

This helps to explain why euro area authorities have never shown any particular interest in promoting the euro as an international currency. Not being able to emerge as an international currency and as a competitor or a substitute for the dollar, the euro is established as a regional currency which is hierarchically subordinate to the dollar. In fact, the euro area, as seen in Sect. 7.3.3, exerts an influence on countries that although not members, gravitate towards it, and, therefore, it has an interest in their financial stability.

China has adopted a quite different stance from the euro area. It has demonstrated that it wishes to promote the spread of the renminbi (RMB) in international exchanges in various ways.[83] The path that they have chosen to achieve this is unusual, differing from that followed by other countries trying to establish and spread an international currency. The Chinese authorities would like the RMB to become the most traded currency in the world before liberalizing their capital market and rendering the currency convertible.[84]

This goal became more explicit after the 2007–2008 financial crisis, in the wake of which the Popular Bank of China promoted currency swap agreements with seven countries,[85] to a total value of RMB 650 billion. The purpose of these operations was to make up for the shortage of dollars and to facilitate trade with the recipient countries.[86]

The regulation of trade using the RMB and the issuance of financial instruments denominated in the RMB on the Hong Kong market constitutes another means of internationalizing the Chinese currency. In 2012, cross-border trade in the RMB rose to reach 10.9% of Chinese trade. Equally, the growth of the offshore market in Hong Kong has been impressive. RMB deposits in this market, which were RMB 263 billion in late 2010, had risen to RMB 587 billion by late 2011 (Zhang, 2012). Despite this explosive growth, international usage of the RMB is still very low. According to the BIS Triennial Survey on the Global Foreign Exchange Markets of 2019, the RMB was used only in about 4.3% of the world's foreign exchange transactions.

The reasons the RMB has had difficulty establishing itself as an international currency are essentially twofold. One lies in the inadequate protection China offers to the property rights of holders of RMB and assets denominated in this currency. Indeed, the rule of law in China is very weak, above all in comparison with the USA (Table 7.11).

As argued by Morelli and Seghezza (2018), this weakness is largely dependent on the structure of the Chinese economy, which still retains many features of a planned economy. The price of assets is not determined by the market but manipulated by the authorities and there is no transparency in the way the markets function. Just as they do not leave it up to the market to determine the exchange rate, the Chinese

[83]See Prasad (2016).

[84]See Eichengreen (2011b).

[85]To be precise: South Korea, Malaysia, Belarus, Indonesia, Argentina, Iceland and Singapore.

[86]According to the People's Bank of China (2009): "In the context of the financial crisis, these new practices will promote bilateral trade and direct investment, and drive economic growth".

Table 7.11 Rule of law indices (2014)

	China		USA	
	Factor score	Global rank	Factor score	Global rank
Constraints on government power	0.35	92/99	0.74	20/99
Absence of corruption	0.48	49/99	0.75	21/99
Open government	0.41	74/99	0.70	17/99
Fundamental rights	0.31	96/99	0.71	27/99
Order and security	0.81	29/99	0.85	18/99
Regulatory enforcement	0.41	78/99	0.67	22/99
Civil justice	0.41	79/99	0.61	27/99
Criminal justice	0.43	51/99	0.65	27/99
Overall score	0.45	76/99	0.71	19/99

Source: World Justice Project (2014)

authorities also do not seem to want to let the market determine the interest rate at which the state can borrow. The continued existence of controls on capital movements points to a will to impose continuing political control over finance.

An inadequate level of rule of law hampers the development of deep and broad financial markets and, thus, the liquidity of assets denominated in RMBs. In fact in the absence of developed financial markets where foreign investors can park their wealth it is unlikely that a fiat national currency will be accepted as a reserve money.

The creation in China of an adequate level of rule of law would presuppose radical political reforms. First and foremost, that the Chinese authorities, in particular the Communist Party of China, would have to relinquish control over the economy and thus also over society. However, as Lo (2013, p. 163) writes: "... changing the political system is easier said than done because communist control has given rise to rent-seeking opportunities that benefit those in power. So there is no urgency for the Communist Party to push for political reform". Therefore, the introduction of the institutional reforms necessary to protect the property rights of holders of RMBs appears problematic since they would "... hit the deep-rooted problems and the political nerve of the system".[87] In short, they could constitute a serious threat to the survival of the regime and the Communist Party of China.

This leads to the conclusion that the dollar is still the key currency in the international monetary system despite the GFC. Indeed, in some respects the dominance of the dollar has strengthened after the GFC.[88] This suggests that the dominance of the dollar seems to be destined to last for a long time to come. At least in part this will depend on the ability of the USA and other powers, especially its allies, to provide adequate responses to the factors of instability that afflict the current international monetary system.

[87] See Lo (2013, p. 172).

[88] On this aspect see, among others, Prasad (2014).

7.8 Problems with the Current International Monetary System

The international monetary system currently in force, the dollar standard, is a continuation of the Bretton Woods system in pursuit of the fundamental objectives of the 1944 Agreements, but differs profoundly from it. Unlike the Bretton Woods system, it does not have an anchor. This is the reason for most of the problems that plague its functioning.[89] The drawbacks in the functioning of the international monetary system mainly concern the following aspects:

(i) *The absence of adjustment mechanisms.* Unlike previous monetary systems, the dollar standard does not provide for the convertibility of currencies into a commodity money or other adjustment mechanisms. This leads to persistent imbalances in the current account balances of member countries. In particular, the USA, issuing the key currency of the system, can have persistent external deficits, while other countries, primarily Germany, China and Japan, have persistent current account surpluses. In fact, these imbalances stem from the lack of coordination of macroeconomic policies and, ultimately, from different growth patterns.[90]

(ii) *The volatility of capital flows.* Financial liberalization has had mixed results. If, on the one hand, it has allowed a better allocation of savings, on the other hand, it has favoured both sudden capital inflows and sudden capital outflows (sudden stops). Sudden capital inflows tend to lead to abnormal increases in asset prices and thus to financial and real bubbles. The latter have been the main cause of financial crises in emerging countries, starting with the 1994 Mexico crisis.

(iii) *High demand for international liquidity.* Contrary to what one would expect in a flexible exchange rate system such as the dollar standard, emerging countries' demand for foreign exchange reserves has increased very markedly since the late 1990s.[91] If this trend continues, and if mechanisms are not put in place to increase the supply of international liquidity, global deflation could occur.

(iv) *Excessive elasticity of credit supply.* As explained by Borio and Disyatat (2011), the global financial crisis of 2008 first affected the advanced countries and resulted from an abnormal increase in gross capital flows between these countries. Its first cause was the high elasticity of credit supply of banks in advanced countries.[92]

These shortcomings have led many scholars and experts to call for a reform of the international monetary system. In reality, however, the institutional architecture in

[89] See Bénassy-Quéré and Pisani-Ferry (2011).

[90] Some countries follow export-led growth models, others growth models driven by domestic demand.

[91] On the causes of this see Aizenman and Lee (2007).

[92] See Bordo et al. (2001), Reinhart and Rogoff (2009).

charge of the functioning of the dollar standard has been changing, albeit not organically. This process has resulted in changes in the responsibilities of existing bodies such as the IMF and the introduction of new institutions and policies.

7.9 Some Directions for Reform of the Current International Monetary System

In the preceding sections we have seen how the emergence of frequent financial crises, in recent years even in the most advanced countries, poses a number of problems and therefore calls for reforms. A first problem is represented by the "excess financial elasticity" of a system based on fiat money. Expansions and contractions of credit through banks and markets tend to exacerbate the booms and busts of the financial cycle generating real estate and financial bubbles and eventually crises.[93]

Limits to financial elasticity may come first of all from improving macro-prudential policies so as not only to strengthen the resilience of the financial system, but also to restrain financial booms.[94]

The amplification of the financial cycle depends not only on the high propensity of banks to create credit, but also on the monetary policy stance. Monetary policy should counteract the emergence of financial imbalances even if the inflation rate is low and stable. In a nutshell, monetary policy has the task of safeguarding the value of money and, therefore, must not only prevent the inflationary erosion of money, but also the impairment of its value due to banking and financial crises.

The reforms outlined above are of a domestic nature, to be implemented by national governments. However, their nature, the institutional mechanisms underlying them should be agreed at the international level. At this level, a global safety net should be defined to safeguard the public good of the stability of the international monetary system.

In the previous chapters, it has been repeatedly stated that the evolution of international money has been driven by the demand for innovations to meet the increased demand for money resulting from the growth of trade between countries. In this chapter, however, it was pointed out that, because of the relative economic decline in the USA, Triffin's dilemma may arise again, albeit in different terms from the past. Hence the possibility of a situation characterized by low international liquidity and the associated risk of global deflation.

Such a risk can be averted either by a decrease in demand or by an increase in the supply of international liquidity, or both. The literature has focused on various ways in which the supply of international liquidity could be increased. One proposal

---

[93]See Borio and Disyatat (2011), Borio (2014), Shin (2012, 2013), Drehmann et al. (2012) and James (2018).

[94]On this aspect see Lim et al. (2011), Claessens et al. (2013) and Kuttner and Shim (2013).

shared by many scholars is to accelerate the transition to a multi-currency system.[95] However, such a system could be characterized by high competition among key currency-issuing countries to grab seigniorage. It could ensure instability in the monetary system and its degeneration into relatively closed monetary blocs.

It would be more feasible to expand the instruments of international liquidity. Among these instruments, BSAs have played an important role since the GFC, and have proven to be an effective instrument in stabilizing markets.[96] Extensive use of this instrument, however, requires prior definition of the treatment of default risk, i.e. the risk that the collateral offered by the counterparty has lost its value. In the case where the central bank of an emerging country wants to enter into a swap lines arrangement with the central bank of a country with a reserve currency, there is an asymmetry of default risk. The lack of definition of this aspect explains why many emerging countries do not have access to swap lines with central banks of advanced countries.

The above problem can be, if not solved, mitigated by regulating these agreements in three ways[97]: by defining eligibility criteria for accessing swap lines, by providing risk compensation mechanisms and by establishing disincentives for moral hazard. The task of regulating the use of BSAs, monitoring the behaviour of the counterparties to these contracts and establishing sanctions for contractual violations should be entrusted to the IMF.

The creation of a network of codified, forward-looking swap agreements should reduce the need for many countries to "self-insure" themselves through the accumulation of international reserves. The demand for international liquidity should be reduced, thus helping to avert the Triffin dilemma.

Lower demand for reserve assets by emerging countries would also allow them to put these resources to productive use. This would result, on the one hand, in higher economic growth in these countries and, on the other hand, in less demand for reserve assets and less downward pressure on interest rates, thus eliminating one of the causes of financial instability.[98]

The advantage of BSAs over extended forms of liquidity by the IMF is that they can be accessed immediately, an important feature when crisis situations arise.

In the absence of a framework allowing emerging countries access to BSAs, IMF credit facilities such as the Flexible Credit Lines (FCLs), Precautionary Credit Lines (PCLs) and Global Stabilization Mechanism (GSM) remain crucial to meeting these countries' demand for liquidity and prevent contagion. Strengthening them, and thus the IMF's capacity to support these countries, would be possible by extending the IMF's borrowing capacity.

---

[95] See Farhi et al. (2011), Bénassy-Quéré et al. (2011) and Bini-Smaghi (2011).

[96] See Aizenman et al. (2010), Allen and Moessner (2010), Goldberg (2010) and Seghezza (2018a, 2018b).

[97] See Truman (2011).

[98] On this point see Farhi et al. (2011).

Some economists have proposed increasing the supply of international liquidity by giving SDRs the role of reserve currency.[99] Not surprisingly, this proposal has been put forward strongly by the governor of the People's Bank of China, Xiaochuan Zhou. It is clear that this would make the SDRs stand alongside the dollar as an international currency: the dominant role of the US currency would therefore be undermined.[100]

However, it is difficult to imagine the creation of an international money that is not issued by a central bank, which has the possibility to issue an unlimited amount of it. Only in this way is there any guarantee that the value of assets denominated in this currency can be stabilized.

The possibility of SDRs becoming international currencies is countered by the fact that the IMF is not and cannot be a central bank. This institution, although not a central bank, has in the past contributed to the stability of the international monetary system. This was despite erroneous interventions, such as in the case of the Asian crisis, which led some to contemplate its abolition.[101]

Recent decades have seen remarkable changes in several respects. If the IMF wants to continue to play an important role in the international monetary system, it must not fail to take these into account. The first of these important changes is a shift in global economic and political power. The weight of advanced economies on global output has declined significantly and, correspondingly, the weight of emerging economies has increased. Therefore, the IMF voting shares should be aligned with the changing economic importance of member countries. At present EU members have 29.6% of votes; the USA, 16.5%; Japan, 6.2%; but China only 6.1% and India 2.6%. If the IMF is to remain a globally relevant institution, the voting shares must be re-weighted, particularly in favour of Asian countries.[102]

A second important change in recent decades, as we have seen, is the pronounced increase in gross capital flows between countries. In the face of this change, the IMF can continue to play a crucial role in contributing to the stability of the international monetary system only under two conditions. The first of these is a significant increase in its financial firepower. At present, the IMF lending capacity is about one trillion dollars, while global foreign exchange reserves are about 12 trillion dollars. Therefore, it appears inadequate for effective crisis prevention. Therefore, IMF's financial capacity has to be increased.

The second condition for the IMF to retain a central role in the international monetary system is that it develops expertise and responsibility in financial surveillance. After the GFC its surveillance policy shifted from bilateral to multilateral surveillance that is to an approach aimed at assessing whether countries' policies have a negative impact, not only on their own financial stability, but also for

[99]See Camdessus (2011) and Padoa-Schioppa (2010).

[100]See Zhou (2009).

[101]See Edwards (1998) and Head (2003).

[102]See Truman (2018).

international financial stability.[103] Financial surveillance should eventually be accompanied by the involvement of the IMF in carrying out—in coordination with central banks and other international institutions, such as the IDB—regulatory and supervisory activities aimed at preventing episodes of amplification of the financial cycle.

7.10 Conclusions

Compared to the spontaneous emergence of an international monetary system, as was the case with the gold standard, the "legalization of monetary affairs" allows for incremental changes to the existing monetary system and, thus, a response to potential instability factors. It has been said that one of these factors is a possible liquidity shortage and its deflationary implications.

Hence the need to find instruments to increase the supply of international liquidity. This objective can be pursued in several ways that tend to be complementary, such as increasing the amount and broadening the scope of SDRs and increasing the IMF's capacity to provide financing.

In the case of the GFC and the sovereign debt crisis the creation of international liquidity through BSAs between central banks of advanced countries proved very effective. Measures to facilitate access to these instruments by emerging countries—and to international liquidity instruments more generally—would probably help reduce the tendency of these countries to accumulate foreign exchange reserves. The likelihood of an international liquidity shortage would diminish and currently unproductive resources could be used to increase output growth in emerging countries.

In a context of "legalization of monetary affairs", the problems mentioned above can only be addressed in a multipolar logic. It is in this logic that the problem of the IMF must be addressed: it does not currently reflect, in any way, the changed and changing weight of advanced and emerging countries in the world economy. Rebalancing the IMF's governance would strengthen its role in crisis prevention and management.

The reluctance of the US to agree to an IMF governance reform stems largely from the fear that it would adversely affect the role of the dollar as an international currency. At present, however, the position of the US currency is not threatened by either the euro or the renminbi.

As seen in Chap. 2, the large size of an economy is not sufficient for the currency to establish itself as an international money. For this to happen, there needs to be a guarantee of the stability of its value and, consequently, of the assets denominated in it. Neither the euro area nor China provides adequate protection for the property rights of holders of the currencies they issue. In China, the Communist Party can

[103] See Moschella (2011).

change *ad libitum* the property rights of holders of renminbi and renminbi-denominated assets. For different reasons, the stability of domestic currencies is also not guaranteed in the euro area. This is due to the fact that in this area the currency is a single one, but the states have maintained their sovereignty and fiscal institutions intact. The protection of ownership rights of securities issued in different countries is therefore different: the degree of integration of the euro area financial market is partial.

To the unsatisfactory protection of the property rights of the holders of local currencies, China and the euro area add the lack of a political-military power that would allow them to guarantee the stability of the international monetary system. In this respect, as James (1990, p. 44) writes: "The US dollar will be the major international currency as long as the USA remain the world's largest concentration of political and military might as well as of economic potential".[104]

References

Aizenman, J., & Lee, J. (2007). International reserves: Precautionary versus mercantilist views, theory and evidence. *Open Economies Review, 18*, 191–214.

Aizenman, J., Jinjarak, Y., & Park, D. (2010). *International reserves and swap lines: Substitutes or complement?*. NBER working paper n. 15804.

Alesina, A., & Ardagna, S. (2009). *Large changes in fiscal policy: Taxes versus spending*. NBER working paper n. 15438.

Allen, F., & Carletti, E. (2010). *International Review of Finance, 10*, 1–26.

Allen, W. A., & Moessner, R. (2010). *Central bank cooperation and international liquidity in the financial crisis of 2008-09*. BIS working paper n. 310.

Angeletos, G. M., & Parroux, V. (2011). Financial integration, entrepreneurial risk and global dynamics. *Journal of Economic Theory, 146*, 863–896.

Antras, P., & Caballero, R. J. (2009). Trade and capital flows: A financial frictions perspective. *Journal of Political Economy, 117*, 701–744.

Ashcraft, A. B., & Schuermann, T. (2007). *Understanding the securitization of subprime mortgage*. Federal Reserve Bank of New York Staff Report n. 318.

Avdjiev, S., Eren, E., & McGuire, P. (2020, April 1). Dollar funding costs during the Covid-19 crisis through the lens of the FX swap markets. *BIS Bulletin, 1*.

Baldwin, R. E. (2009). The great trade collapse: What caused it and what does it mean? In R. E. Baldwin (Ed.), *The great trade collapse: Causes, consequences, and prospects*. CEPR.

Basel Committee on Banking Supervision. (2010). *Basel III: A global regulatory framework for more resilient banks and banking systems*. Bank for International Settlements.

Beckley, M. (2011). China's century? Why America's edge will endure. *International Security, 36*, 41–78.

Bénassy-Quéré, A. (2015). *The international monetary system in perpetual search of stability*. Rice University's Baker Institute for Public Policy working paper n. 91.

Bénassy-Quéré, A., & Pisani-Ferry, J. (2011). *The long march towards a multipolar monetary regime*. Lettre du CEPII 308, Paris, Centre d'Etudes Prospectives et d'Informations Internationales.

[104] A similar thought can be found in Mundell (1971).

Bénassy-Quéré, A., Pisani-Ferry, J., & Yu, Y. (2011). *Reform of the international monetary system. Some concrete steps*. Policy contributions n. 516, Bruegel.
Bergsten, F. C. (1997). The dollar and the euro. *Foreign Affairs, 76*, 83–95.
Bergsten, C. F. (2011, February 15). Why the world needs three global currencies. *Financial Times*.
Bergsten, C. F., & Williamson, J. (2003). *Dollar overvaluation in the world economy*. Institute for International Economics.
Bernanke, B. (2005). *The global saving glut and the US current account deficit*. Remarks of the Governor at the Sandridge Lecture, Virginia Association of Economists. Richmond, March 10.
Bernanke, B. (2009). *Financial reform to address systemic risk*. Speech at the Council on Foreign Relations. Washington, 10 March.
Bini-Smaghi, L. (2011). *The reform of the international monetary system*. Paper presented at the Bank of Italy conference in memory of Tommaso Padoa-Schioppa. Rome, December 16.
BIS. (2019). *Triennial central bank survey of foreign exchange and over-the-counter (OTC) derivatives markets*. Basel.
Blinder, A. S. (2014). *What did we learn from the financial crisis, the great recession, and the pathetic recovery*. Griswold Center for Economic Policy Studies working paper n. 243.
Bordo, M., & McCauley, R. N. (2016). The current account version of the Triffin Dilemma. *Atlantic Economic Journal, 44*, 171–182.
Bordo, M., Eichengreen, B., Klingebiel, D., & Martinez-Peria, M. S. (2001). Financial crises: Lessons from the last 120 years. *Economic Policy, 16*, 51–82.
Borio, C. (2014). *The Achilles' heel of the international monetary system: What it is and what to do about it*. Paper prepared for a keynote lecture at the festschrift in honor of Niels Thygesen. University of Copenhagen, December 5.
Borio, C. (2020). The Covid-19 economic crisis: Dangerously unique. *Business Economics, 55*, 181–190.
Borio, C., & Disyatat, P. (2011). *Global imbalances and the financial crisis: Link or not link?*. BIS working paper n. 346.
Borio, C., & Disyatat, P. (2015). *Capital flows and the current account: Taking financing (more) seriously*. BIS working paper n. 525.
Broz, L. (2015). The politics of rescuing the world's financial system: The Federal Reserve as a global lender of last resort. *Korean Journal of International Studies, 13*, 323–351.
Caballero, R., Farhi, E., & Gourinchas, P. (2008). An equilibrium model of global imbalances and low interest rates. *American Economic Review, 98*, 358–393.
Caballero, R.J., & Krishnamurty, A. (2009). Global imbalances and financial fragility. *American Economic Review, 99*, 584–588.
Calleo, D. P. (2009). Twenty-first century geopolitics and the erosion of the dollar order. In E. Helleiner & J. Kirshner (Eds.), *The future of the dollar*. Cornell University Press.
Camdessus, M. (2011). Towards a new international monetary system. In J. T. Boorman & A. Icard (Eds.), *Reform of the international monetary system: The Palais Royal Initiative*. Sage.
Caruana, J. (2010). *Macroprudential policy: Working towards a new consensus*. Remarks at the high-level meeting on 'The emerging framework for financial regulation and monetary policy' jointly organized by the BIS's Financial Stability Institute and the IMF.
Cetorelli, N., Goldberg, L. S., & Ravazzolo, F. (2020, May 22). Have the fed swap lines reduced dollar funding strains during the Covid-19 outbreak?. *Liberty Street Economics*.
Chang, M., & Leblond, P. (2015). All in: Market expectations of eurozone integrity in the sovereign debt crisis. *Review of International Political Economy, 22*, 626–665.
Chinn, M., & Frankel, J. A. (2007). Will the euro eventually surpass the dollar as leading international reserve currency? In R. H. Clarida (Ed.), *G7 current account imbalances: Sustainability and adjustment*. University of Chicago Press.
Chinn, M., & Frankel, J. (2008). Why the euro will rival the dollar. *International Finance, 11*, 49–73.
Christiano, L. J., Eichenbaum, M. S., & Trabandi, M. (2015). Understanding the great recession. *American Economic Journal: Macroeconomics, 7*, 110–167.

Claessens, S. (2015). An overview of macroprudential policy tools. *Annual Review of Financial Economics, 7*, 397–422.
Claessens, S., Ghosh, S. R., & Mihet, R. (2013). Macroprudential policies to mitigate financial system vulnerabilities. *Journal of International Money and Finance, 29*, 153–185.
Cohen, B. (2010). *The future of global currency: The euro vs the dollar*. Routledge.
Cohen, B. (2015). The demise of the dollar? *Revue de la Régulation, 18*, 1–22.
Cohen, B. (2017). *Renminbi internationalization: A conflict of statecrafts*. Chatham House International Economics Department Research Paper, March 2017.
Cohen, B., & Benney, T. M. (2013). What does the international currency system really look like? *Review of International Political Economy, 21*, 1017–1041.
Constancio, V. (2012). Contagion and the European debt crisis. *Banque de France Financial Stability Review, 16*, 109–121.
Coombs, C. (1976). *The arena of international finance*. Wiley.
Curcuru, S. E., Dvorak, T., & Warnock, F. E. (2008). Cross-border returns differentials. *Quarterly Journal of Economics, 123*, 1495–1530.
De Grauwe, P. (2013a). Foreword. In I. Sanchis & M. Marco (Eds.), *The economics of the monetary union and the eurozone crisis*. Springer.
De Grauwe, P. (2013b). *Design failures in the Eurozone: Can they be fixed?* European Economy, Economic Papers n. 491.
Desai, R. M., & Vreeland, J. M. (2011). Global governance in a multipolar world: The case for regional monetary funds. *International Studies Review, 13*, 109–121.
Despres, E., Kindleberger, C., & Salant, W. (1966). The dollar and world liquidity: A minority view. *The Economist, 218*, 526–529.
Dooley, M., Folkerts-Landau, D., & Garber, P. (2003). *An essay on the revived Bretton Woods system*. NBER working paper n. 9971.
Dornbusch, R. (1996, September–October). Euro fantasies. *Foreign Affairs*, 25–37.
Drehmann, M., Borio, C., & Tsatsaronis, K. (2012). *Characterising the financial cycle: Don't lose right of the medium term*. Bank of International Settlement working paper n. 380.
Drezner, D. W. (2014). The system worked. Global economic governance during the great recession. *World Politics, 66*, 123–164.
Duran, S. V. (2015). *The international lender of last resort for emerging countries: A bilateral currency swap*. Global Economic Governance working paper n. 2015/108.
ECB. (2012). *The international role of the euro*. ECB.
Edwards, S. (1998, November 13). Abolish the IMF. *Financial Times*.
Eggertsson, G. B., & Krugman, P. (2012). Debt, deleveraging, and the liquidity trap: A Fisher-Minsky-Koo approach. *Quarterly Journal of Economics, 127*, 1469–1513.
Eichengreen, B. (1998). The euro as a reserve currency. *Journal of the Japanese and International Economies, 12*, 483–506.
Eichengreen, B. (2009). *The financial crisis and global policy reforms*. Federal Reserve Bank of San Francisco, Asia Economic Policy Conference, October 18–20.
Eichengreen, B. (2010). *Global imbalances and the lessons of Bretton Woods*. MIT.
Eichengreen, B. (2011a). *Exorbitant privilege: The rise and fall of the dollar and the future of the international monetary system*. Oxford University Press.
Eichengreen, B. (2011b). The renminbi as an international currency. *Journal of Policy Modeling, 33*, 723–730.
Eichengreen, B., & Wyplosz, C. (2016). How the euro crisis was successfully resolved. In R. E. Baldwin & F. Giavazzi (Eds.), *How to fix Europe's monetary union: Views of leading economists*. CEPR.
Eren, E., Schrimpf, A., & Sushko, V. (2020, May 12). US dollar funding markets during the Covid-19 crisis – The international dimension. *BIS Bulletin, 15*.
Farhi, E., Gourinchas, P., & Rey, H. (2011). *Reforming the international monetary system*. CEPR.
Fratianni, M. (2012). The future international monetary system: Dominant currencies or supranational money? An introduction. *Open Economies Review, 23*, 1–12.

Freixas, X., & Parigi, B. M. (2012). Lender of last resort and bank closure policy. In A. N. Berger, P. Molyneux, & J. O. S. Wilson (Eds.), *The Oxford handbook of banking*. Oxford University Press.

Friedman, M., & Schwartz, A. (1963). *The monetary history of the United States*. Princeton University Press.

Gilpin, R. (1975). *US power and the multinational corporation: The political economy of foreign direct investment*. Basic Books.

Gilpin, R. (1981). *War and change in world politics*. Cambridge University Press.

Goldberg, L. S. (2010). Is the international role of the dollar changing? *Federal Reserve Bank of New York Current Issues in Economics and Finance, 16*, 1–7.

Goodfriend, M., & King, R. (1988). Financial deregulation, monetary policy and central banking. In W. Haraf & R. M. Kushmeider (Eds.), *Restructuring banking and financial services in America*. American Enterprise Institute Studies n. 481.

Gopinath, G. (2015). *The international price system*. NBER working paper n. 21646.

Gourinchas, P. O., & Rey, H. (2007). From world banker to world venture capitalist: US external adjustment and the exorbitant privilege. In R. Clarida (Ed.), *Current account imbalances sustainability and adjustment*. University of Chicago Press.

Gourinchas, P. O., & Rey, H. (2014). External adjustment, global imbalances, valuation effects. In G. Gopinath, E. Helpman, & K. Rogoff (Eds.), *Handbook of international economics* (Vol. IV). Elsevier.

Gourinchas, P. O., Rey, H., & Govillot, N. (2010). *Exorbitant privilege and exorbitant duty*. Mimeo.

Guerrieri, V., & Lorenzoni, G. (2012). *Credit crises, precautionary savings and the liquidity trap*. NBER working paper n. 19313.

Head, J. W. (2003). Seven deadly sins: An assessment of criticism directed at the International Monetary Fund. *University of Kansas Law Review, 52*, 521–582.

Helleiner, E. (2008). Political determinants of international currencies: What future for the US dollar? *Review of International Political Economy, 15*, 354–378.

Helleiner, E. (2014). *The status quo crisis: Global financial governance after the 2008 meltdown*. Oxford University Press.

Helleiner, E., & Kirshner, J. (2009). The future of the dollar: Whither the key currency? In E. Helleiner & J. Kirshner (Eds.), *The future of the dollar*. Cornell University Press.

Henning, C. R. (2015). *The global liquidity safety net: Institutional cooperation on precautionary facilities and central bank swaps*. Center for International Governance Innovation working paper n. 5.

Ikenberry, G. J. (2011). *Liberal leviathan*. Princeton University Press.

Ilzetzki, E., Reinhart, C. M., & Rogoff, K. S. (2020). *Will the secular decline in exchange rate and inflation volatility survive Covid-19?*. NBER working paper n. 28108.

IMF. (2005, April). *World economic outlook*.

IMF. (2016). *Adequacy of the global financial safety net*. IMF.

James, H. (1990). Enduring international preeminence of dollar. In E. Helleiner & J. Kirshner (Eds.), *The future of dollar*. Cornell University Press.

James, H. (2018). Learning lessons from previous crises: The capital account and the current account. In A. R. Ghosh & M. S. Qureshi (Eds.), *From great depression to great recession*. International Monetary Fund.

Johnson, K. H. (2009). *Gross or net international financial flows*. Council on Foreign Relations working paper, July 2009.

Kenen, P. (2002). The euro versus the dollar: Will there be a struggle for dominance. *Journal of Policy Modeling, 24*, 347–354.

Keohane, R. O. (1984). *After hegemony: Cooperation and discord in the world political economy*. Princeton University Press.

Kindleberger, C. (1965). *Balance of payments deficits and the international market for liquidity*. Princeton Studies in International Finance n. 46.

Kindleberger, C. (1973). *The world in depression, 1929–1939*. University of California Press.

Kindleberger, C. (2000). *Manias, panics and crashes*. Cambridge University Press.

Kohn, D. (2010). *Global imbalances*. Speech delivered at the high-level conference on the international monetary system. Zurich, May 11.

Kopf, C. (2011). Restoring financial stability in the euro area. *CEPS Policy Brief.*

Kose, M. A., Matsuoka, M., Panizza, U., & Vorisek, D. (2018). Inflation expectations: Review and evidence. In World Bank, *Inflation in emerging and developing economies*. World Bank.

Kose, M. A., Prasad, E., Rogoff, K., & Wei, S. J. (2009). Financial globalization: a reappraisal. *IMF Staff Papers, 56*, 8–62.

Kose, M. A., Prasad, E. S., & Terrones, M. E. (2009). Does financial globalization promote risk sharing? *Journal of Development Economics, 89*, 258–270.

Krasner, S. (1983). *International regimes*. Cornell University Press.

Krugman, P. (2009, March 1). Revenge of the glut. *The New York Times*.

Krugman, P. (2011, January 12). Can Europe be saved? *The New York Times*.

Kuttner, K. N., & Shim, I. (2013). *Can non-interest rate policies stabilize housing markets? Evidence from a panel of 57 economies*. BIS working paper n. 433.

Lake, D. (2009). Open economy politics: A critical review. *Review of International Organizations, 4*, 219–244.

Lane, P. (2012). The European sovereign debt crisis. *Journal of Economic Perspectives, 26*, 49–67.

Lane, P., & Milesi-Ferretti, G. (2001). The external wealth of nations: Measures of foreign assets and liabilities for industrial and developing countries. *Journal of International Economics, 55*, 263–294.

Lane, P., & Milesi-Ferretti, G. (2009). Where did all the borrowing go? A forensic analysis of the US external position. *Journal of the Japanese and International Economies, 23*, 177–199.

Levy-Yeyati, E., Sturzenegger, F., & Gluzmann, F. A. (2013). Fear of appreciation. *Journal of Development Economics, 101*, 233–247.

Lim, E., Columba, C. F., Costa, A., Kongsamut, P., Otani, A., Saiyid, M., Wezel, T., & Wu, X. (2011). *Macroprudential policy, what instruments and how to use them? Lessons from country experiences*. IMF working paper 11/238.

Lo, C. (2013). *The renminbi rises: Myths, hypes, and realities of RMB internationalization and reforms in the post-crisis world*. Palgrave Macmillan.

McDowell, D. (2011). The US as 'sovereign international last resort lender': The Fed's currency swap programme during great panic of 2007-08. *New Political Economy, 17*, 157–178.

McDowell, D. (2017). The emergent international liquidity network: Central bank cooperation after the global financial crisis. *Journal of International Relations and Development, 22*, 1–27.

McGuire, P., & von Peter, G. (2009). *The US dollar shortage in global banking and the international policy response*. BIS working paper n. 291.

McKinnon, R. (1998). The euro threat is exaggerated. *International Economy, 12*, 32–60.

Mendoza, E. G., Quadrini, V., & Rios Rull, J. V. (2009). Financial integration, financial development, and global imbalances. *Journal of Political Economy, 117*, 371–416.

Minsky, H. (1982). *Can "it" happen again?: Essays on instability and finance*. Sharpe.

Mody, A. (2018). *Euro tragedy. A drama in nine acts*. Oxford University Press.

Moessner, R., & Allen, W. (2010). *Banking crises and the international monetary system in the great depression and now*. BIS working paper n. 333.

Morelli, P., & Seghezza, E. (2018). Rule of law and balance of power sustain US dollar preeminence. *Journal of Policy Modeling, 40*, 16–36.

Moschella, M. (2011). Lagged learning and the response to equilibrium shock: The global financial crisis and IMF surveillance. *Journal of Public Policy, 31*, 121–141.

Mundell, R. (1971). *The dollar and the policy mix*. Essay in International Finance n. 85, International Finance Section, Princeton University.

Mundell, R. (1998). What the euro means for the dollar and the international monetary system. *Atlantic Economic Journal, 26*, 227–237.

Mundell, R. (2000). The euro and the stability of the international monetary system. In R. Mundell & A. Cleese (Eds.), *The euro as a stabilizer in the international economic system*. Kluwer Academic.

Norrlof, C. (2010). *America's global advantage: US hegemony and international cooperation*. Cambridge University Press.

Norrlof, C., & Reich S. (2015). American and Chinese leadership during the global financial crisis: testing Kindleberger's stabilization functions. *International Area Studies Review, 18*, 227-250.

Obstfeld, M. (2011). *International liquidity: The fiscal dimension*. NBER working paper n. 17379.

Obstfeld, M. (2013). The international monetary system: Living with asymmetry. In R. C. Feenstra & A. M. Taylor (Eds.), *Globalization in an age of crisis, multilateral economic cooperation in the twenty-first century*. University of Chicago Press.

Obstfeld, M. (2018). *Twenty-five years of global imbalances*. CEPR Discussion Paper: DP13066.

Obstfeld, M., & Rogoff, K. (2009). *Global imbalances and the financial crisis: Products of common causes*. Asia and the Global Financial Crisis. Asia Economic Policy Conference, Santa Barbara, October 18–20, Federal Reserve Bank of San Francisco.

Obstfeld, M., Shambaugh, J. C., & Taylor, A. M. (2009). Financial instability, reserves, and central bank swap lines in the panic of 2008. *American Economic Review, 99*, 480–486.

Olson, M. (1982). *The rise and decline of nations: Economic growth, stagflation and social rigidities*. Yale University Press.

Padoa-Schioppa, T. (2010). *The ghost of bancor: The economic crisis and global monetary disorder*. Speech at the Conference in Louvain la Neuve, February 25.

People's Bank of China. (2009). *Strengthen regional financial cooperation and actively conduct currency swap*. March 31, People's Bank of China, Beijing.

Portes, R. (2009). Global imbalances. In M. Dewatripont, X. Freixas, & R. Portes (Eds.), *Macroeconomic stability and financial regulation: Key issues for the G-20*. CEPR.

Portes, R. (2012). A reassessment of the Triffin dilemma. In J. Koeune & A. Lamfalussy (Eds.), *In search of a new world monetary order. Proceedings of a conference to celebrate the 100th anniversary of Robert Triffin (1911-1993)*. Brussels: P.I.E. Peter Lang for the Foundation International Triffin.

Portes, R., & Rey, H. (1998). The emergence of the euro as an international currency. *Economic Policy, 13*, 305–343.

Posen, A. (2008). Why the euro will not rival the dollar. *International Finance, 11*, 75–100.

Prasad, E. (2014). The dollar reigns supreme by default. *Finance and Development, 51*, 34–37.

Prasad, E. (2016). *China's efforts to expand the international use of the Renminbi*. Report prepared for the US-China Economic and Security Review Commission.

Rajan, R. G. (2005). *Has financial development made the world riskier?* Federal Reserve Bank of Kansas City, Symposium Proceedings.

Reinhart, C., & Rogoff, K. (2009). *This time is different*. Princeton University Press.

Rey, H. (2013). *Dilemma not trilemma: The global financial cycle and monetary policy independence*. Federal Reserve Bank of Kansas City Economic Policy Symposium.

Rodrik, D. (1998). Who needs capital account convertibility?. In Kenen (Ed.), *Should the IMF pursue capital account convertibility?* Princeton Essays in International Finance, n. 207.

Rodrik, D. (2000). How far will international economic integration go? *Journal of Economic Perspectives, 14*, 177–186.

Rogoff, K. (2003). *Globalization and global disinflation*. Paper prepared for the Federal Reserve Bank of Kansas City conference on 'Monetary Policy and Uncertainty: Adapting to a Changing Economy', Jackson Hole, August 29.

Sayers, R. (1976). *The Bank of England, 1891–1944*. Cambridge University Press.

Seghezza, E. (2018a). *L'evoluzione del sistema monetario internazionale. Il ruolo della domanda di innovazioni e della produzione di fiducia*. Soveria Mannelli.

Seghezza, E. (2018b). Can swap line arrangements help solve the Triffin dilemma? How? *The World Economy, 41*, 2691–2708.

Shin, H. (2012). Global banking glut and loan risk premium. Mundell-Fleming lecture. *IMF Economic Review, 60*, 155–192.

Shin, H. (2013). *The second phase of global liquidity and its impact on emerging economies*. Keynote address at the Federal Reserve Bank of San Francisco, Asia Economic Policy Conference, San Francisco, November 3–5.

Smith, T. (1981). *The pattern of imperialism*. Cambridge University Press.

Steiner, A. (2014). Current account balance and dollar standard: Exploring the linkages. *Journal of International Money and Finance, 41*, 65–94.

Strange, S. (1971a). *Sterling and British policy: A political study of an international currency in decline*. Oxford University Press.

Strange, S. (1971b). The politics of international currencies. *World Politics, 23*, 215–231.

Strange, S. (1987). The persistent myth of lost hegemony. *International Organization, 41*, 551–574.

Stulz, R. M. (2005). The limits of financial globalization. *Journal of Finance, 60*, 1595–1638.

Subramanian, A. (2011). *Eclipse: Living in the shadow of China's economic dominance*. Institute for International Economics.

Swoboda, A. (2012). International monetary reform and global imbalances. In J. C. Koeune & A. Lamfalussy (Eds.), *In search of a new world monetary order: Proceedings of a conference to celebrate the 100th anniversary of Robert Triffin (1911–1993)*. Peter Lang for the Fondation Internationale Triffin.

Toniolo, G. (2005). *Central bank cooperation at the Bank for International Settlements, 1930–1973*. Cambridge University Press.

Trichet, J. C., & Papademos, L. (2008). Introductory statement with Q&A. *European Central Bank*, June 5.

Truman, E. (2011). *Three evolutionary proposals for reform of the international monetary system*. Paper presented at the Bank of Italy conference in memory of Tommaso Padoa-Schioppa. Rome, December 16.

Truman, E. (2018). *IMF quota and governance reform once again*. Policy Brief 18-9. Peterson Institute for International Economics.

World Bank. (2011). *Multipolarity: The new global economy*. The International Bank for Reconstruction and Development/The World Bank.

Zhang, C. (2012). *The development of the offshore RMB business*. Paper presented at the Round Table organized by ADBI and OECD on 'Capital Market Reform in Asia'.

Zhou, X. (2009). Reform the international monetary system. *BIS Review, 41*, 1–3.

Chapter 8
Conclusions

The international monetary system currently in force is a hierarchically organized system of flexible exchange rates. At the top of this hierarchy is the dollar, at a lower level the other reserve currencies and below that the other currencies.

It is inevitable to ask what the prospects are for the dollar's predominant role in a context in which major new players are appearing in the international economic arena, namely the eurozone and China.

Already in the late 1990s, when the EMU was being formed, several scholars put forward the hypothesis that the pre-eminence of the dollar would be threatened by the euro. Their hypothesis was based on the Mengerian theory of the origin of money. Since the economic size of the euro area was similar to, if not larger than, the USA, it was inevitable that the European currency would establish itself as an international currency. The European currency would first flank and then replace the dollar as the international currency.

This has not occurred. The euro remains a regional currency and has little prospect of becoming an international one. It is a currency issued by a central bank, not by a sovereign state. This has two implications. On the one hand, the euro area does not have the political-military power needed to guarantee the stability of a monetary system based on a fiat currency. On the other, the euro area lacks political unity and still has significant institutional and economic differences within it. Consequently, the degree of rule of law within the area is not homogenous. The same applies to the fiscal soundness of EMU member countries. These two factors contribute to a fragmented eurozone financial market. The degree of liquidity of euro-denominated securities suffers as a result.

Several scholars have put forward the hypothesis that the economic and geopolitical decline of the USA makes the replacement of the dollar with the Chinese renminbi as the international currency imminent. This hypothesis is shared both by scholars who refer to Mengerian theory and by some who refer to the theory of hegemonic stability.

In fact, the rise of the renminbi as an international currency, although facilitated by China's growing economic size in terms of both output and exports, is made

G. B. Pittaluga, E. Seghezza, *Building Trust in the International Monetary System*, Frontiers in Economic History, https://doi.org/10.1007/978-3-030-78491-1_8

problematic by China's low level of protection of property rights. Thus, on the one hand, there is a lack of adequate institutional guarantee of the stability of the value of the renminbi, and on the other, the low level of rule of law hinders the development of a large and thick domestic financial market, i.e. one that ensures a high degree of liquidity of assets denominated in the Chinese currency.

On the basis of the above, it is likely that the dollar will remain prominent in the international monetary system for a long time to come.

However, the stability of the international monetary system is threatened by several factors. The first of these is that the large amount of gross capital flows makes it easier than in the past for the financial cycle to amplify, for credit booms and systemic crises to occur. This risk can be countered by reforms and policies aimed at controlling the elasticity of credit supply, similar to what was done in the 1980s to control governments' exploitation of the high elasticity of fiat money. The tightening of constraints in micro-prudential banking supervision and the coupling of macro-prudential policies to monetary policy management point in this direction.

A second factor of instability in the current international monetary system is a possible shortage of international liquidity. This could lead to a situation similar to that which occurred in the early 1930s, when the decline in world money helped turn a cyclical recession into the Great Depression.

A liquidity shortage could result from either demand or supply factors. On the demand side, in fact, emerging countries tend to accumulate very high amounts of reserves, given their large and persistent current account surpluses. On the supply side, Triffin's dilemma reappears, albeit in new forms. The relative decline in the comparative size of the United States economy, especially with regard to the issuance of dollar-denominated government securities, adversely affects the supply of international liquidity. In this context, the introduction of new liquidity instruments and the strengthening of existing ones, in particular SDRs, become important. Among the new instruments, the role of Bilateral Swap Lines appears extremely promising. Access to this instrument is currently only possible for advanced countries. Institutional mechanisms facilitating its access to emerging countries could induce these countries to slow the accumulation of reserves and reduce their demand for international liquidity.

A third critical factor lies in the governance of the international institutions responsible for ensuring the stability of the international monetary system, in particular the IMF. If its authority is to be preserved, its governance structure must be adapted to the changes in the structure of the world economy.

These are crucial issues, however, the "legalization of monetary affairs" that began with Bretton Woods has proved to be an extremely flexible instrument for responding to the demand for monetary innovations, often manifested in crises, that have emerged in recent decades.

Appendix

To take into account the role of states in the creation of an international money, we have built a search-theoretic model with three characteristics. First, we assume the government of a leading country invests to make its currency acceptable as an international money. Secondly, the follower country, being concerned about the relative gains that the leader country derives from the possibility of exploiting the right of seigniorage, decides whether or not to allow its citizens to accept the currency of the leader country as a means of payment. Third, the two countries differ in the degree of internal protection of property rights.

Therefore, we consider two countries, $c = 1{,}2$. Country 1 is the leading country and country 2 is the follower country. The leading country is a large economy. It has to decide whether or not it is convenient for it to make its currency an international currency, that is, also used in Country 2. The latter is, however, sensitive to the effects that the possibility of Country 1 exploiting international seigniorage has on relative gains and, therefore, on the balance of power existing at the international level.

Time is discrete and lasts indefinitely. Country 2 is populated by a continuum of [0,1] individuals operating in two distinct markets: a centralized market, CM, and a decentralized market, DM, where buyers and sellers meet and trade goods bilaterally. In each period, each subject first trades in the decentralized market and then in the centralized one.

In the centralized market they trade a consumer good X of which all subjects can produce 1 unit with a unit of labour H. The utility individuals get from this good is: $U(X) - H$. In DM we are dealing with another good, q, which gives individuals a utility equal to $u(q)$ and whose production entails a cost for them equal to $c(q)$. Goods cannot be stored. It is assumed that $u' > 0$, $u'' < 0$, $c' > 0$, $c'' > 0$. $X^*$and $q^*$are the values of X and q that maximize the utility of individuals. In DM, each individual has an equal probability of being a buyer or seller. So, denoting 2λ the probability of encountering another subject in DM, the likelihood of being, in this market, a buyer is λ.

G. B. Pittaluga, E. Seghezza, *Building Trust in the International Monetary System*, Frontiers in Economic History, https://doi.org/10.1007/978-3-030-78491-1

There are four assets, a_j, with $j \in (1,4)$: two real assets and two fiat currencies, θ_j is the price of asset j. Real assets give a return equal to δ_j and their supply is fixed, equal to A_j, In each period the money supply is given by $M_j = (1 + \gamma_j)M_j^{-1}$ with $j = 1,2$. Changes in the money supply are obtained by transfers from the government to individuals, for each of them of the same amount, in CM; while γ_j is the inflation rate.

Assets also differ in relation to the *rule of law*, i.e. the protection of property rights in force in the country of issue. The *rule of law* is denoted $r_j \in (0,1)$: an increase in r means a higher protection of property rights. As in Lester et al. (2012), in the decentralized market, DM, there is the problem of recognize the quality of assets: a seller of goods is not prepared to accept in payment an asset whose quality he is not able to recognize. It is assumed that the quality of real assets in DM is not recognizable, therefore, only currencies can be used to make payments in this market. It is also assumed that sellers are always able to recognize the local currency, but have difficulty in recognizing the quality of the foreign currency. They can recognize the latter and accept it as payment only if Country 1 has incurred costs, equal to k, to make it recognizable. The amount of investments made by Country 1 to make its currency recognizable is known to all.

Initially the information structure is considered given. S indicates any type of meeting in DM, in order to circumscribe the subset of assets that the seller recognizes (a seller can recognize either only the currency of Country 2 or both the currency of Country 1 and the currency of Country 2).

ρ_s is the probability of encountering a vendor-type S.

As we will see later, the value of ρ_s depends on the investment strategy of Country 1. Let us assume that P_j is the set of encounters in which the seller recognizes the currency j, In a type S encounter, a buyer with a portfolio a has liquid, that is, recognizable, wealth equal to, $\sum_{j \in S} \theta_j a_j$.

As mentioned above, and unlike Lester et al. (2012), another element of friction is introduced that distinguishes the two countries: the *rule of law*. Assets are assumed to differ in the degree of protection of property rights. This means that, at the time of payment, a portion equal to (1-r_j) of the buyer's recognizable assets can be destroyed. Payment to the seller $p_s(a)$ is bound by $p_s(a) \leq y_s(a) = \sum_{j \in S} r_j \theta_j a_j$, where r_j represents the *rule of law* level. The higher r is, the higher is the amount of wealth available for trade.

Suppose that $V(a)$ is the utility function of a subject in DM. In CM, where assets are recognized, all that matters to the individual is the amount of wealth, $y(a)$. Therefore, the utility function in CM can be written as $W[y(a)]$. The problems of the *rule of law* also exist in CM: at the moment of payment the available wealth is $y(a) = \sum_{j=1}^{4} r_j(\delta_j + \theta_j)a_j$.

Now we are able to write the equilibrium conditions of the model. In CM the problem of maximization of an individual is the following:

$$W(y) = \max_{X,H,a}[U(X) - H + \beta V(a)] \text{ s.t. } X = H + y(a) - \sum_j \theta_j a_j + T. \quad (A.1)$$

i.e., when the individual is in the centralized market, he maximizes the utility function $W(y)$, choosing the consumption of good X, the amount of labour H and the amount and composition of its asset portfolio, a. The latter choice will affect its utility in the following period, V, when he will be in the decentralized market. β is the discount factor, while T is the transfer to individuals from the state to make changes in the money supply. Eliminating H, Eq. (A.1) becomes:

$$W(y) = U(X^*) - X^* + y(a) + T + \max_a \left[-\sum_j \theta_j a_j + \beta V(a) \right] \quad (A.2)$$

The choice of a satisfies the first-order condition:

$$-\theta_j + \beta \frac{\partial V(a)}{\partial a} = 0 \quad (A.3)$$

Now return to the equilibrium in DM. As in Lester et al. (2012), the terms of trade are determined on the basis of proportional bargaining: a buyer buys goods in exchange for payment and receives a constant share, assuming ½, of the seller's surplus. The buyer's surplus that gets q by paying p to the seller is $u(q) - p$, Similarly, the seller surplus is $p - c(q)$.

Consider a meeting between two individuals, where the buyer has liquid wealth available $y_s(a) = \sum_{j \in S} r_j \theta_j a_j$. The solution to proportional bargaining is given by a payment $p = p_s(a)$ and a quantity $q = q_s(a)$ that solve:

$$\max_{p,q} u(q) - p \text{ s.t. } u(q) - p = \frac{1}{2}[p - c(q)] \text{ and } p \leq y_s(a). \quad (A.4)$$

We define $z(q) = \frac{1}{2}[u(q) + c(q)]$ and $y^* = z(q^*)$, where $u'(q^*) = c'(q^*)$. The buyer pays $p_s(a) = y^*$ and gets $q_s(a) = q^*$ if its liquid wealth $y_s(a)$ exceeds y^*; otherwise it gives all its available liquid wealth in exchange for $q_s(a) < q^*$. In this latter case, $p_s(a) = y_s(a)$ and $q_s(a)$ solves $z(q) = y_s(a)$.

The utility function in DM is:

$$V(a) = W[y(a)] + \lambda \sum_S \rho_s [u(q_s(a) - p_s(a)] + \zeta \quad (A.5)$$

where the first term is the utility that comes from passing in CM with wallet a intact. The second term is the probability of being a buyer λ multiplied by the surplus expected from the exchanges according to the types of encounters. The last term, ζ, is the expected surplus if you are a seller, which does not depend on a. Differentiating we obtain:

$$\frac{\partial V(a)}{\partial a_j} = r_j(\delta_j + \theta_j)\left[1 + \lambda \sum_{S \in P_j} \rho_s l(q_s(a))\right] \tag{A.6}$$

where $l(q) = \left(\frac{u'(q)}{z'(q)} - 1\right)$ is a liquidity premium, i.e. the pay-off of a marginal unit of wealth that is liquid, and can be used to buy more q in DM. The liquidity premium is decreasing in q, when we have $q = q^*$, $l(q^*) = 0$ and all individuals are satisfied with liquidity. By combining Eqs. (A.3) and (A.6), we get:

$$\theta_{j,t-i} = \beta r_j(\delta_j + \theta_j)\left[1 + \lambda \sum_{S \in P_j} \rho_s l(q_s(a))\right] \tag{A.7}$$

Equation (A.7) represents the equilibrium prices of the assets. We now turn to what it implies for fiat currencies, that is, for $j = 1{,}2$. In a stationary equilibrium, the inflation rate is $\frac{\theta_{j,t-1}}{\theta_{j,t}} = 1 + \gamma$, and Eq. (A.7) implies that:

$$\frac{1 + \gamma_j - \beta r_j}{\beta r_j} = \lambda \sum_{S \in P_j} \rho_s l(q_s(a)) \tag{A.8}$$

The first term of Eq. (A.8) is the nominal interest rate on money j, Indeed, the real asset denominated in currency j, which is not used in DM transactions, has a real interest rate equal to $\frac{1}{\beta r_j} - 1$. Using Fisher's equation, the nominal interest rate satisfies the condition $1 + i_j = (1 + \gamma_j)\frac{1}{\beta r_j}$.

Equation (A.8) allows us to arrive at the First Proposition.

Proposition 1 *An increase in the rule of law level determines a decrease in the nominal interest rate and the liquidity premium on one's own currency and, at the same time, an increase in the quantity traded in DM.*

A high *rule of law* makes a fiat currency recognizable, i.e. it mitigates the problem of information asymmetries and, therefore, the possibility that the holder of it is subject to fraud. This favours the acceptability of this currency.

At this point we can use Eq. (A.8) to clarify how an international currency emerges. Consider a situation where all the sellers accept the local currency and some accept the foreign currency as well: ρ_2 is the probability that the sellers recognize only the local currency, while ρ_{12} is the probability that they recognize both currencies. The condition of Eq. (A.8) becomes:

$$i_1 = \frac{1+\gamma_1-\beta r_1}{\beta r_1} = \lambda \rho_{12} l(q_{12}) \text{ and } i_2 = \frac{1+\gamma_2-\beta r_2}{\beta r_2}$$
$$= \lambda(\rho_2 l(q_2) + \rho_{12} l(q_{12})) \tag{A.9}$$

From Eq. (A.9) we get:

$$i_2 - i_1 = \frac{1+\gamma_2-\beta r_2}{\beta r_2} - \frac{1+\gamma_1-\beta r_1}{\beta r_1} = \lambda(\rho_2 l(q_2)) \tag{A.10}$$

From Eq. (A.10) it is deduced that for the currency issued by Country 1 to become the international currency, the interest rate on it must be lower than the interest rate in Country 2. Otherwise, the liquidity premium on the currency of Country 2 would be zero and the individuals of that country would have enough local currency to satisfy all their exchange needs ($q = q^*$).

All this allows us to arrive at the Second Proposition.

Proposition 2 *The probability that a currency becomes an international currency is higher the lower the inflation and the higher the rule of law level of the issuing country.*

It is certainly no coincidence that the countries that recently issued currencies with the rank of international money, namely the United Kingdom and the USA, have been characterized by low inflation rates and a high level of *rule of law*.

We now proceed to endogenize the probability, ρ_{12}, that the foreign currency is recognized. We assume that two conditions must be met for a currency to be recognizable. First, the leading country must invest to make its currency recognizable abroad. The cost of this investment is k. The leading country will make this investment only if the revenues from the seigniorage it enjoys are higher than the costs it incurs. The seigniorage is given by $\theta_1 M_1 \gamma_1$, therefore, the first condition is:

$$\theta_1 M_1 \gamma_1 \geq k \tag{A.11}$$

where the first term of Eq. (A.11) is the seigniorage enjoyed by country 1 and the second term is the cost that this country incurs in making its currency the international currency.

The second condition concerns the follower country. For an international currency to exist, the latter must have the convenience of using it. To this end, the follower compares the benefits it derives from the use of an international currency with the costs associated with the fact that Country 1 benefits from seigniorage. These costs are weighted with the parameter ψ which reflects the structure of the balance of power in the international context. This second condition is satisfied if:

$$[u(q_{12}) - c(q_{12})] - [u(q_2) - c(q_2)] \geq \psi \theta_1 M_1 \gamma_1 \tag{A.12}$$

where the first term is the sum of the surpluses of sellers and buyers when they recognize both currencies, while the second term represents their surpluses when they recognize only the local currency. The last term is the seigniorage enjoyed by the leading country, weighting by ψ.

Conditions (A.11) and (A.12) are both satisfied when:

$$\frac{[u(q_{12}) - c(q_{12})] - [u(q_2) - c(q_2)]}{\psi} \geq k \tag{A.13}$$

Equation (A.13) shows that for an international currency to exist it is necessary that the utility that the follower country receives from it is greater than the product of the cost of Country 1 to make its currency recognizable and the weight attributed by the follower country to the seigniorage that this country appropriates.

The following Proposition summarizes the above.

Proposition 3 *A fiat-type international currency exists when:*

1. *The leader country revenue from seigniorage is greater than the costs of producing trust in its currency.*
2. *The follower benefits from using the international currency are higher than the costs due to changes in the international balance of power.*
3. *The net benefit for the follower countries to accept the leader currency, is higher than the cost for the leader country to produce trust in it.*

Reference

Lester, B., Postlewaite, A., & Wright, R. (2012). Information, liquidity, asset prices and monetary policy. *Review of Economic Studies, 79*, 1209–1238.

The manufacturer's authorised representative in the EU is Springer
Nature Customer Service Centre GmbH, Europaplatz 3, 69115 Heidelberg,
Germany. If you have any concerns regarding our products, please
contact ProductSafety@springernature.com

Printed and bound by CPI Group (UK) Ltd, Croydon, CR0 4YY
28/09/2026
02224091-0011